# Quiet Girl in a Noisy World

## An Introvert's Story

Debbie Tung

Andrews McMeel
PUBLISHING®

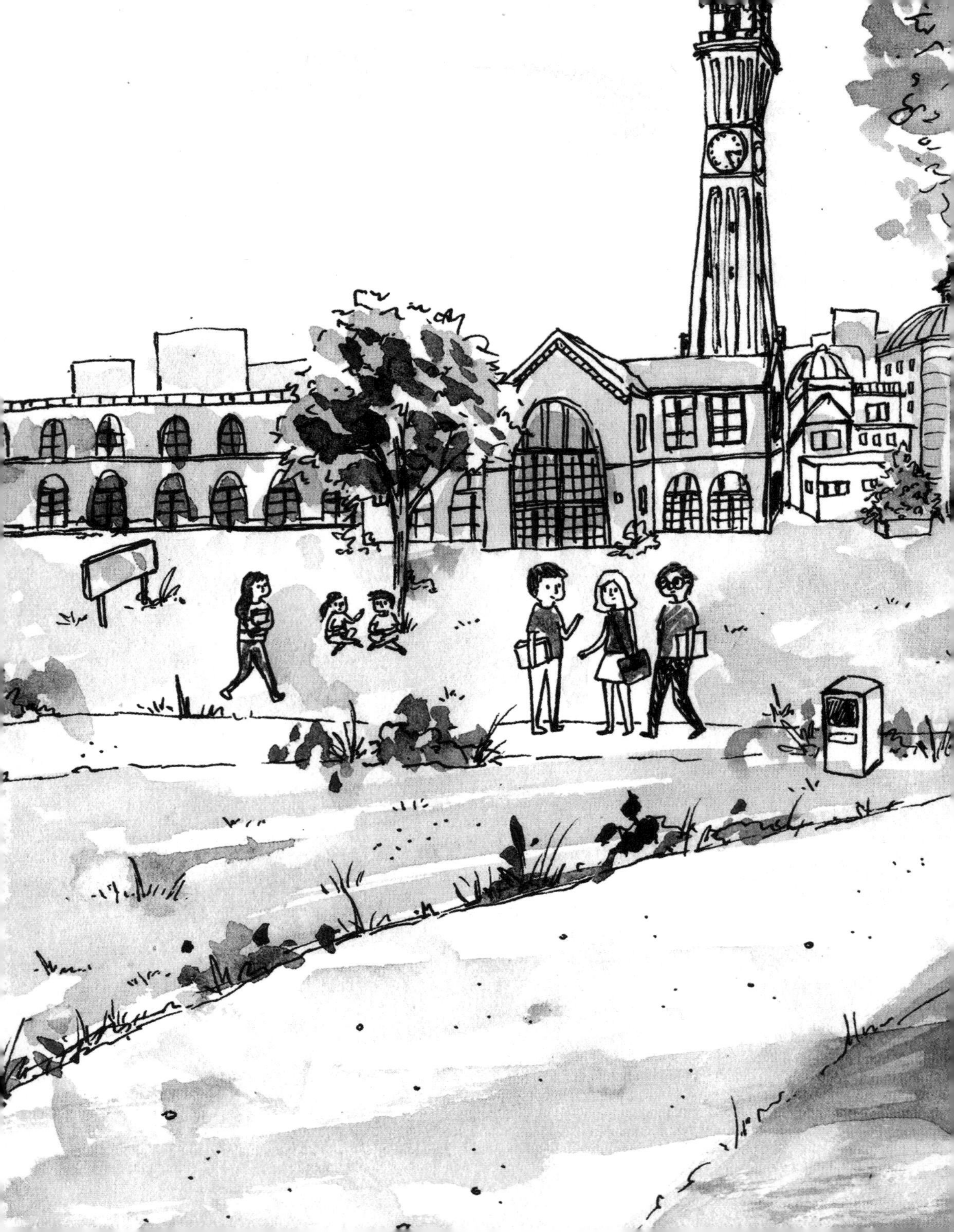

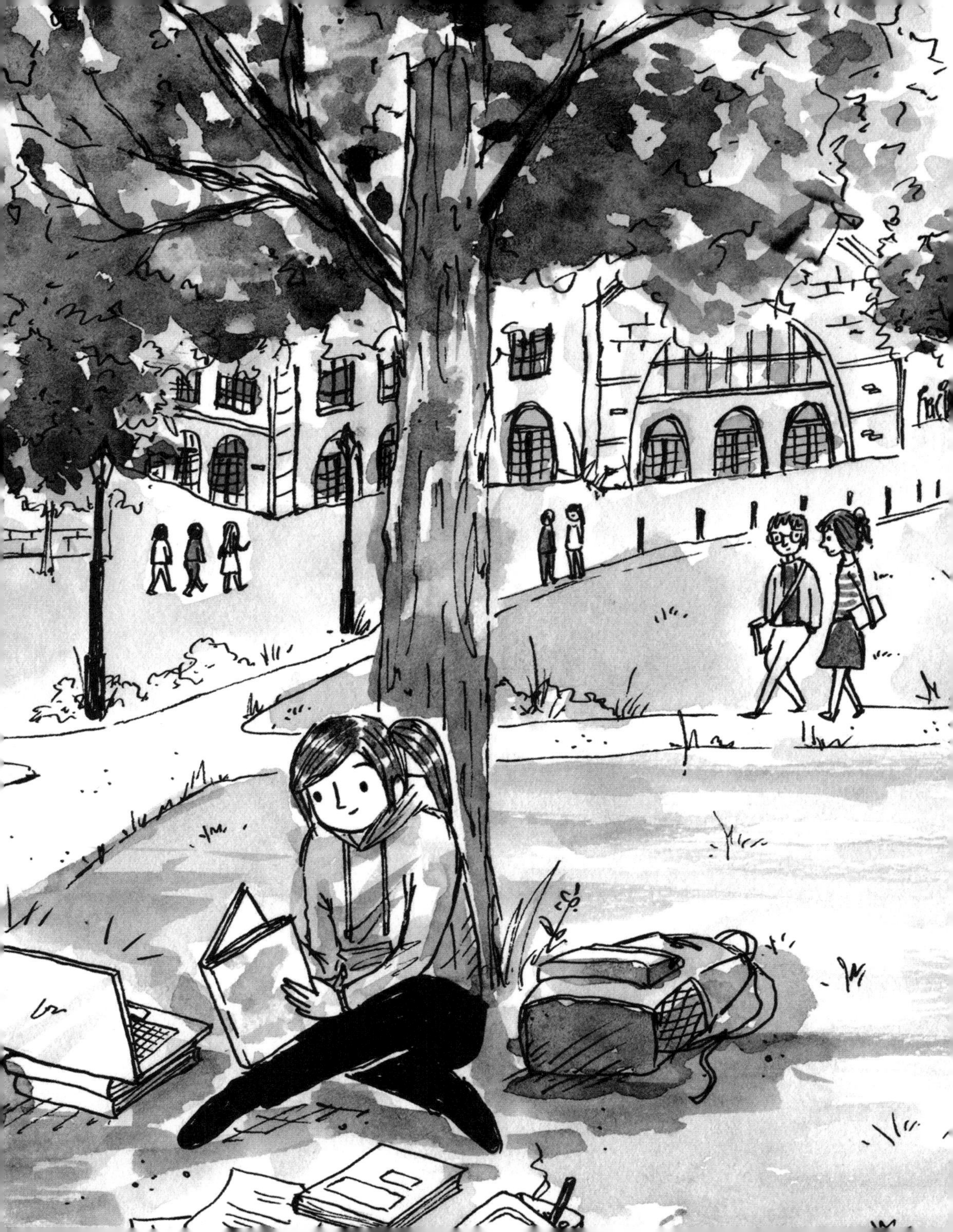

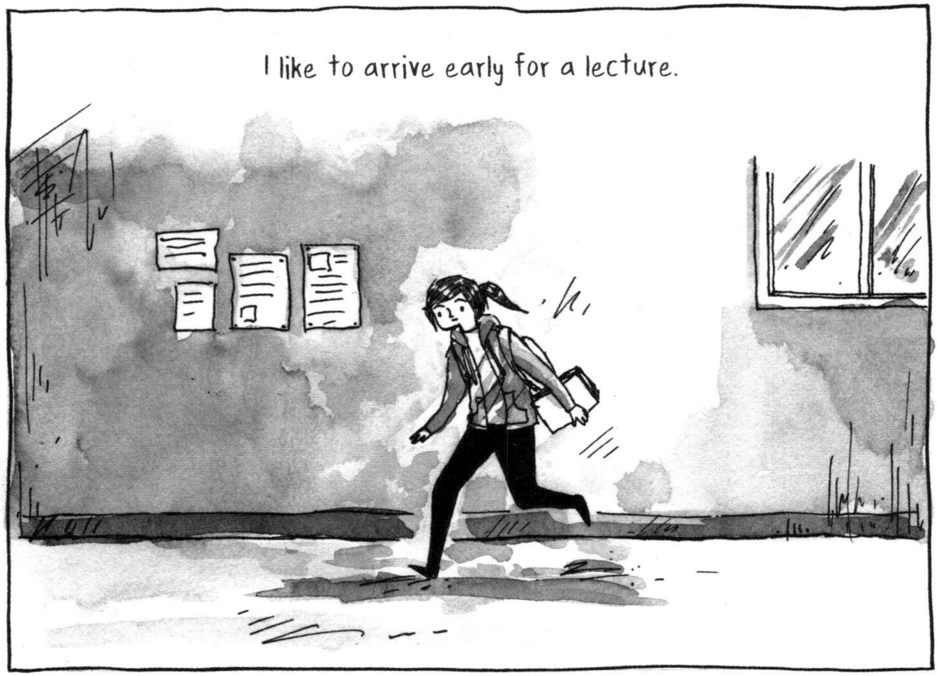
I like to arrive early for a lecture.

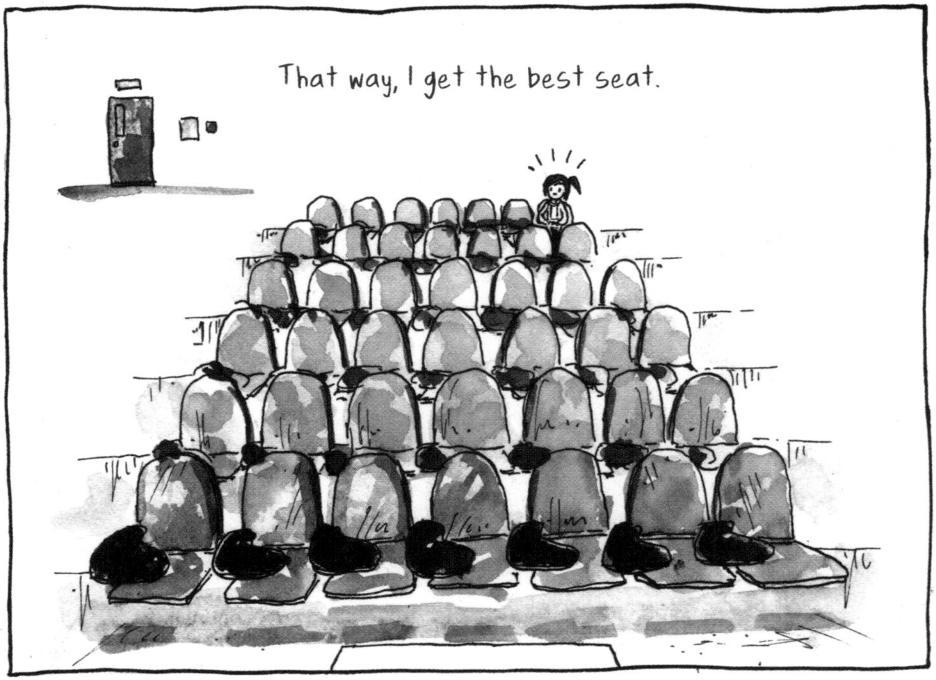
That way, I get the best seat.

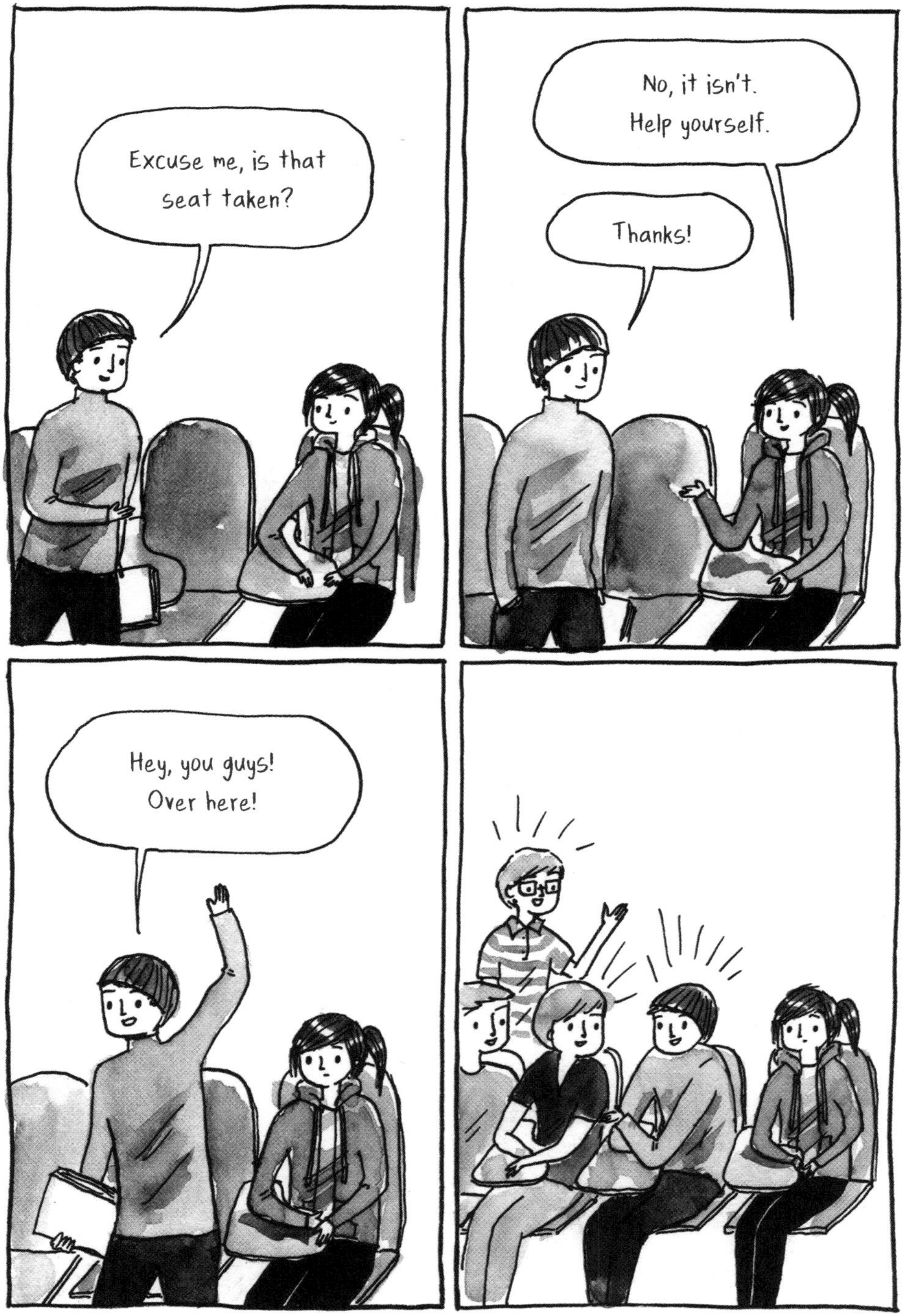
Excuse me, is that seat taken?
No, it isn't. Help yourself.
Thanks!
Hey, you guys! Over here!

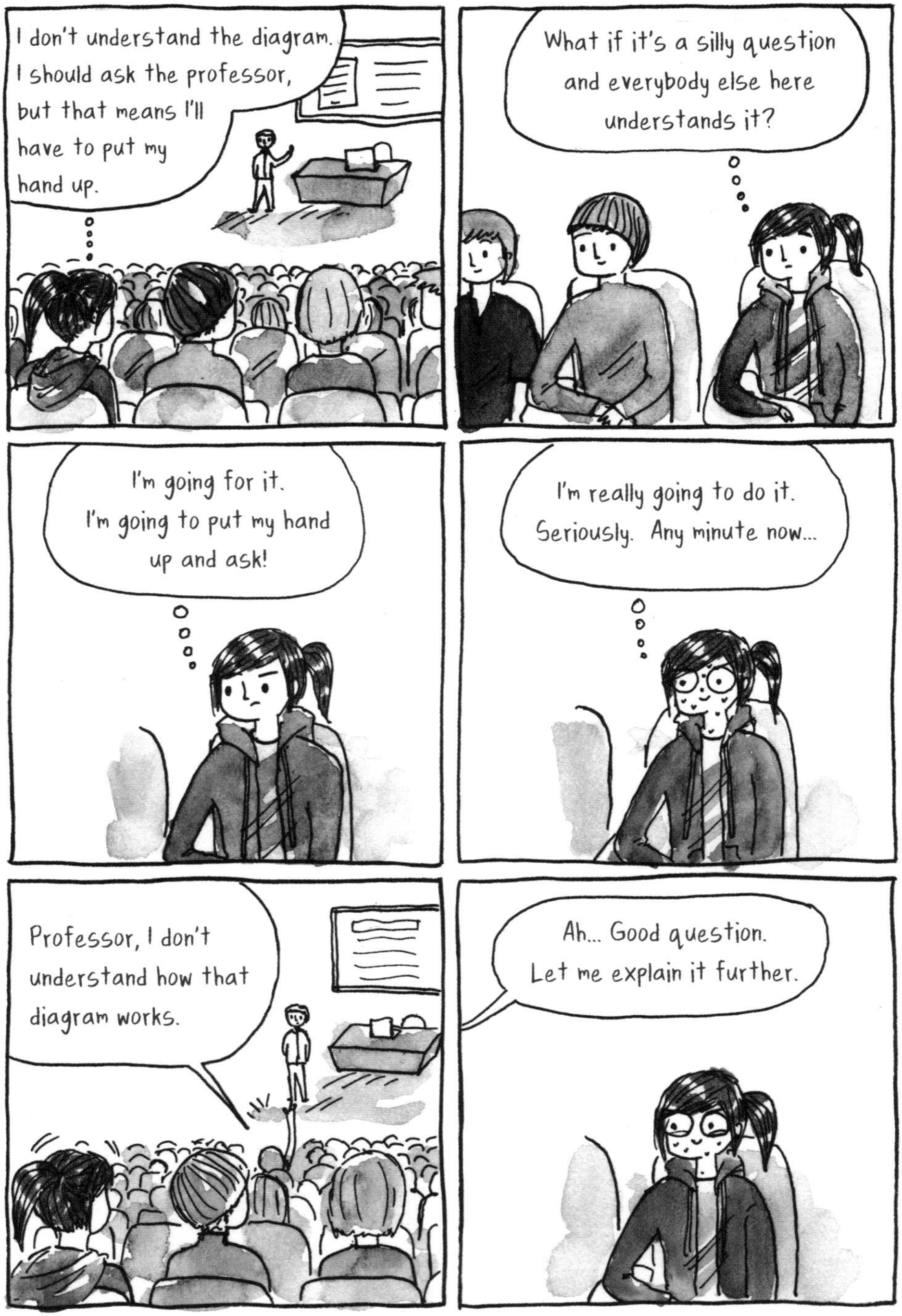
I don't understand the diagram. I should ask the professor, but that means I'll have to put my hand up.
What if it's a silly question and everybody else here understands it?
I'm going for it. I'm going to put my hand up and ask!
I'm really going to do it. Seriously. Any minute now...
Professor, I don't understand how that diagram works.
Ah... Good question. Let me explain it further.

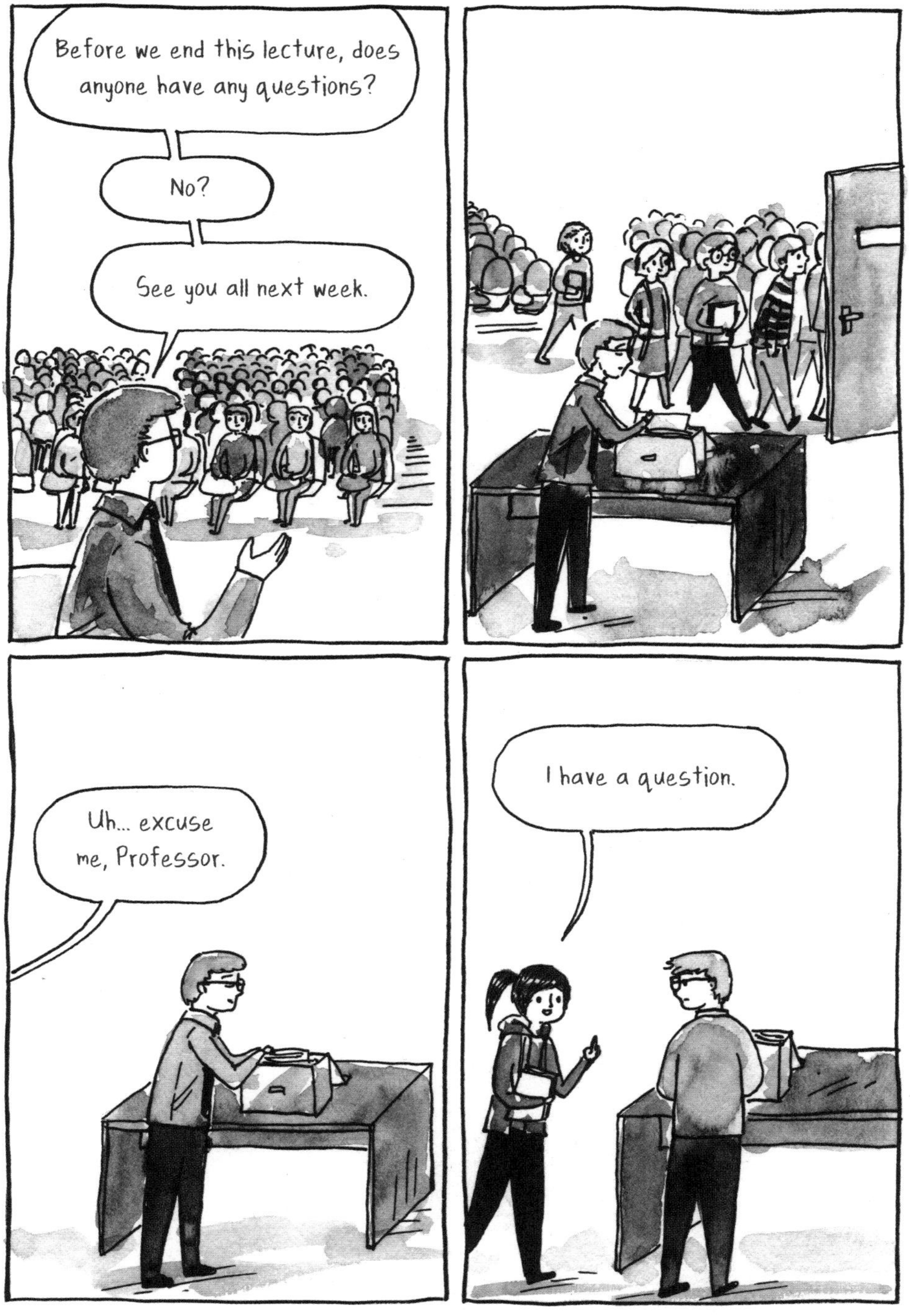
Before we end this lecture, does anyone have any questions?
No?
See you all next week.
Uh... excuse me, Professor.
I have a question.

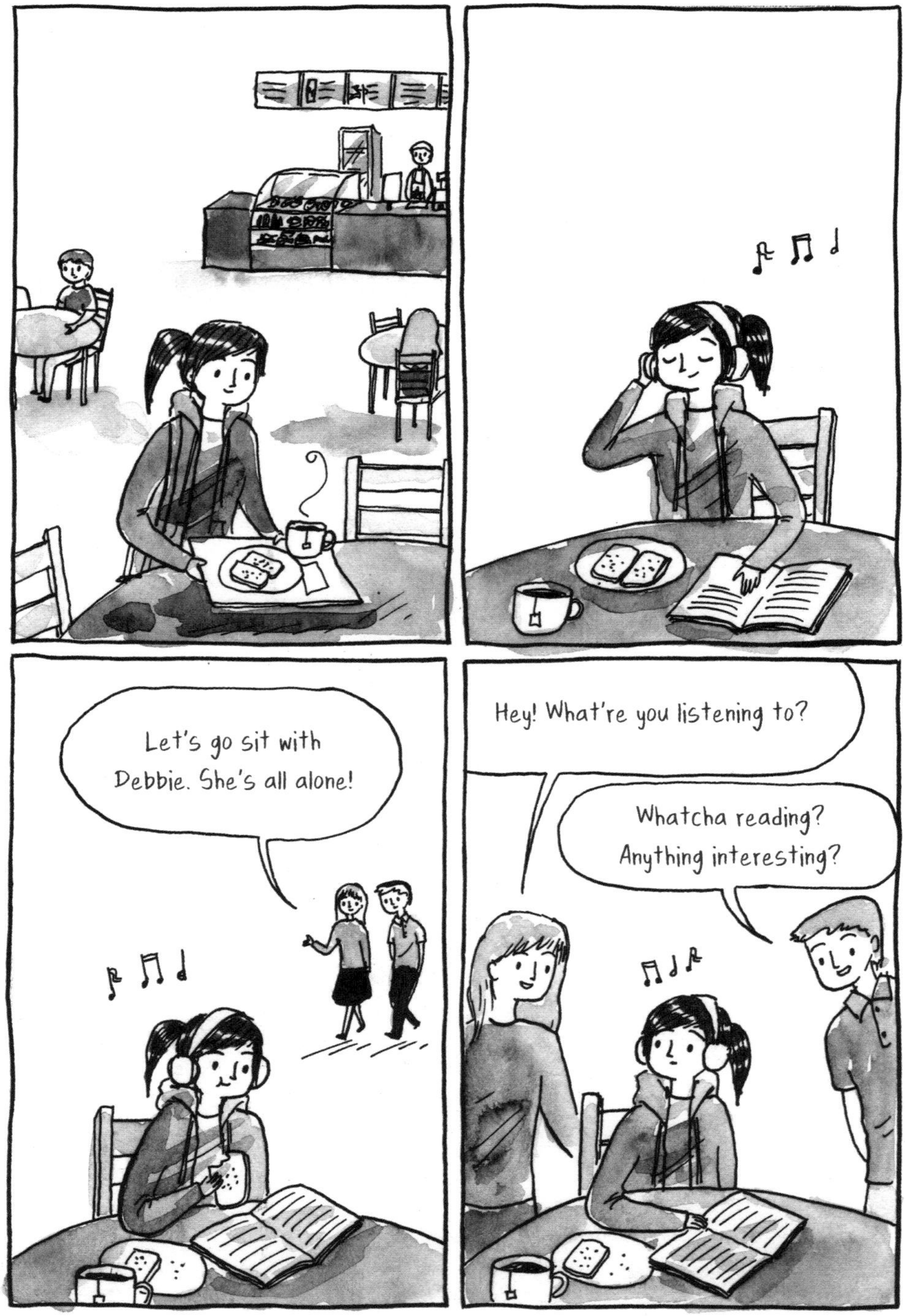
Let's go sit with Debbie. She's all alone!
Hey! What're you listening to?
Whatcha reading? Anything interesting?

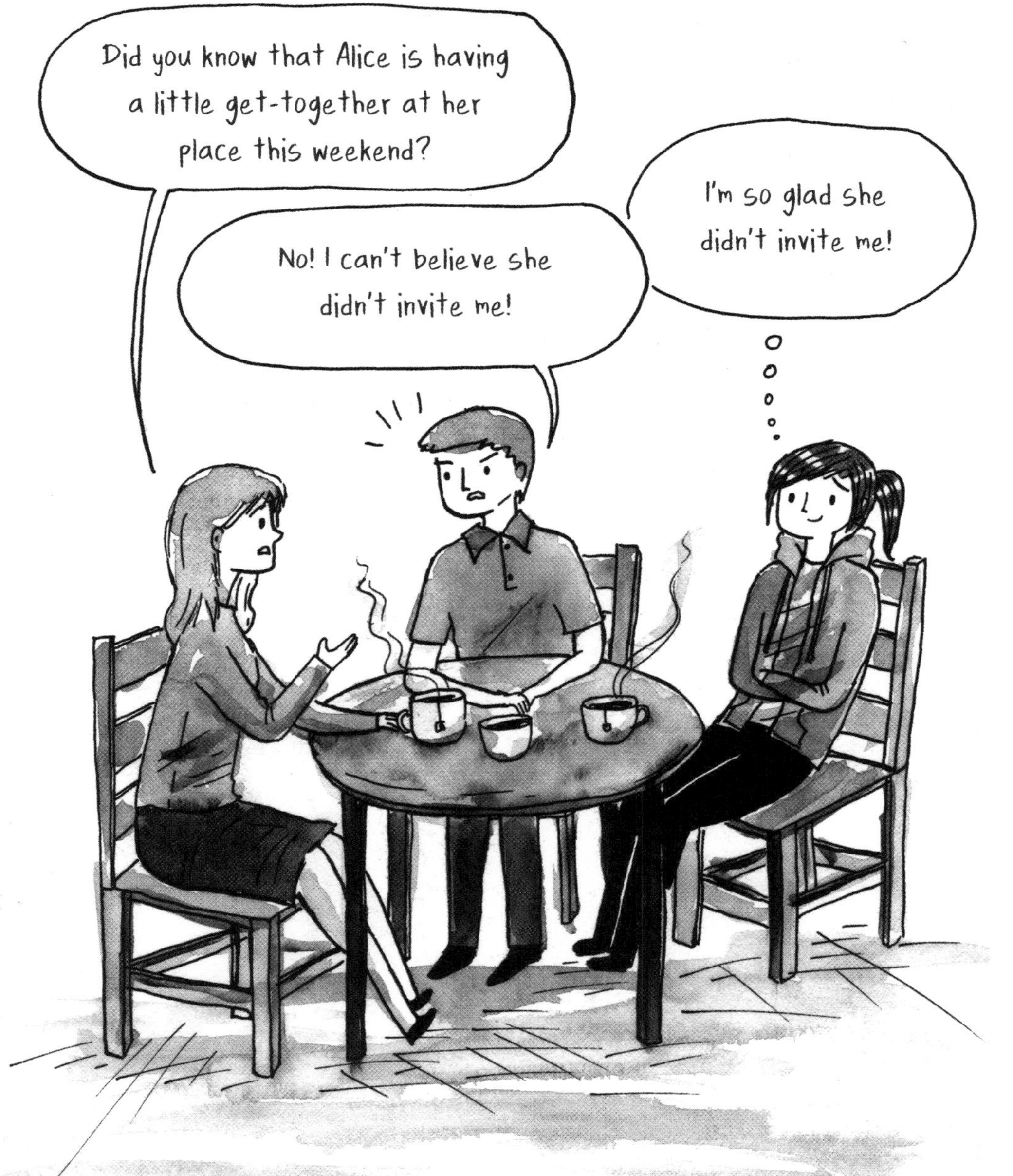
Did you know that Alice is having a little get-together at her place this weekend?
No! I can't believe she didn't invite me!
I'm so glad she didn't invite me!

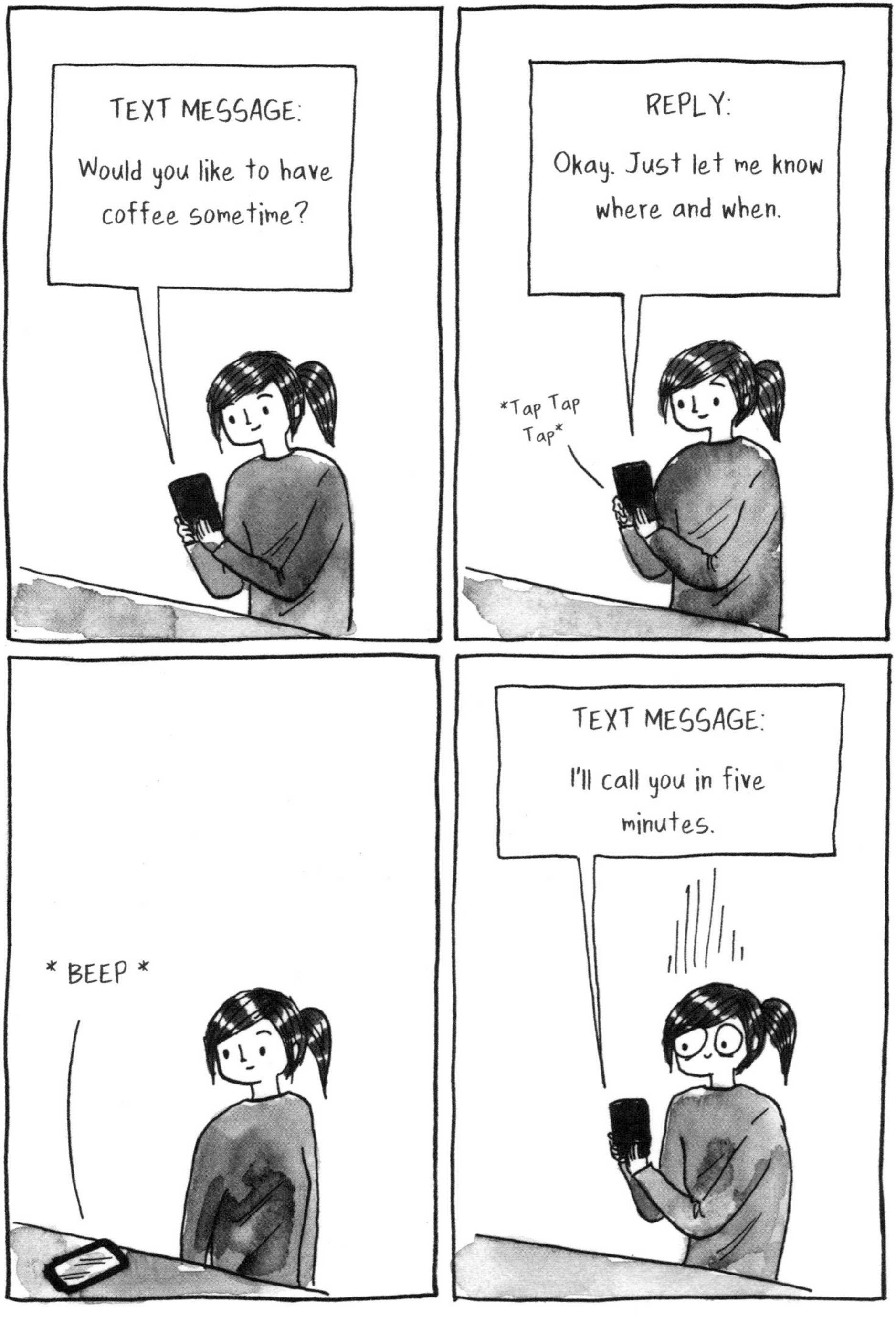
TEXT MESSAGE:
Would you like to have coffee sometime?
REPLY:
Okay. Just let me know where and when.
*Tap Tap Tap*
* BEEP *
TEXT MESSAGE:
I'll call you in five minutes.

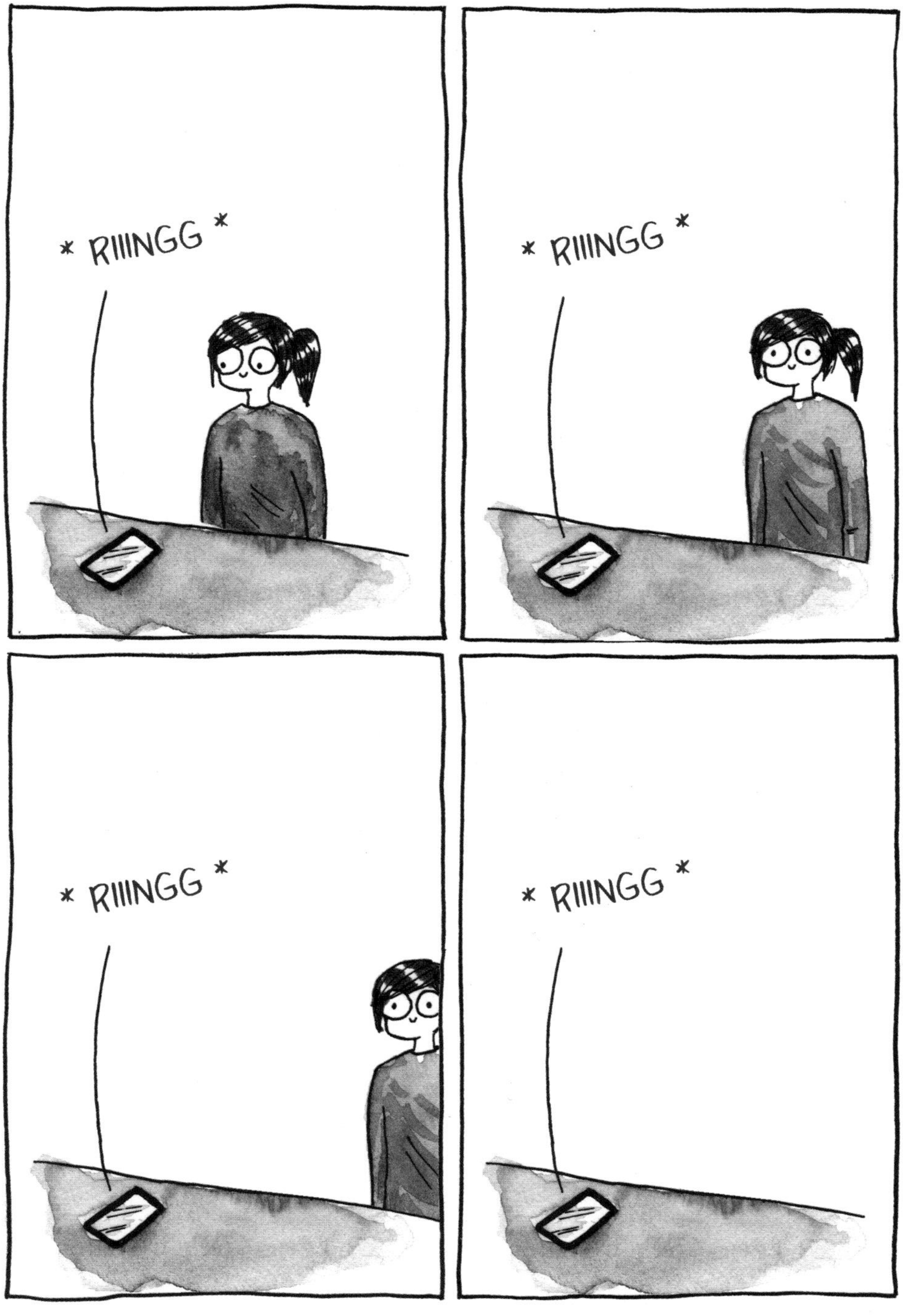
* RIIINGG *
* RIIINGG *
* RIIINGG *
* RIIINGG *

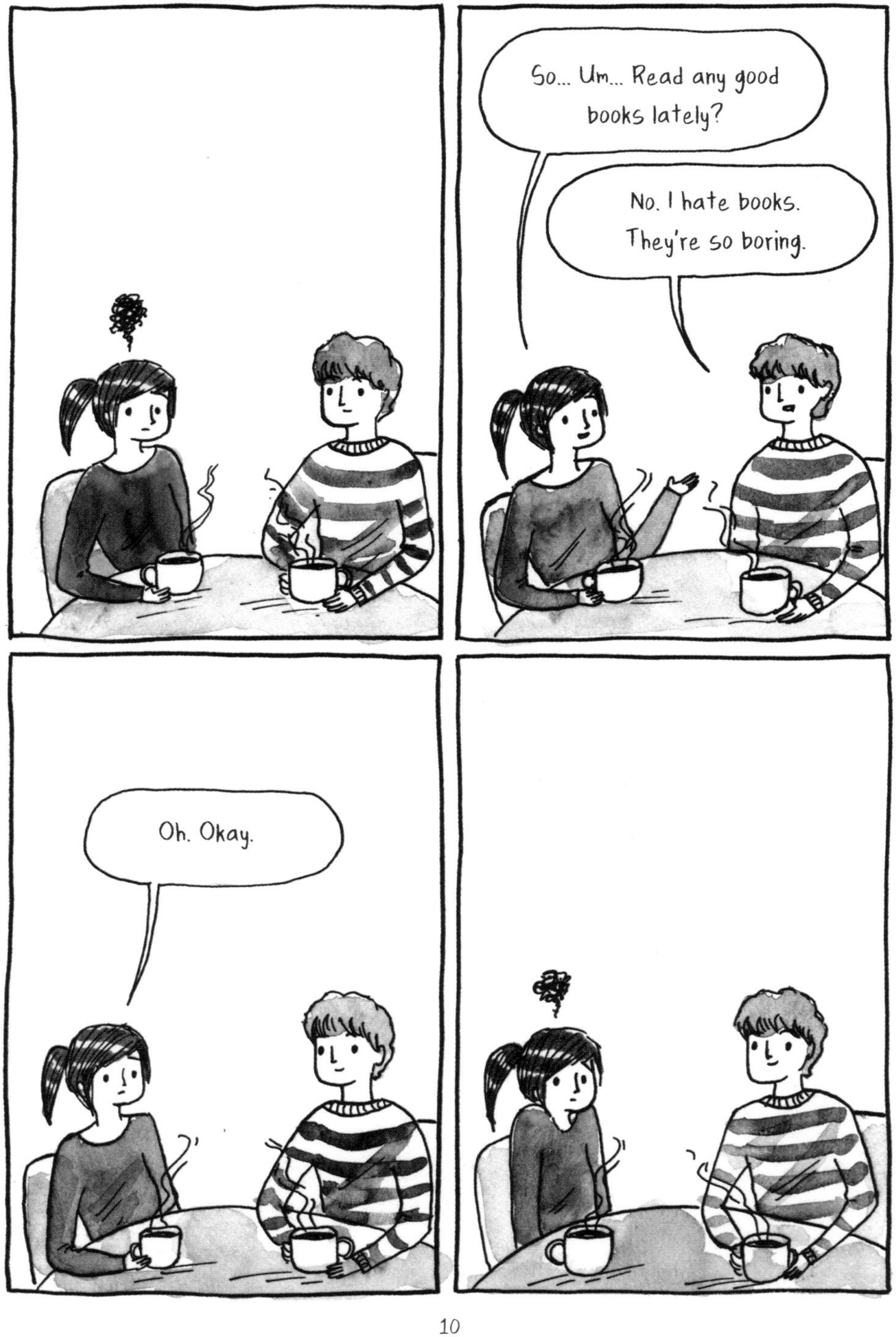
So... Um... Read any good books lately?
No. I hate books. They're so boring.
Oh. Okay.

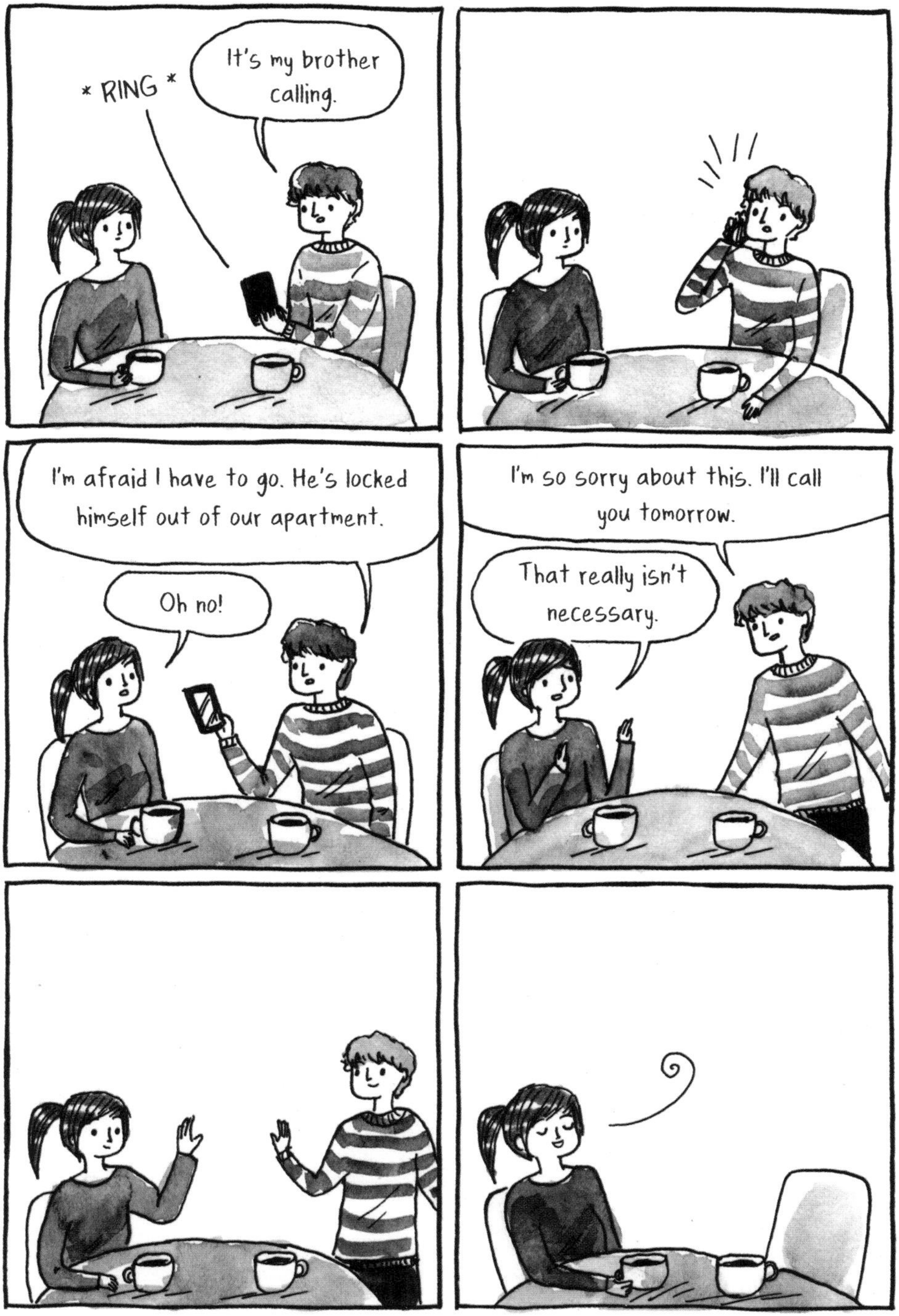
* RING *
It's my brother calling.
I'm afraid I have to go. He's locked himself out of our apartment.
Oh no!
I'm so sorry about this. I'll call you tomorrow.
That really isn't necessary.

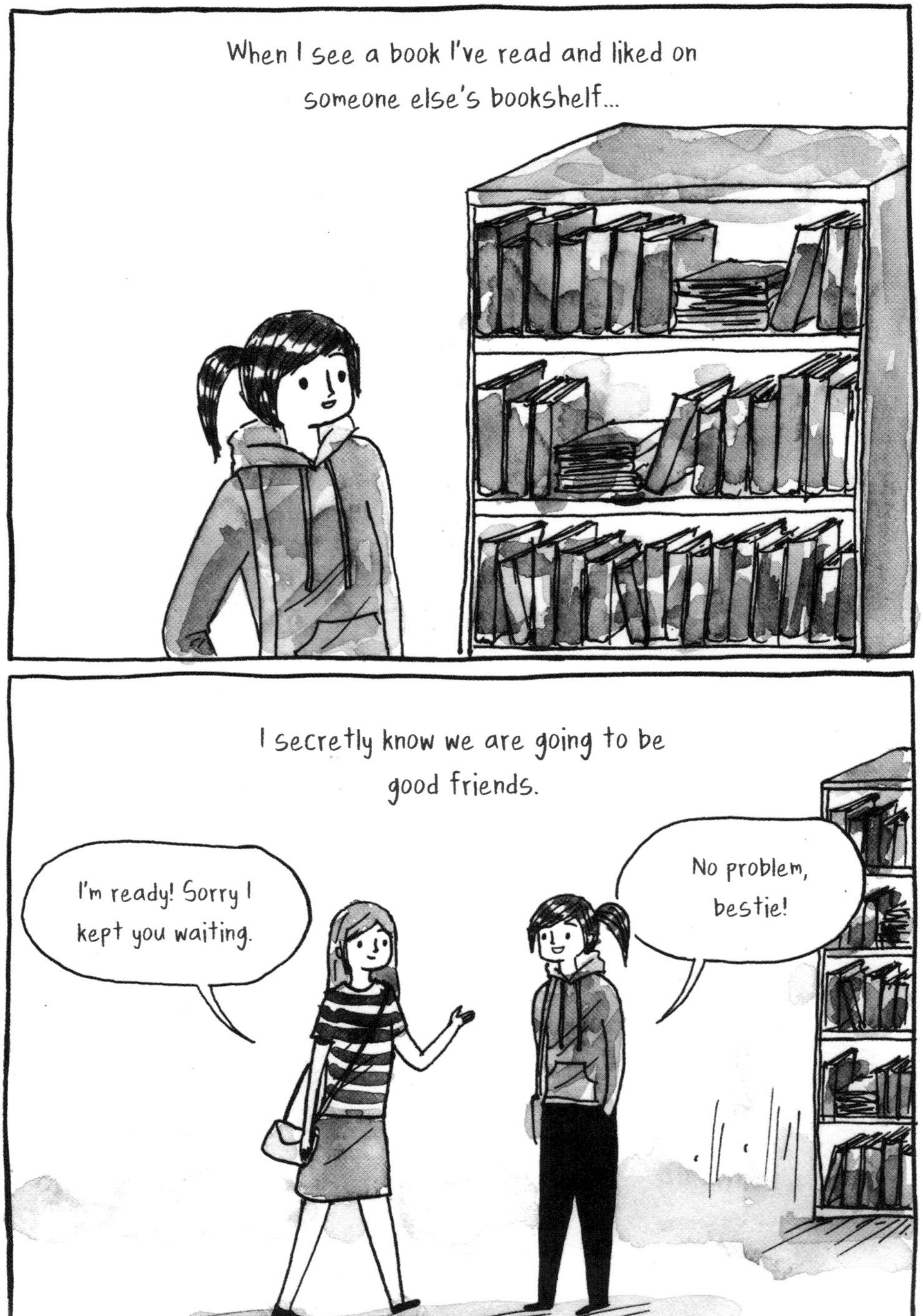
When I see a book I've read and liked on someone else's bookshelf...
I secretly know we are going to be good friends.
I'm ready! Sorry I kept you waiting.
No problem, bestie!

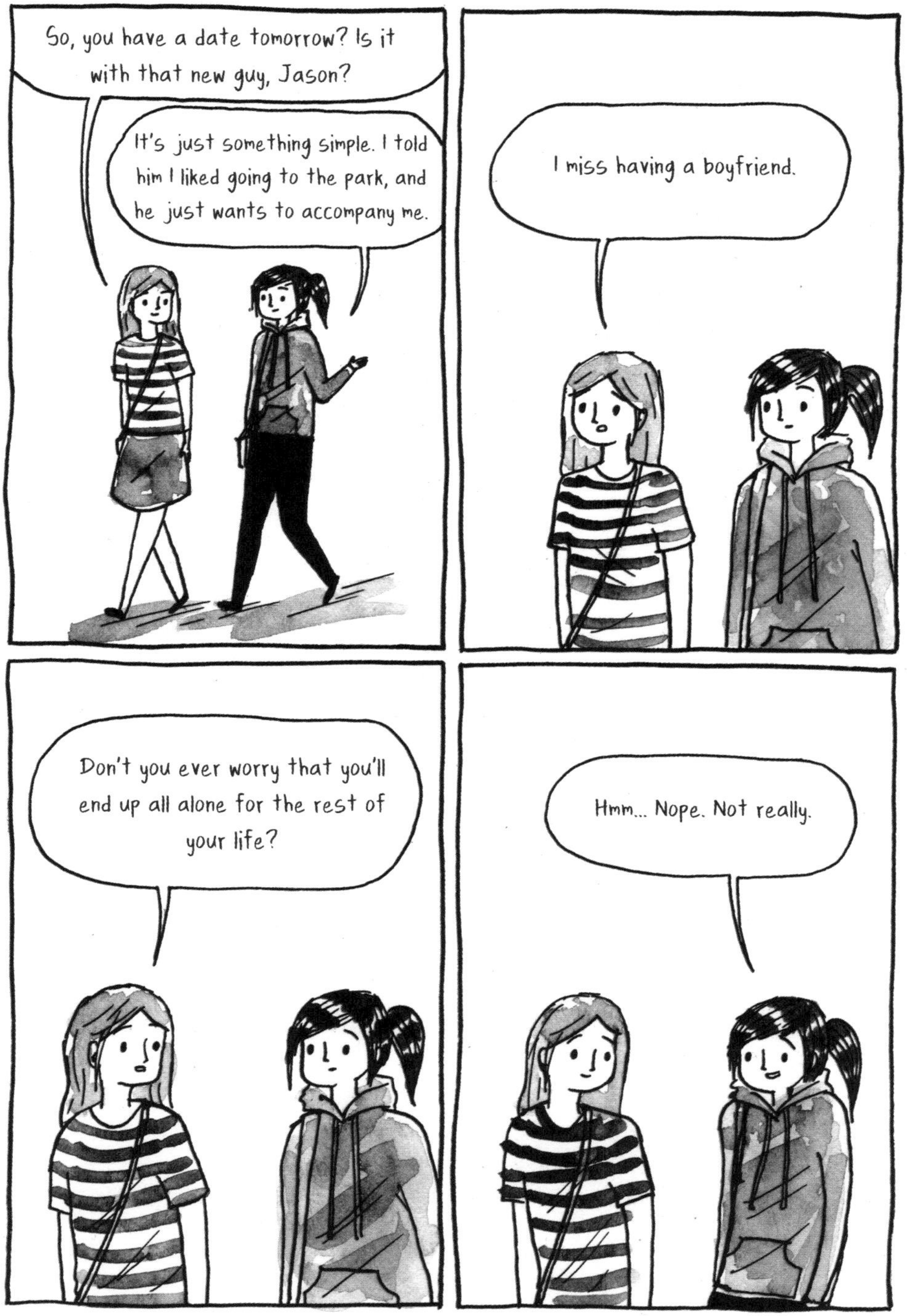
So, you have a date tomorrow? Is it with that new guy, Jason?
It's just something simple. I told him I liked going to the park, and he just wants to accompany me.
I miss having a boyfriend.
Don't you ever worry that you'll end up all alone for the rest of your life?
Hmm... Nope. Not really.

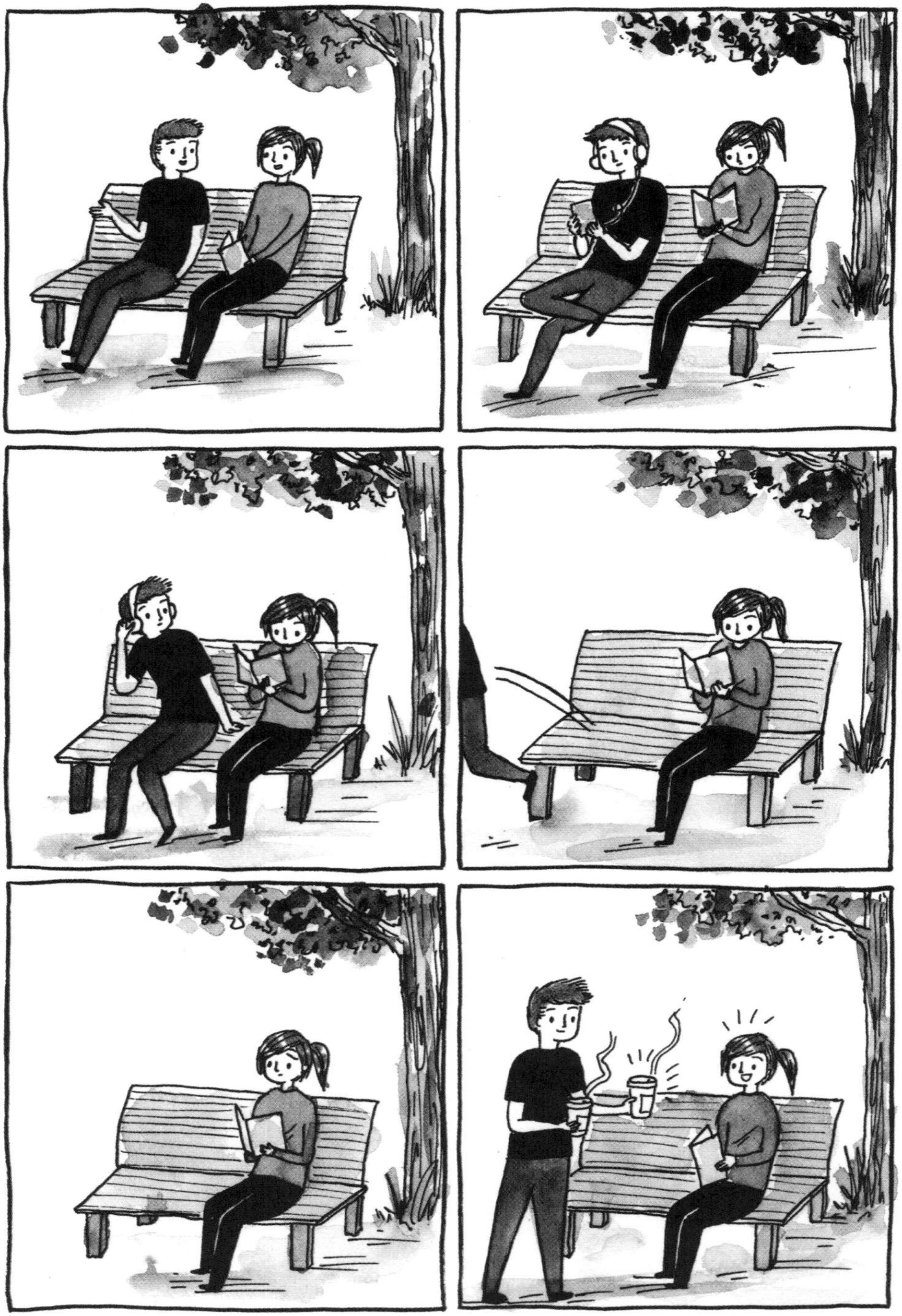

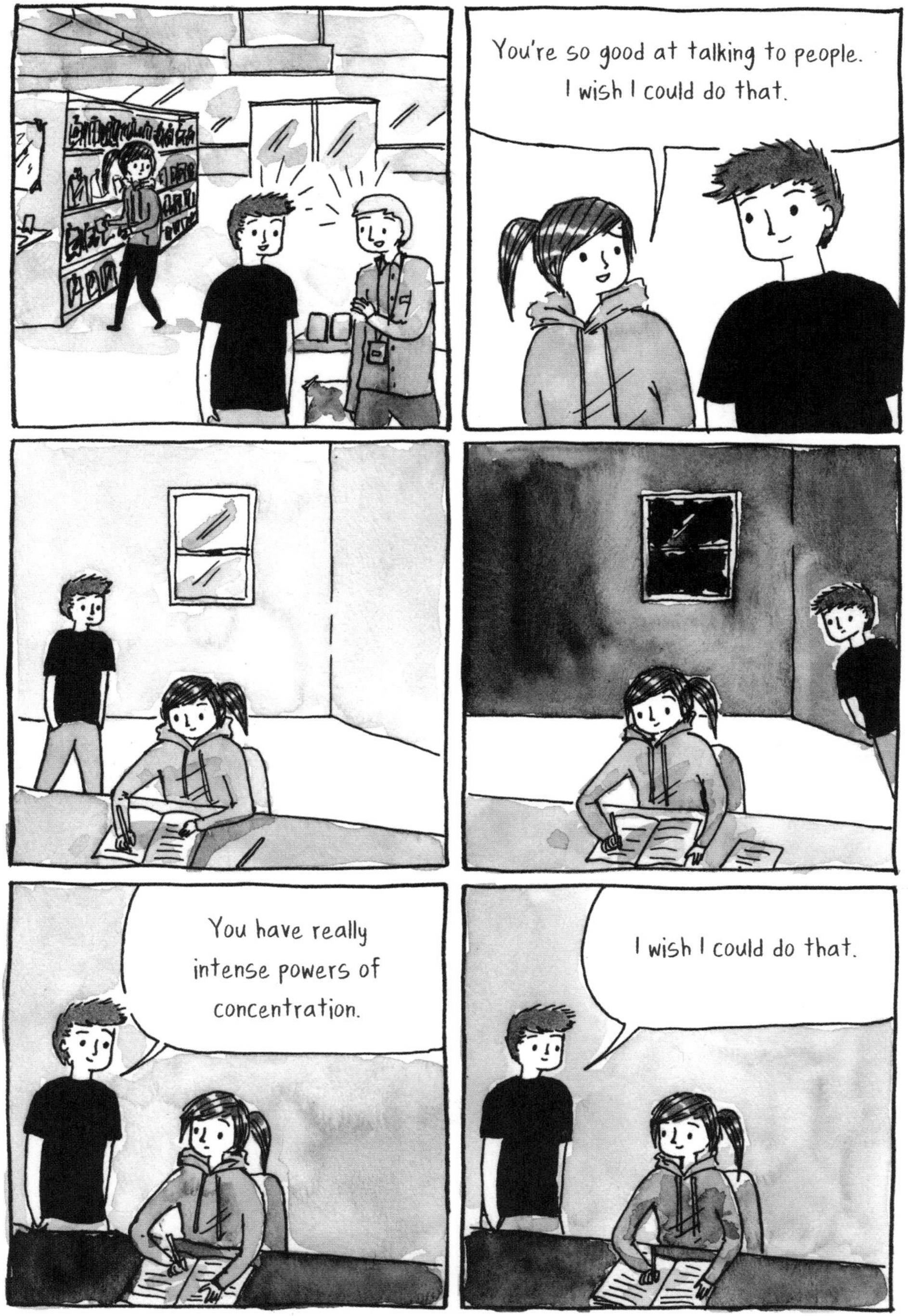
You're so good at talking to people. I wish I could do that.
You have really intense powers of concentration.
I wish I could do that.

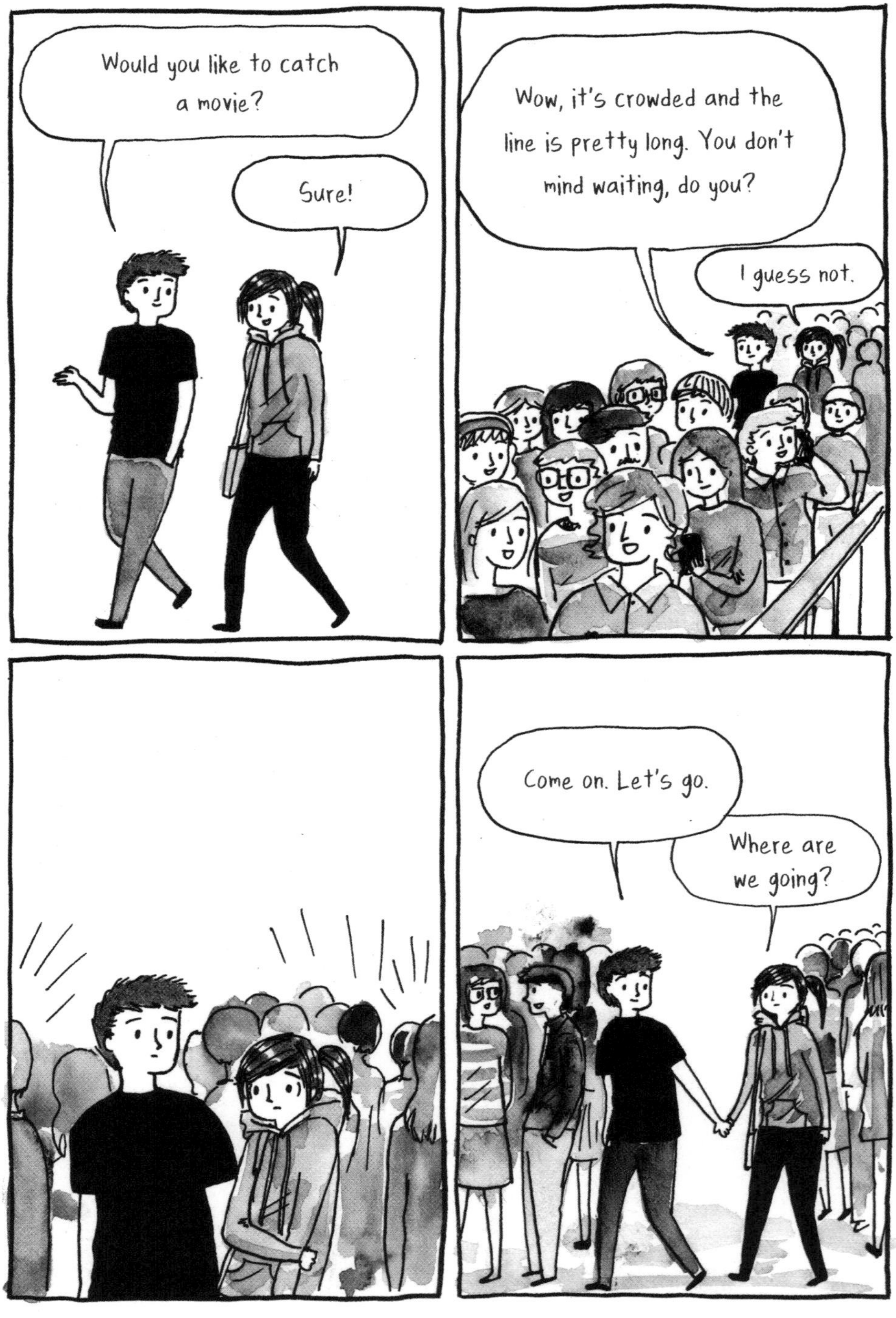
Would you like to catch a movie?
Sure!
Wow, it's crowded and the line is pretty long. You don't mind waiting, do you?
I guess not.
Come on. Let's go.
Where are we going?

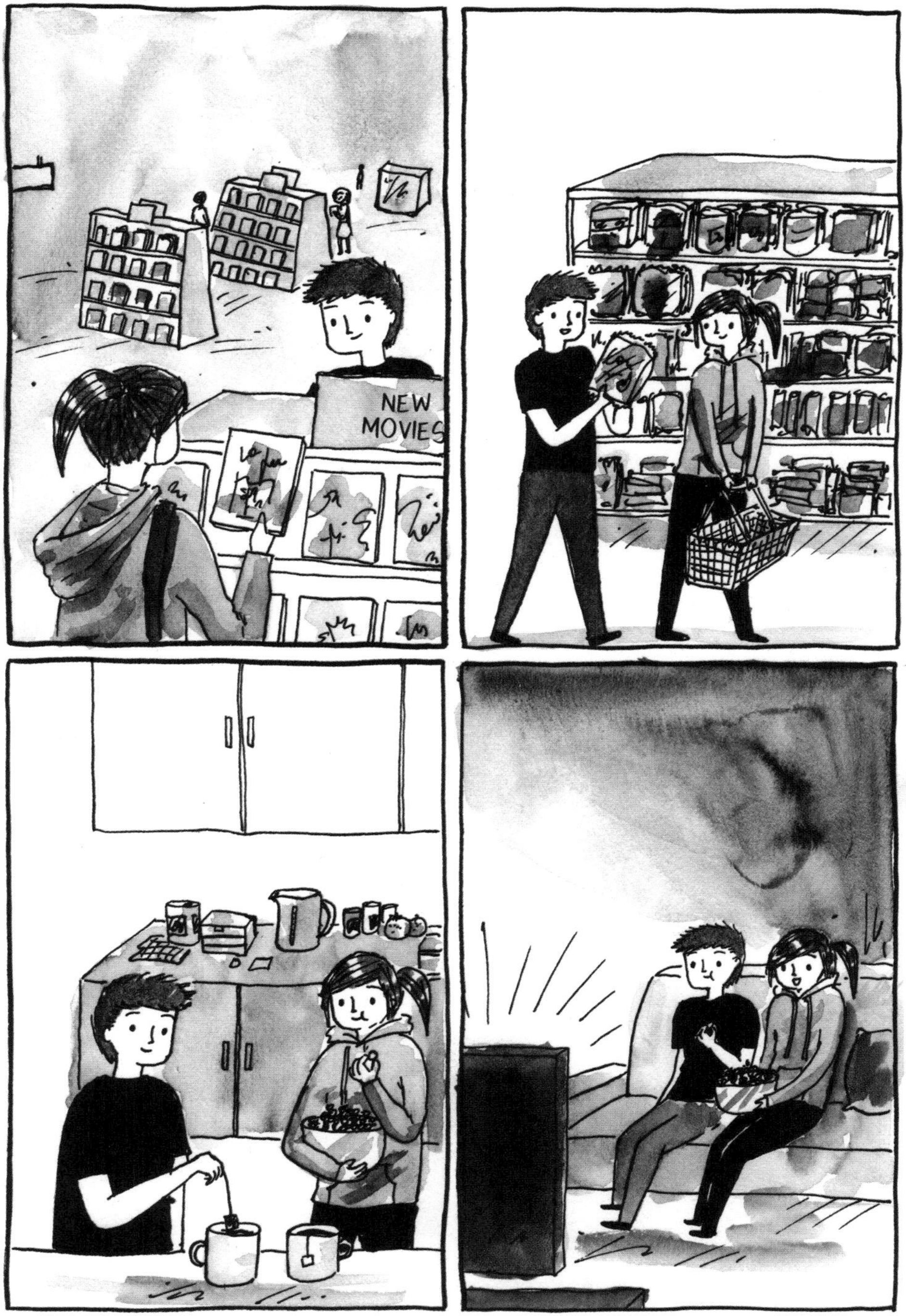
NEW
MOVIES

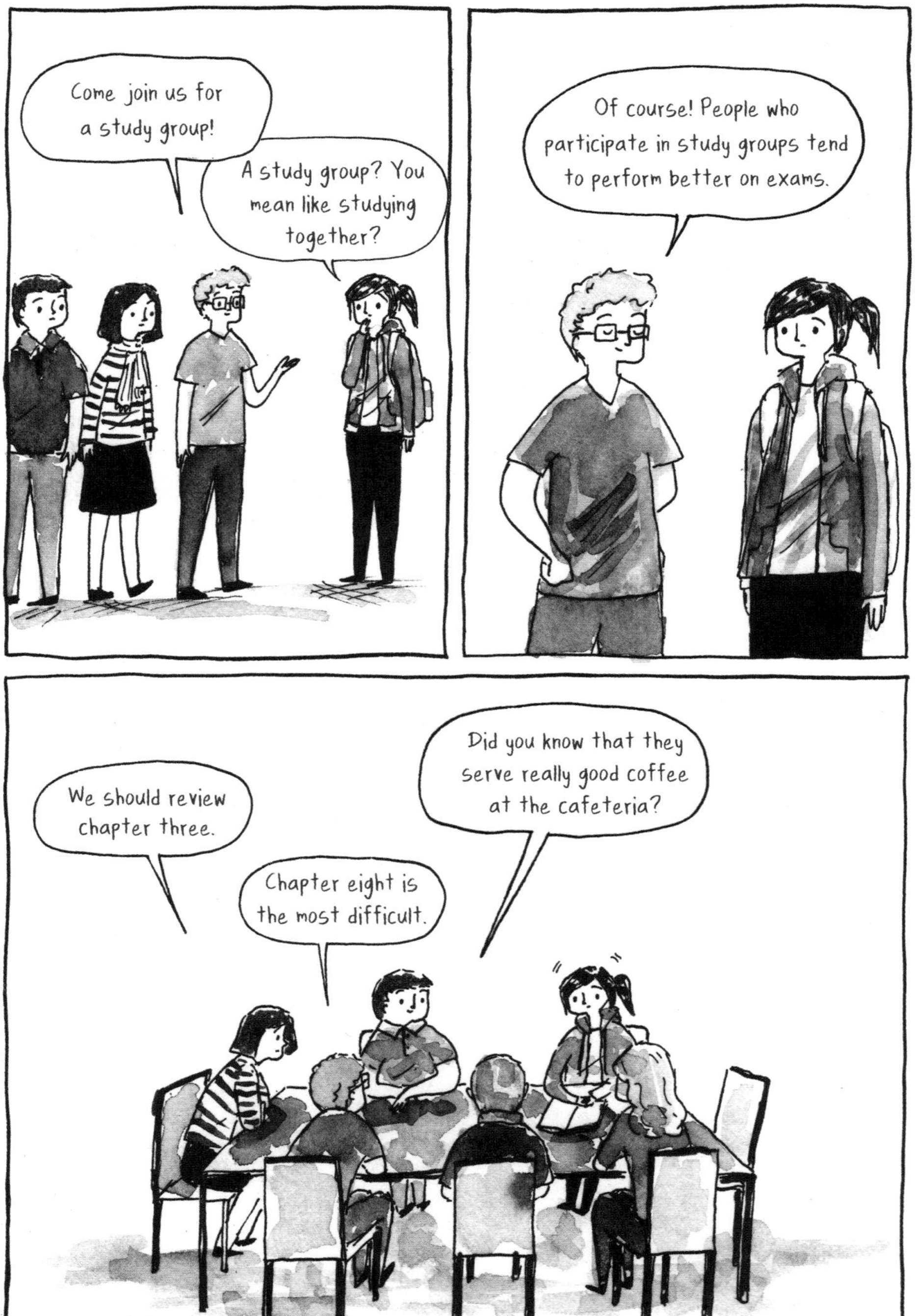
Come join us for a study group!
A study group? You mean like studying together?
Of course! People who participate in study groups tend to perform better on exams.
We should review chapter three.
Chapter eight is the most difficult.
Did you know that they serve really good coffee at the cafeteria?

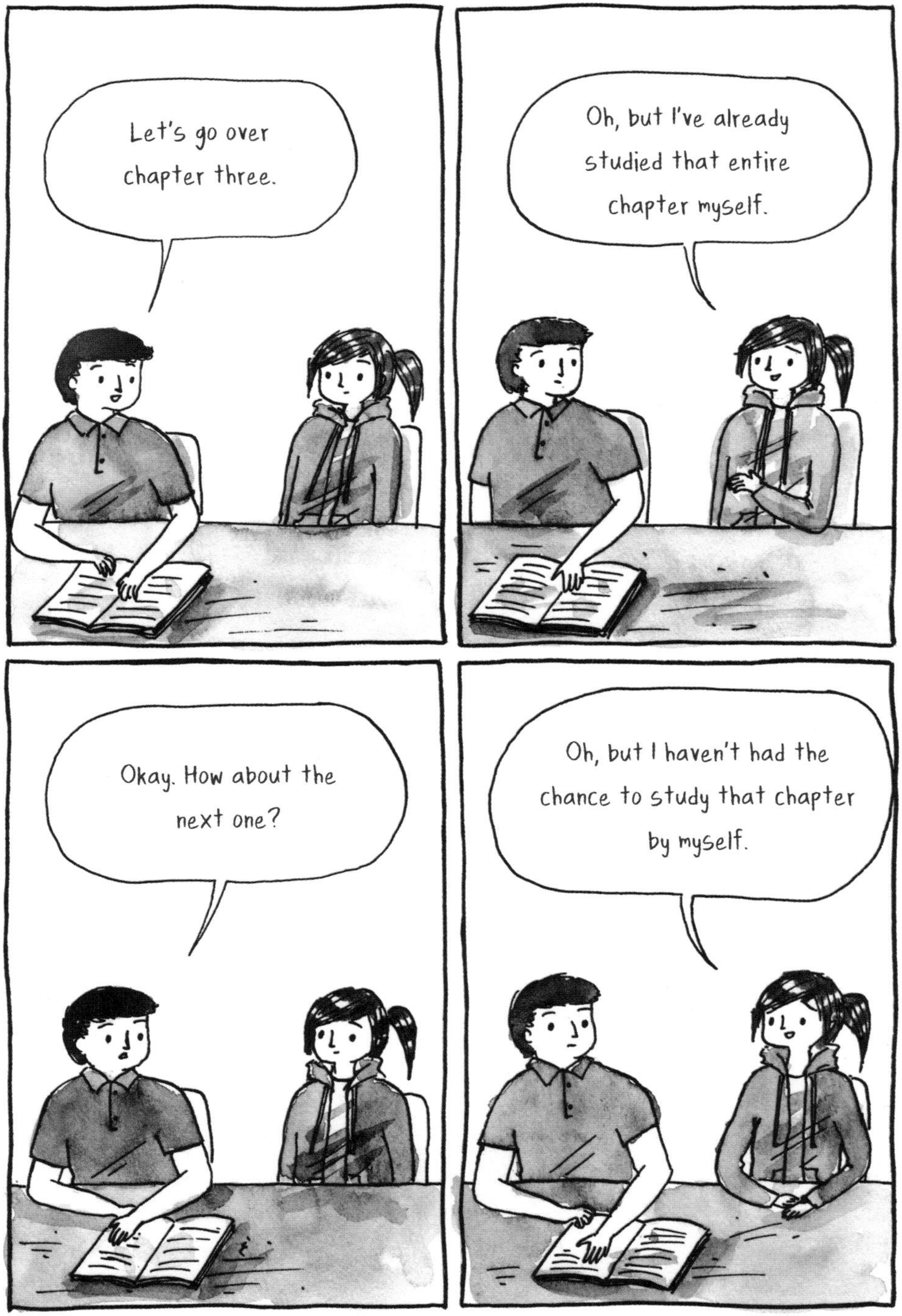
Let's go over chapter three.
Oh, but I've already studied that entire chapter myself.
Okay. How about the next one?
Oh, but I haven't had the chance to study that chapter by myself.

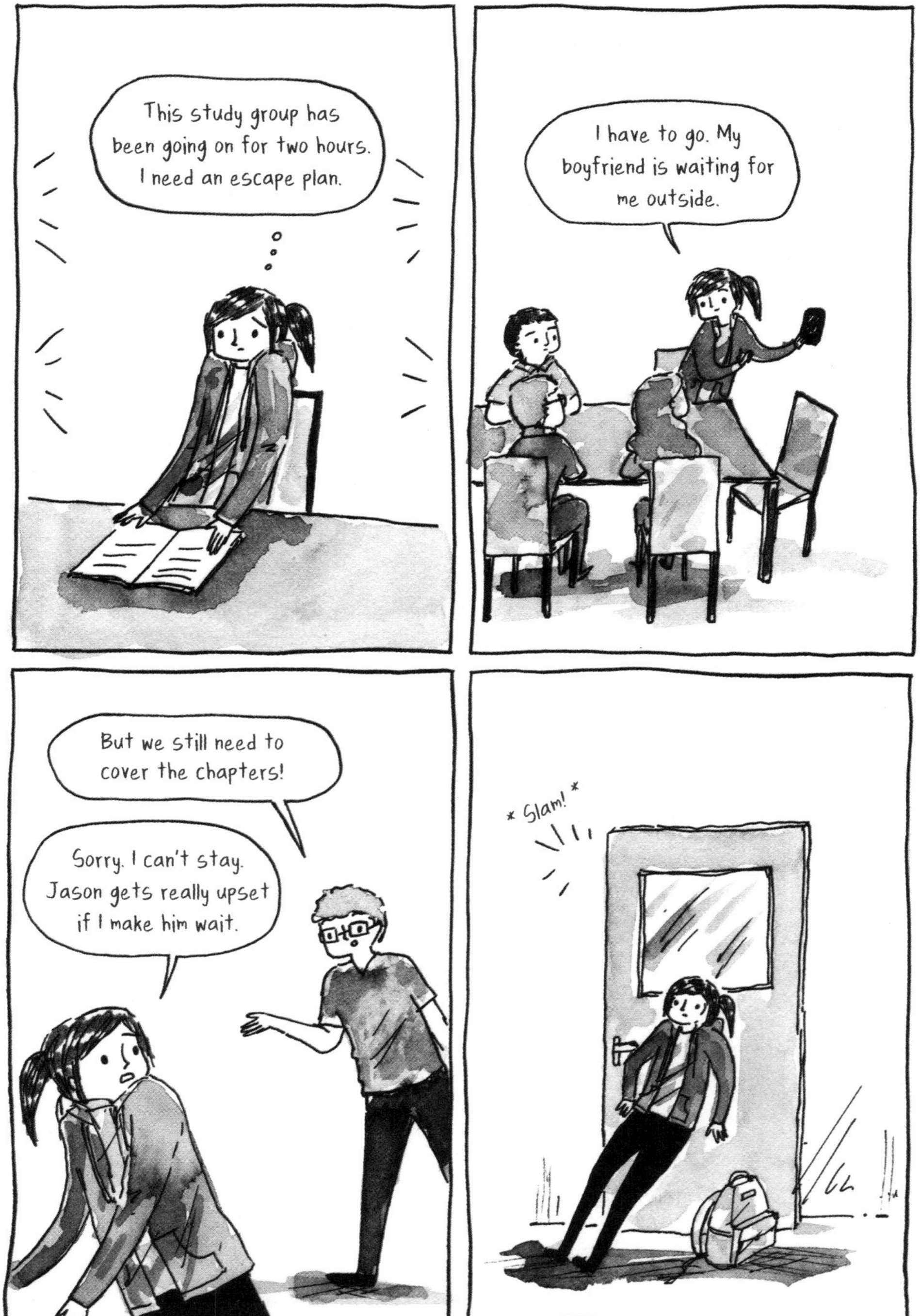
This study group has been going on for two hours. I need an escape plan.
I have to go. My boyfriend is waiting for me outside.
But we still need to cover the chapters!
Sorry. I can't stay. Jason gets really upset if I make him wait.
* Slam! *

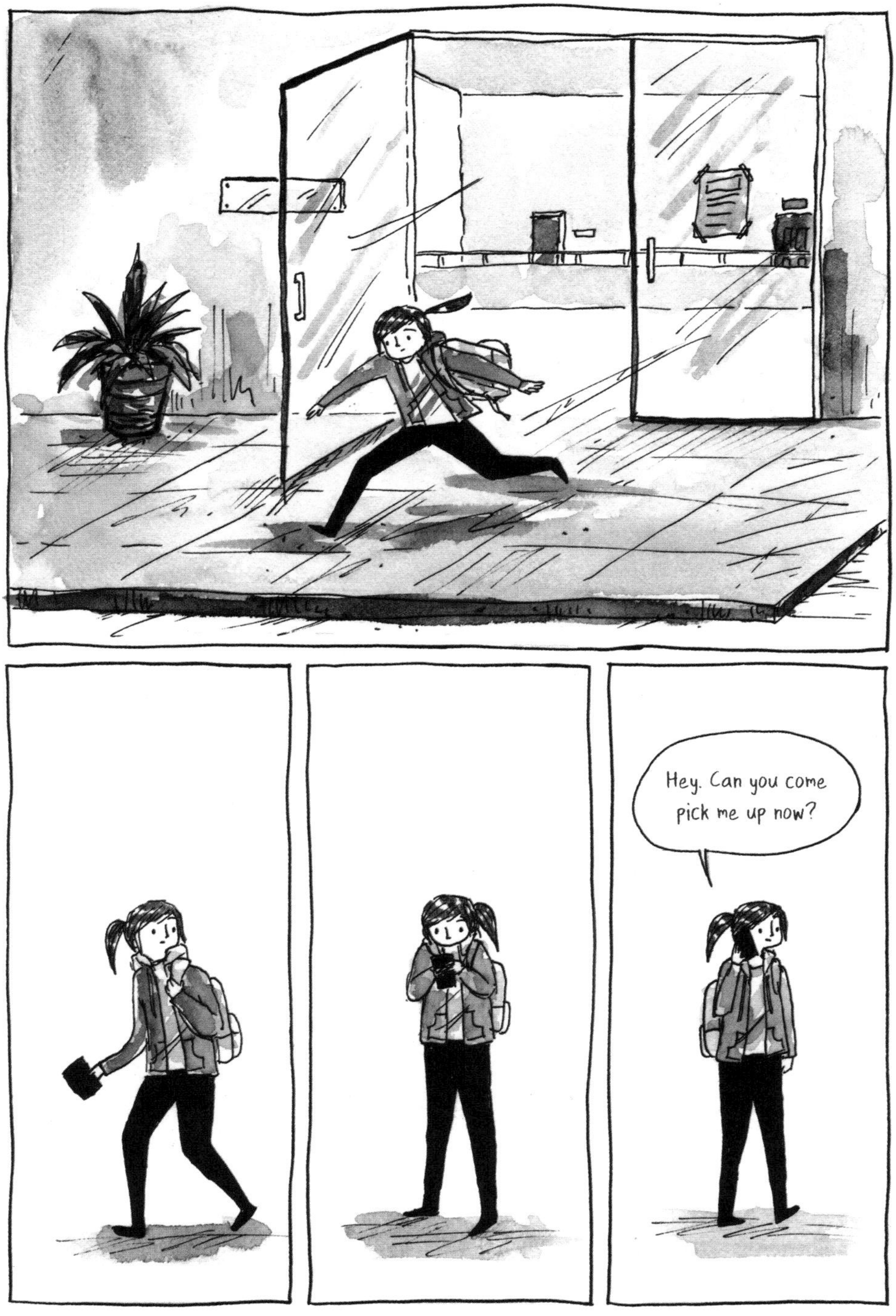
Hey. Can you come pick me up now?

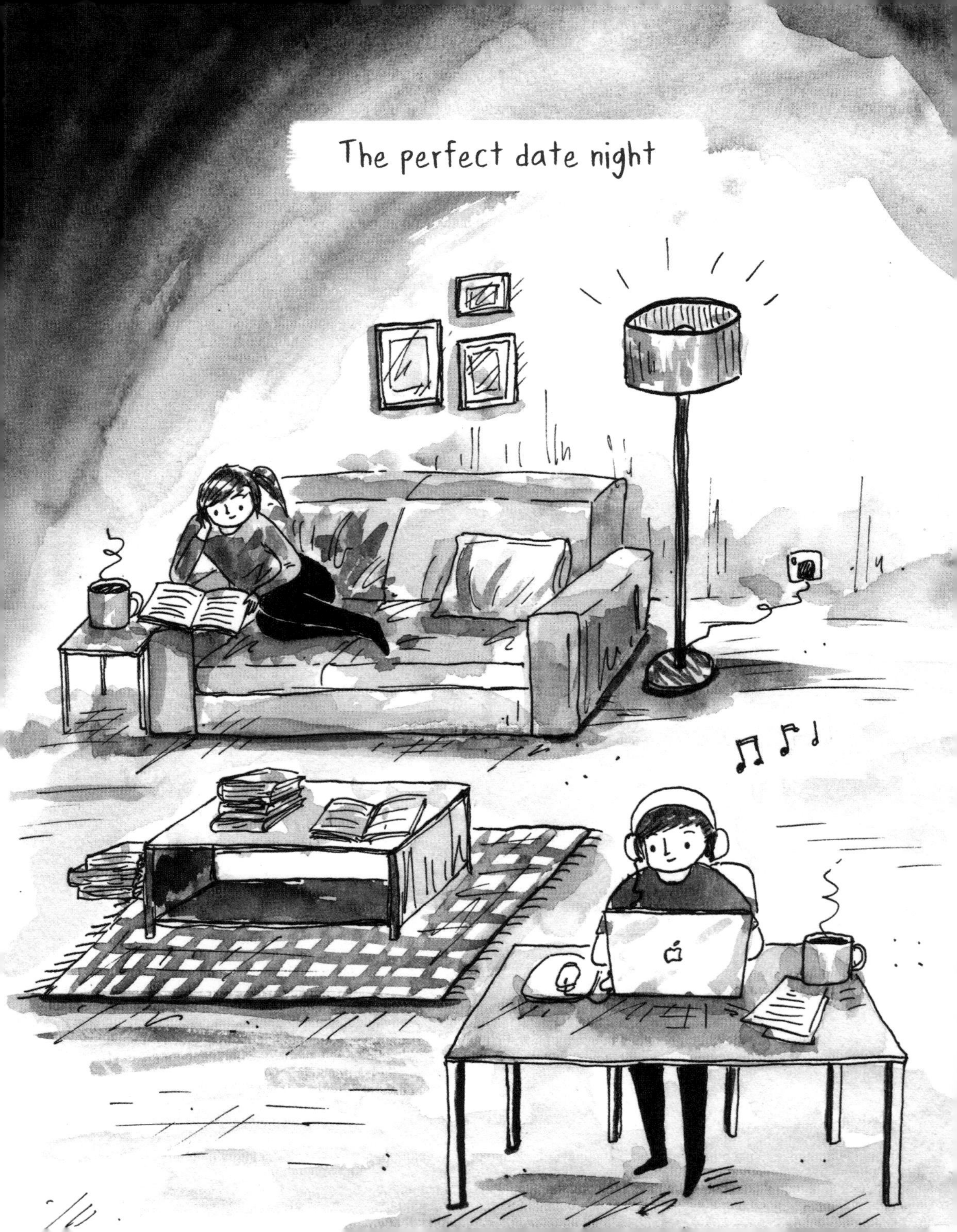
The perfect date night

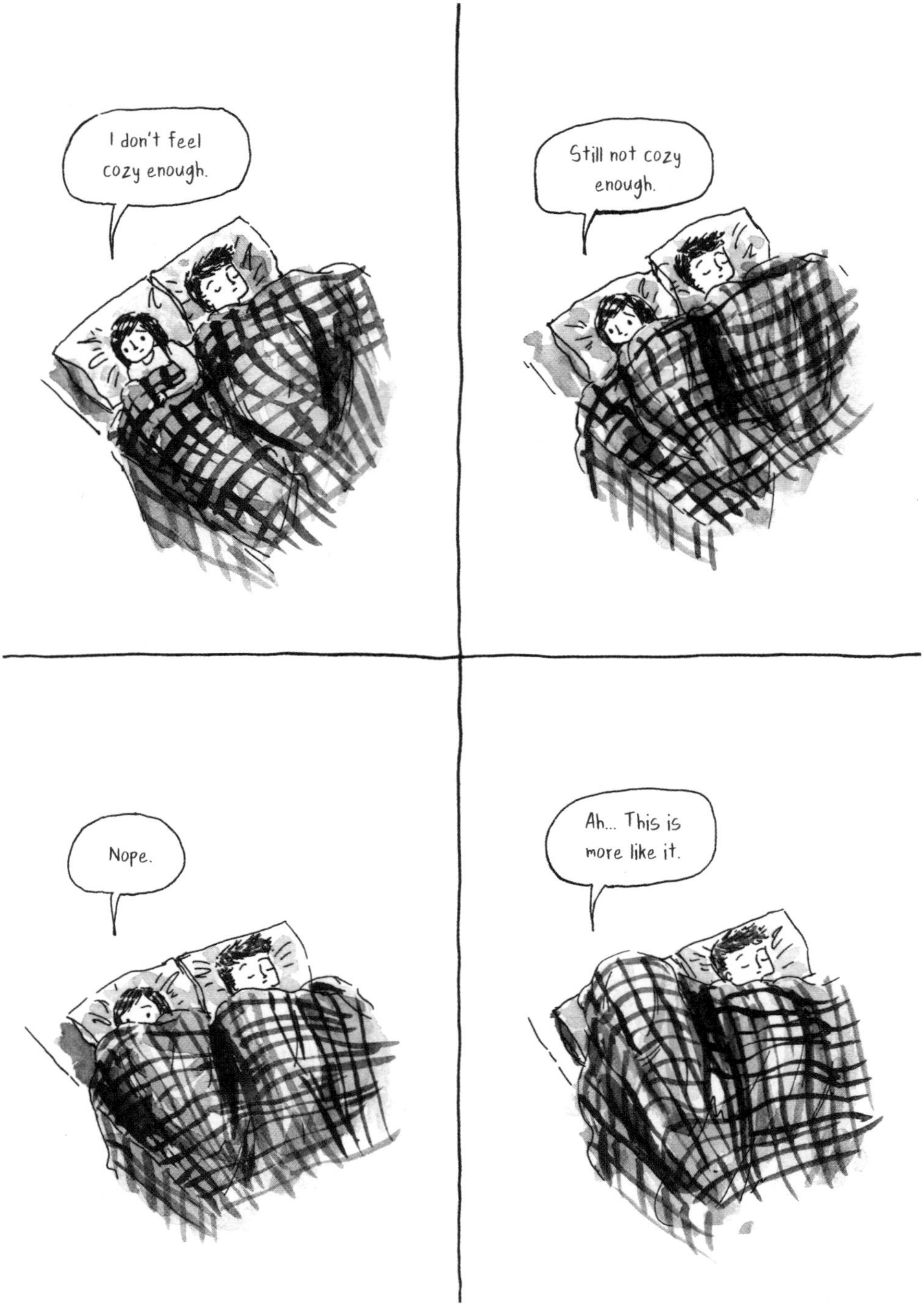
I don't feel cozy enough.
Still not cozy enough.
Nope.
Ah... This is more like it.

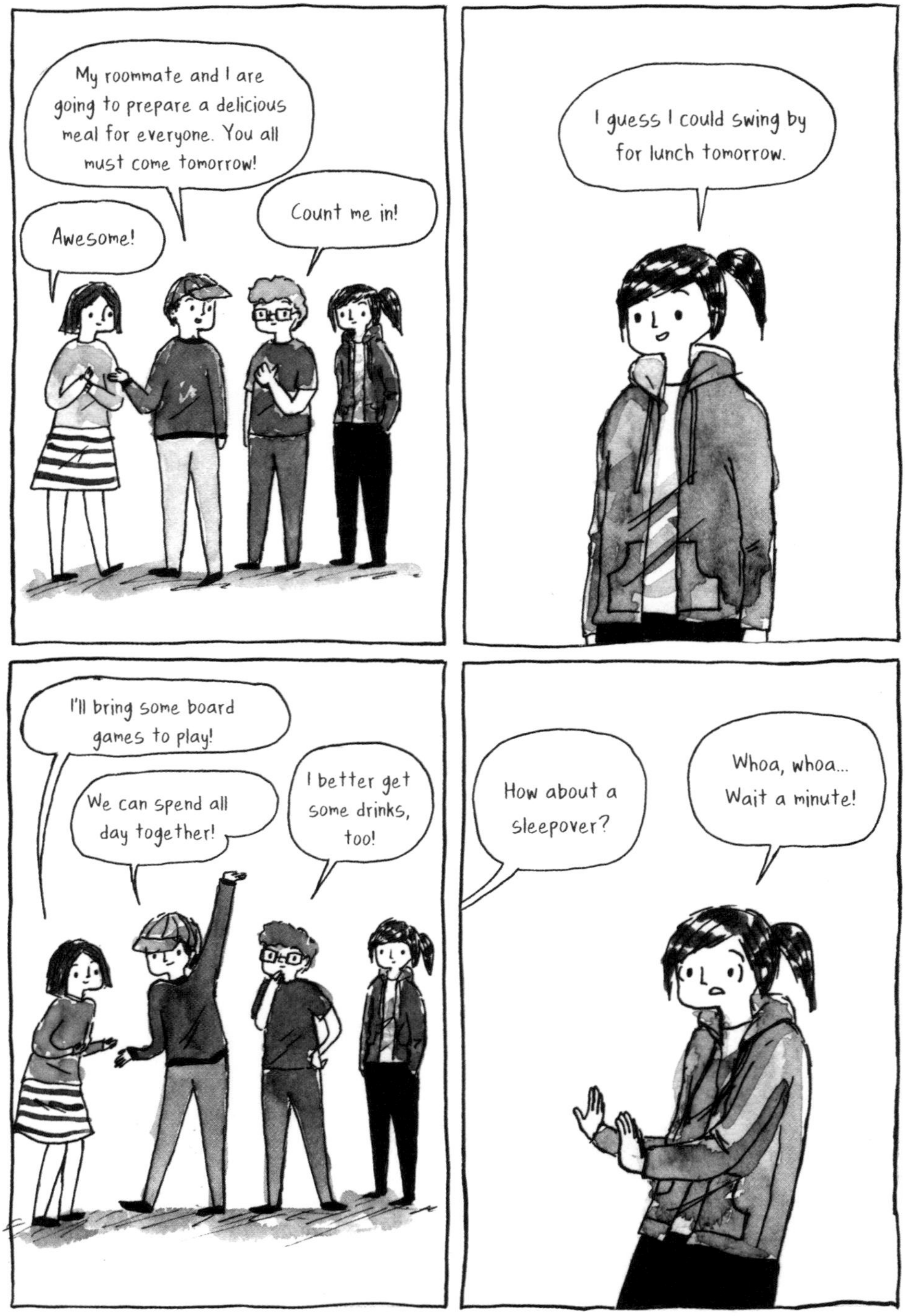
My roommate and I are going to prepare a delicious meal for everyone. You all must come tomorrow!
Awesome!
Count me in!
I guess I could swing by for lunch tomorrow.
I'll bring some board games to play!
We can spend all day together!
I better get some drinks, too!
How about a sleepover?
Whoa, whoa... Wait a minute!

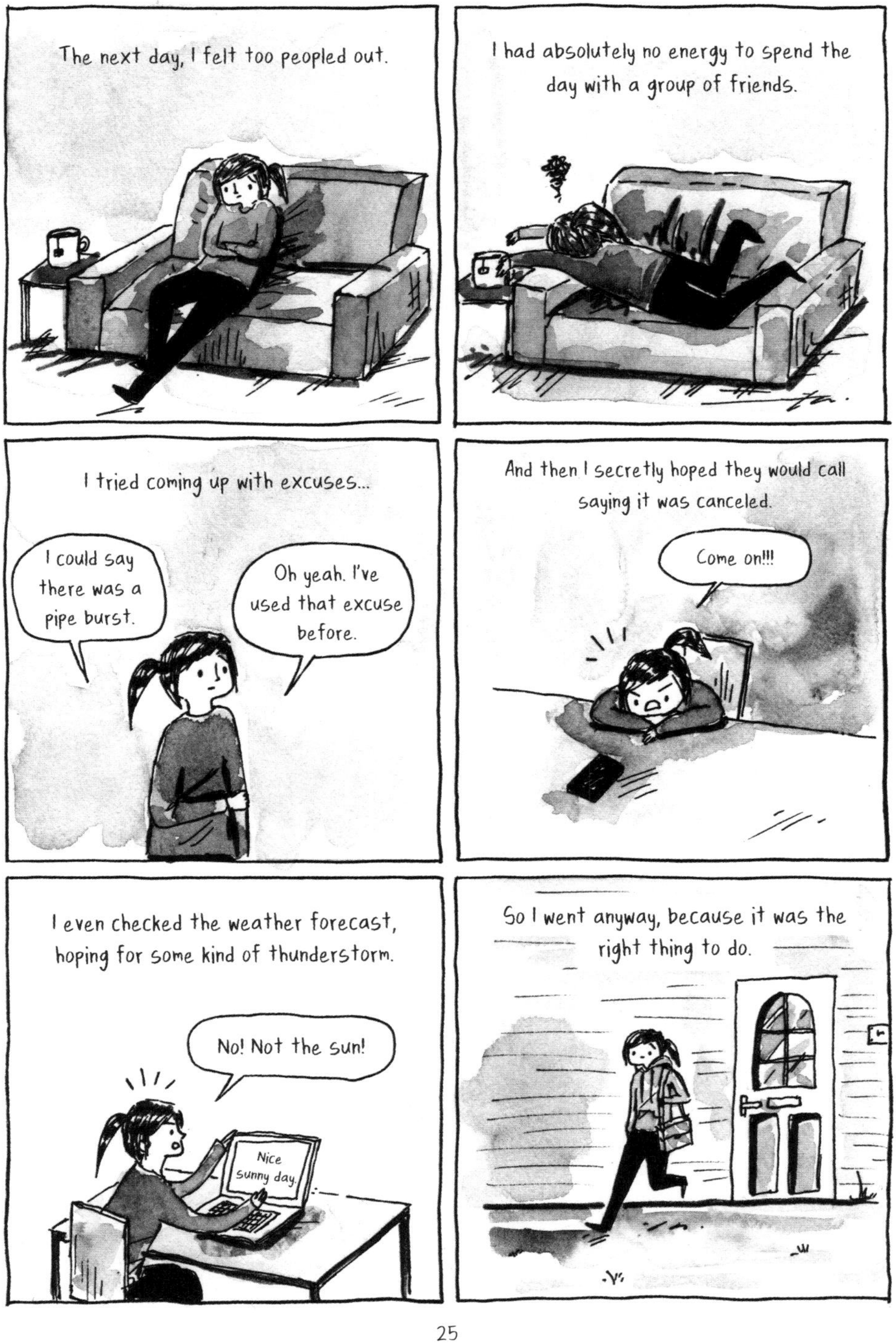
The next day, I felt too peopled out.
I had absolutely no energy to spend the day with a group of friends.
I tried coming up with excuses...
I could say there was a pipe burst.
Oh yeah. I've used that excuse before.
And then I secretly hoped they would call saying it was canceled.
Come on!!!
I even checked the weather forecast, hoping for some kind of thunderstorm.
No! Not the sun!
Nice sunny day.
So I went anyway, because it was the right thing to do.

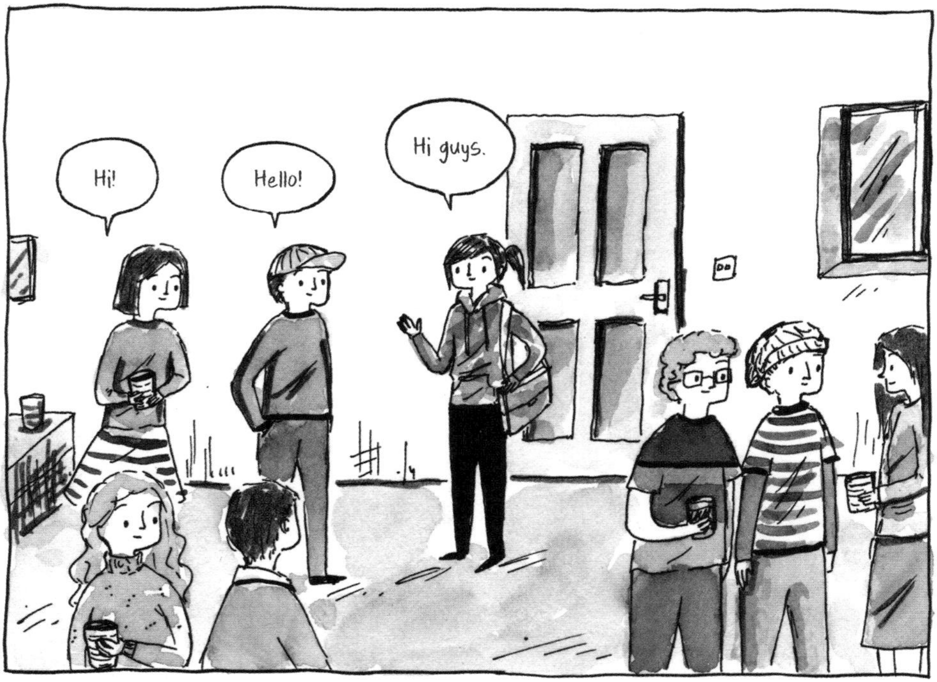
Hi!
Hello!
Hi guys.

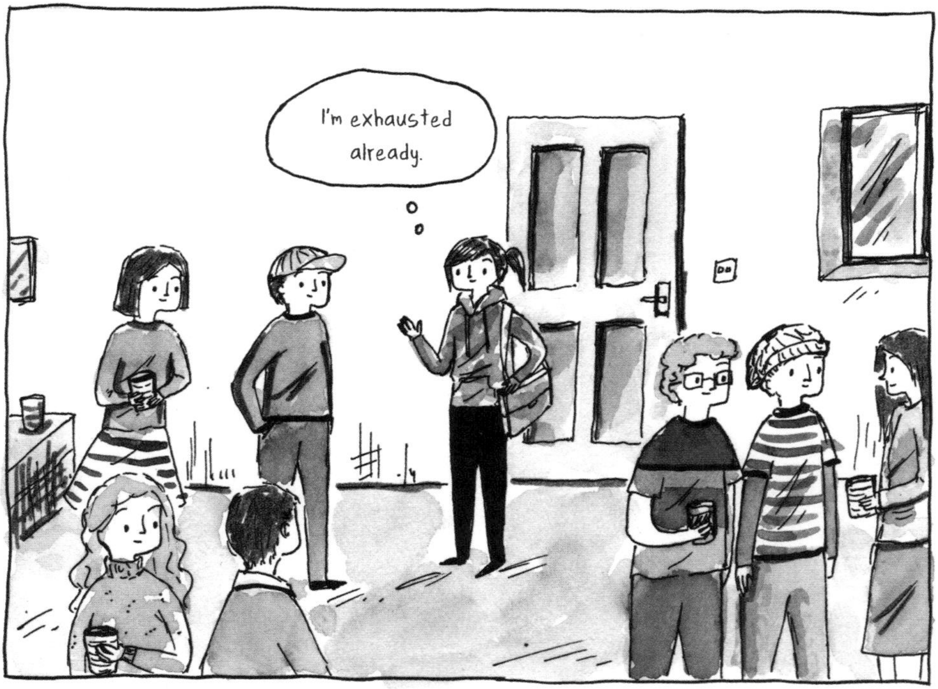
I'm exhausted already.

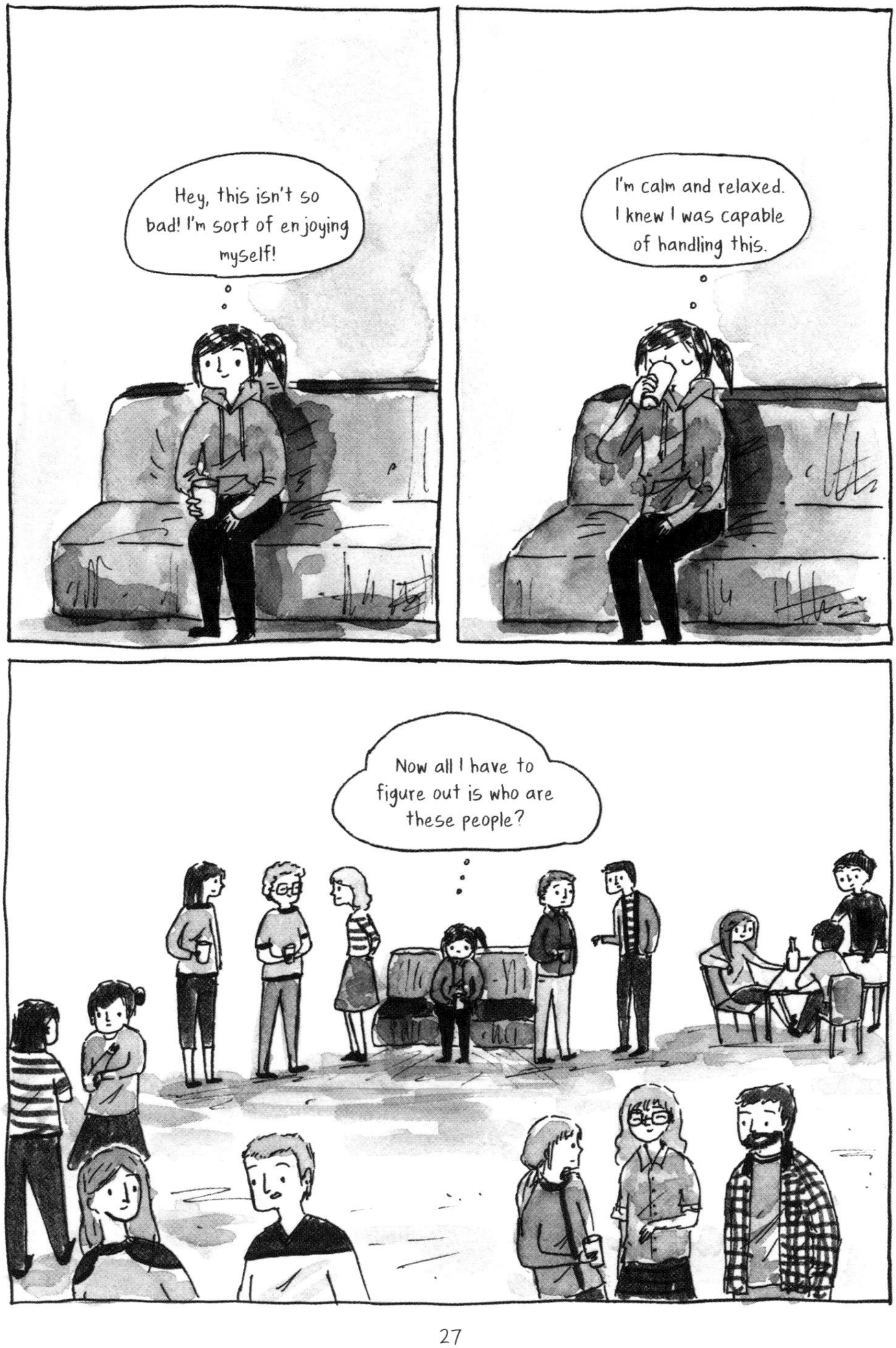
Hey, this isn't so bad! I'm sort of enjoying myself!
I'm calm and relaxed. I knew I was capable of handling this.
Now all I have to figure out is who are these people?

Me meeting new people

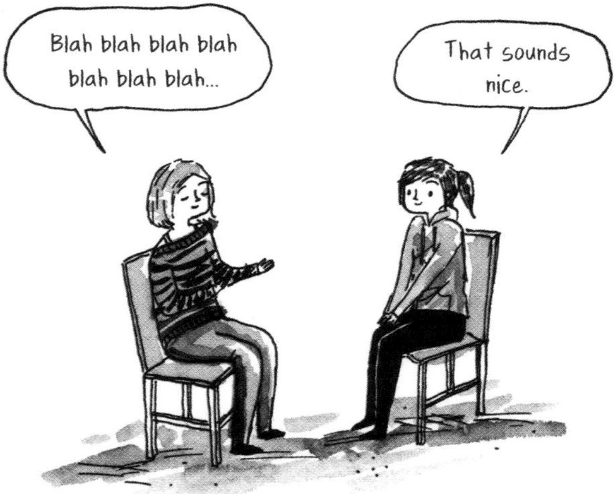
Blah blah blah blah blah blah blah...
That sounds nice.

Me with family and close friends

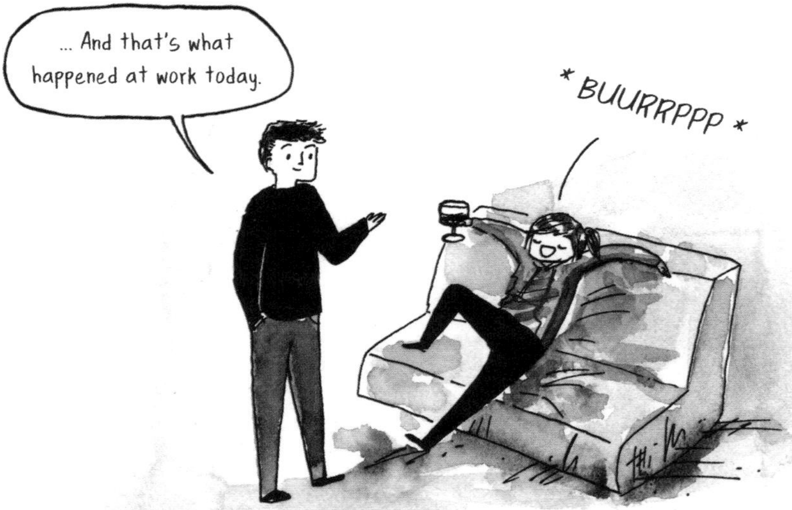
... And that's what happened at work today.
*BUURRPPP*

# What small talk does to me...

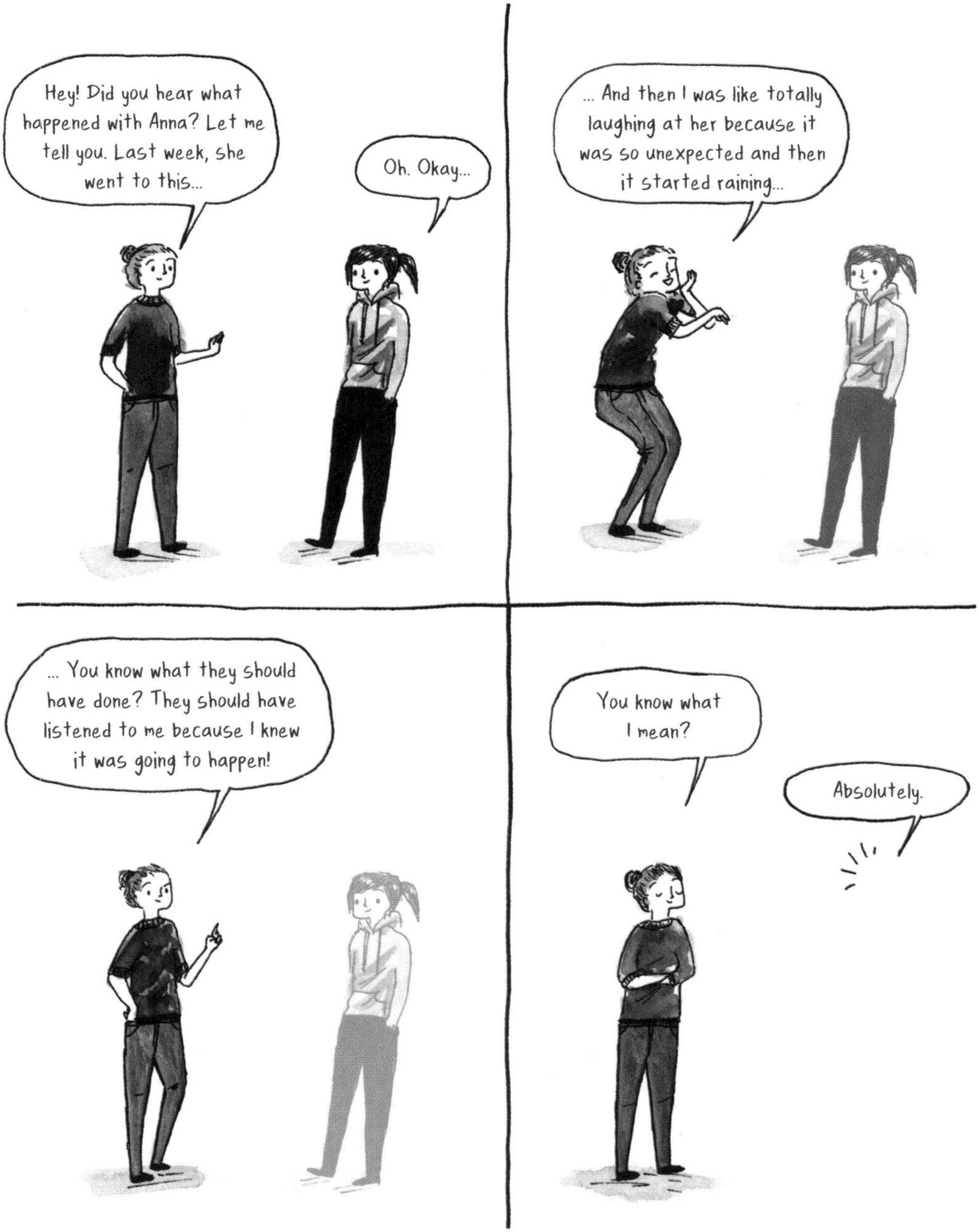
Hey! Did you hear what happened with Anna? Let me tell you. Last week, she went to this...
Oh. Okay...
... And then I was like totally laughing at her because it was so unexpected and then it started raining...
... You know what they should have done? They should have listened to me because I knew it was going to happen!
You know what I mean?
Absolutely.

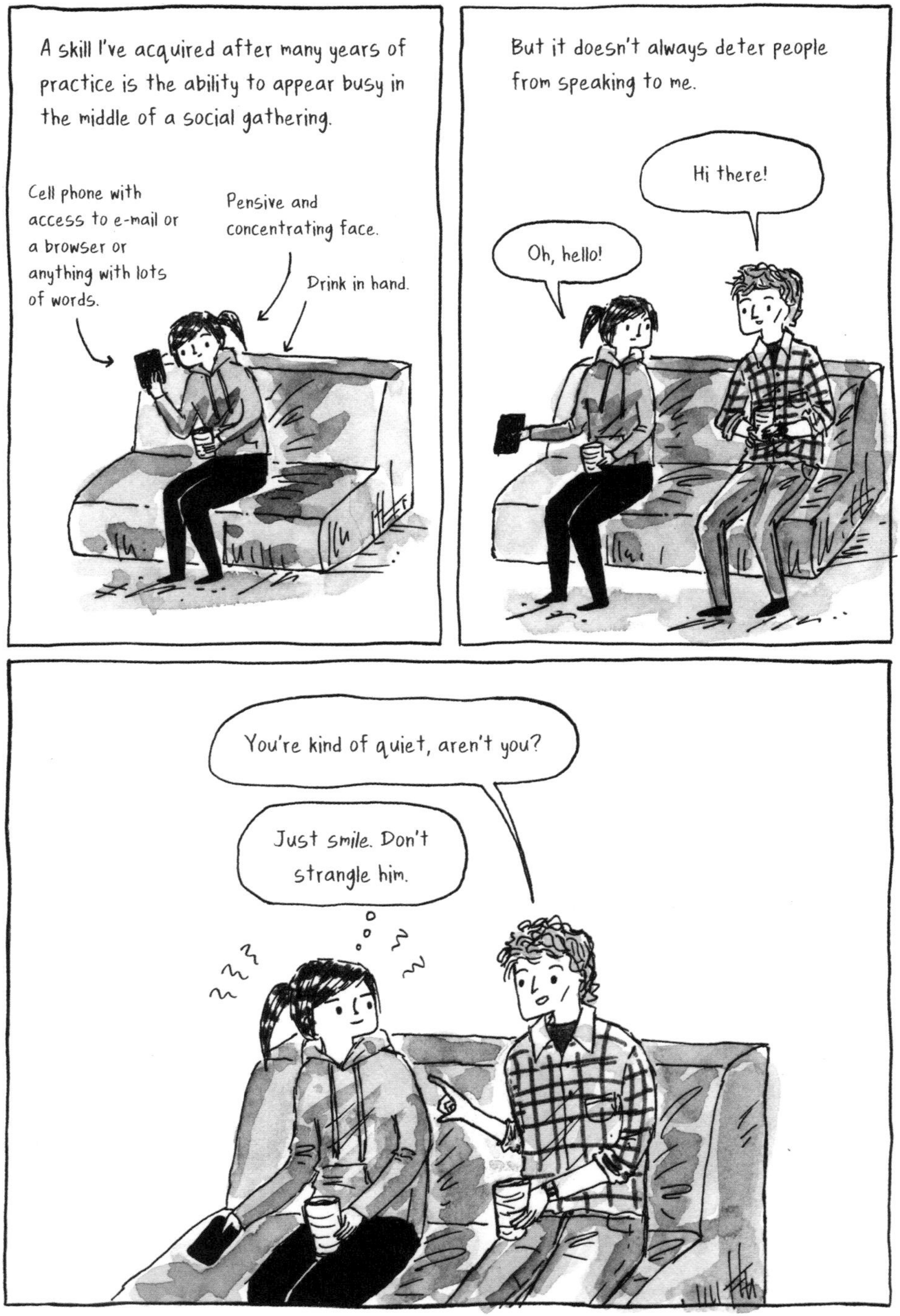
A skill I've acquired after many years of practice is the ability to appear busy in the middle of a social gathering.
Cell phone with access to e-mail or a browser or anything with lots of words.
Pensive and concentrating face.
Drink in hand.
But it doesn't always deter people from speaking to me.
Hi there!
Oh, hello!
You're kind of quiet, aren't you?
Just smile. Don't strangle him.

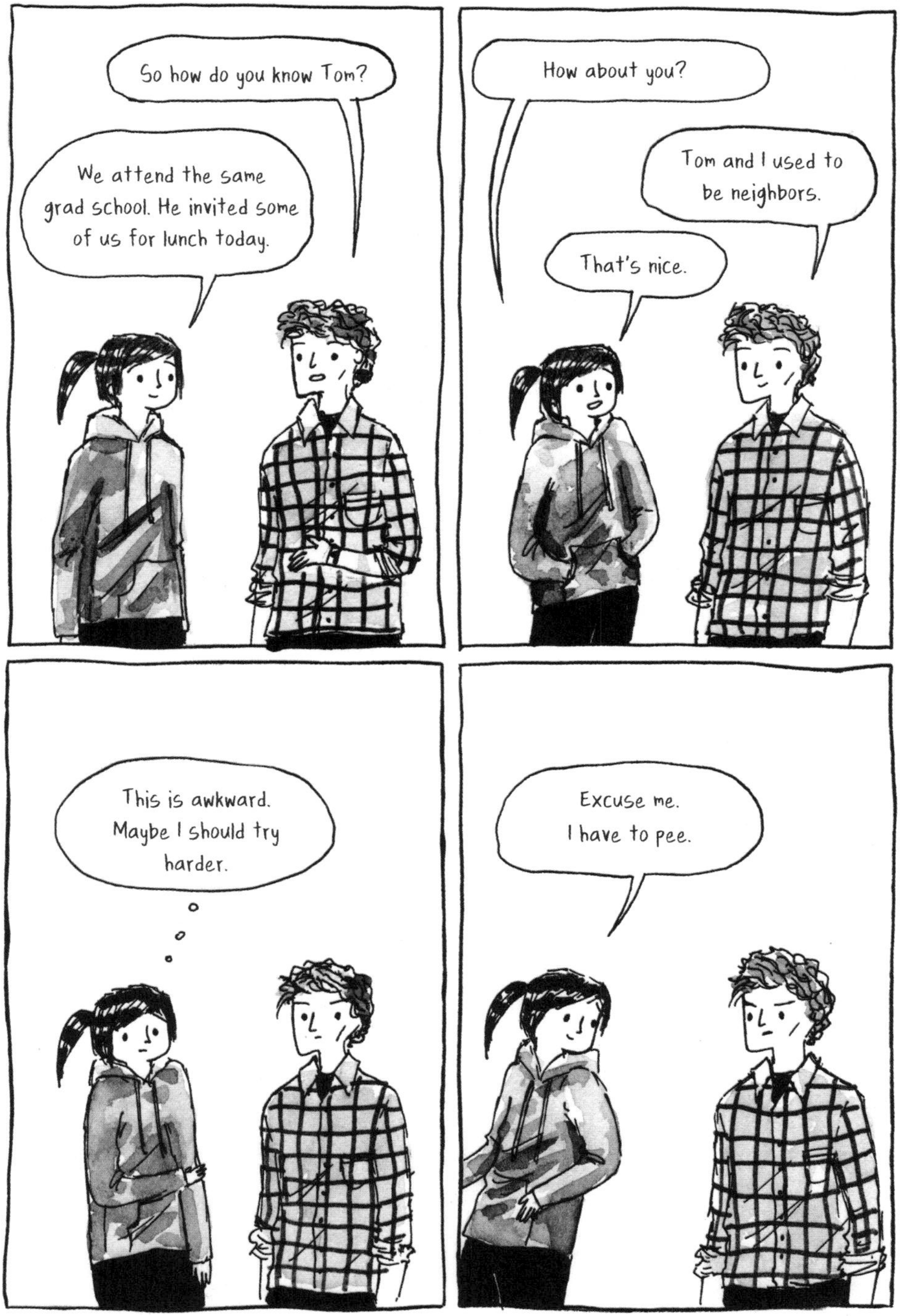
So how do you know Tom?
We attend the same grad school. He invited some of us for lunch today.
How about you?
Tom and I used to be neighbors.
That's nice.
This is awkward. Maybe I should try harder.
Excuse me. I have to pee.

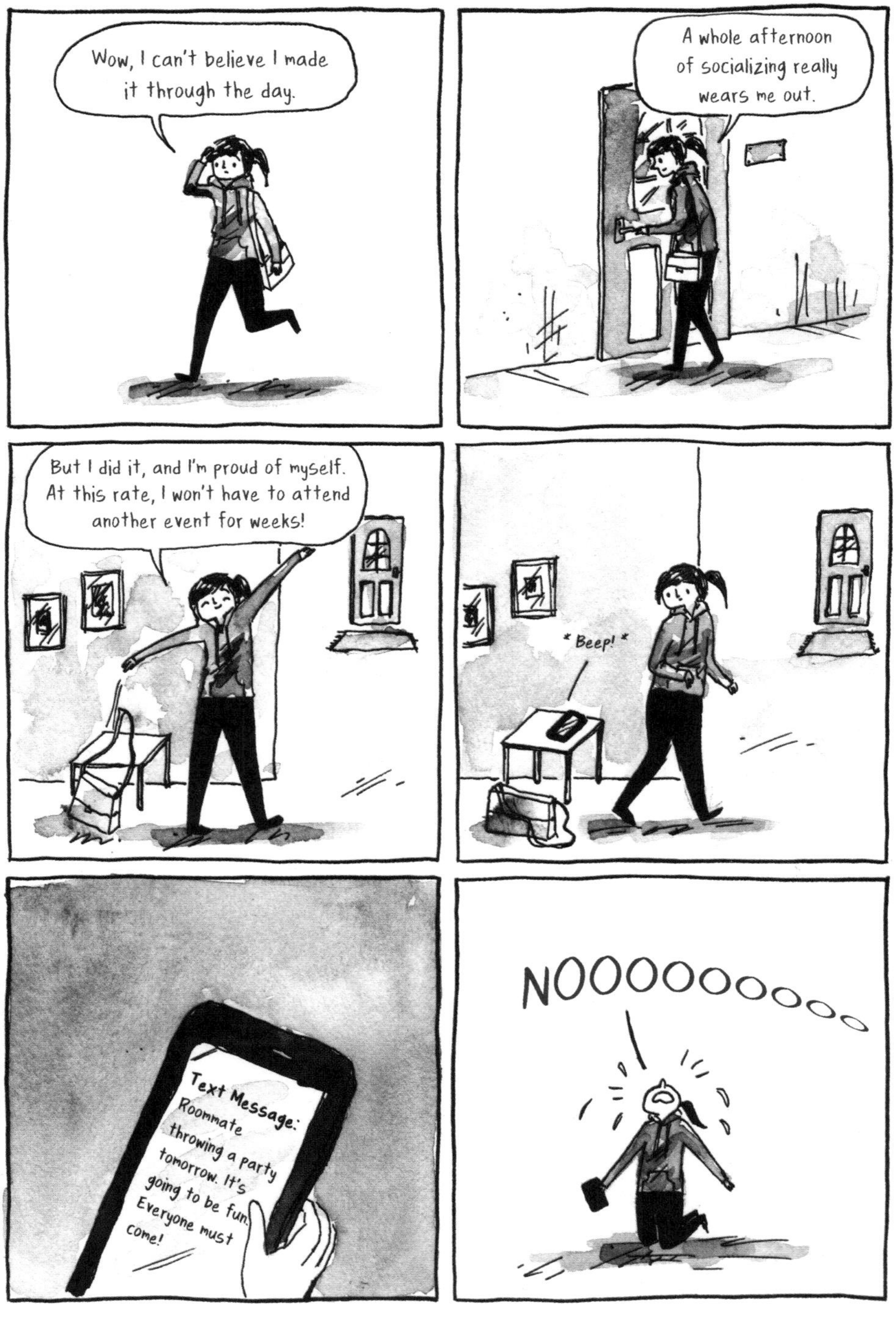
Wow, I can't believe I made it through the day.
A whole afternoon of socializing really wears me out.
But I did it, and I'm proud of myself. At this rate, I won't have to attend another event for weeks!
*Beep!*
Text Message: Roommate throwing a party tomorrow. It's going to be fun. Everyone must come!
NOOOOOOOOOO

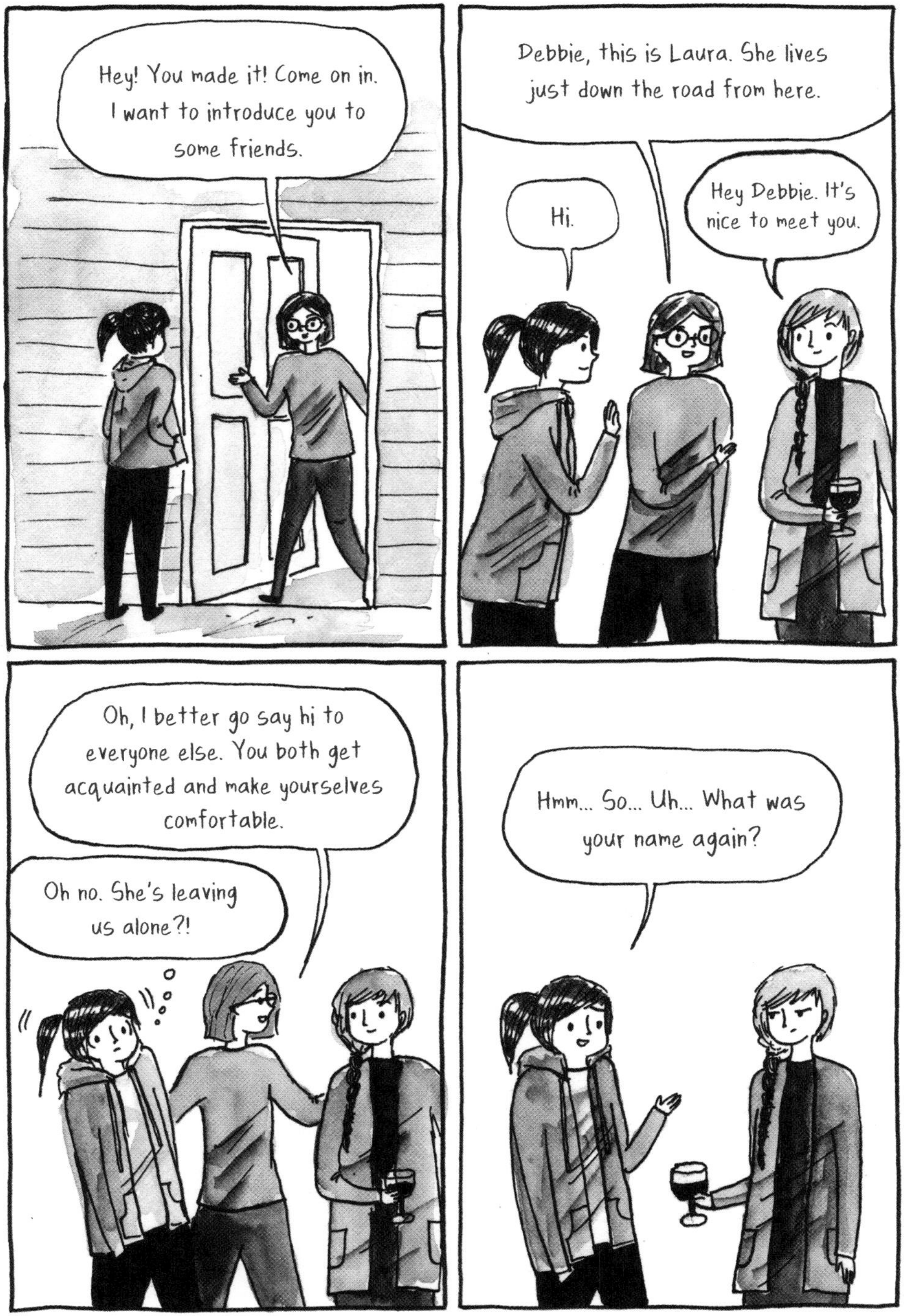
Hey! You made it! Come on in. I want to introduce you to some friends.
Debbie, this is Laura. She lives just down the road from here.
Hi.
Hey Debbie. It's nice to meet you.
Oh, I better go say hi to everyone else. You both get acquainted and make yourselves comfortable.
Oh no. She's leaving us alone?!
Hmm... So... Uh... What was your name again?

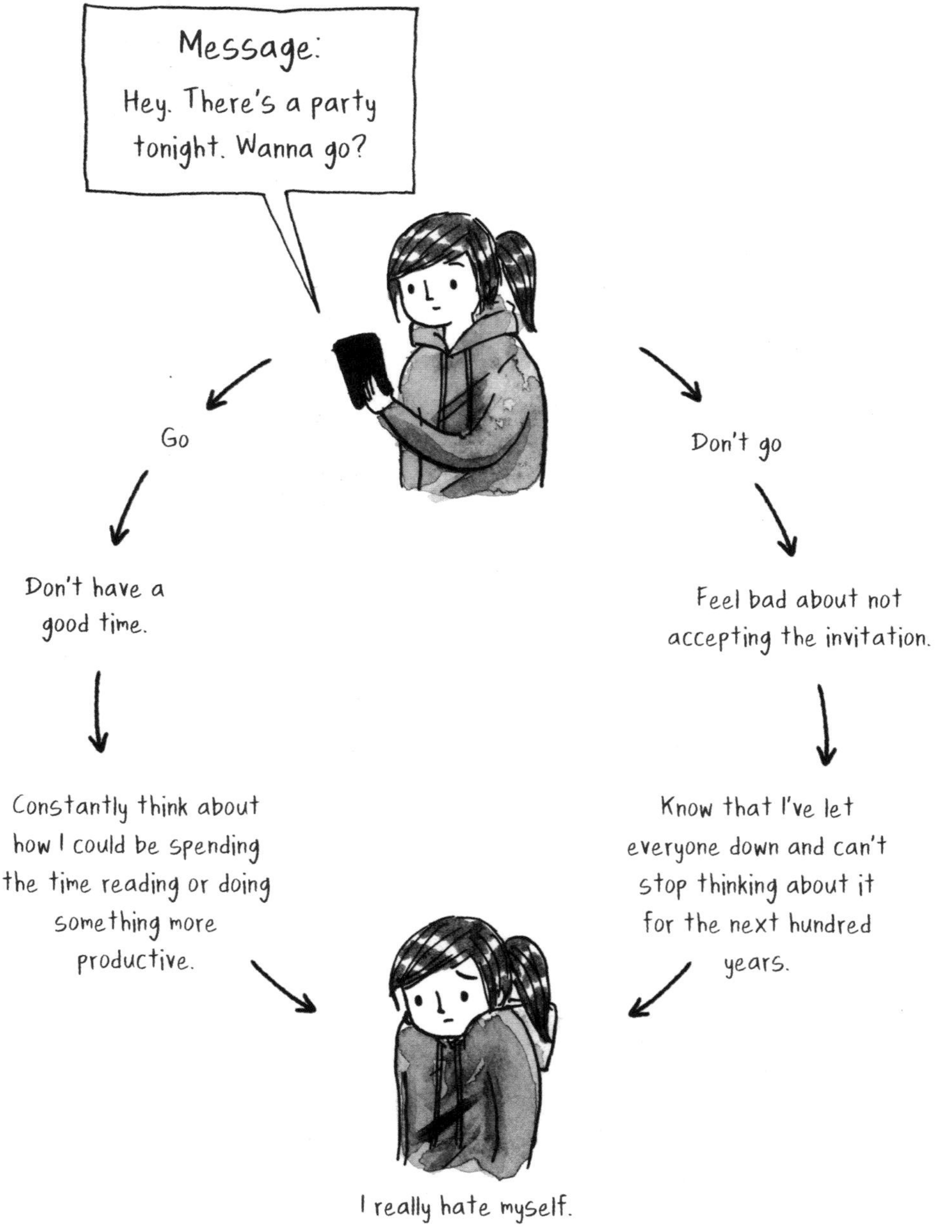
Message:
Hey. There's a party tonight. Wanna go?
Go
Don't have a good time.
Constantly think about how I could be spending the time reading or doing something more productive.
Don't go
Feel bad about not accepting the invitation.
Know that I've let everyone down and can't stop thinking about it for the next hundred years.
I really hate myself.

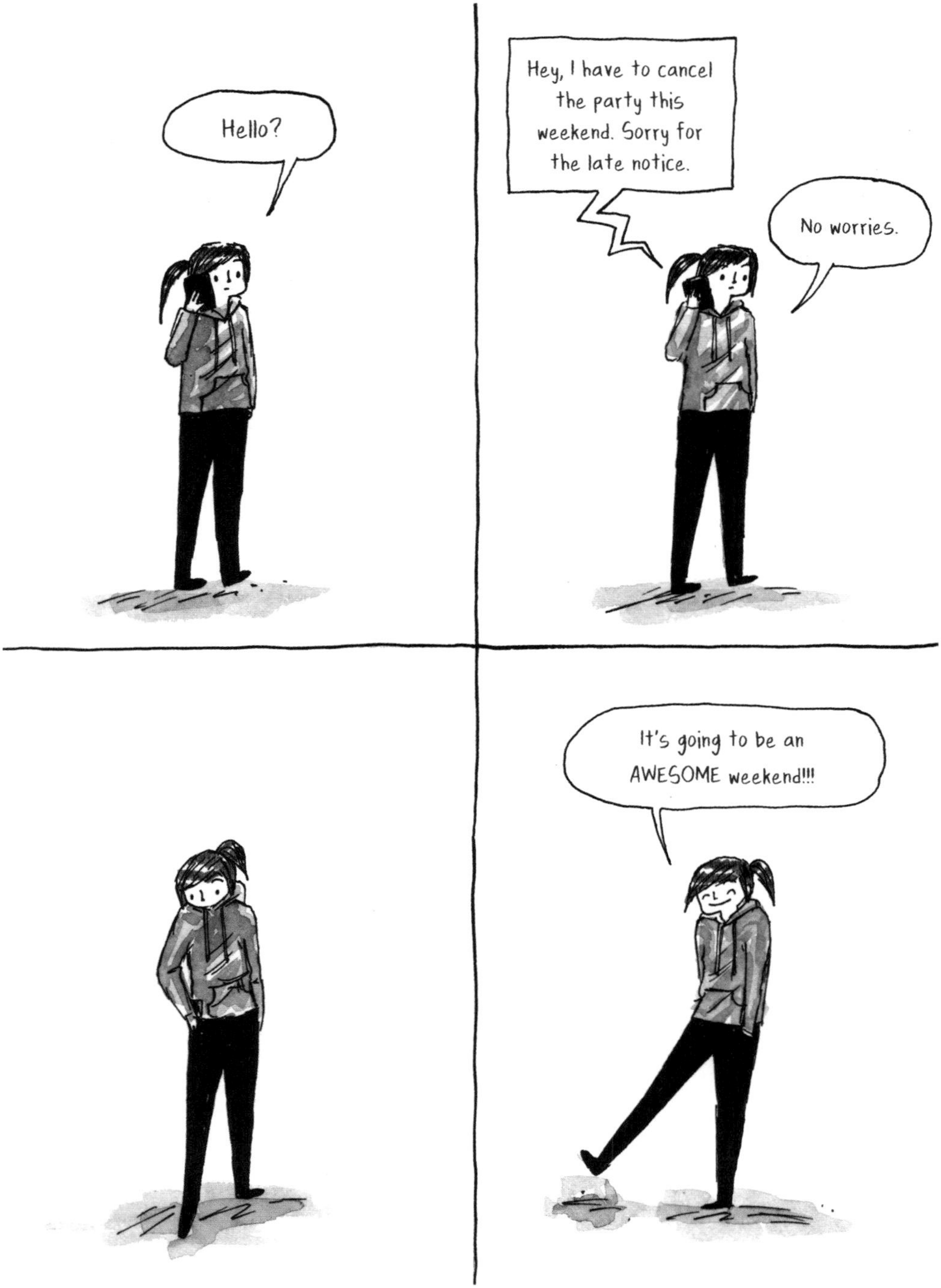
Hello?
Hey, I have to cancel the party this weekend. Sorry for the late notice.
No worries.
It's going to be an AWESOME weekend!!!

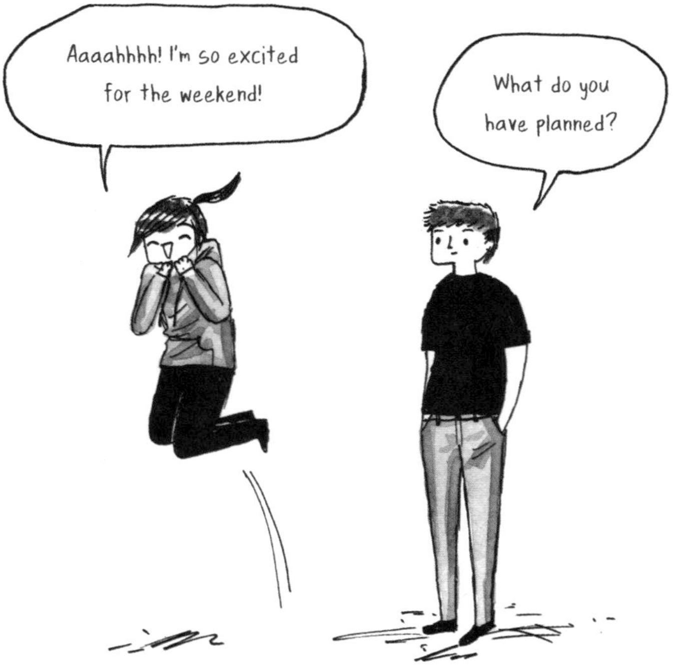
Aaaahhhh! I'm so excited for the weekend!
What do you have planned?

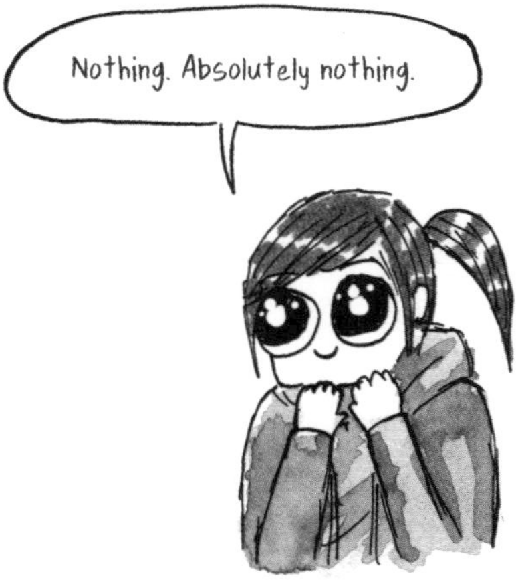
Nothing. Absolutely nothing.

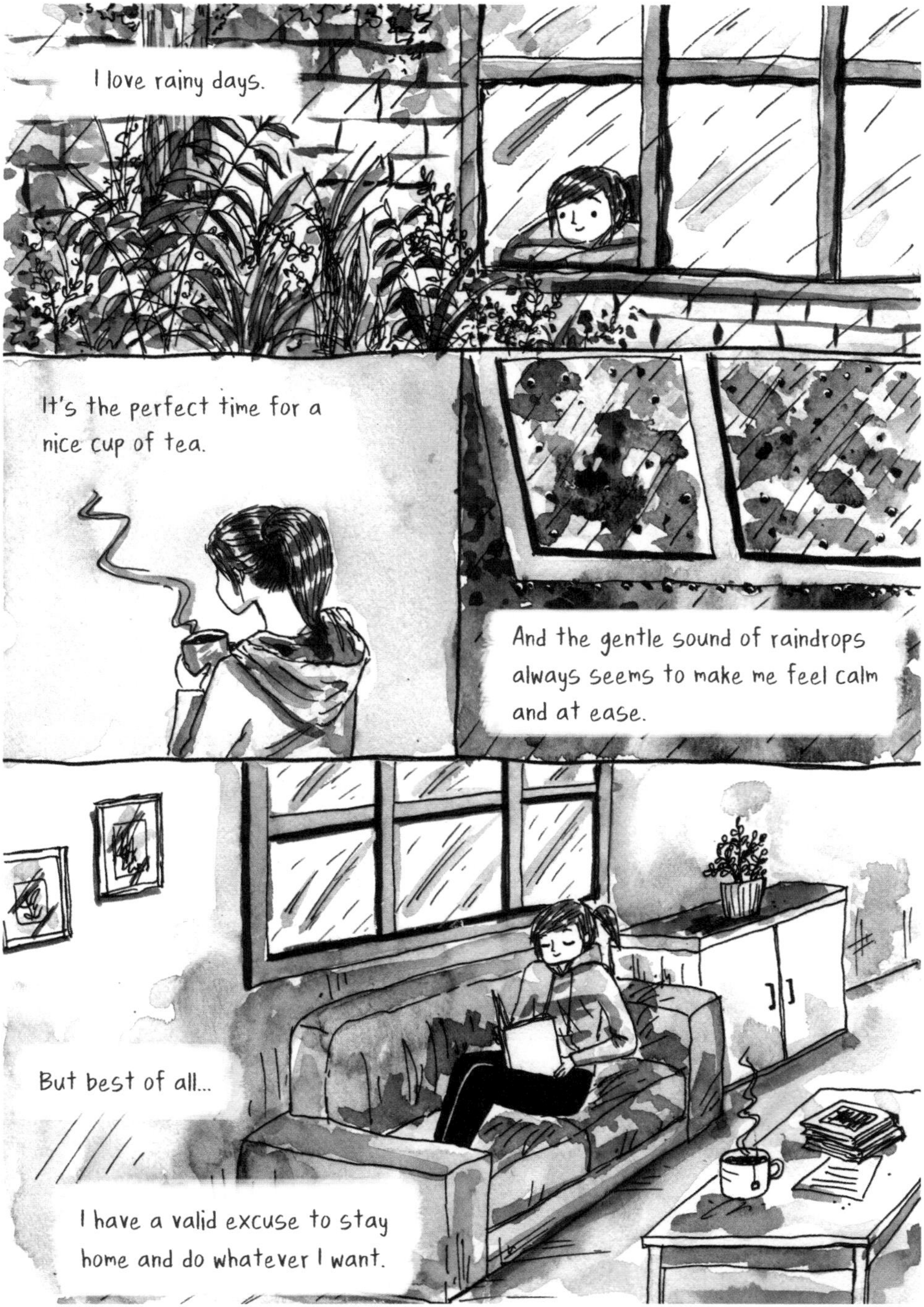
I love rainy days.
It's the perfect time for a nice cup of tea.
And the gentle sound of raindrops always seems to make me feel calm and at ease.
But best of all...
I have a valid excuse to stay home and do whatever I want.

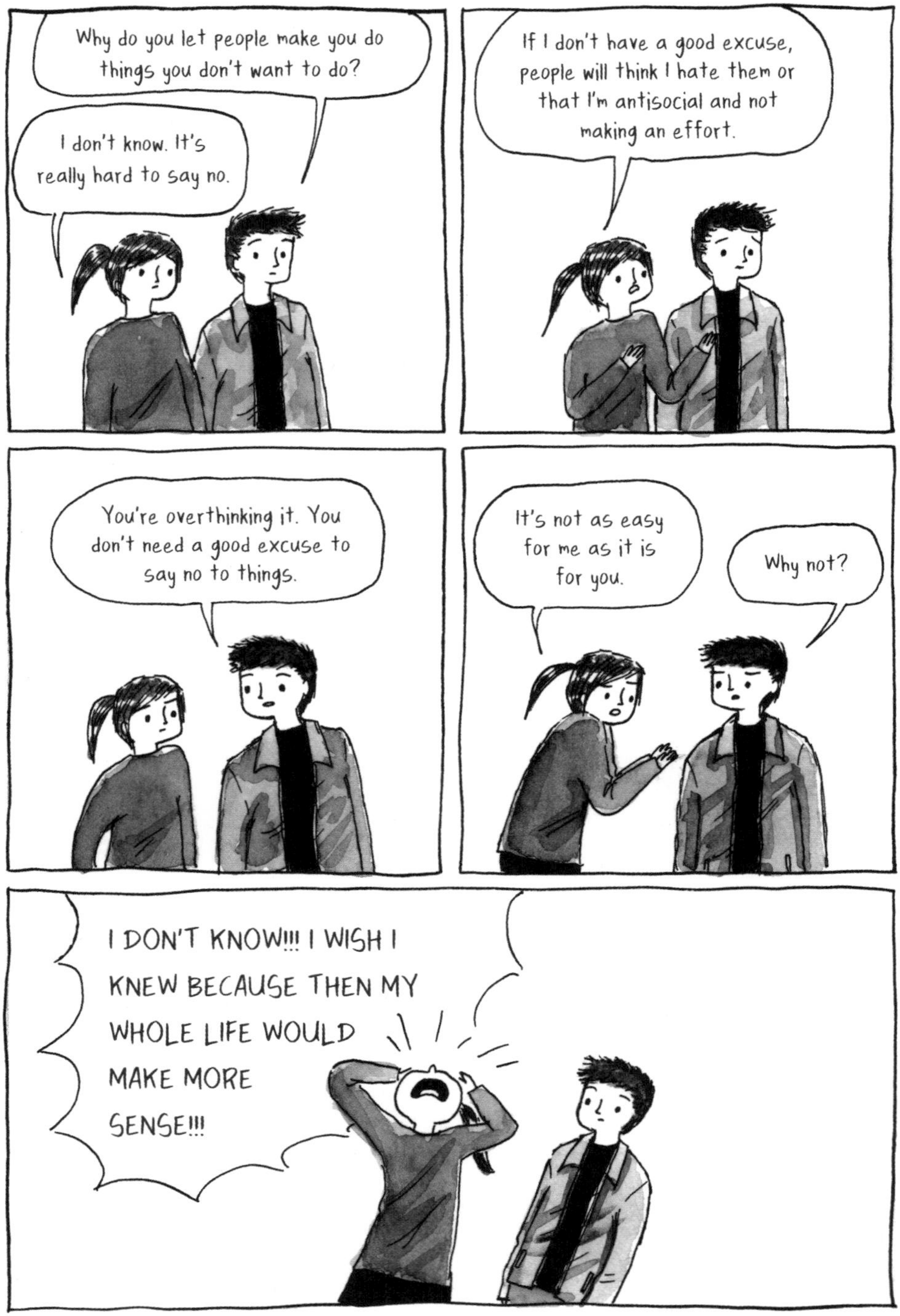
Why do you let people make you do things you don't want to do?
I don't know. It's really hard to say no.
If I don't have a good excuse, people will think I hate them or that I'm antisocial and not making an effort.
You're overthinking it. You don't need a good excuse to say no to things.
It's not as easy for me as it is for you.
Why not?
I DON'T KNOW!!! I WISH I KNEW BECAUSE THEN MY WHOLE LIFE WOULD MAKE MORE SENSE!!!

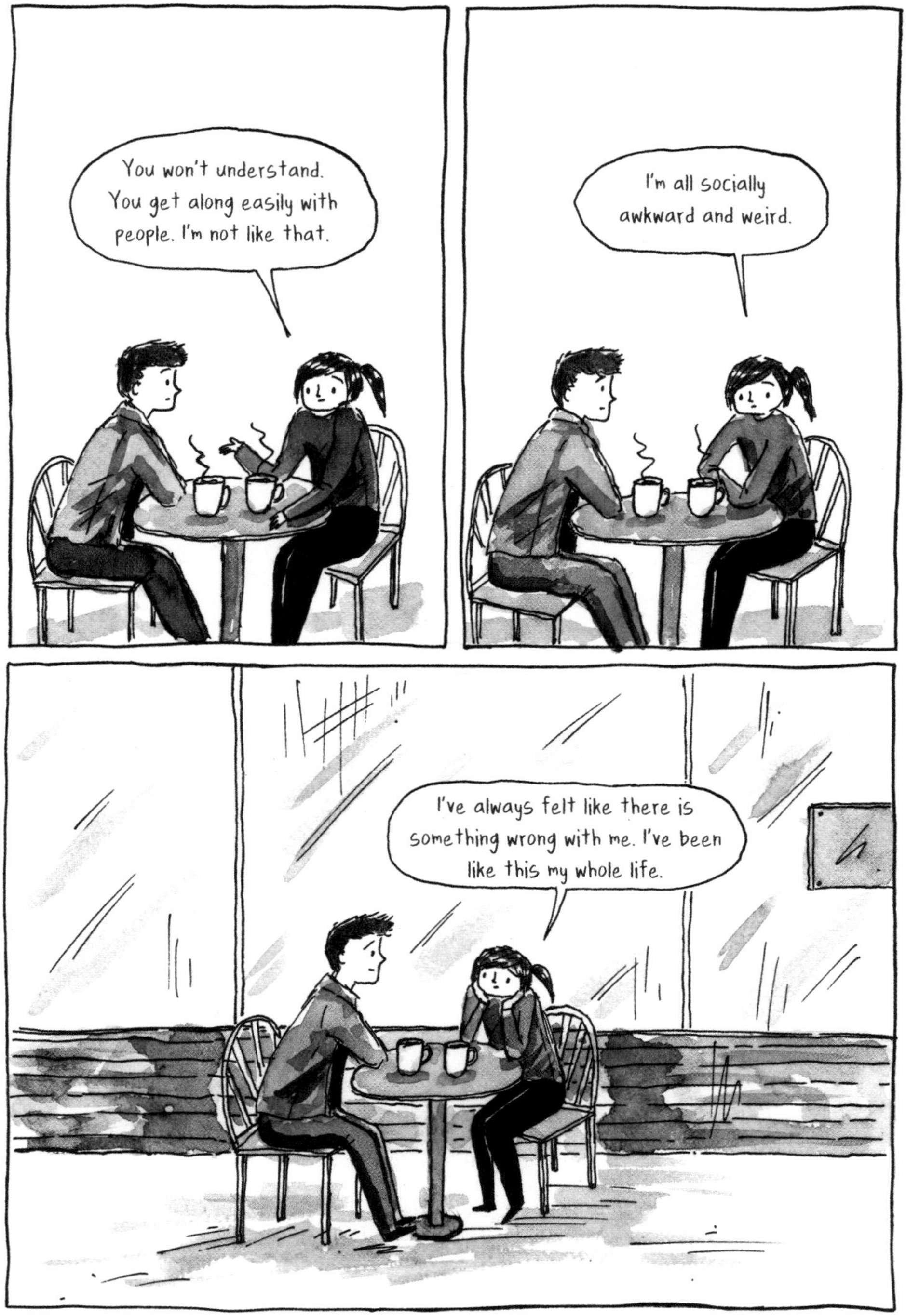
You won't understand. You get along easily with people. I'm not like that.
I'm all socially awkward and weird.
I've always felt like there is something wrong with me. I've been like this my whole life.

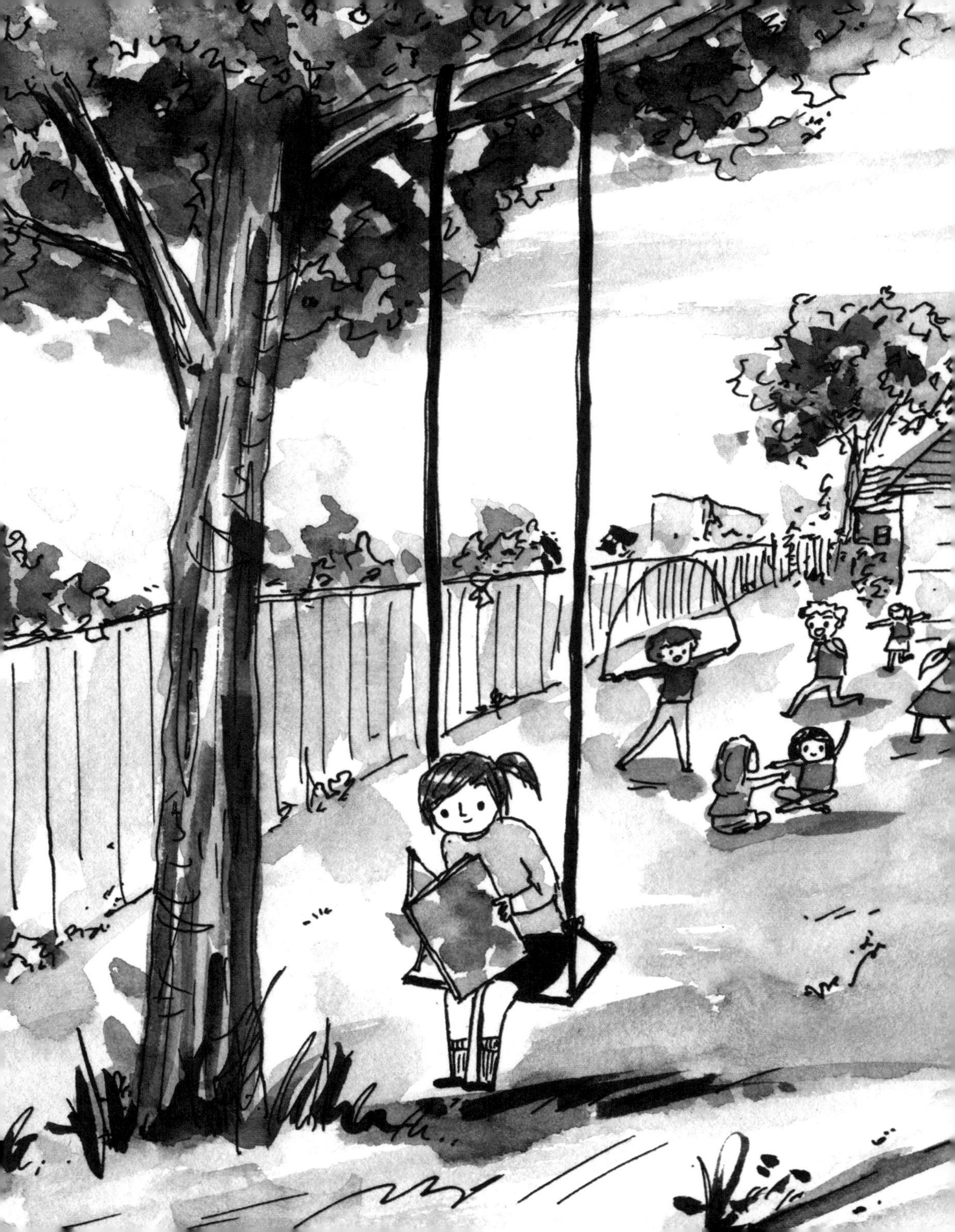

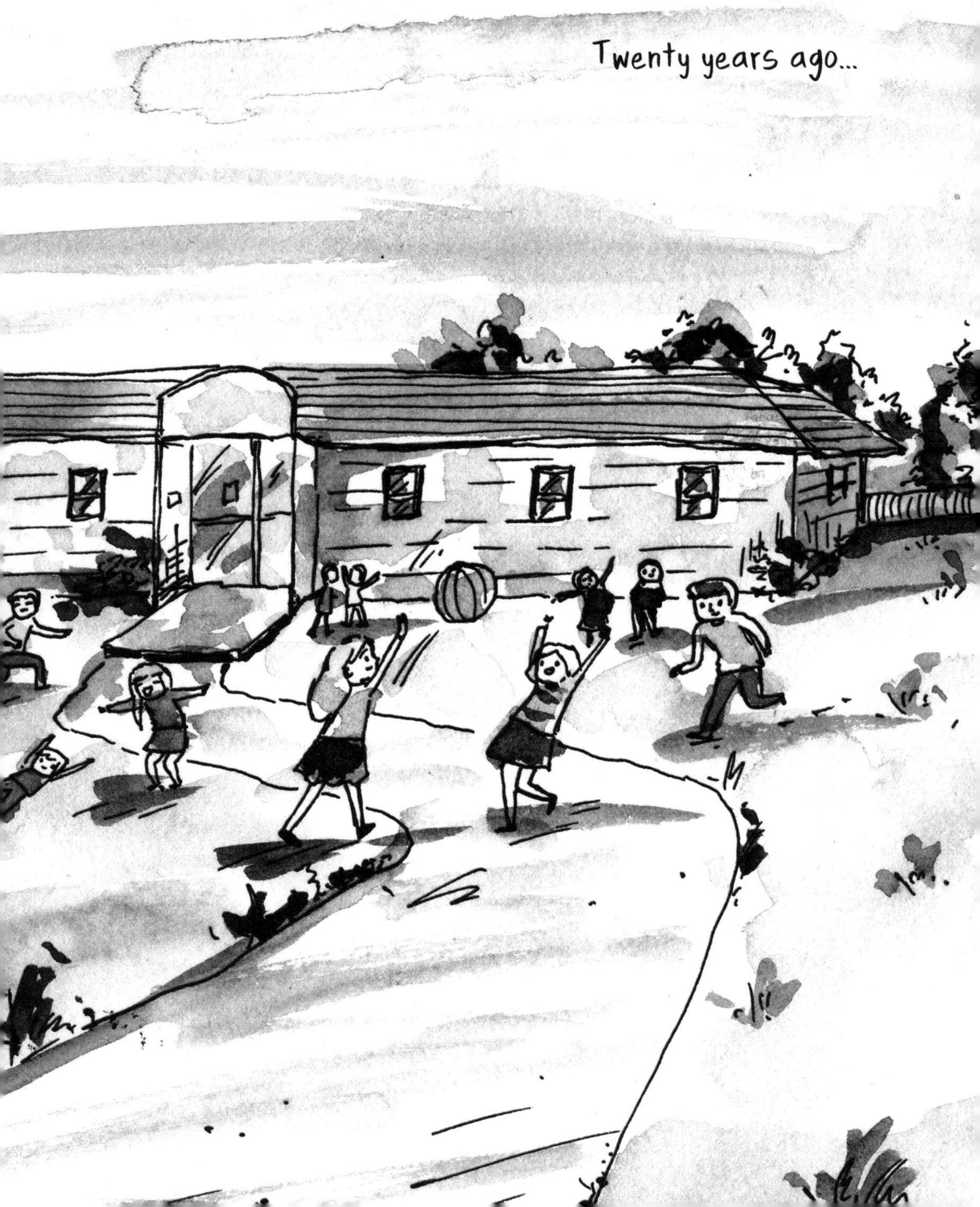
Twenty years ago...

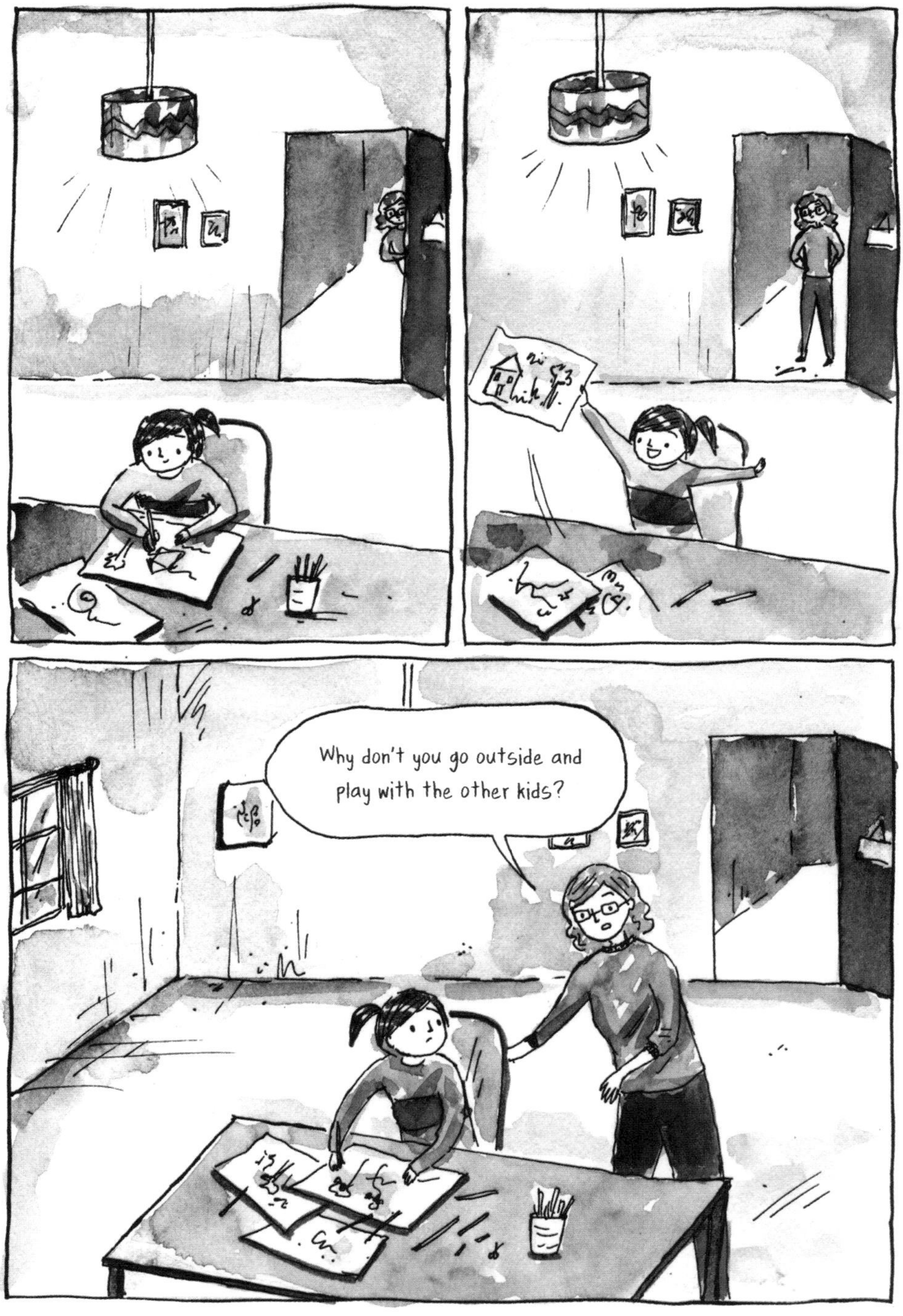
Why don't you go outside and play with the other kids?

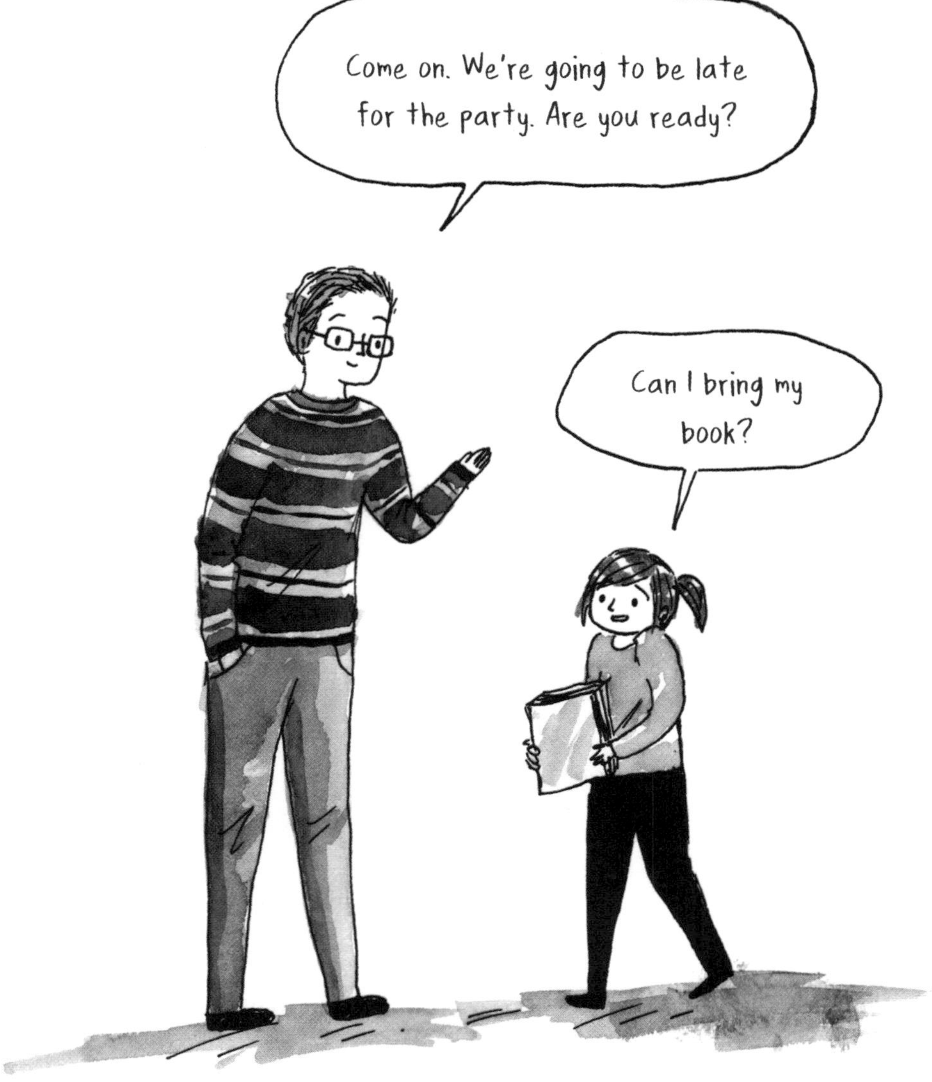
Come on. We're going to be late for the party. Are you ready?
Can I bring my book?

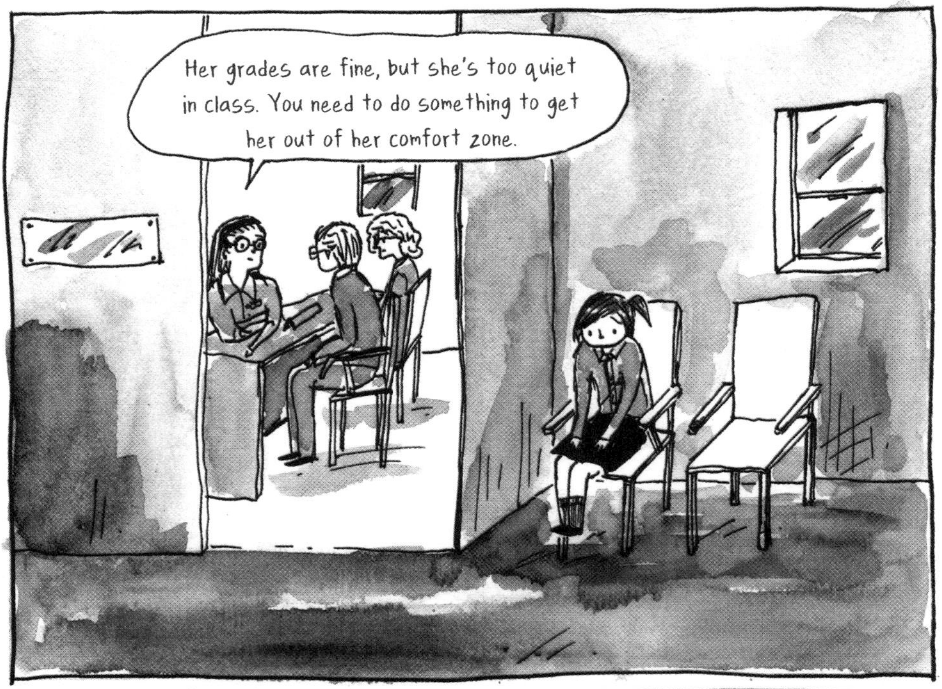
Her grades are fine, but she's too quiet in class. You need to do something to get her out of her comfort zone.

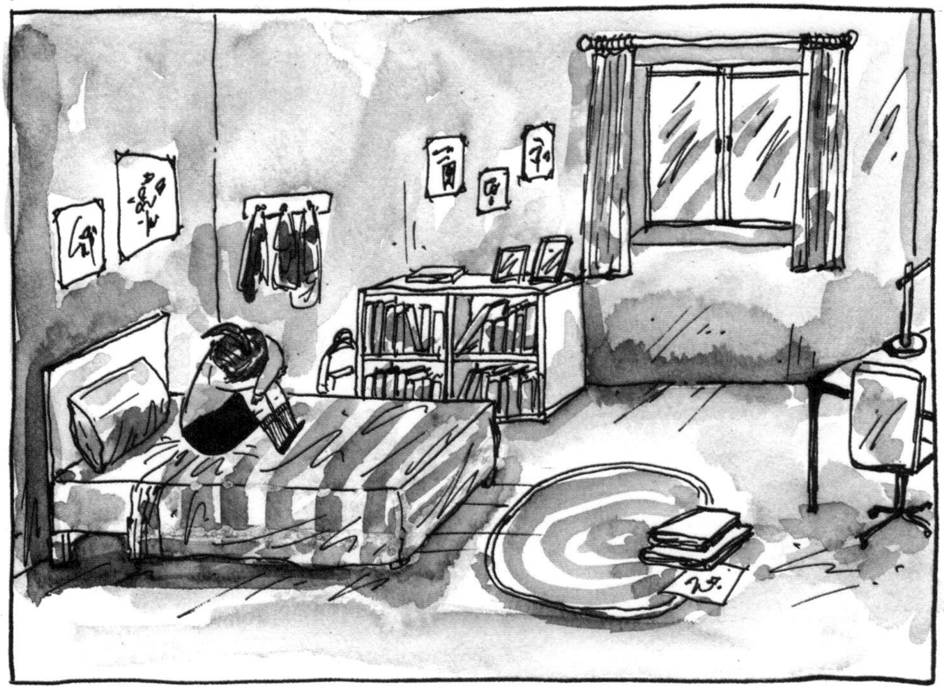

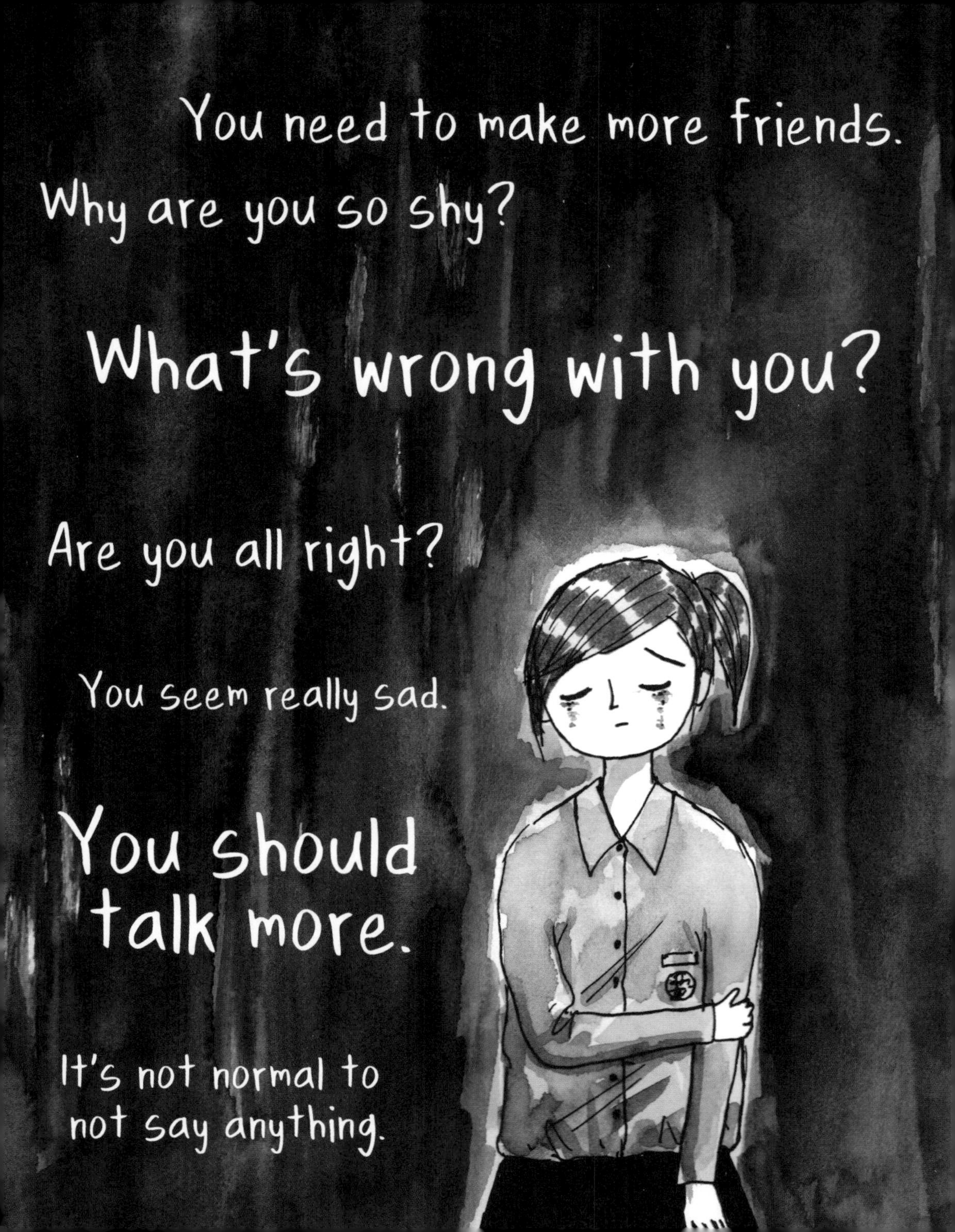
You need to make more friends.
Why are you so shy?
What's wrong with you?
Are you all right?
You seem really sad.
You should talk more.
It's not normal to not say anything.

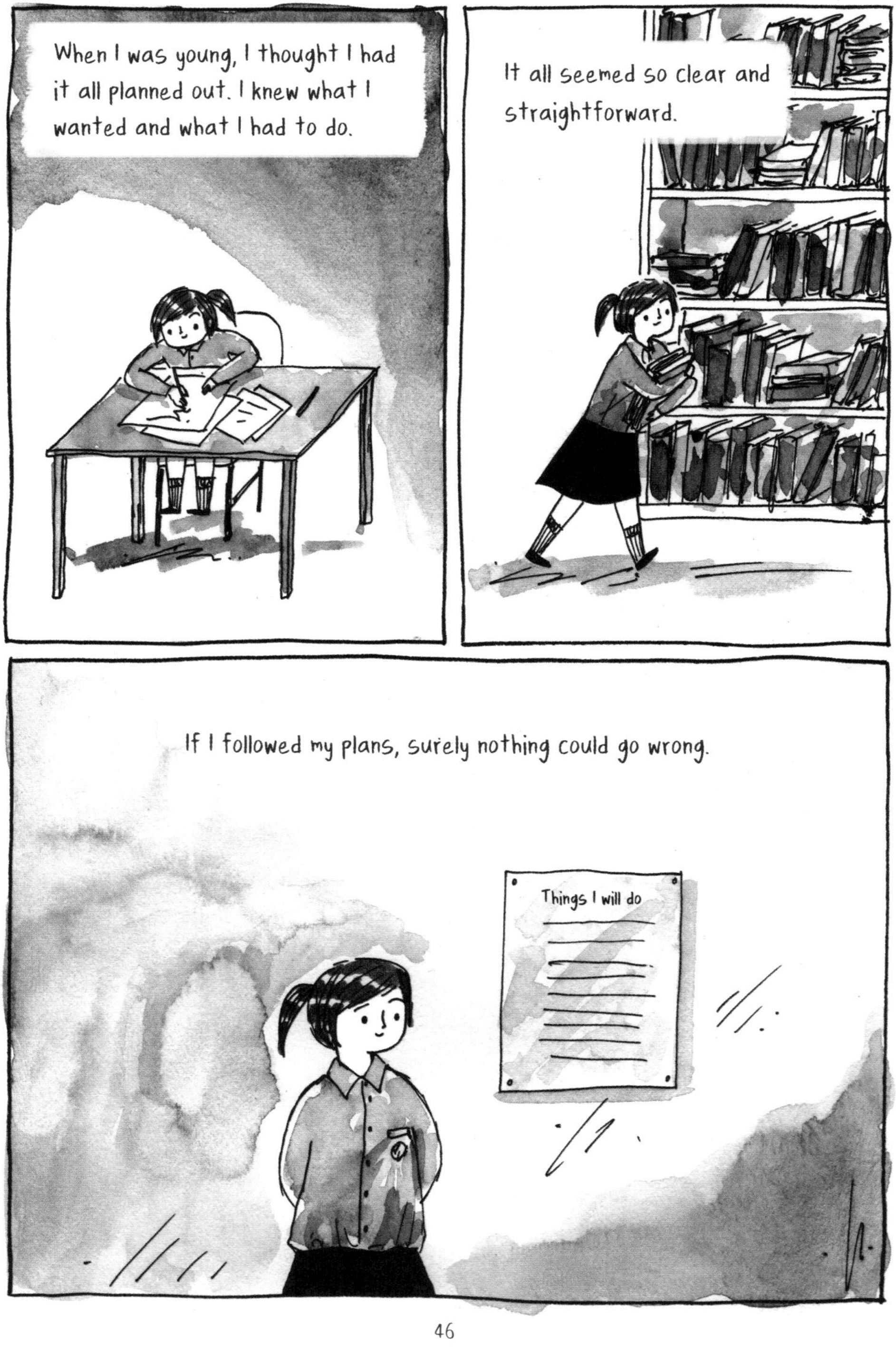
When I was young, I thought I had it all planned out. I knew what I wanted and what I had to do.
It all seemed so clear and straightforward.
If I followed my plans, surely nothing could go wrong.
Things I will do

Present Day...

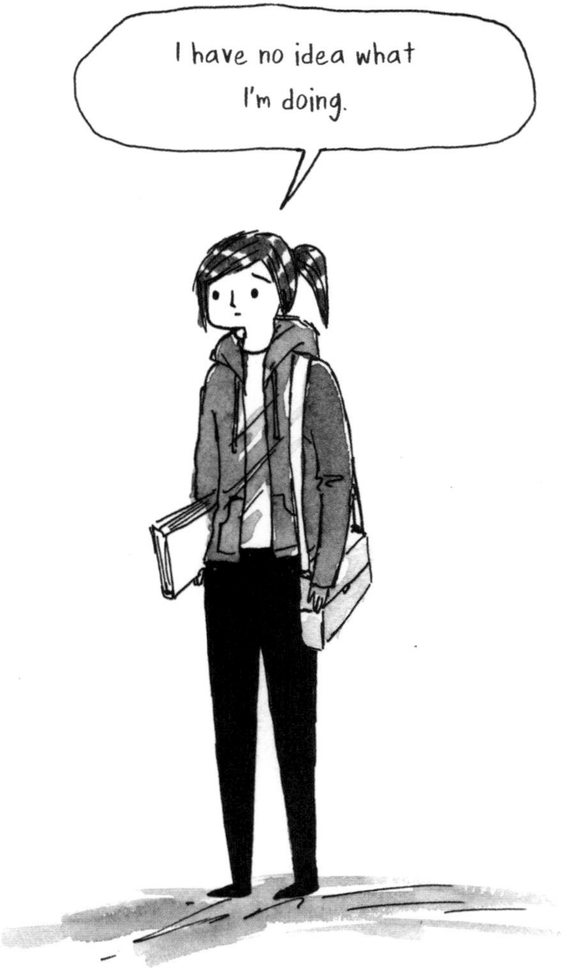
I have no idea what I'm doing.

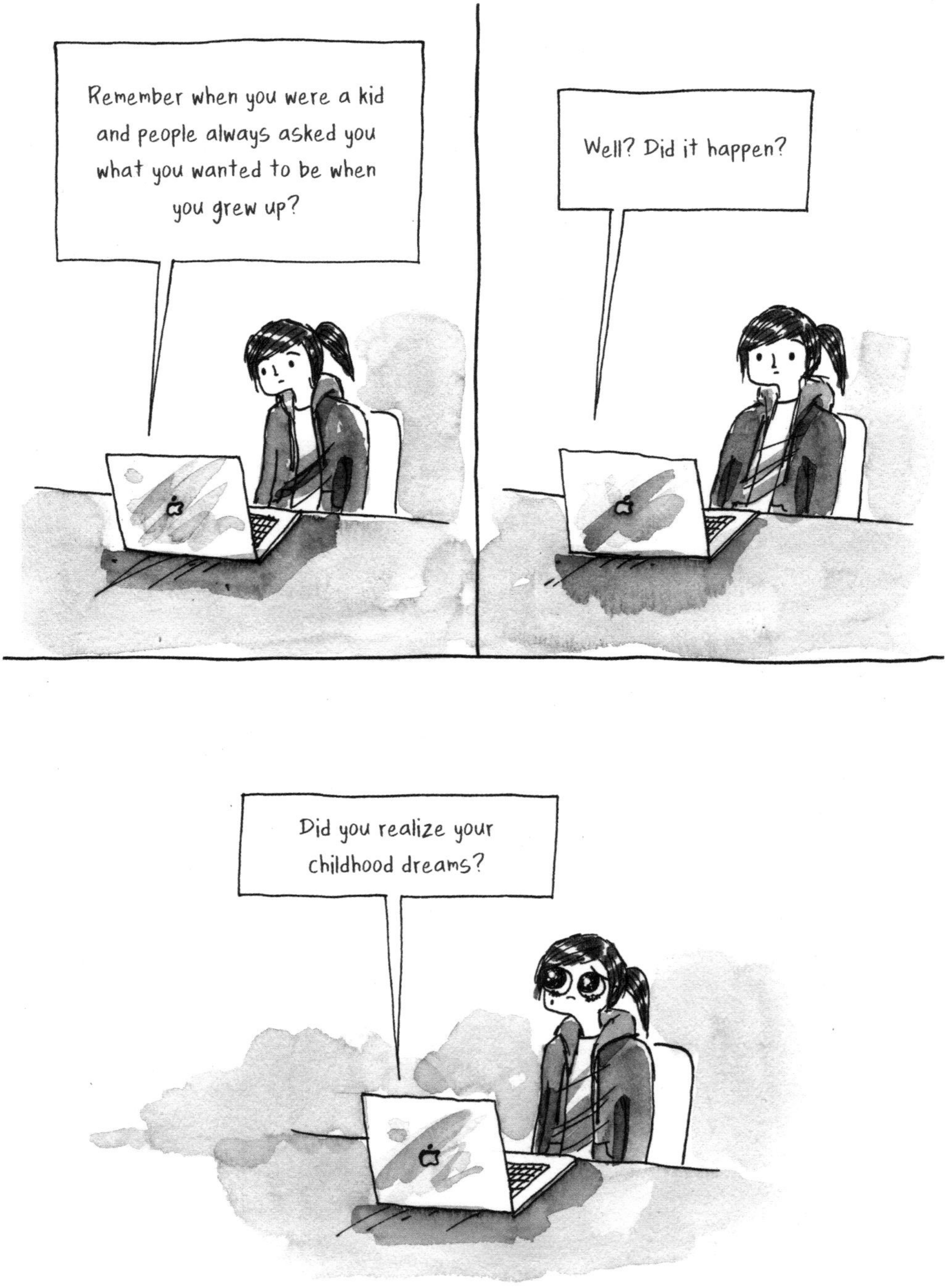
Remember when you were a kid and people always asked you what you wanted to be when you grew up?
Well? Did it happen?
Did you realize your childhood dreams?

\* SOB \*
I'M SORRY, YOUNGER SELF!!!
I'M SORRY!!!

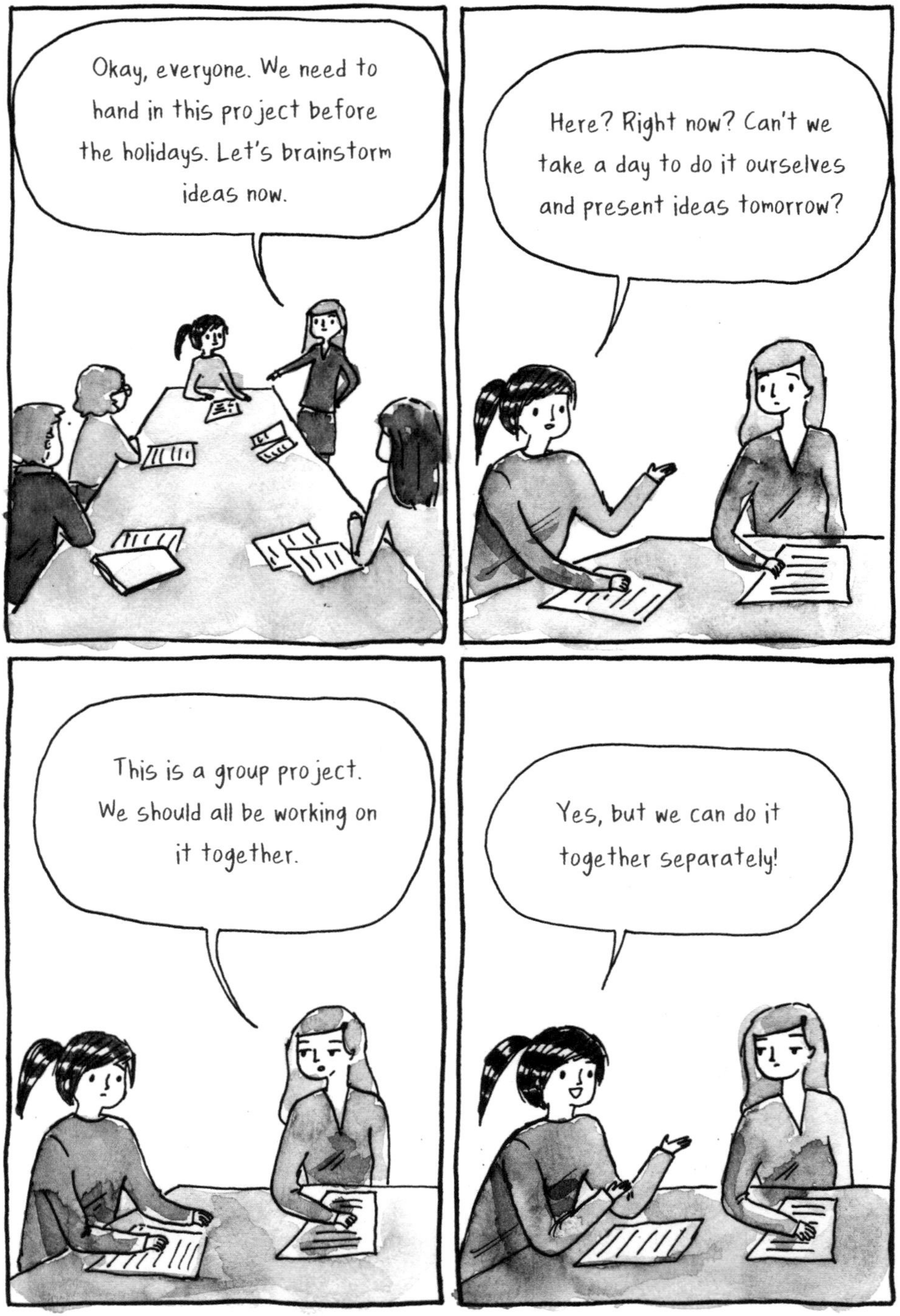

Okay, everyone. We need to hand in this project before the holidays. Let's brainstorm ideas now.
Here? Right now? Can't we take a day to do it ourselves and present ideas tomorrow?
This is a group project. We should all be working on it together.
Yes, but we can do it together separately!

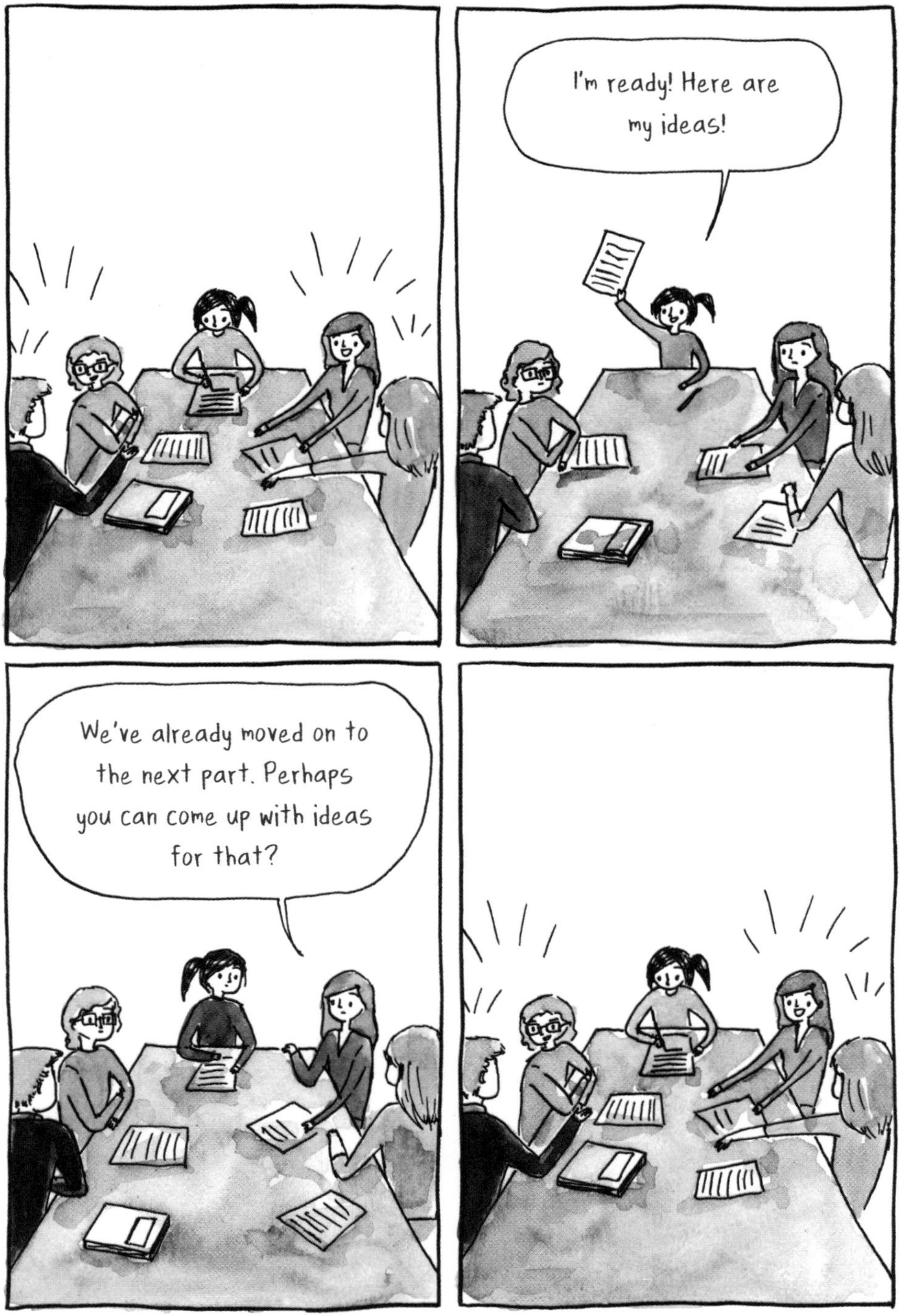
I'm ready! Here are my ideas!
We've already moved on to the next part. Perhaps you can come up with ideas for that?

How other people party

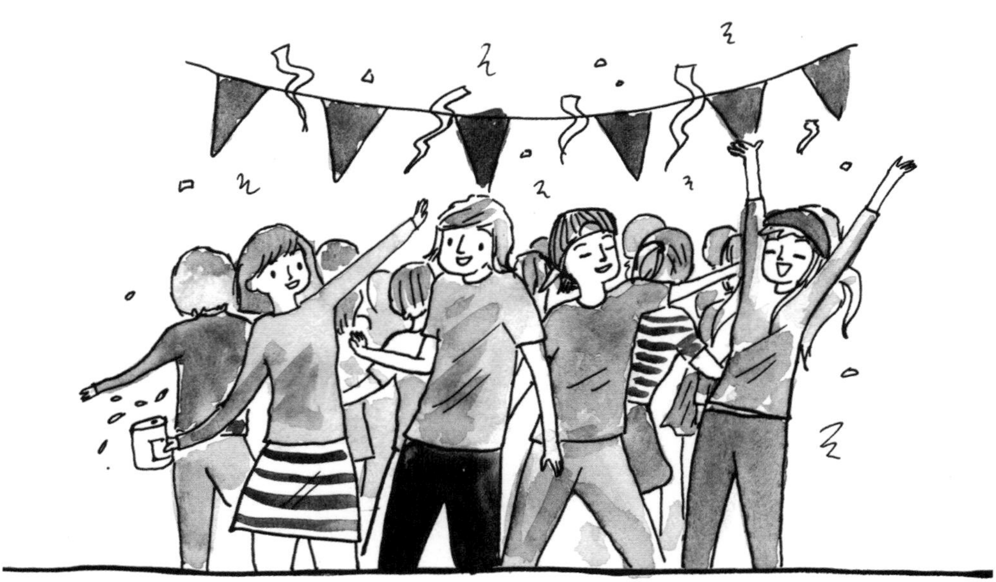

How I party

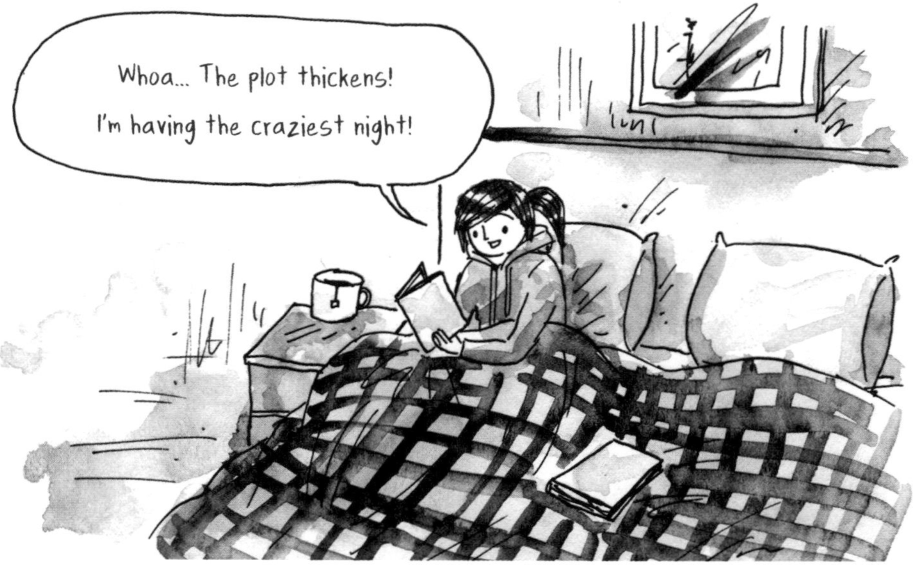
Whoa... The plot thickens!
I'm having the craziest night!

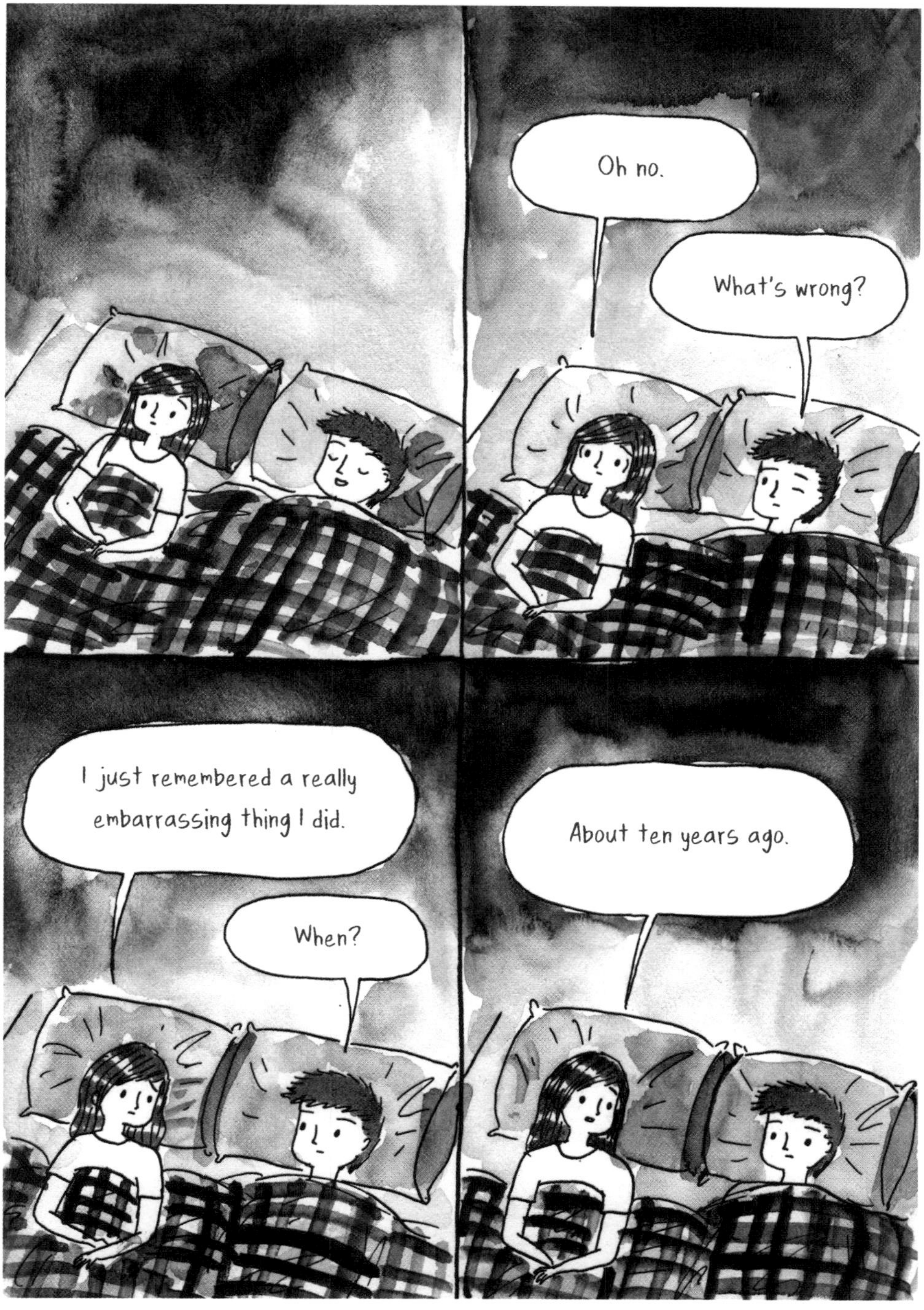
Oh no.
What's wrong?
I just remembered a really embarrassing thing I did.
When?
About ten years ago.

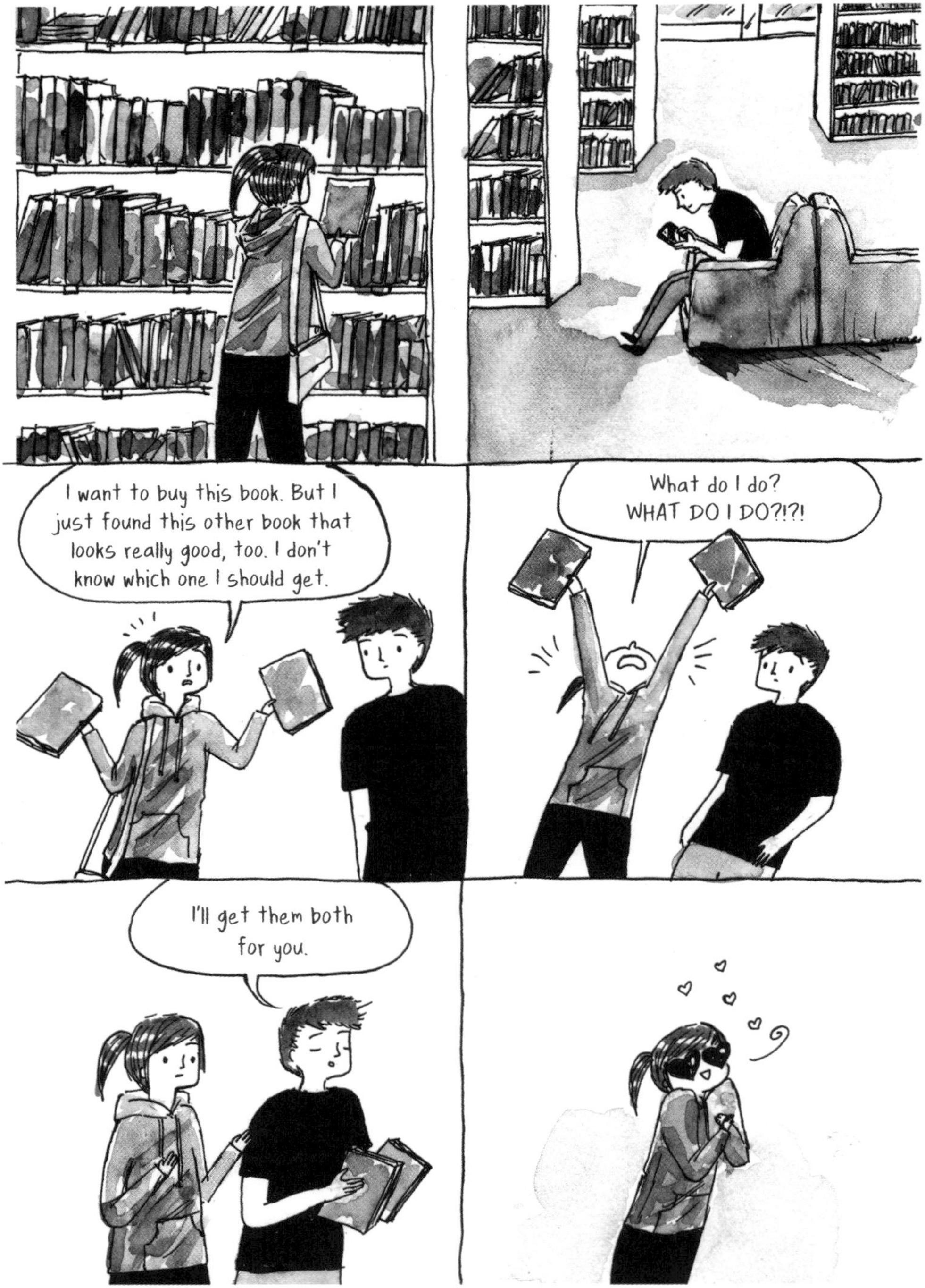
I want to buy this book. But I just found this other book that looks really good, too. I don't know which one I should get.
What do I do?
WHAT DO I DO?!?!
I'll get them both for you.

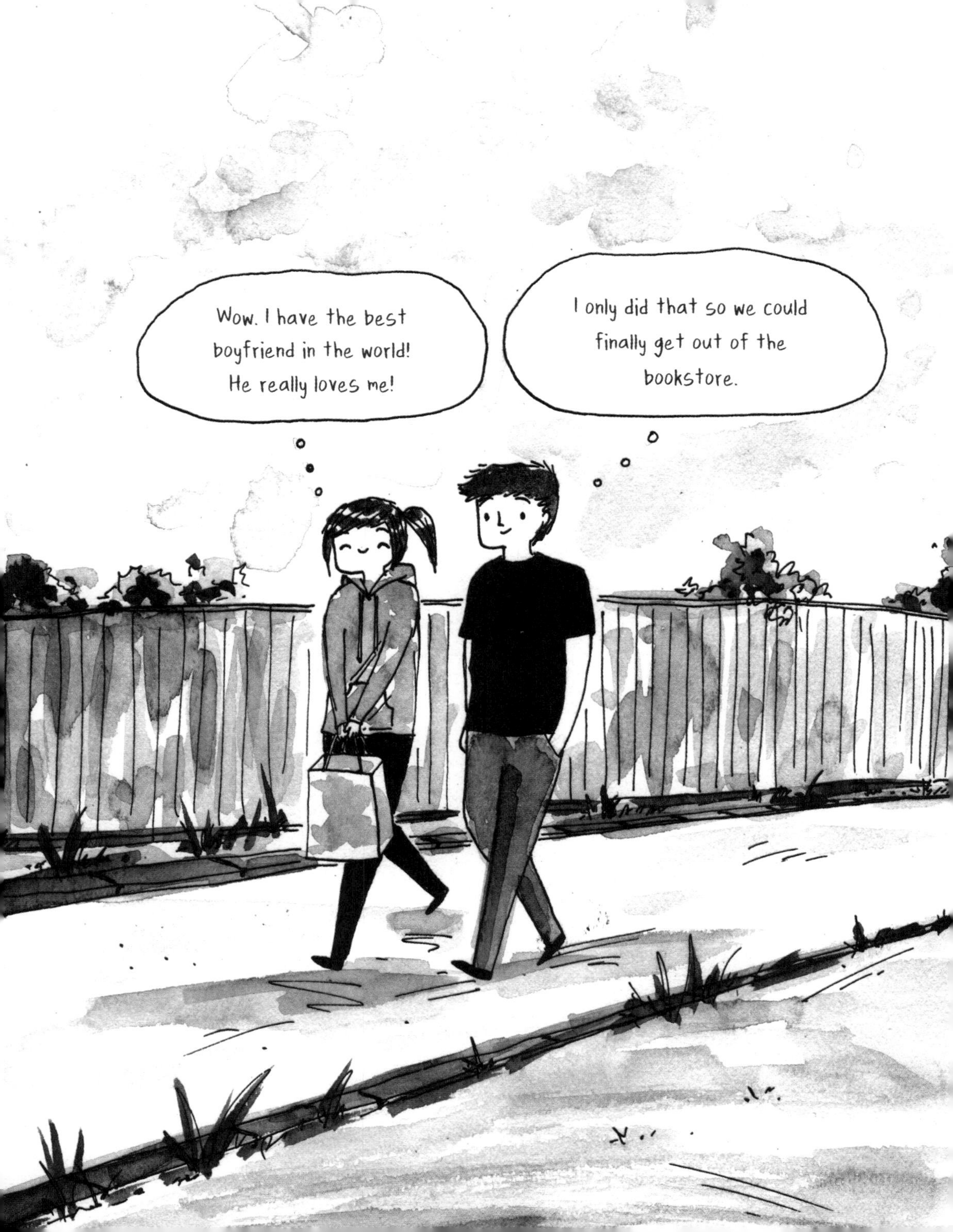
Wow. I have the best boyfriend in the world! He really loves me!
I only did that so we could finally get out of the bookstore.

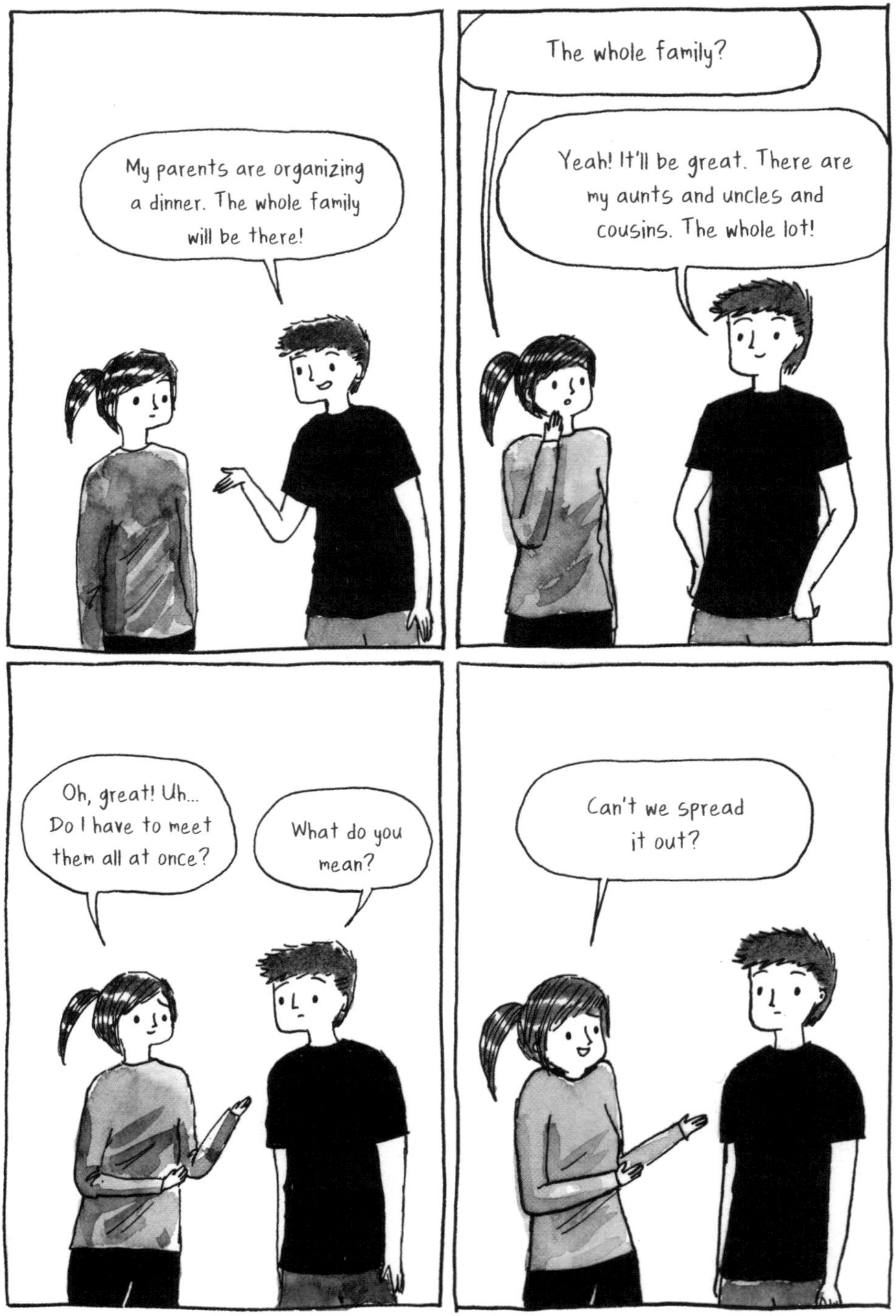
My parents are organizing a dinner. The whole family will be there!
The whole family?
Yeah! It'll be great. There are my aunts and uncles and cousins. The whole lot!
Oh, great! Uh... Do I have to meet them all at once?
What do you mean?
Can't we spread it out?

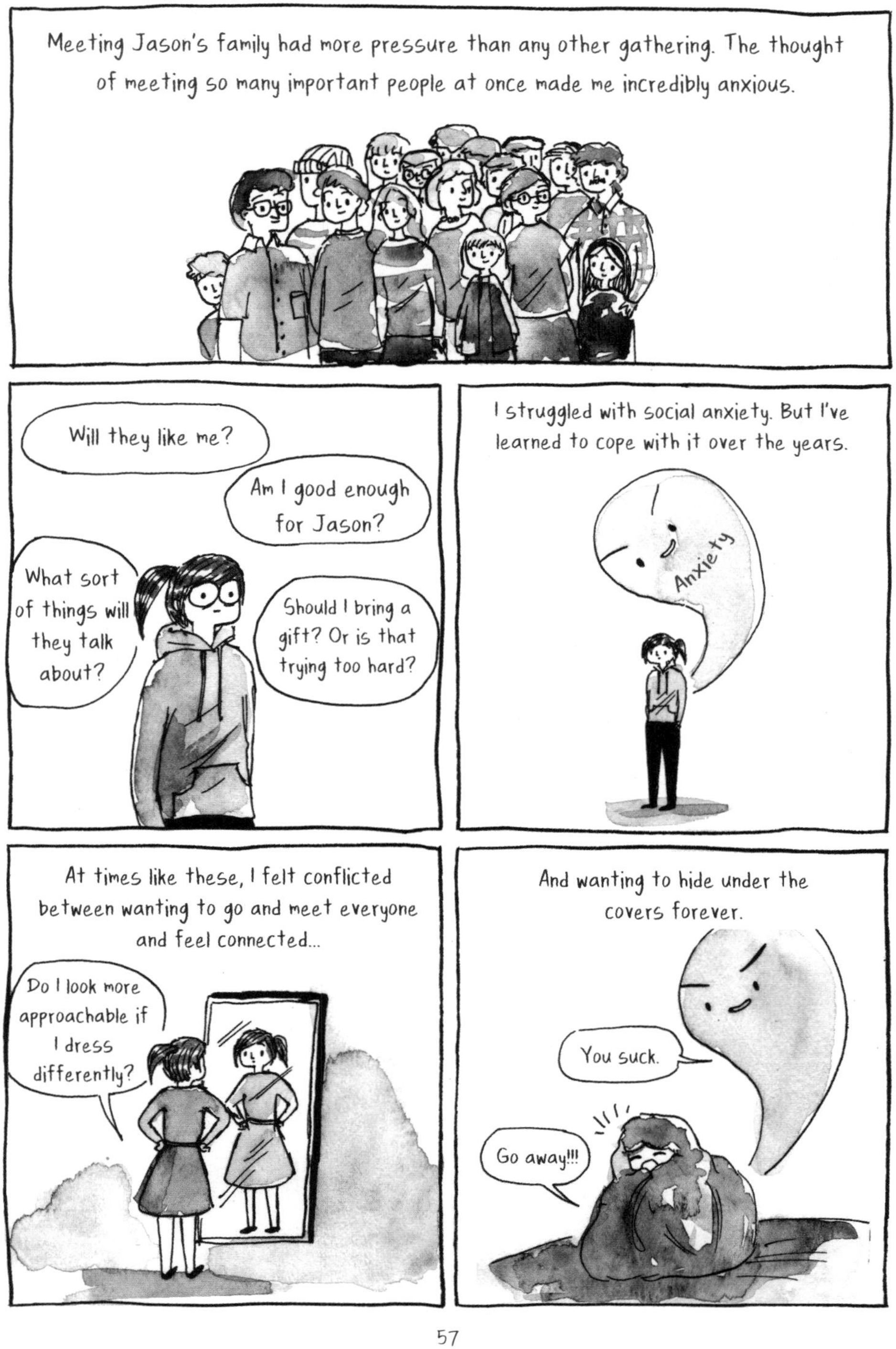
Meeting Jason's family had more pressure than any other gathering. The thought of meeting so many important people at once made me incredibly anxious.
Will they like me?
Am I good enough for Jason?
What sort of things will they talk about?
Should I bring a gift? Or is that trying too hard?
I struggled with social anxiety. But I've learned to cope with it over the years.
Anxiety
At times like these, I felt conflicted between wanting to go and meet everyone and feel connected...
Do I look more approachable if I dress differently?
And wanting to hide under the covers forever.
You suck.
Go away!!!

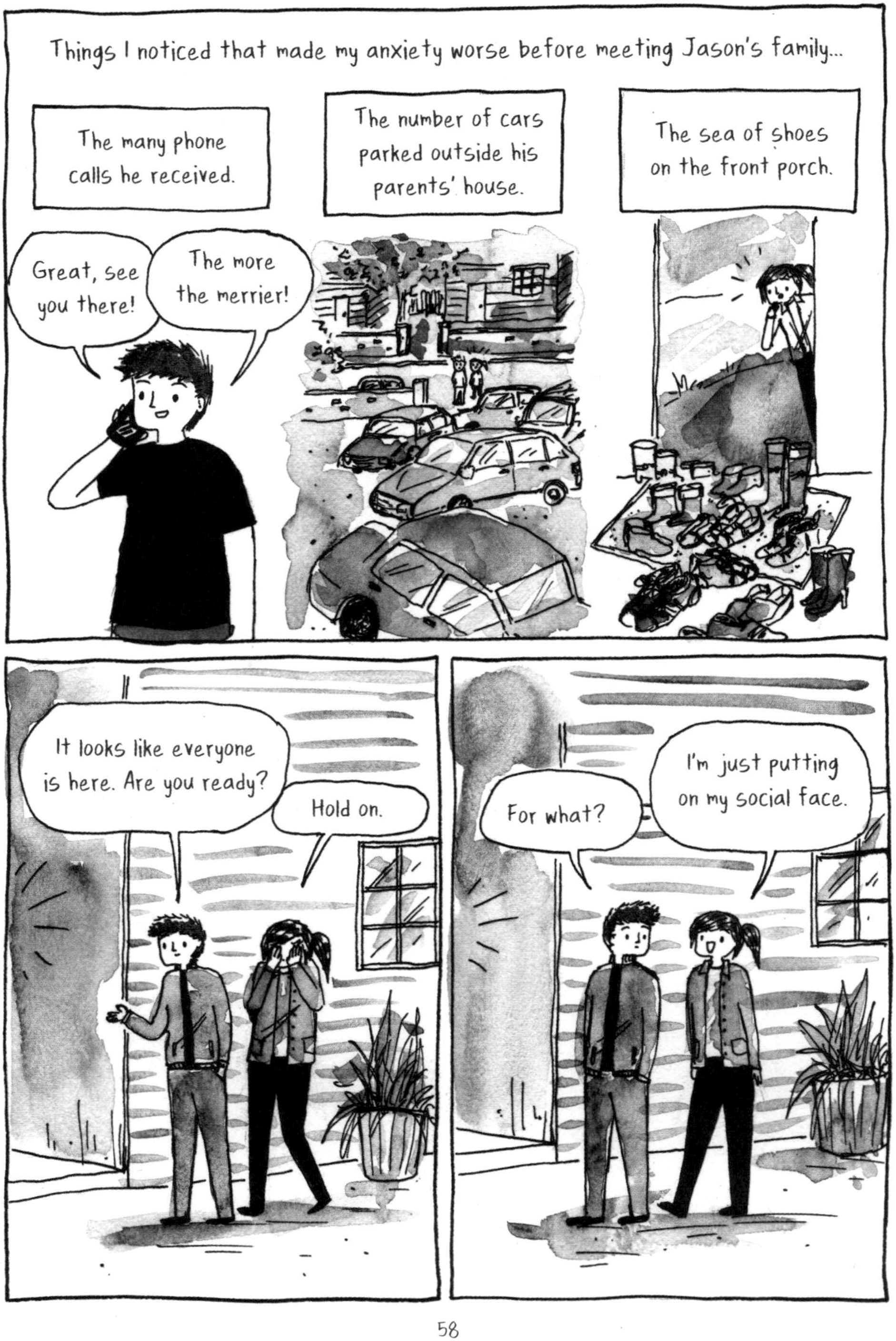
Things I noticed that made my anxiety worse before meeting Jason's family...
The many phone calls he received.
Great, see you there!
The more the merrier!
The number of cars parked outside his parents' house.
The sea of shoes on the front porch.
It looks like everyone is here. Are you ready?
Hold on.
For what?
I'm just putting on my social face.

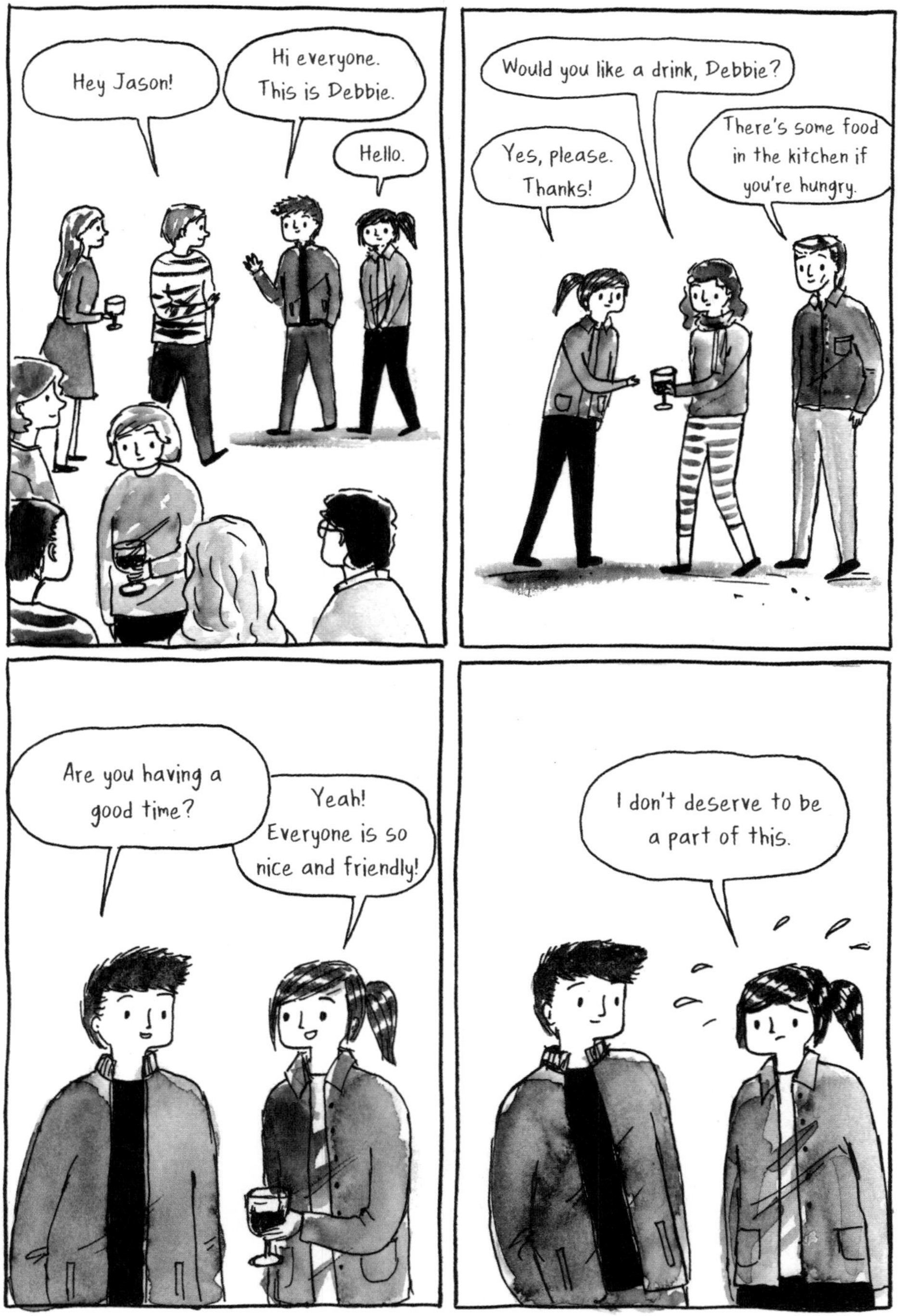
Hey Jason!
Hi everyone. This is Debbie.
Hello.
Would you like a drink, Debbie?
Yes, please. Thanks!
There's some food in the kitchen if you're hungry.
Are you having a good time?
Yeah! Everyone is so nice and friendly!
I don't deserve to be a part of this.

One of the perks of having an
extrovert partner...

is that he can do all the small talk and
socializing for both of you.

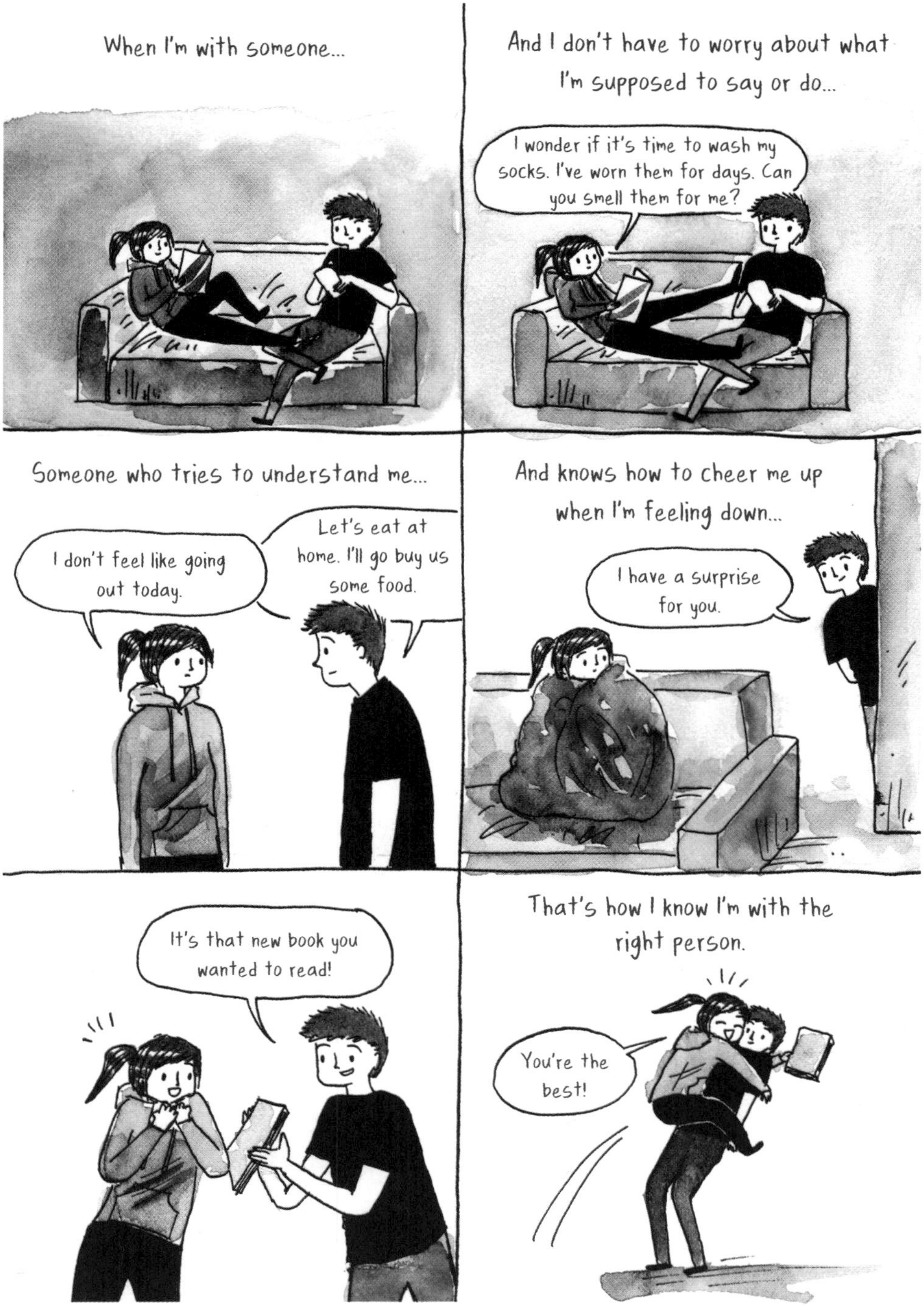
When I'm with someone...
And I don't have to worry about what I'm supposed to say or do...
I wonder if it's time to wash my socks. I've worn them for days. Can you smell them for me?
Someone who tries to understand me...
I don't feel like going out today.
Let's eat at home. I'll go buy us some food.
And knows how to cheer me up when I'm feeling down...
I have a surprise for you.
It's that new book you wanted to read!
That's how I know I'm with the right person.
You're the best!

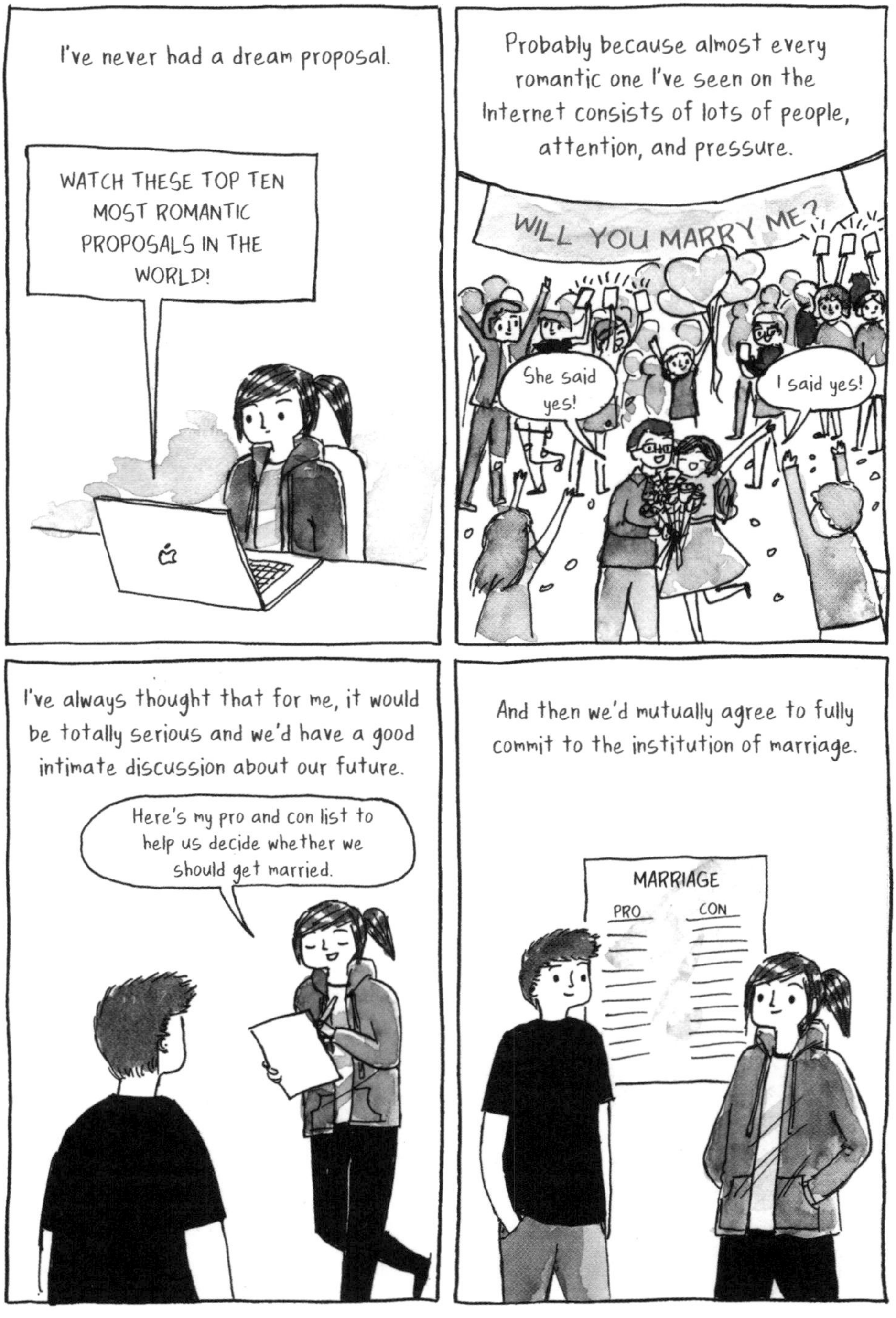
I've never had a dream proposal.
WATCH THESE TOP TEN MOST ROMANTIC PROPOSALS IN THE WORLD!
Probably because almost every romantic one I've seen on the Internet consists of lots of people, attention, and pressure.
WILL YOU MARRY ME?
She said yes!
I said yes!
I've always thought that for me, it would be totally serious and we'd have a good intimate discussion about our future.
Here's my pro and con list to help us decide whether we should get married.
And then we'd mutually agree to fully commit to the institution of marriage.
MARRIAGE
PRO
CON

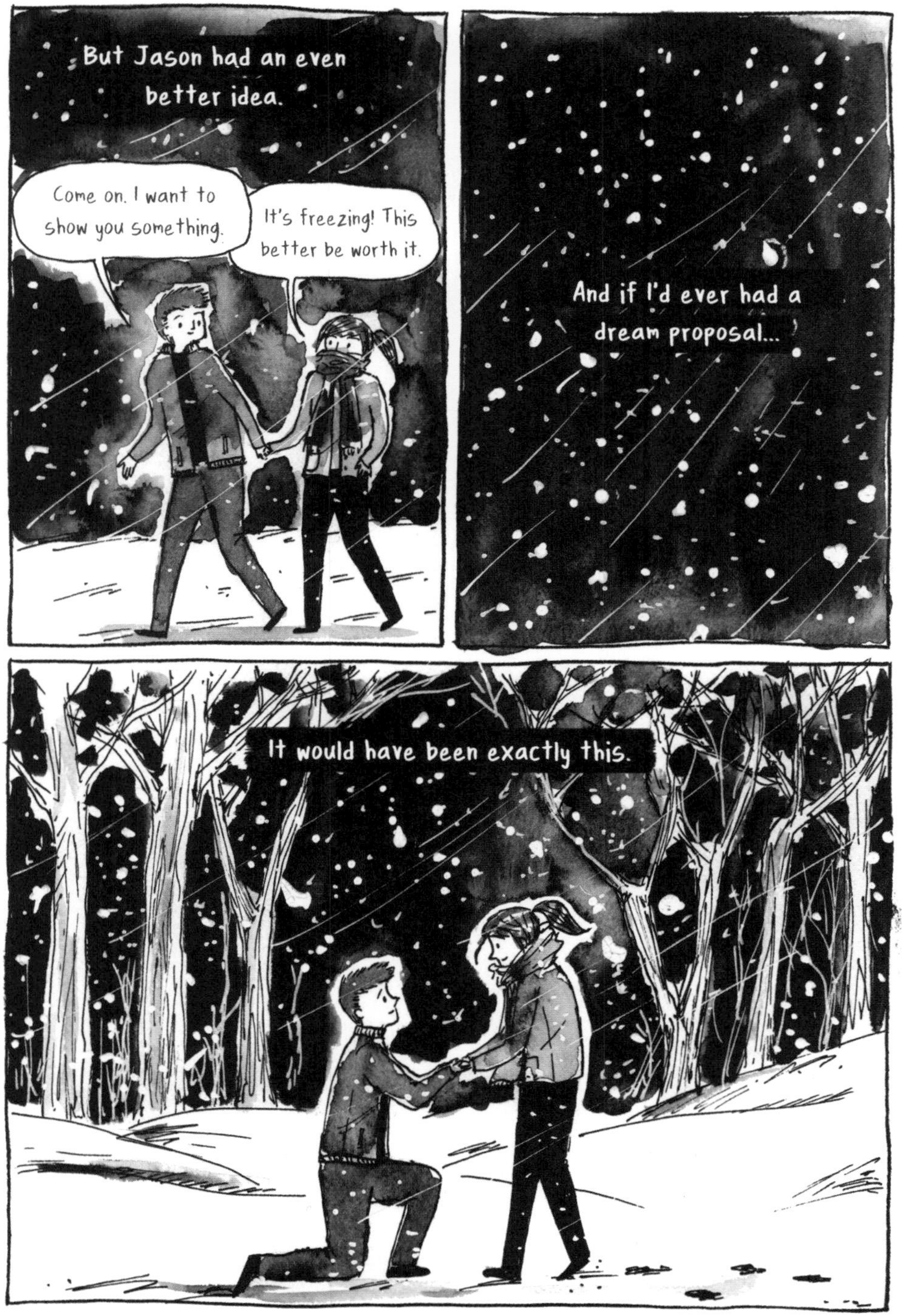
But Jason had an even better idea.
Come on. I want to show you something.
It's freezing! This better be worth it.
And if I'd ever had a dream proposal...
It would have been exactly this.

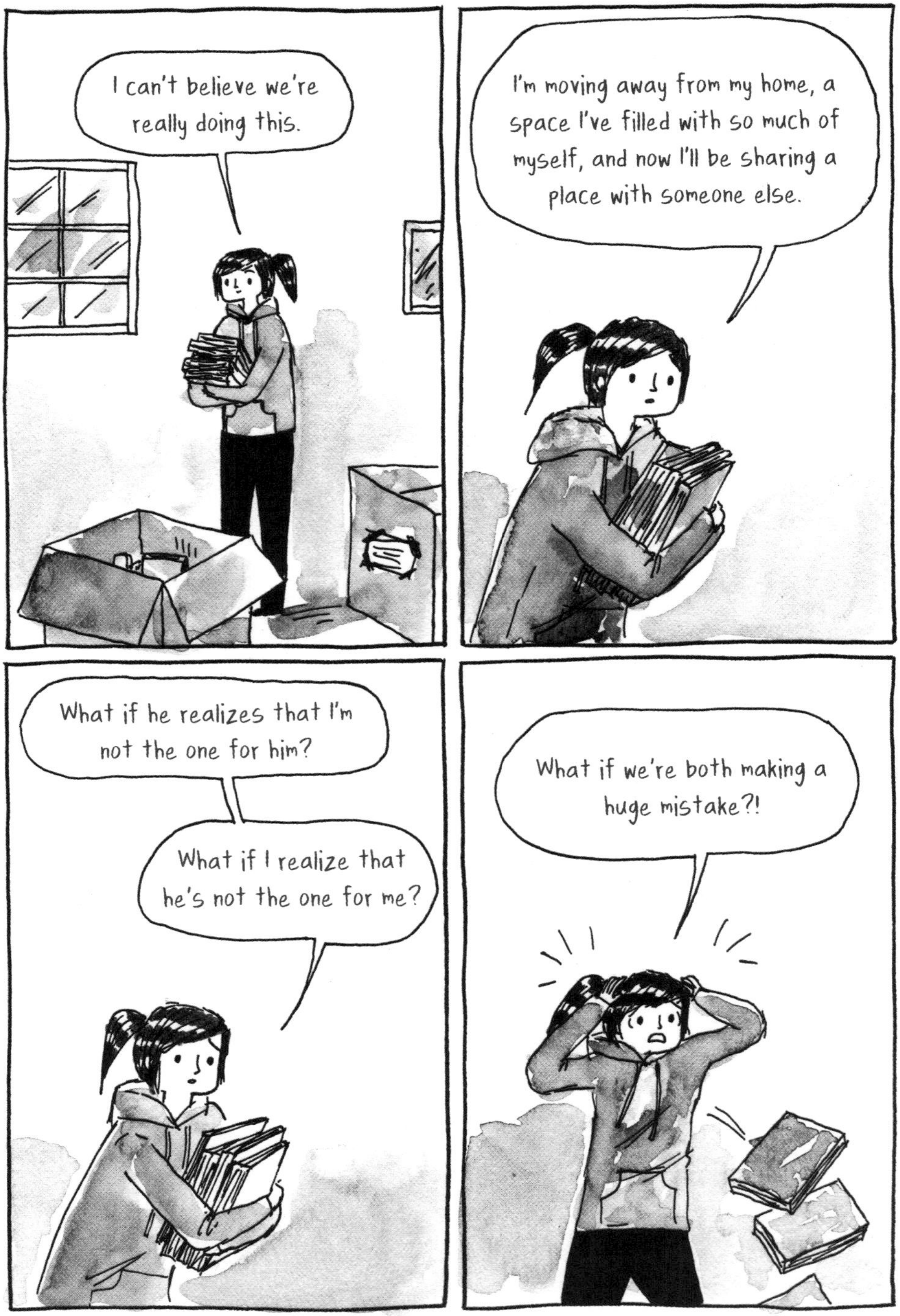
I can't believe we're really doing this.
I'm moving away from my home, a space I've filled with so much of myself, and now I'll be sharing a place with someone else.
What if he realizes that I'm not the one for him?
What if I realize that he's not the one for me?
What if we're both making a huge mistake?!

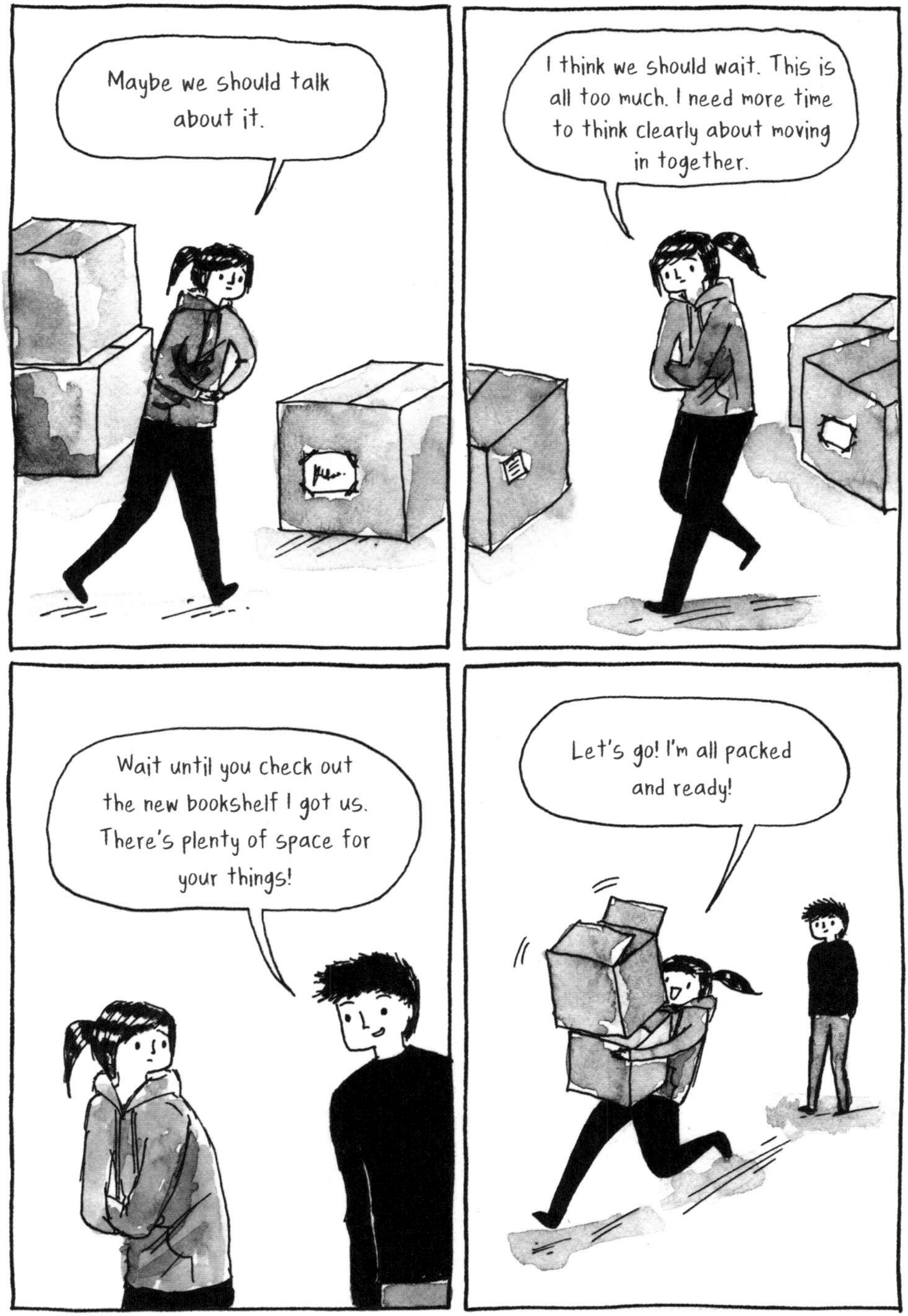
Maybe we should talk about it.
I think we should wait. This is all too much. I need more time to think clearly about moving in together.
Wait until you check out the new bookshelf I got us. There's plenty of space for your things!
Let's go! I'm all packed and ready!

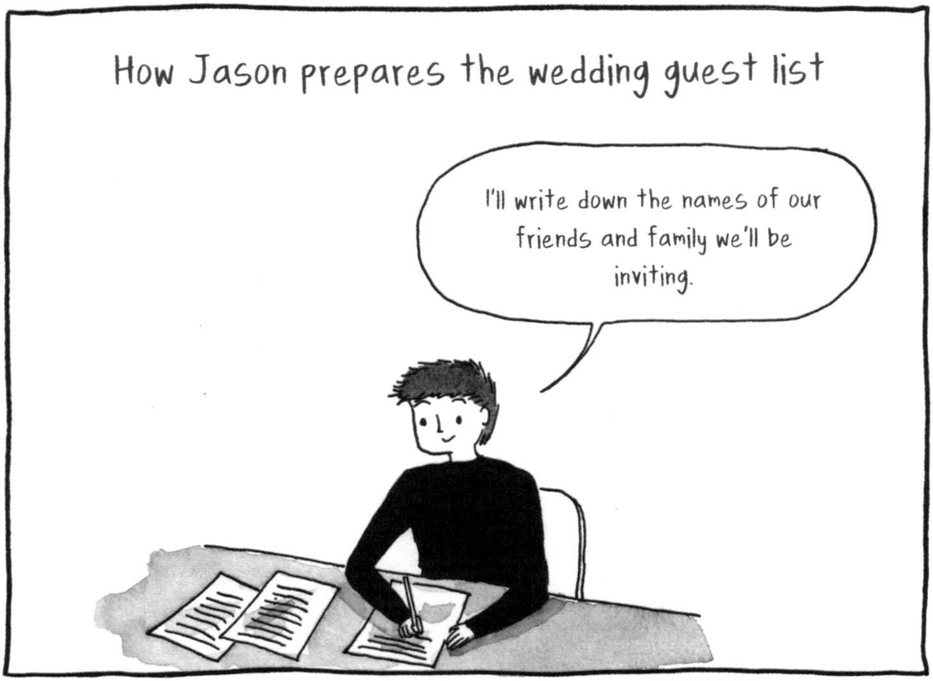
How Jason prepares the wedding guest list
I'll write down the names of our friends and family we'll be inviting.

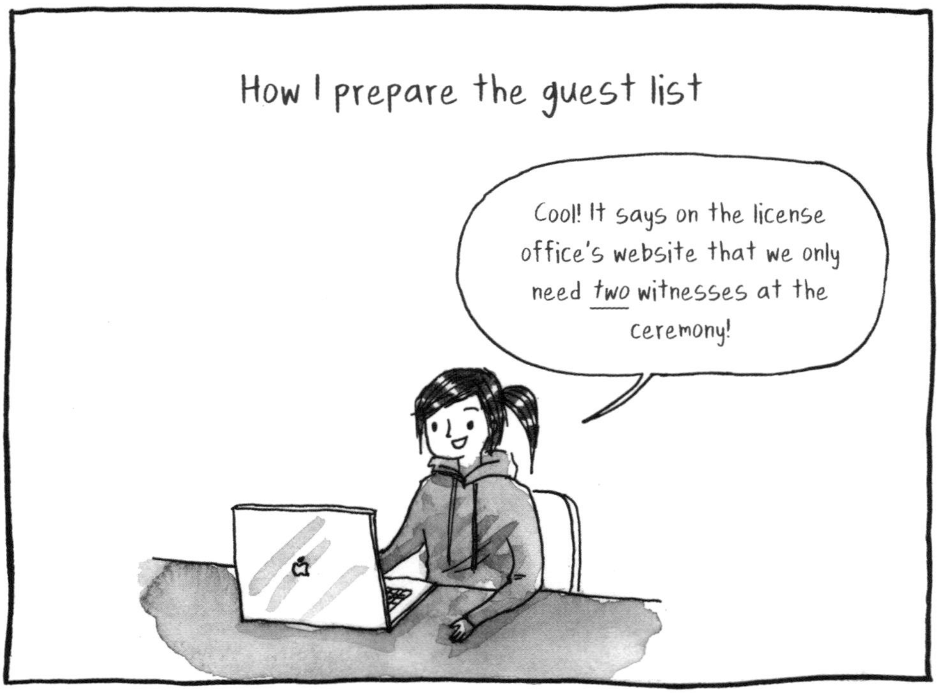
How I prepare the guest list
Cool! It says on the license office's website that we only need two witnesses at the ceremony!

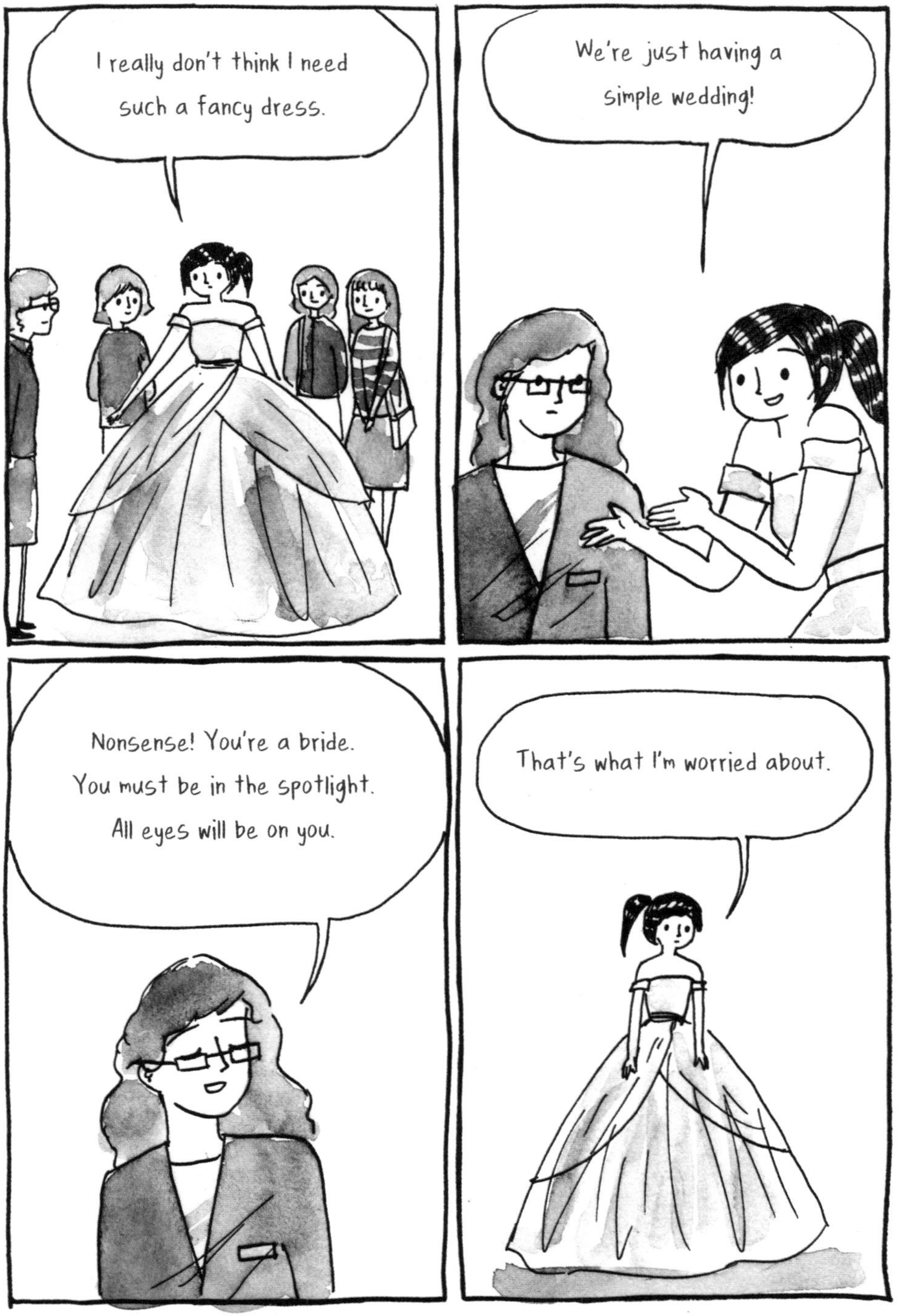
I really don't think I need such a fancy dress.
We're just having a simple wedding!
Nonsense! You're a bride. You must be in the spotlight. All eyes will be on you.
That's what I'm worried about.

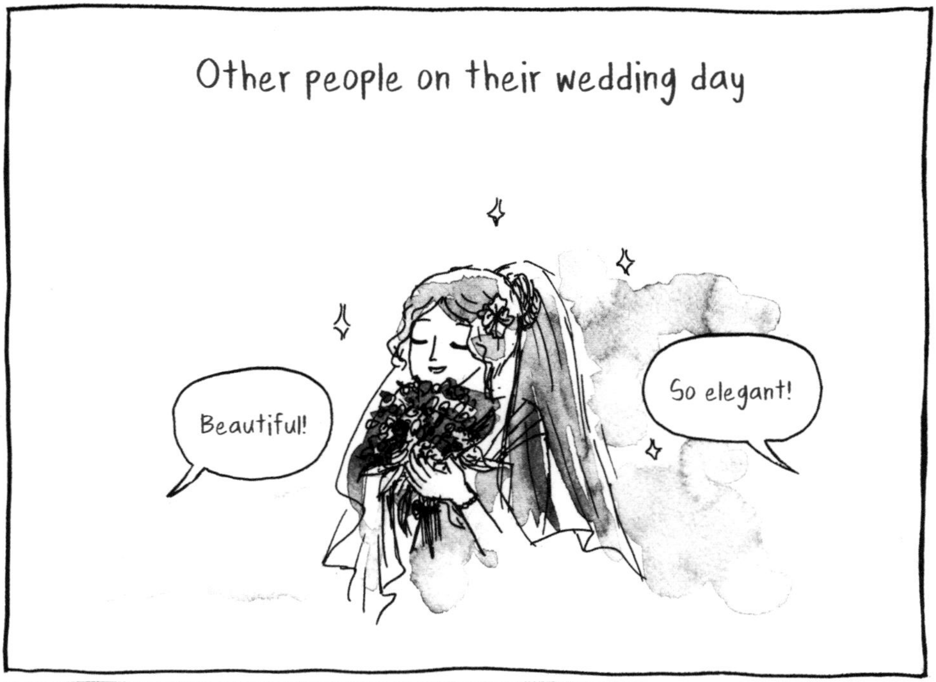
Other people on their wedding day
Beautiful!
So elegant!

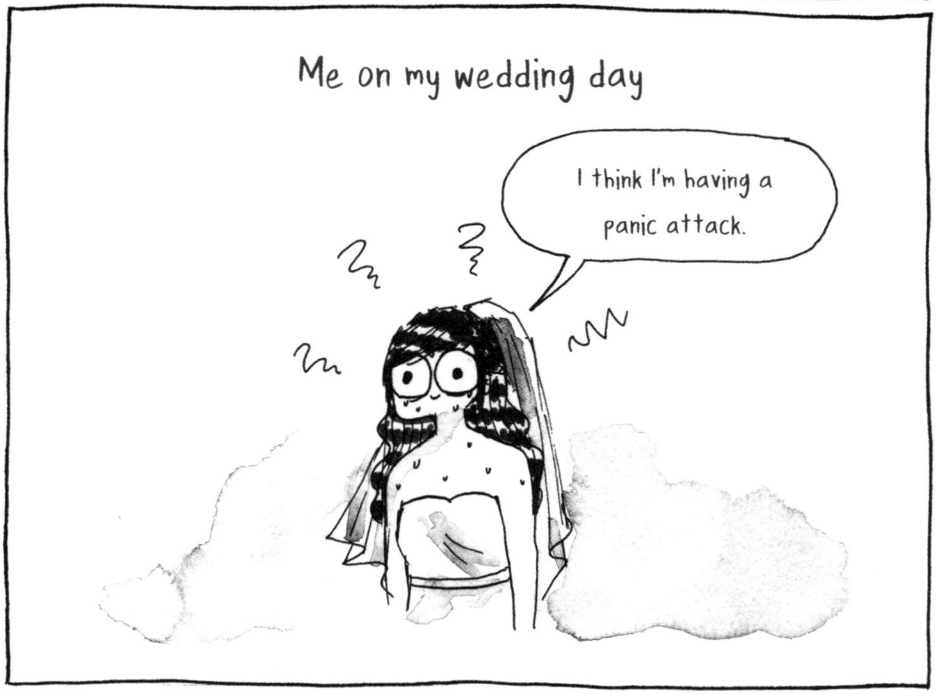
Me on my wedding day
I think I'm having a panic attack.

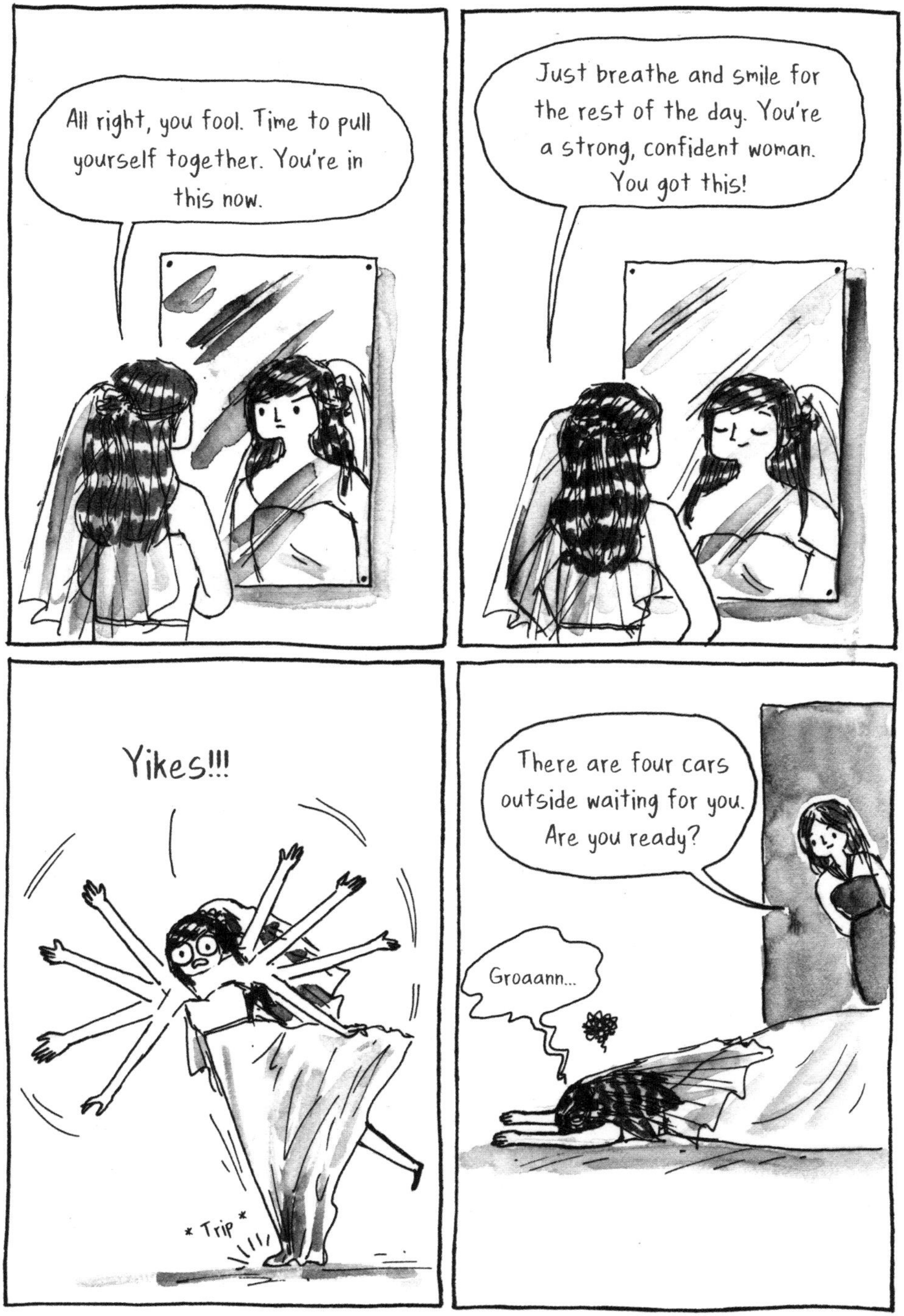
All right, you fool. Time to pull yourself together. You're in this now.
Just breathe and smile for the rest of the day. You're a strong, confident woman. You got this!
Yikes!!!
* Trip *
There are four cars outside waiting for you. Are you ready?
Groaann...

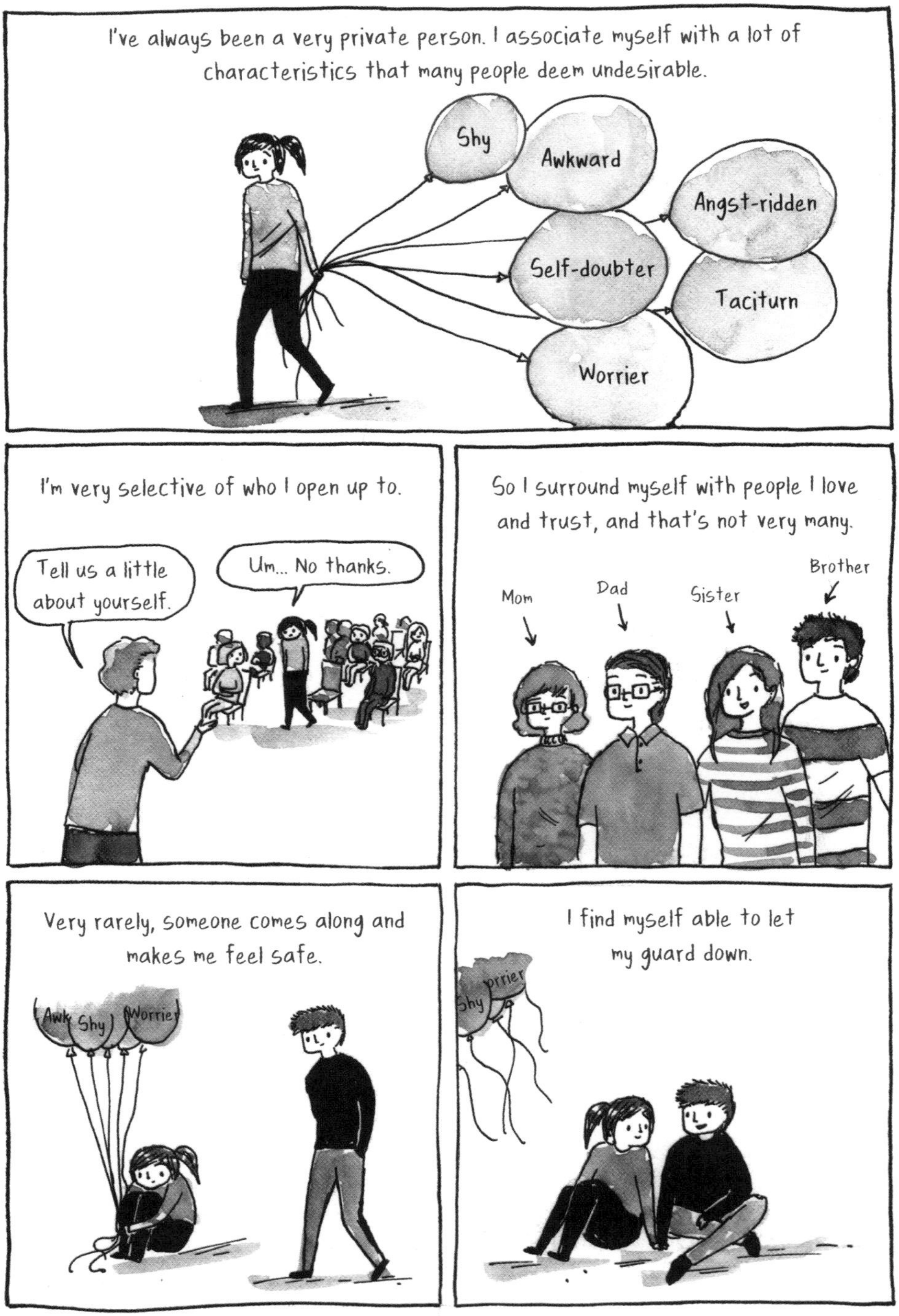
I've always been a very private person. I associate myself with a lot of characteristics that many people deem undesirable.
Shy
Awkward
Angst-ridden
Self-doubter
Taciturn
Worrier
I'm very selective of who I open up to.
Tell us a little about yourself.
Um... No thanks.
So I surround myself with people I love and trust, and that's not very many.
Mom
Dad
Sister
Brother
Very rarely, someone comes along and makes me feel safe.
Shy
I find myself able to let my guard down.
Shy

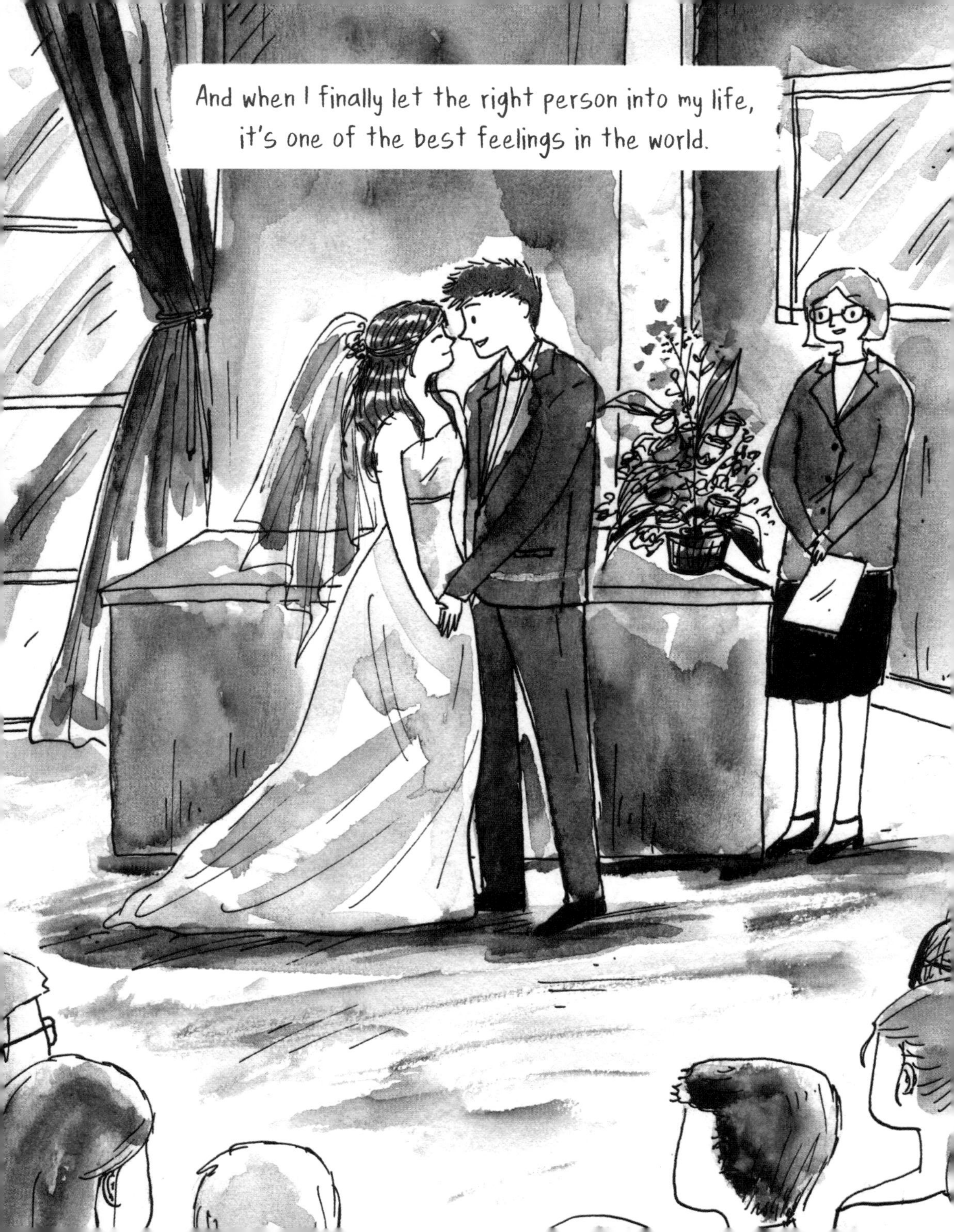
And when I finally let the right person into my life,
it's one of the best feelings in the world.

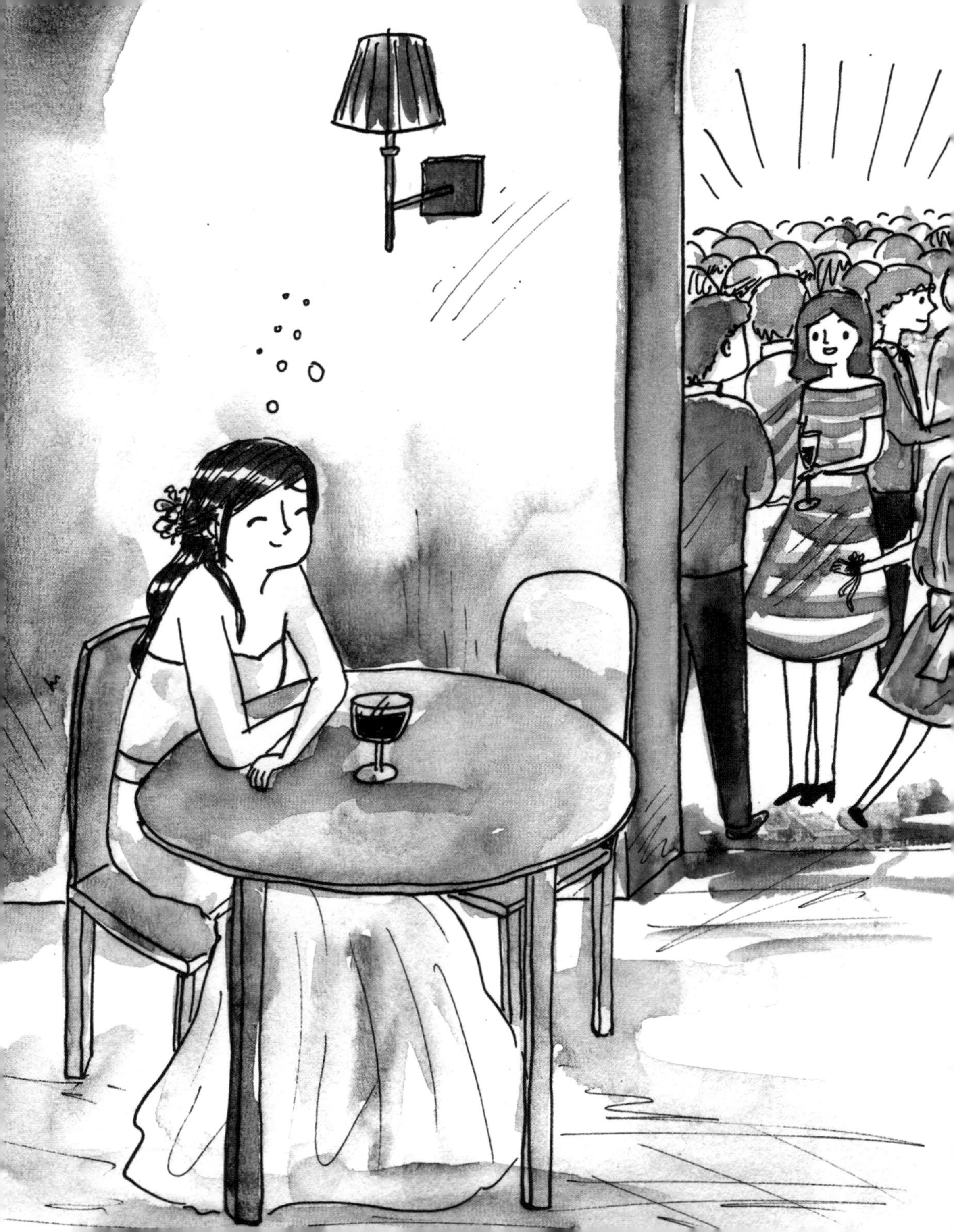

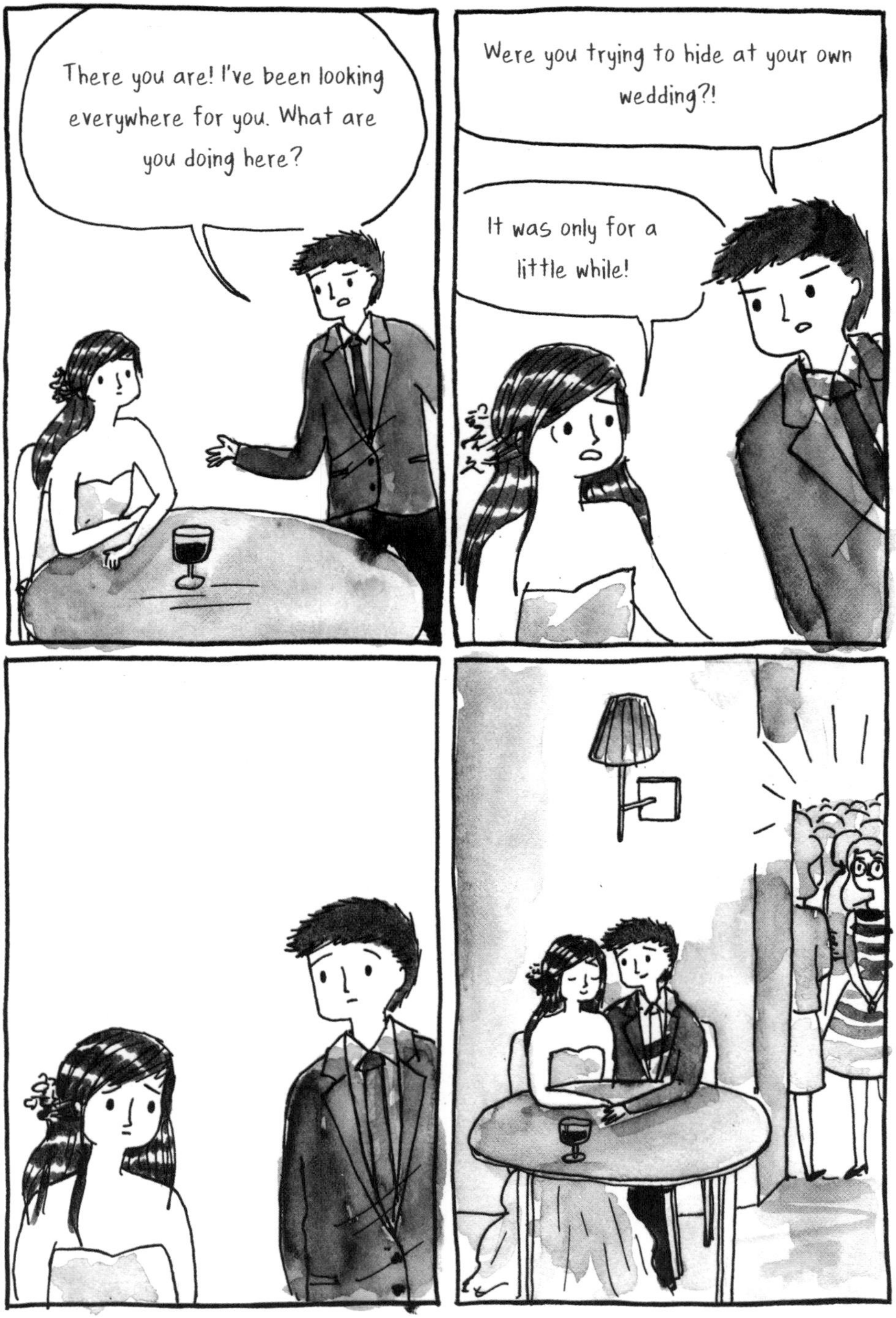
There you are! I've been looking everywhere for you. What are you doing here?
Were you trying to hide at your own wedding?!
It was only for a little while!

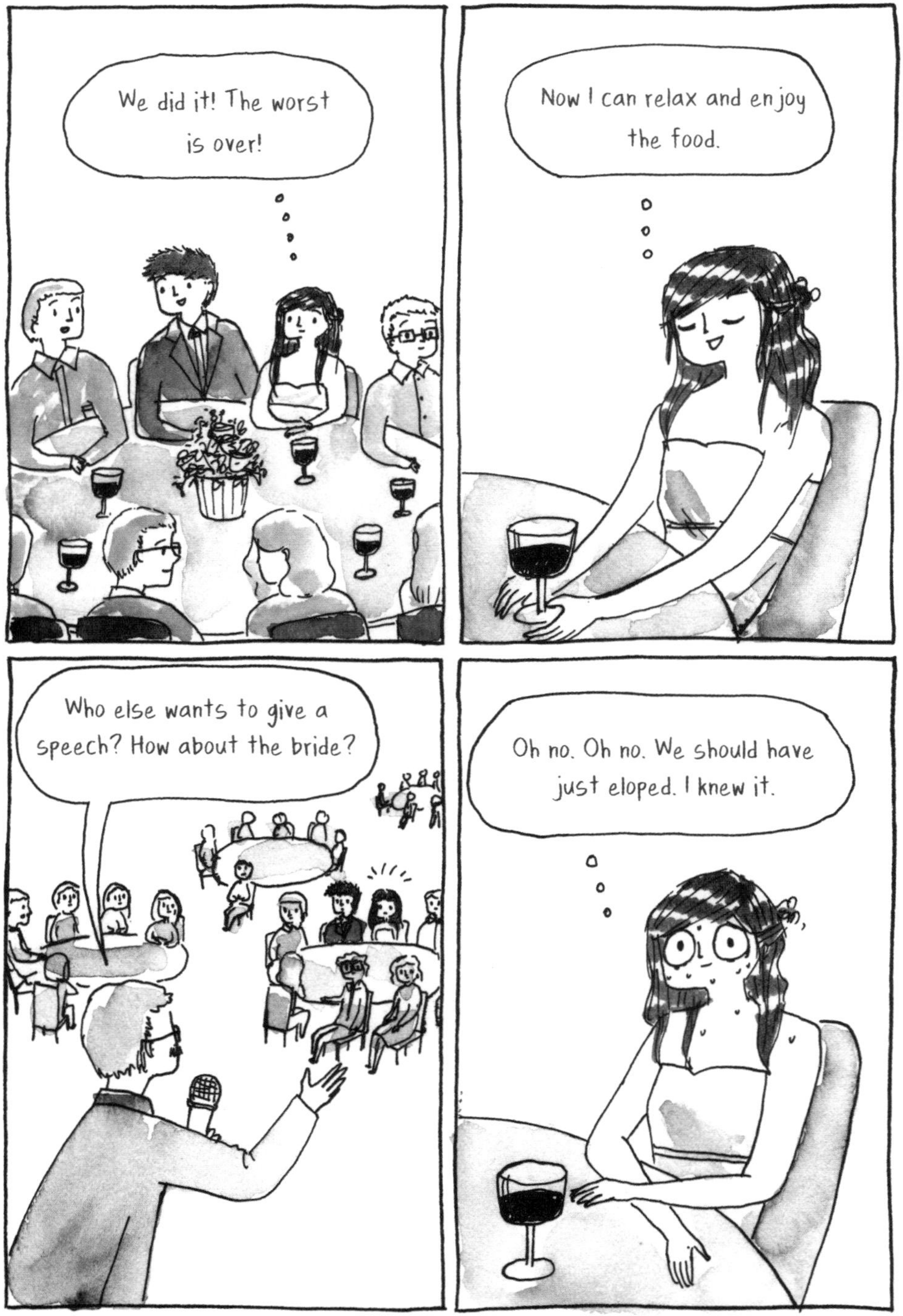
We did it! The worst is over!
Now I can relax and enjoy the food.
Who else wants to give a speech? How about the bride?
Oh no. Oh no. We should have just eloped. I knew it.

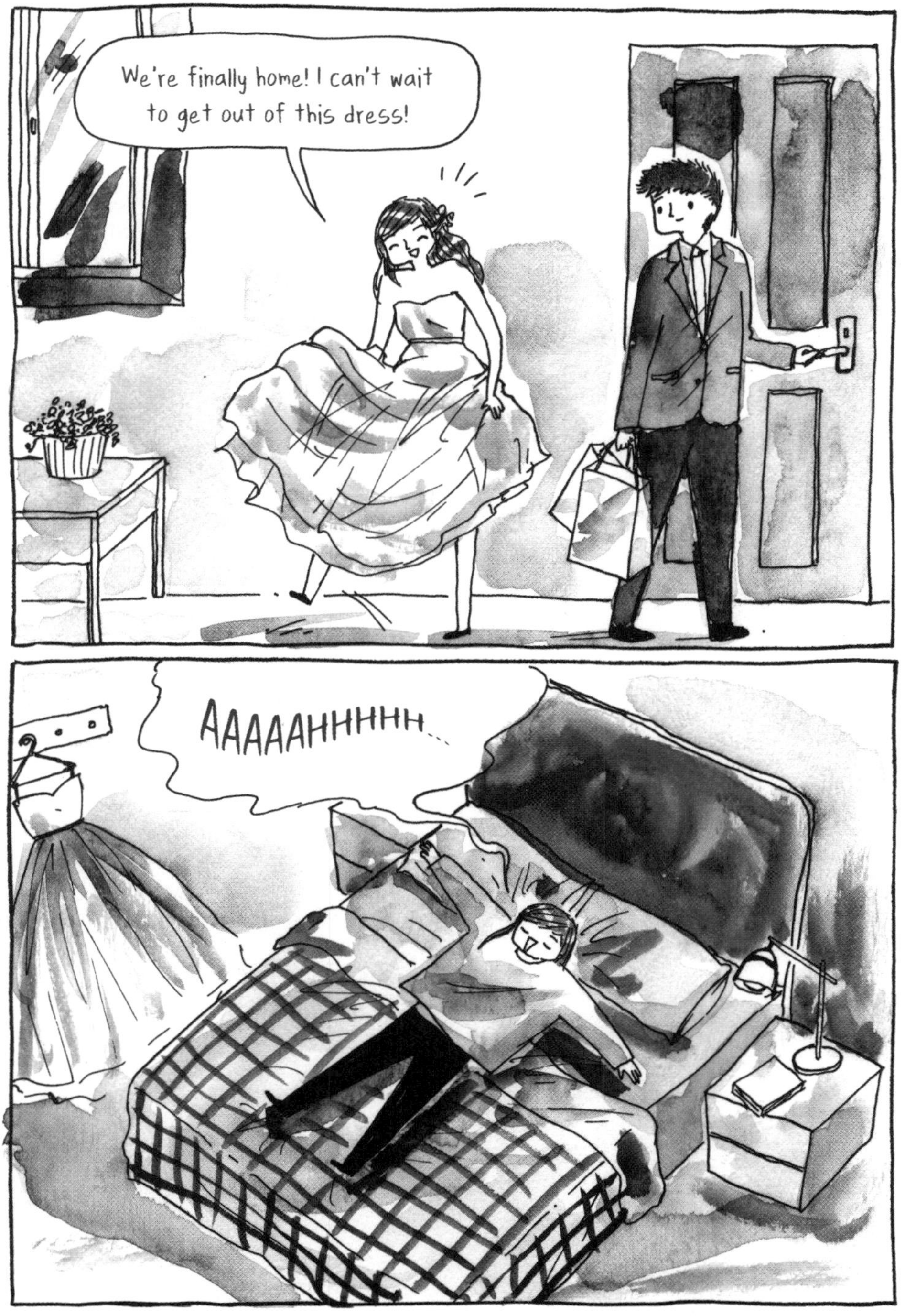
We're finally home! I can't wait to get out of this dress!
AAAAAHHHHH...

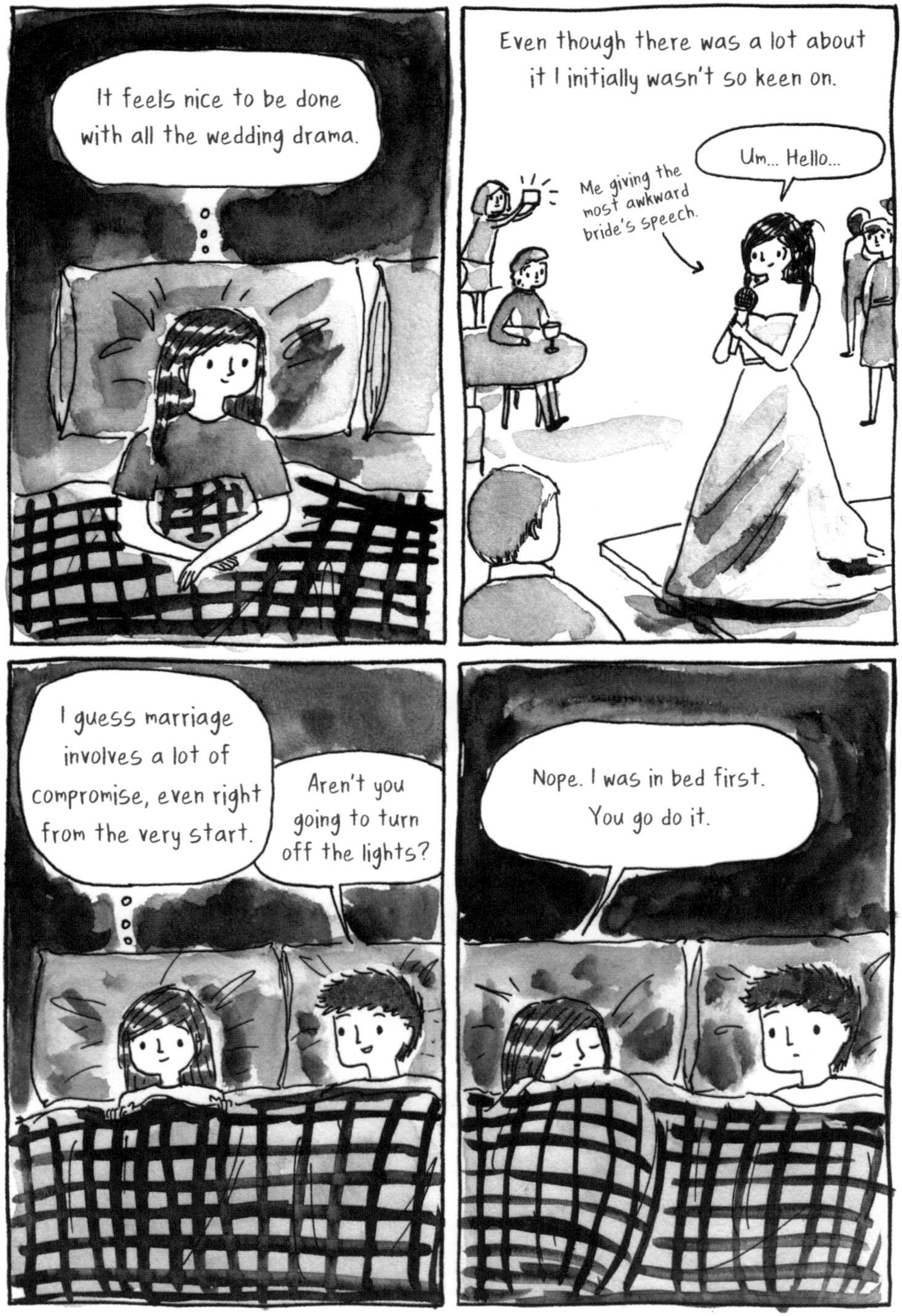

It feels nice to be done with all the wedding drama.
Even though there was a lot about it I initially wasn't so keen on.
Me giving the most awkward bride's speech.
Um... Hello...
I guess marriage involves a lot of compromise, even right from the very start.
Aren't you going to turn off the lights?
Nope. I was in bed first. You go do it.

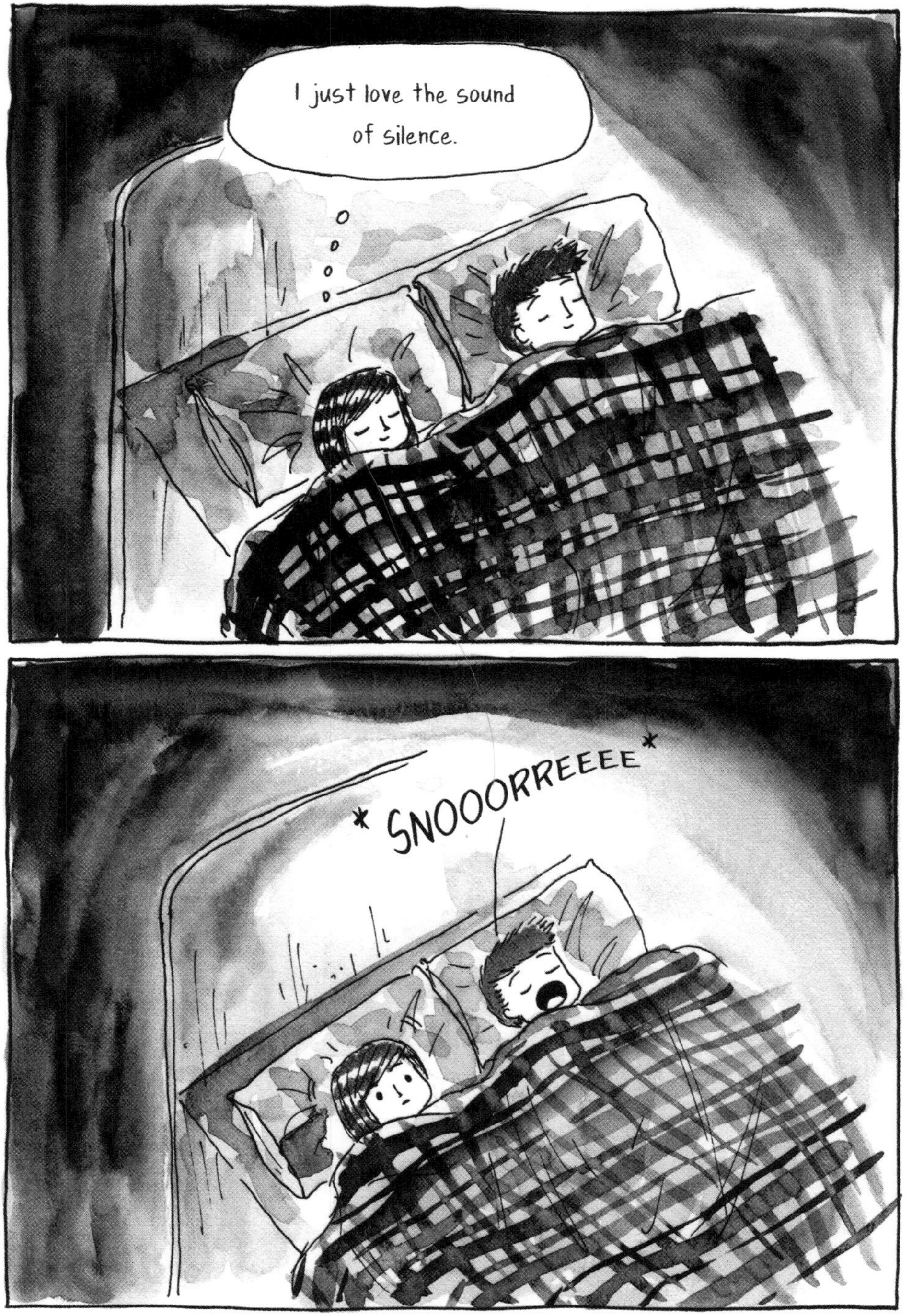
I just love the sound of silence.
*SNOOORREEEE*

# Social Hangover Symptoms

Headache

Fatigue

Dejection

Anger and frustration

Feeling the need to disappear from the world

# Social Hangover Cures

Comfort food

Good books

Favorite music

Quiet time alone

Warm hugs from a loved one

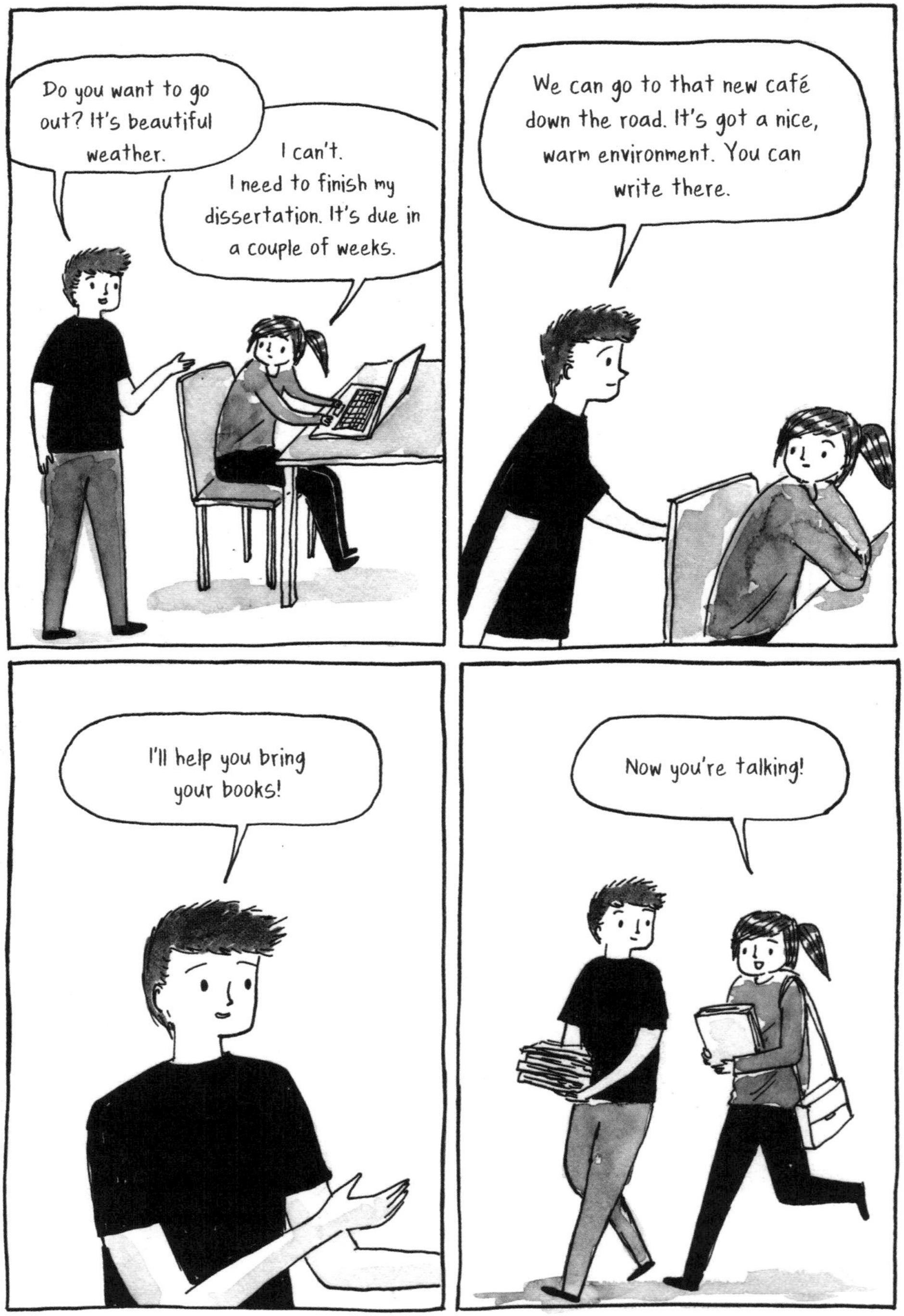
Do you want to go out? It's beautiful weather.
I can't. I need to finish my dissertation. It's due in a couple of weeks.
We can go to that new café down the road. It's got a nice, warm environment. You can write there.
I'll help you bring your books!
Now you're talking!

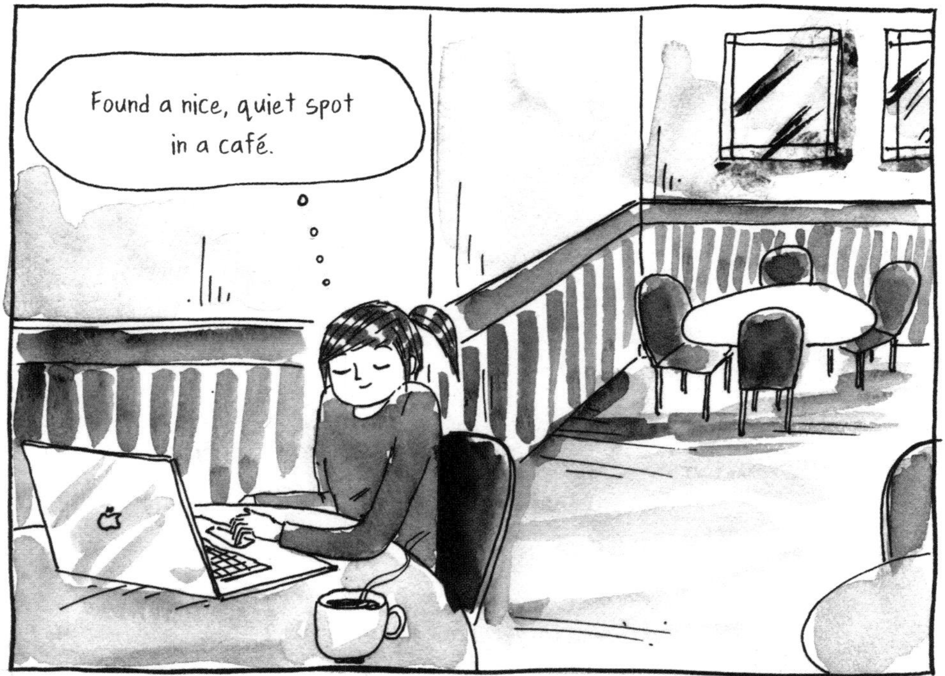
Found a nice, quiet spot in a café.

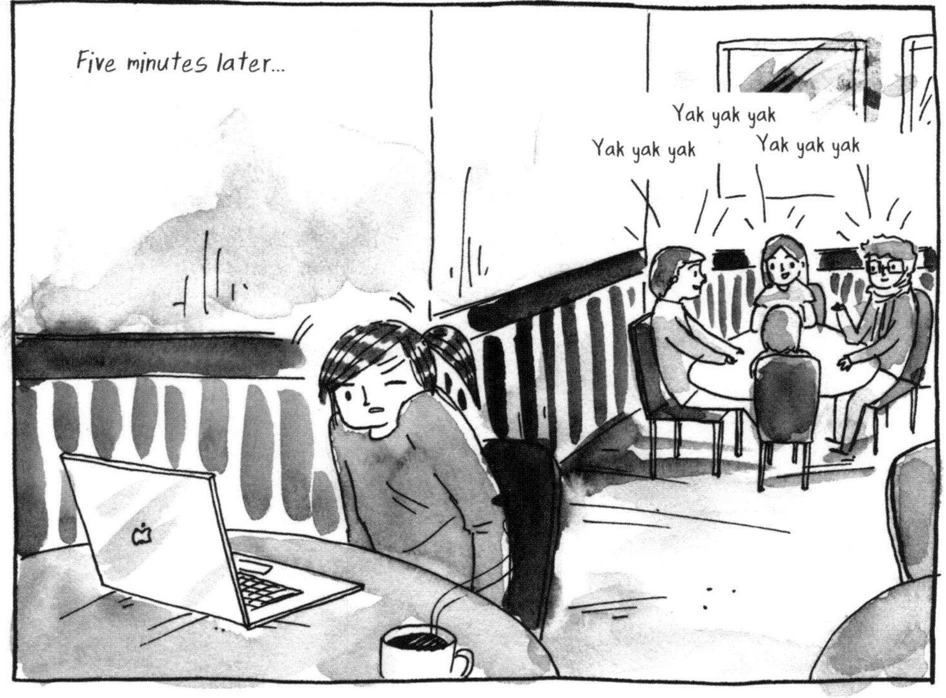
Five minutes later...
Yak yak yak
Yak yak yak
Yak yak yak

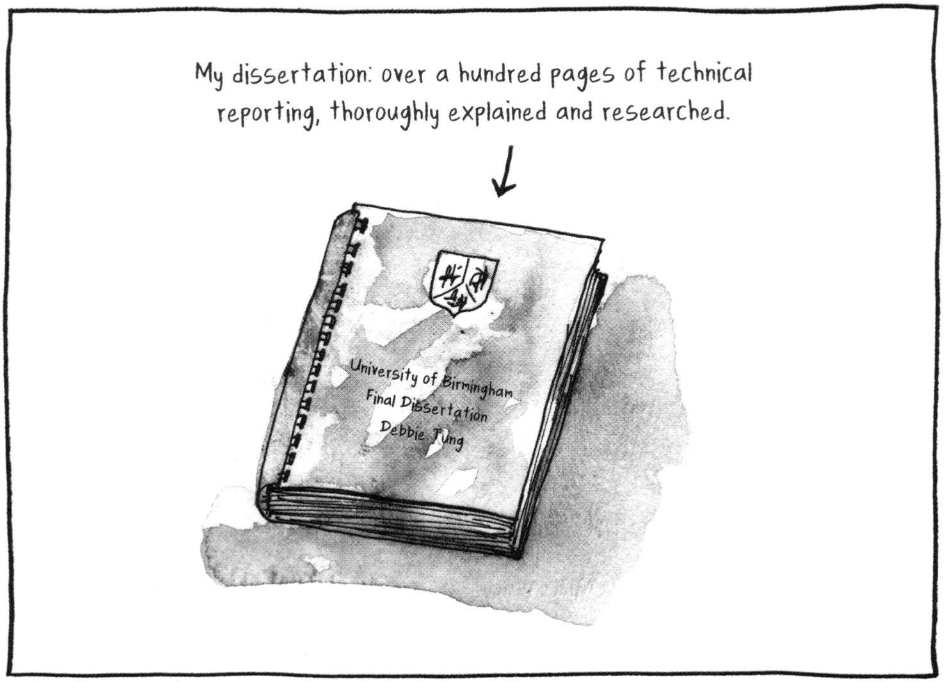
My dissertation: over a hundred pages of technical reporting, thoroughly explained and researched.
University of Birmingham
Final Dissertation
Debbie Tung

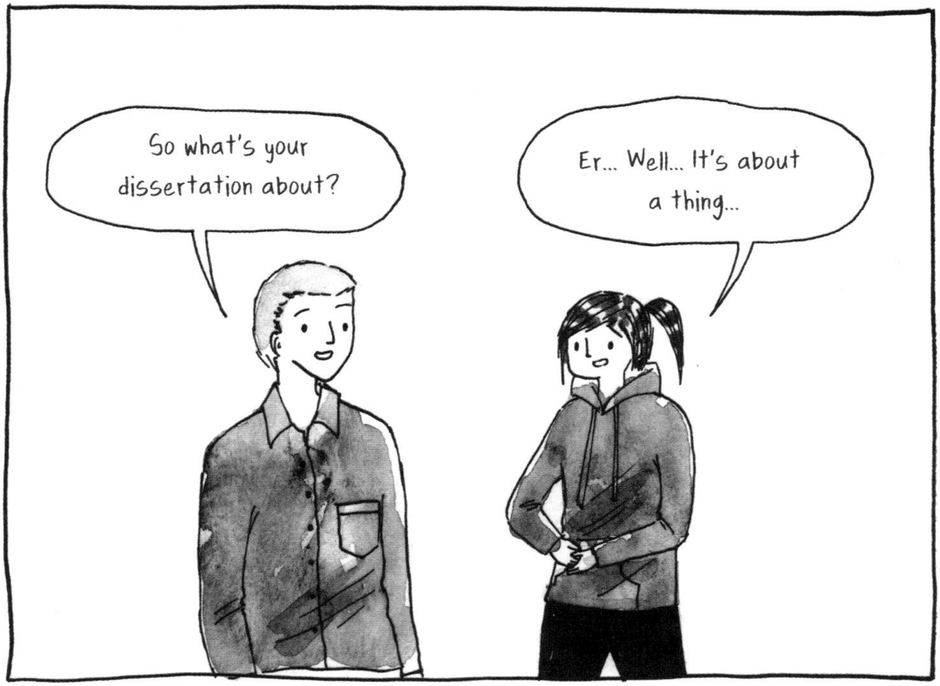
So what's your dissertation about?
Er... Well... It's about a thing...

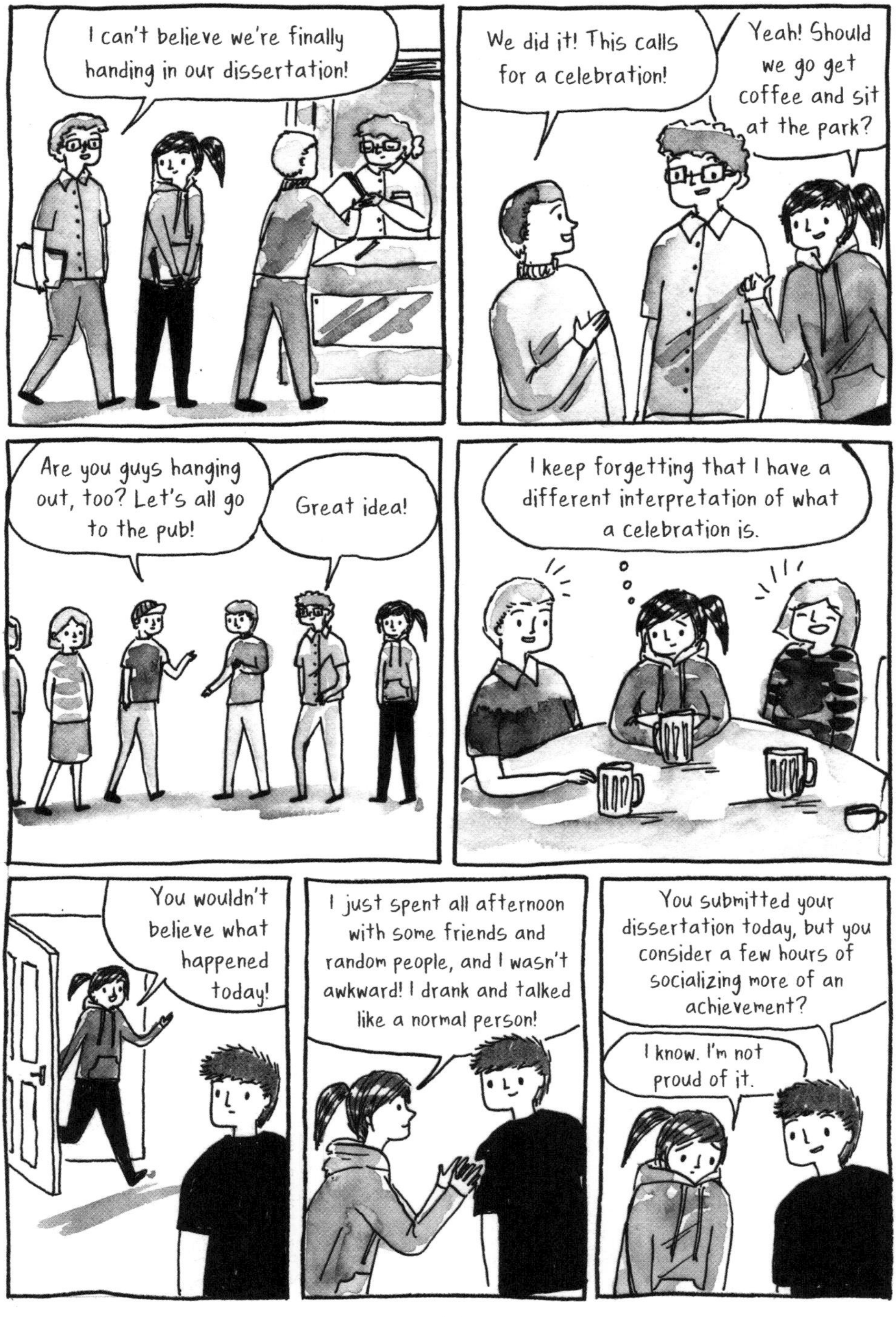
I can't believe we're finally handing in our dissertation!
We did it! This calls for a celebration!
Yeah! Should we go get coffee and sit at the park?
Are you guys hanging out, too? Let's all go to the pub!
Great idea!
I keep forgetting that I have a different interpretation of what a celebration is.
You wouldn't believe what happened today!
I just spent all afternoon with some friends and random people, and I wasn't awkward! I drank and talked like a normal person!
You submitted your dissertation today, but you consider a few hours of socializing more of an achievement?
I know. I'm not proud of it.

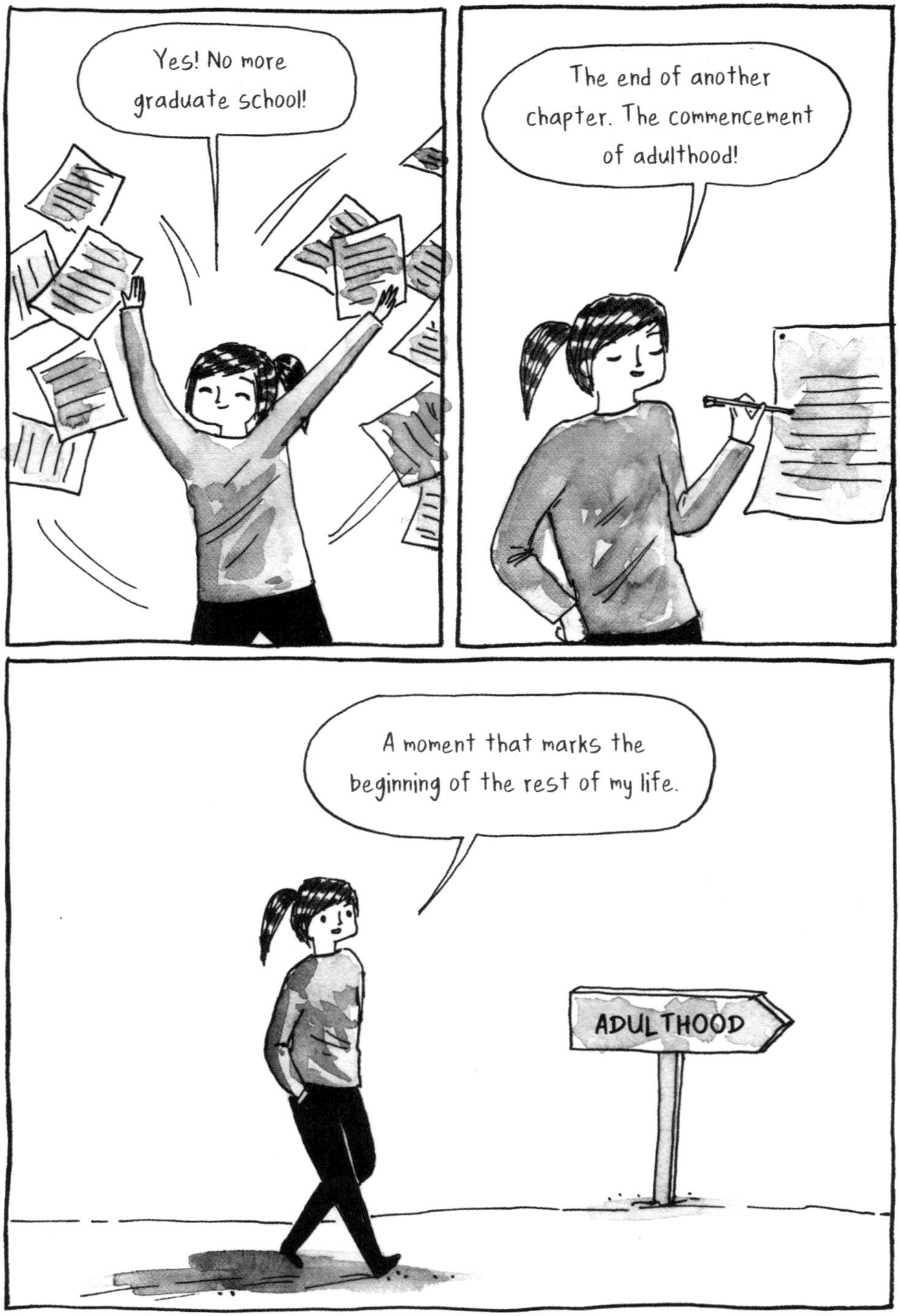
Yes! No more graduate school!
The end of another chapter. The commencement of adulthood!
A moment that marks the beginning of the rest of my life.
ADULTHOOD

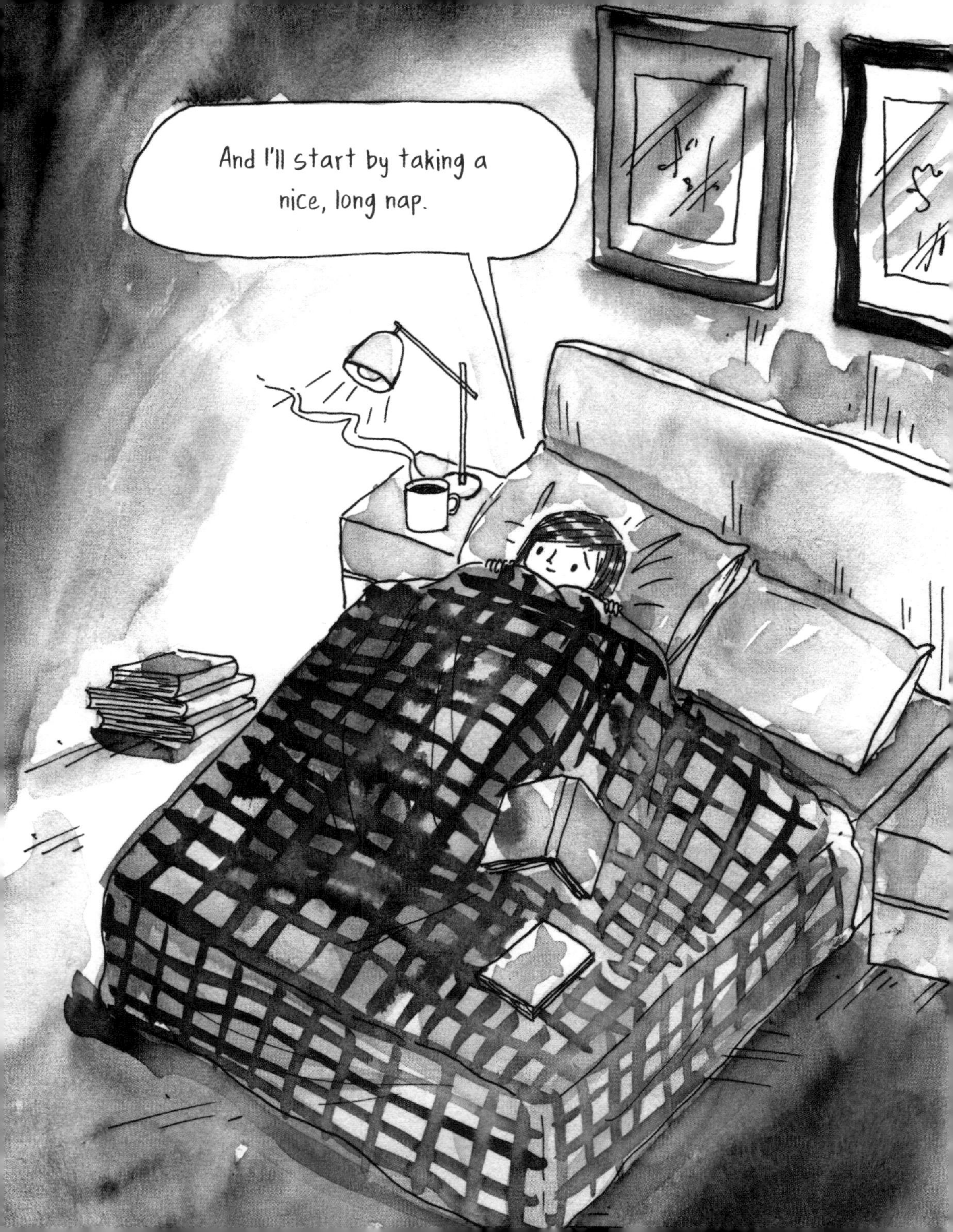
And I'll start by taking a nice, long nap.

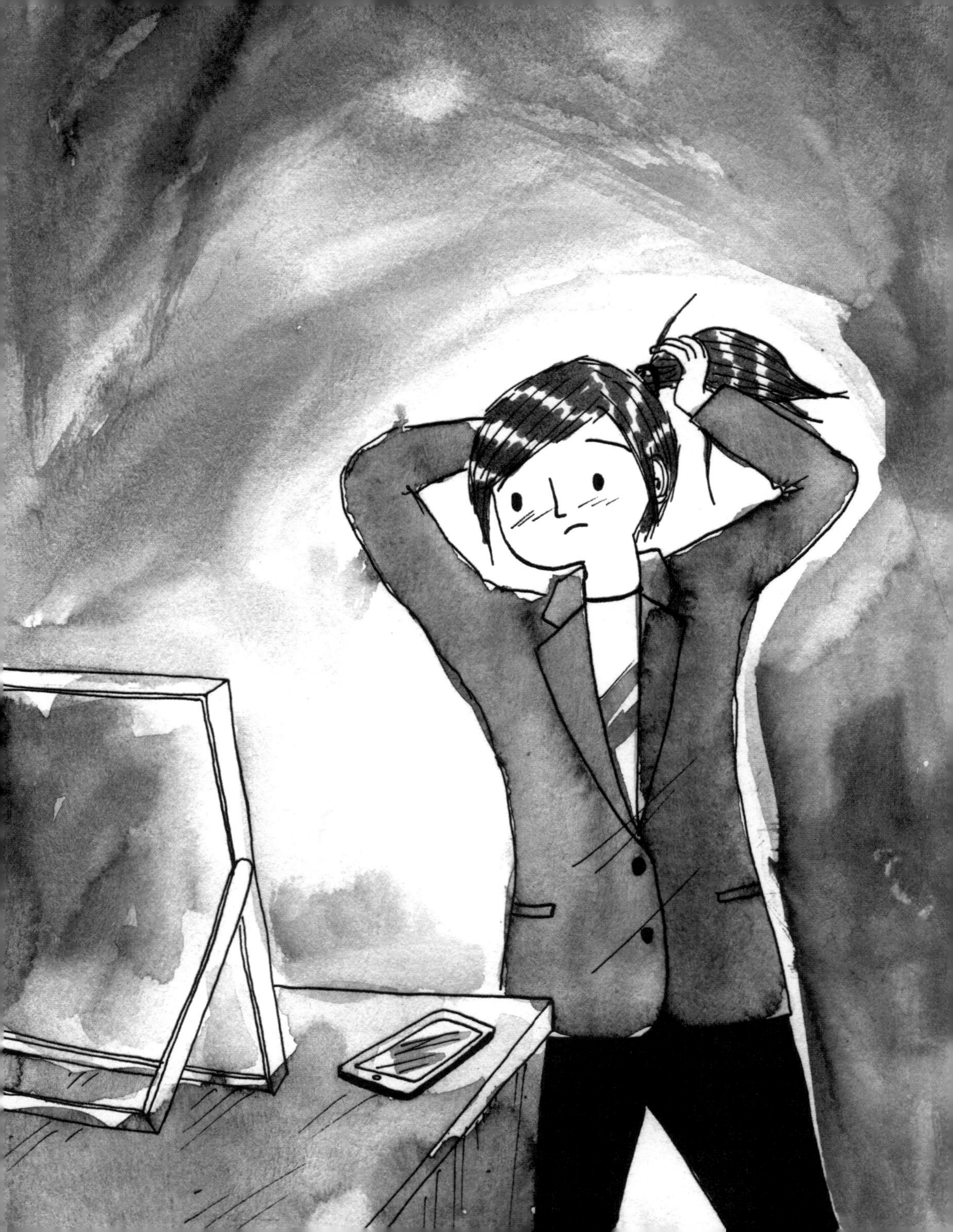

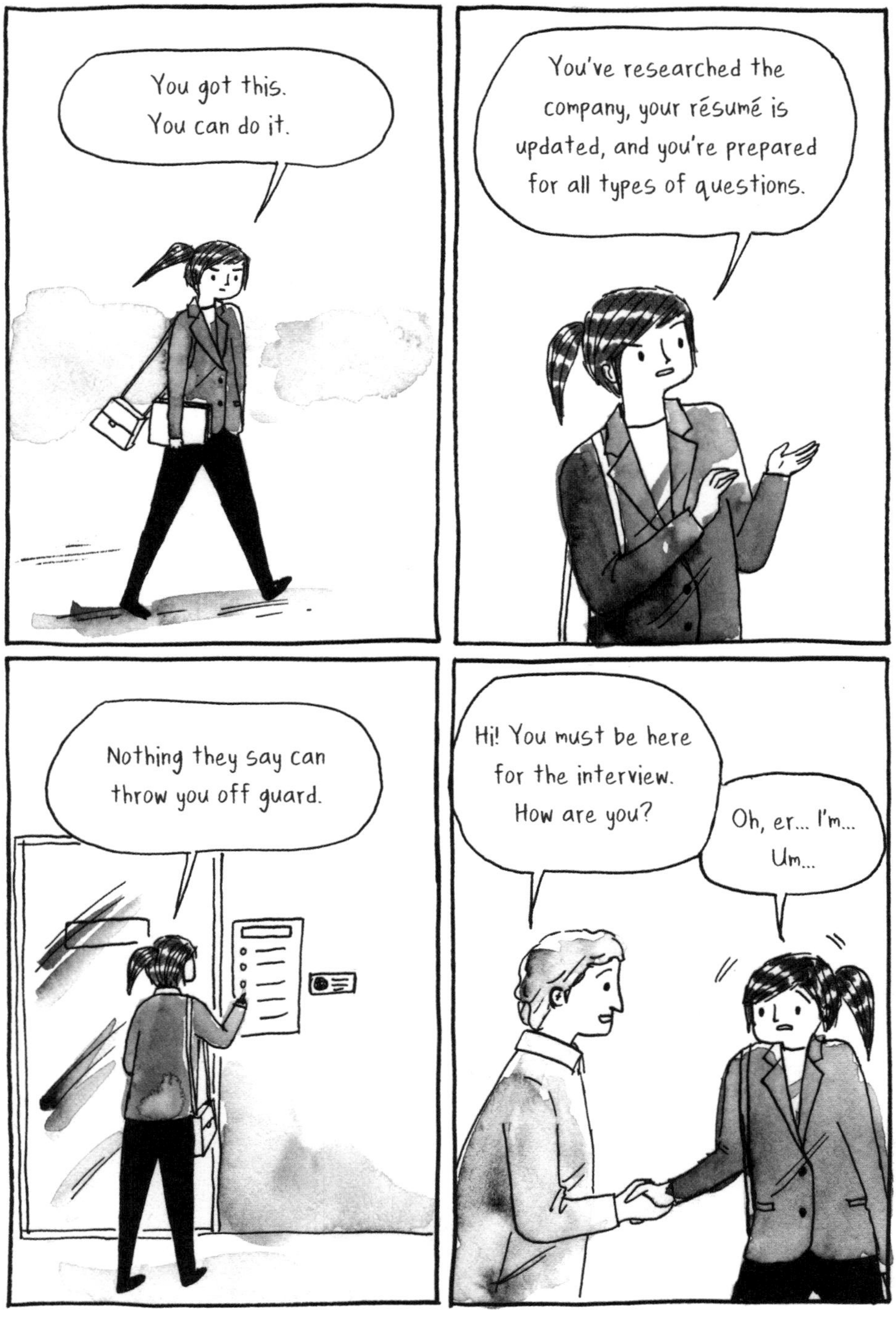
You got this. You can do it.
You've researched the company, your résumé is updated, and you're prepared for all types of questions.
Nothing they say can throw you off guard.
Hi! You must be here for the interview. How are you?
Oh, er... I'm... Um...

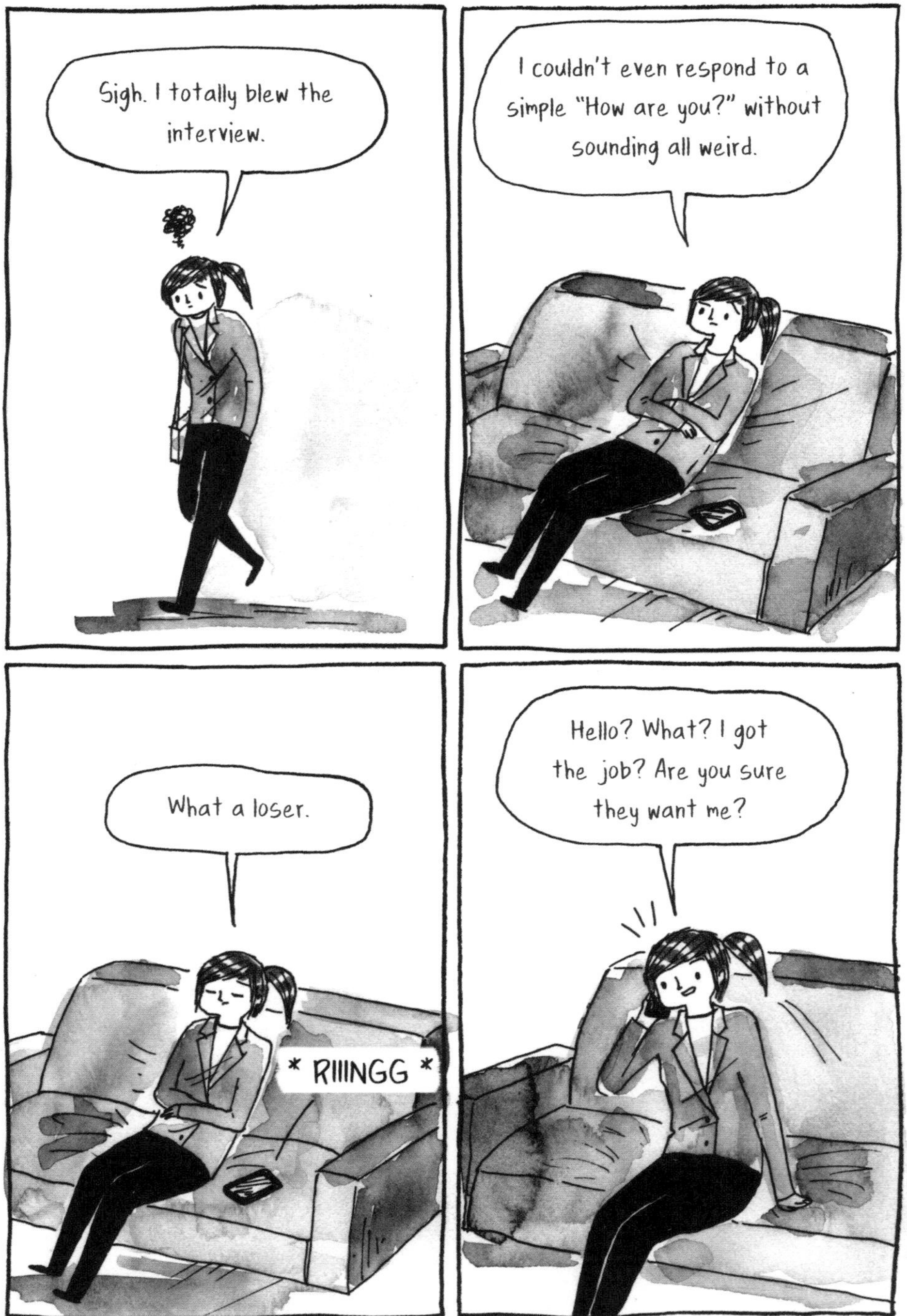
Sigh. I totally blew the interview.
I couldn't even respond to a simple "How are you?" without sounding all weird.
What a loser.
* RIIINGG *
Hello? What? I got the job? Are you sure they want me?

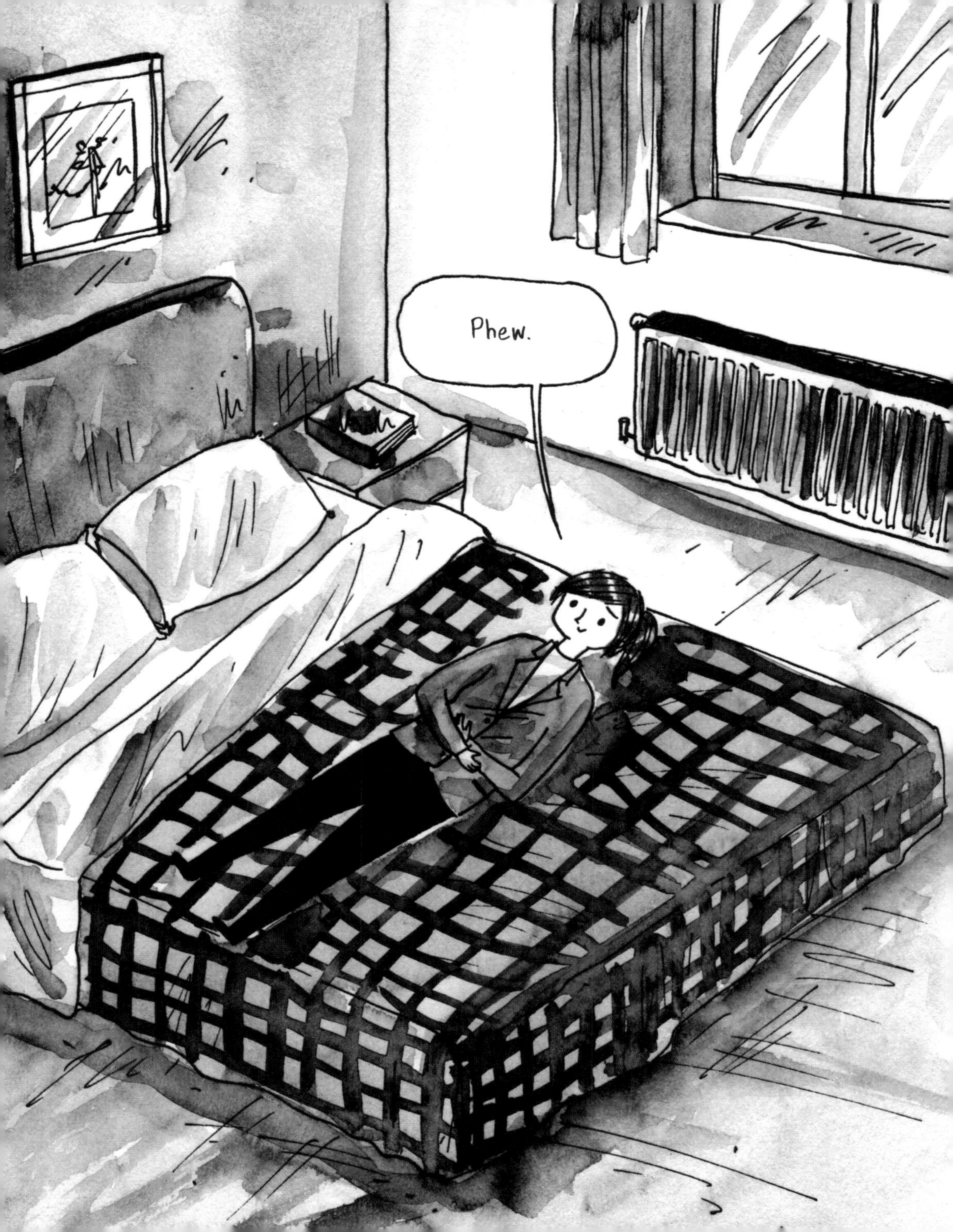
Phew.

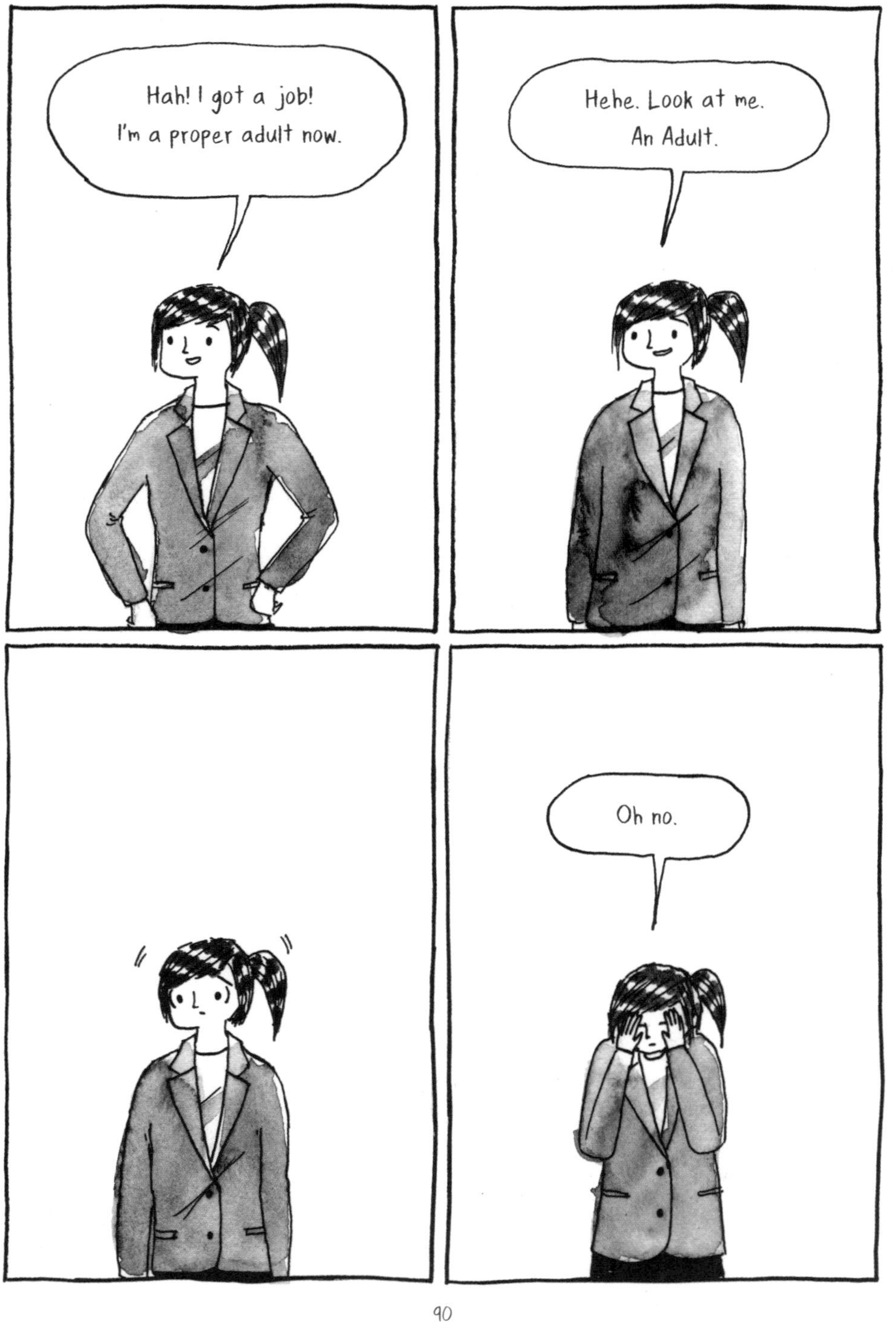
Hah! I got a job!
I'm a proper adult now.
Hehe. Look at me.
An Adult.
Oh no.

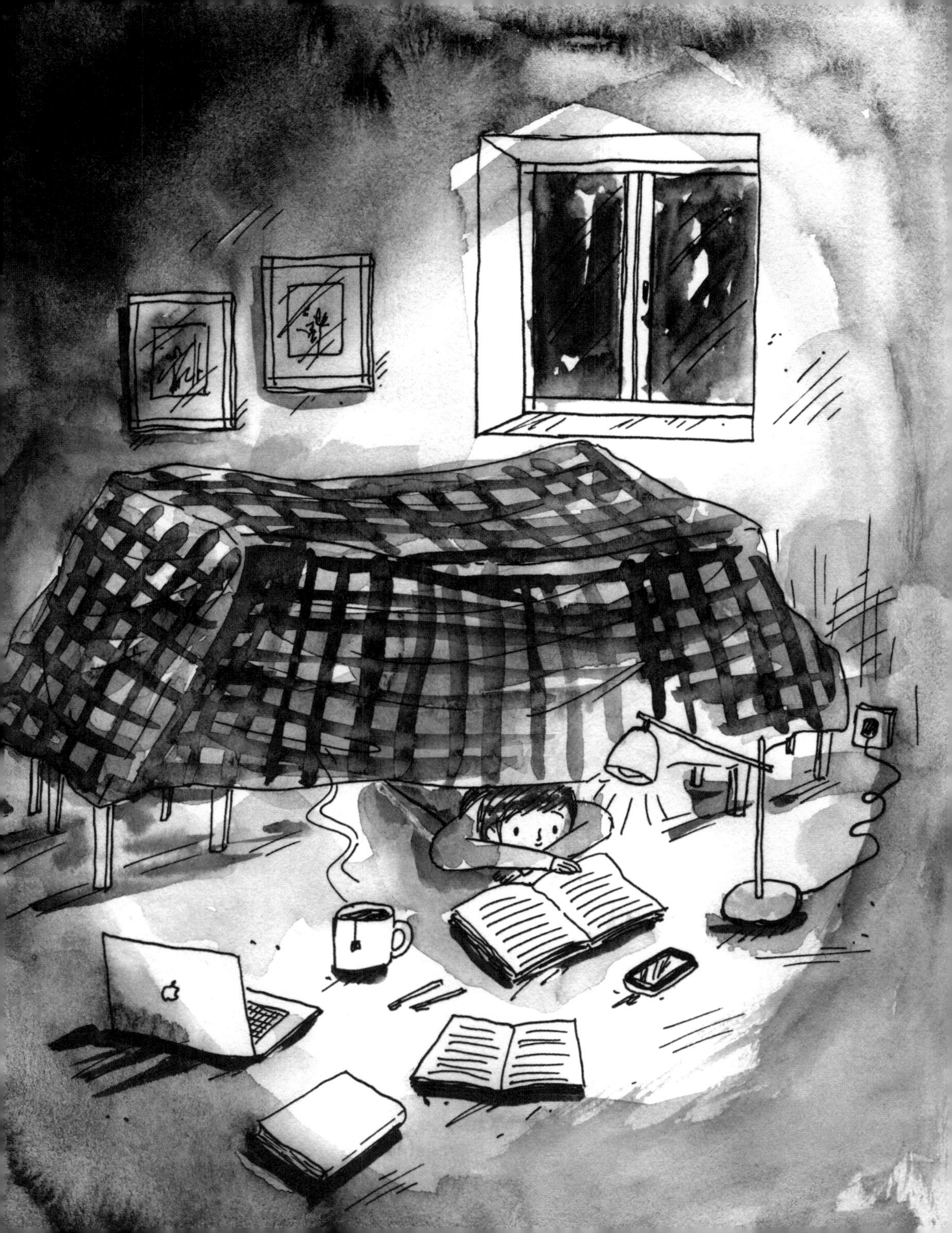

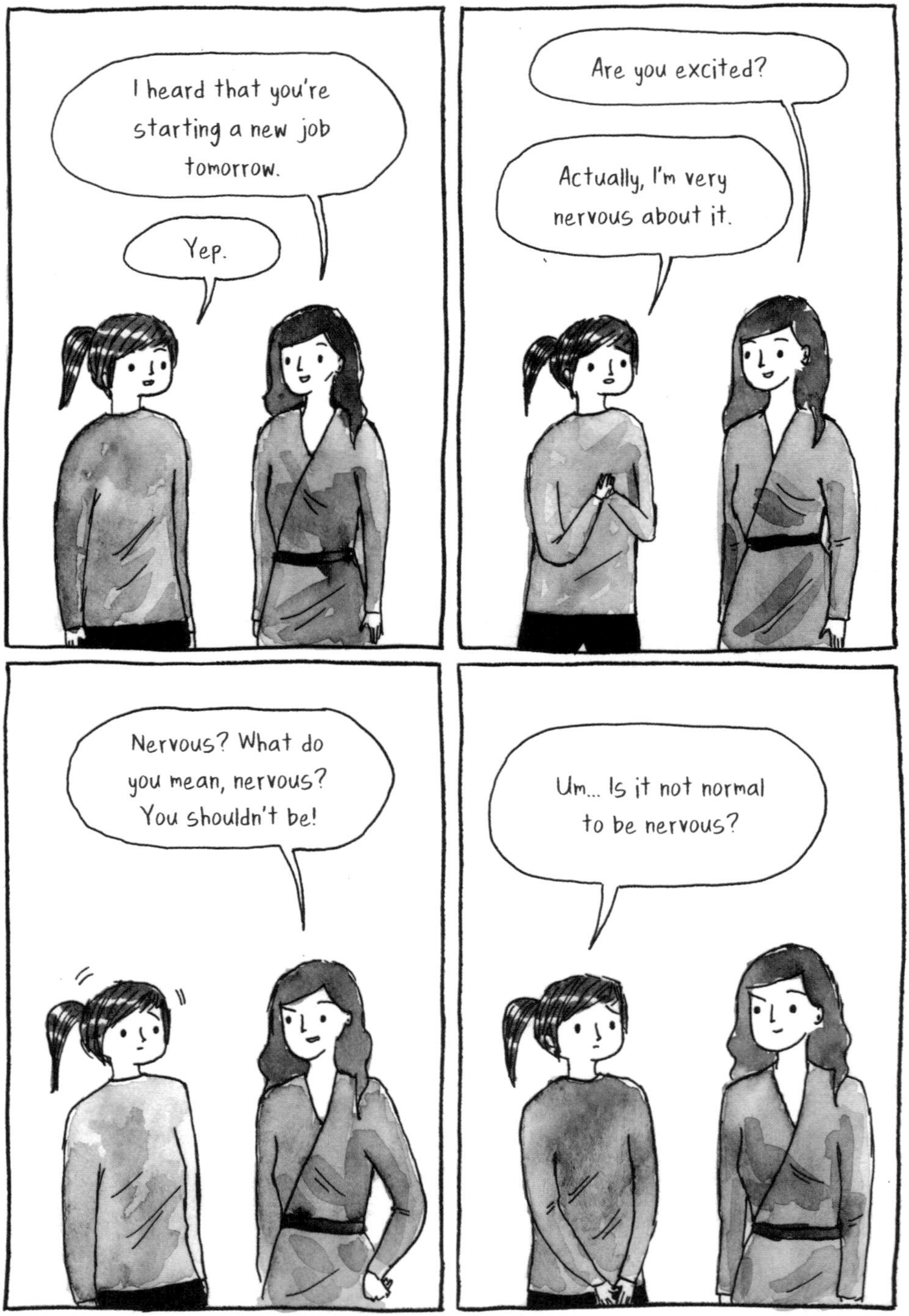
I heard that you're starting a new job tomorrow.
Yep.
Are you excited?
Actually, I'm very nervous about it.
Nervous? What do you mean, nervous? You shouldn't be!
Um... Is it not normal to be nervous?

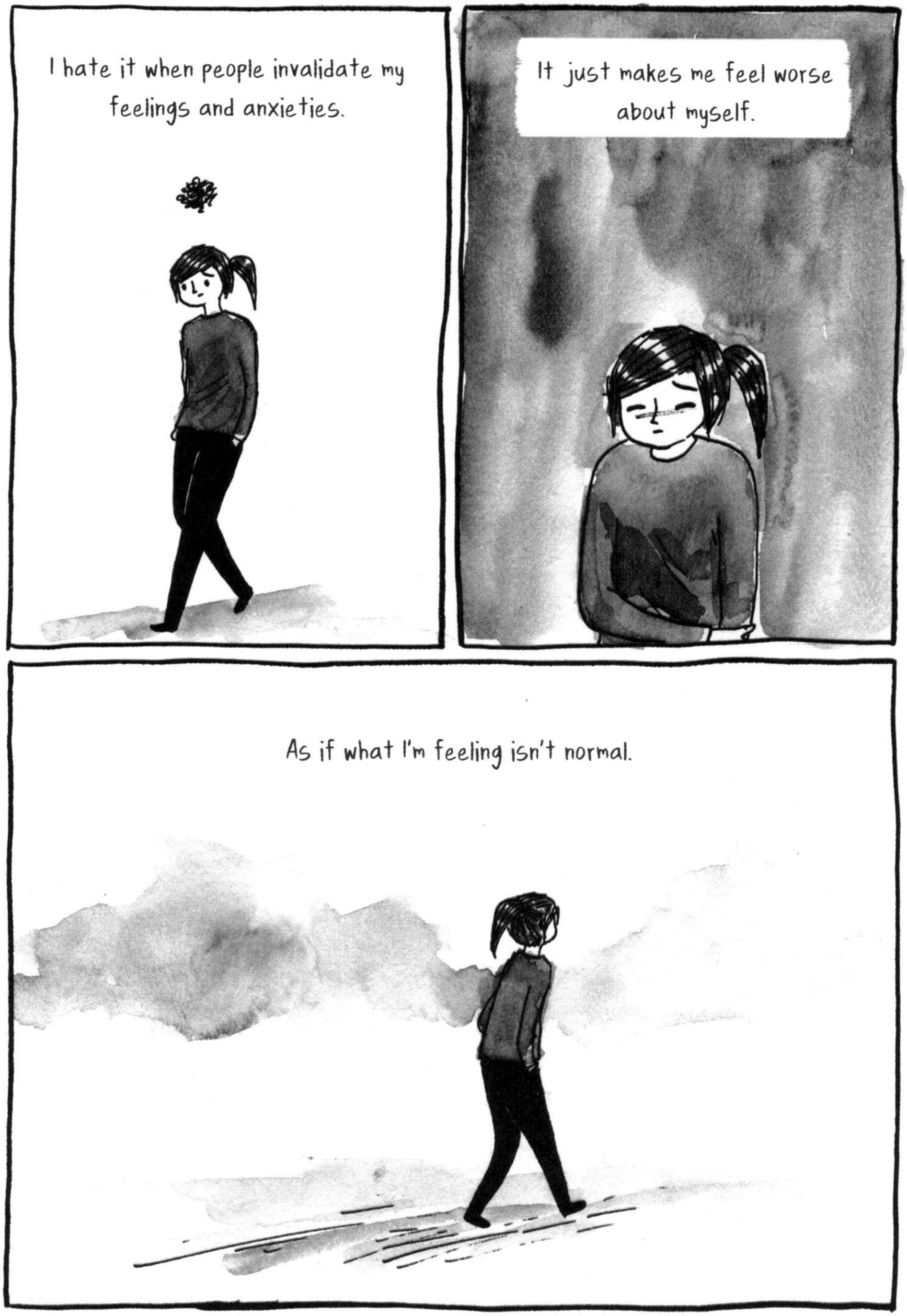
I hate it when people invalidate my feelings and anxieties.
It just makes me feel worse about myself.
As if what I'm feeling isn't normal.

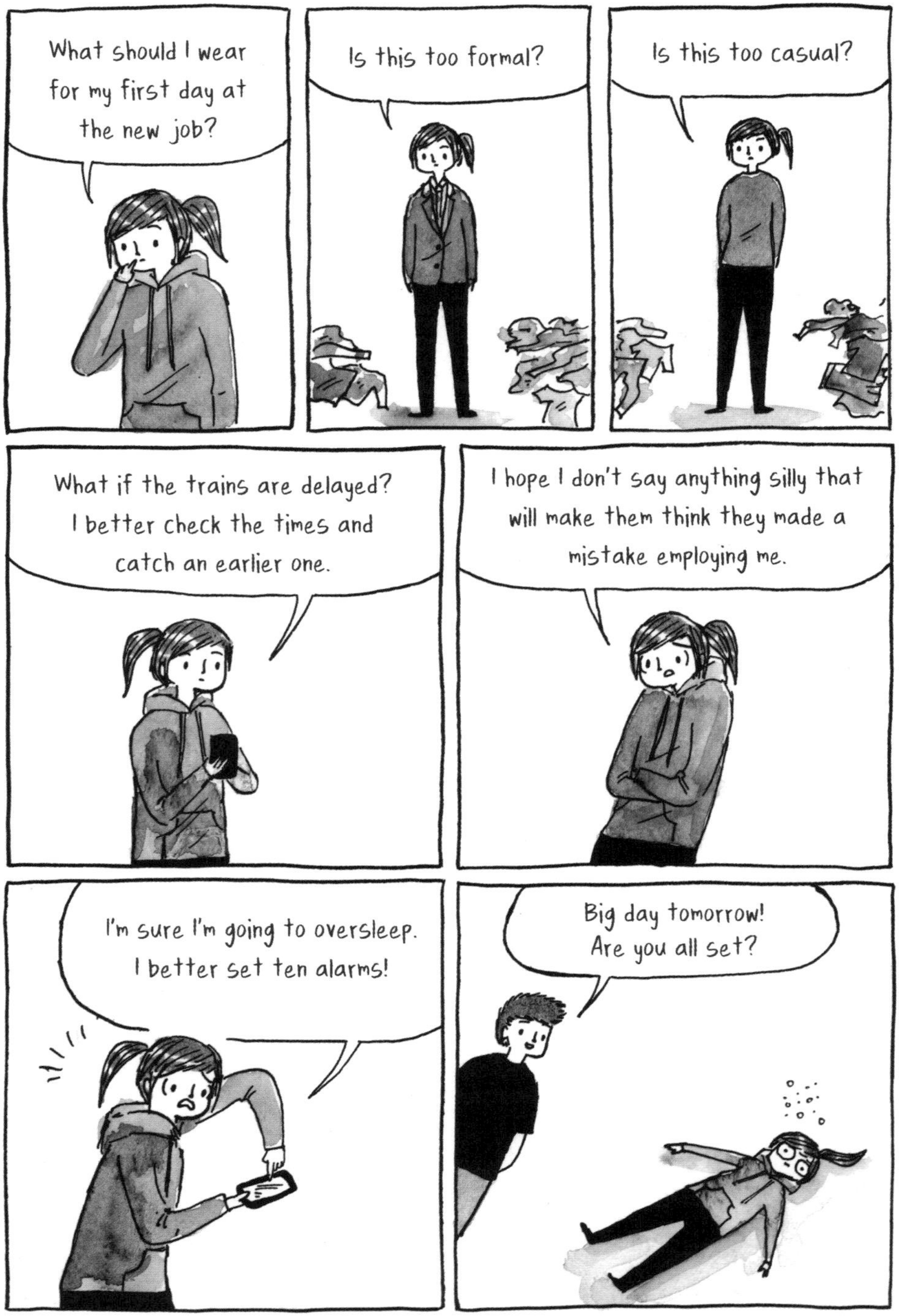
What should I wear for my first day at the new job?
Is this too formal?
Is this too casual?
What if the trains are delayed? I better check the times and catch an earlier one.
I hope I don't say anything silly that will make them think they made a mistake employing me.
I'm sure I'm going to oversleep. I better set ten alarms!
Big day tomorrow! Are you all set?

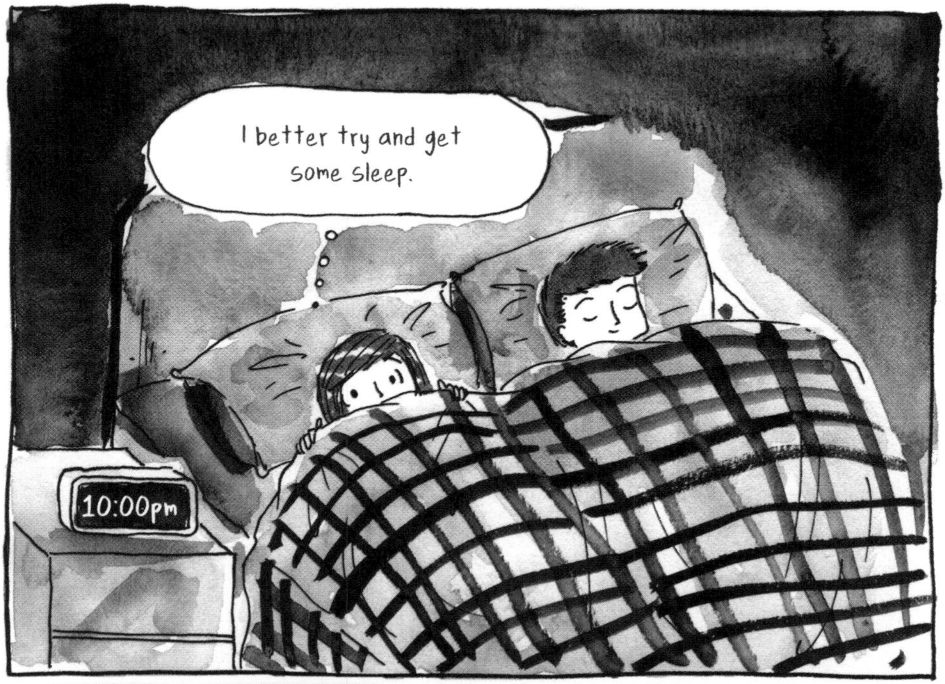
I better try and get some sleep.
10:00pm

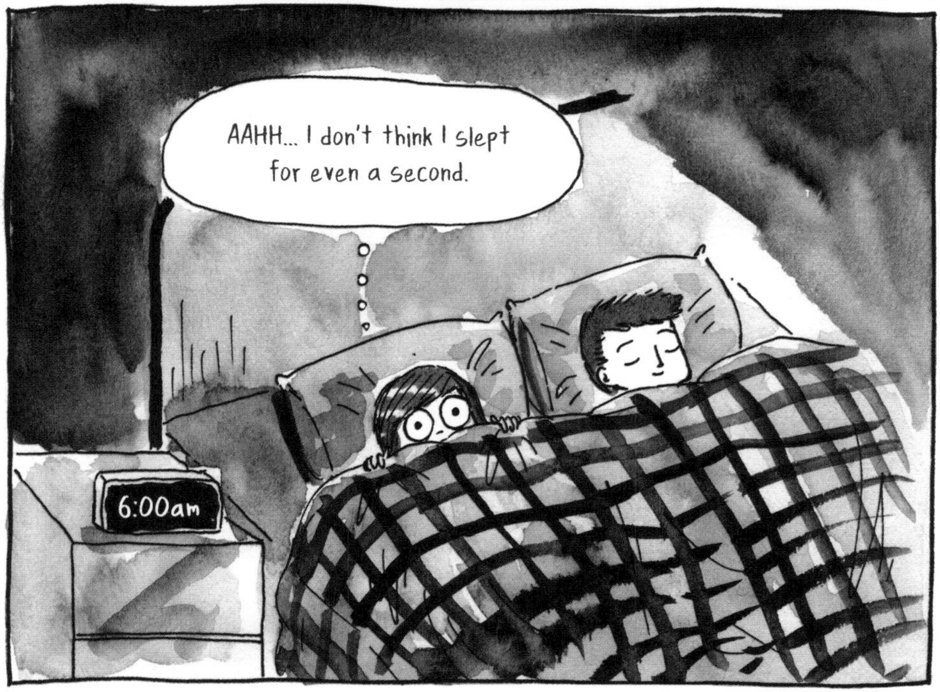
AAHH... I don't think I slept for even a second.
6:00am

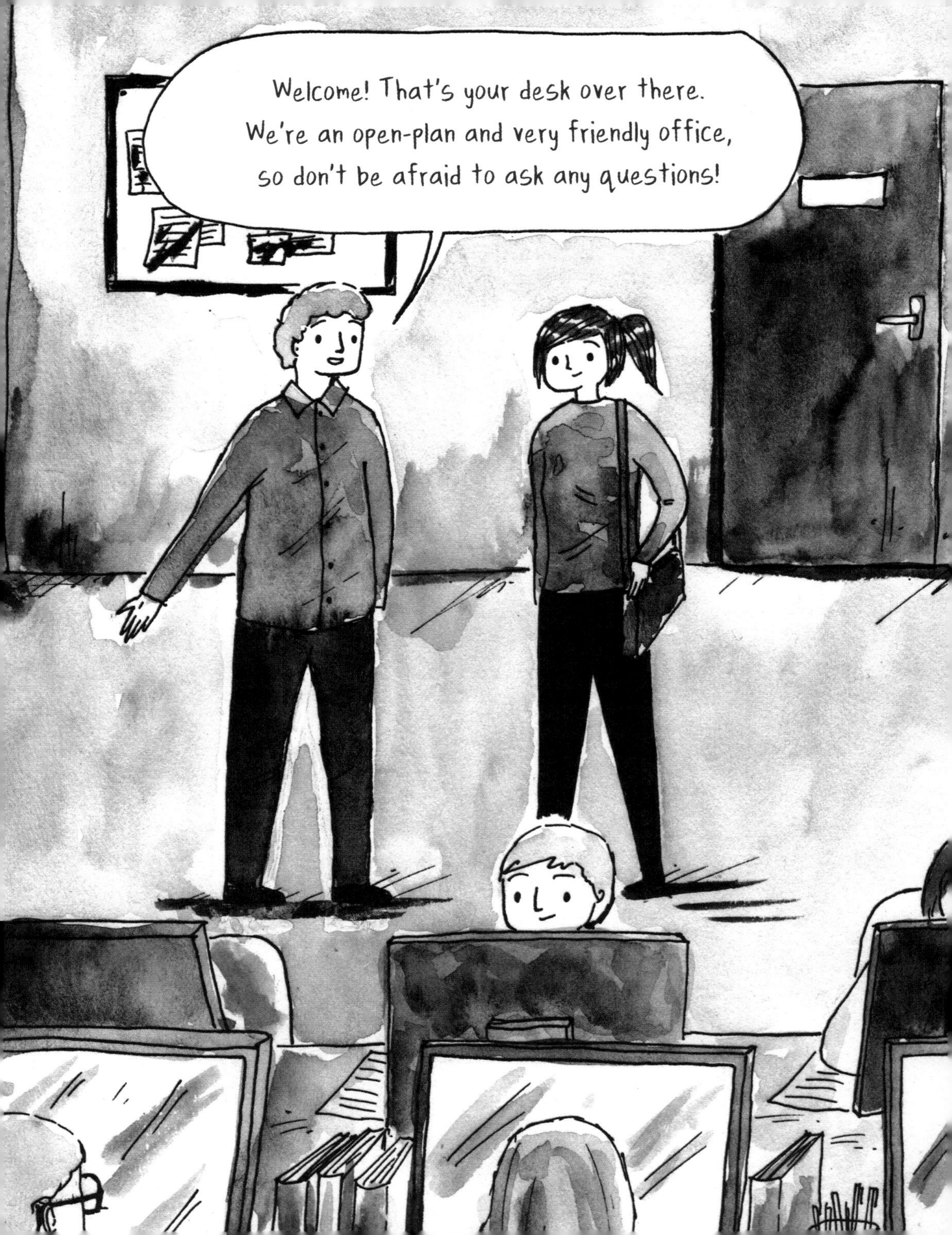
Welcome! That's your desk over there. We're an open-plan and very friendly office, so don't be afraid to ask any questions!

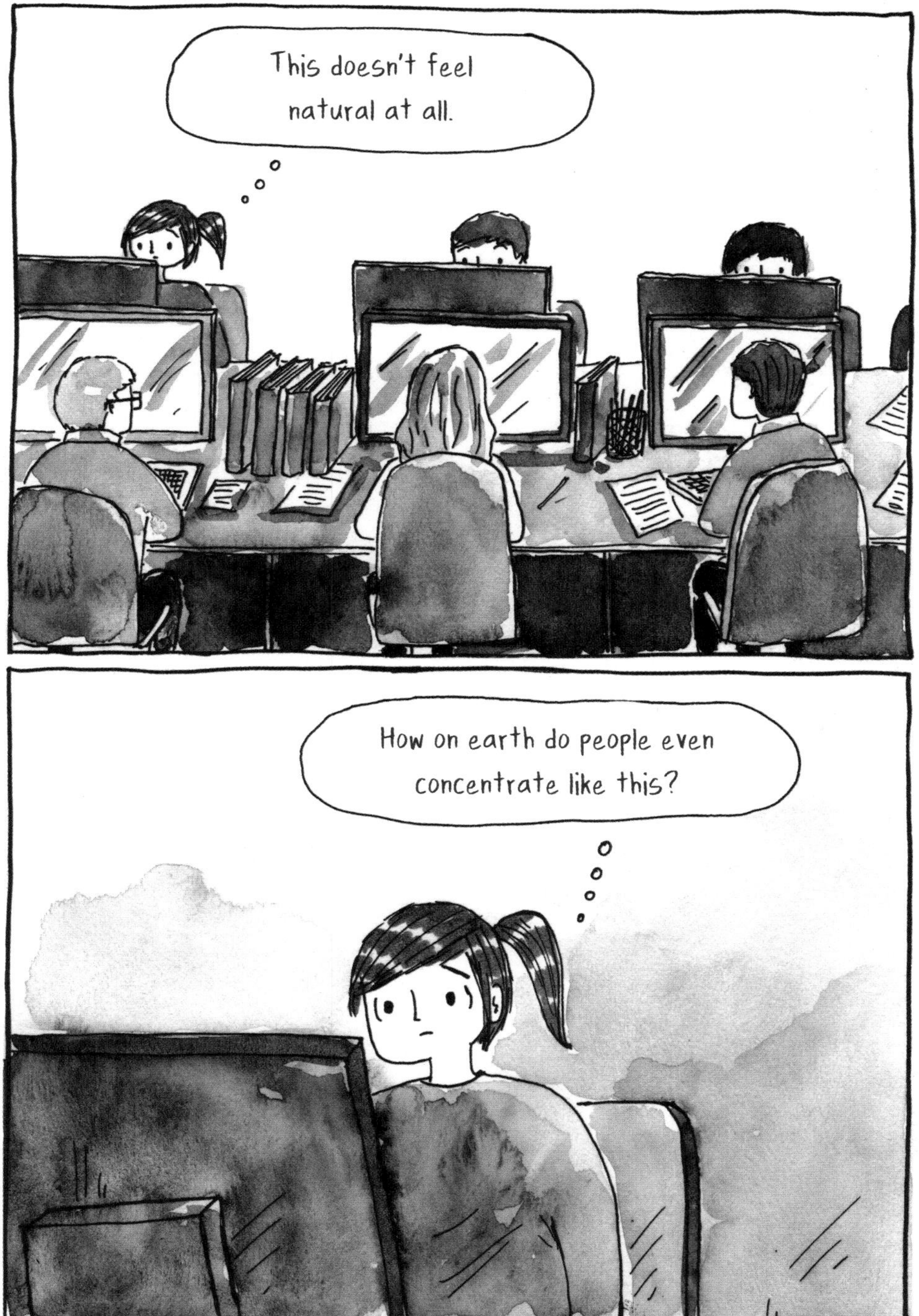
This doesn't feel natural at all.
How on earth do people even concentrate like this?

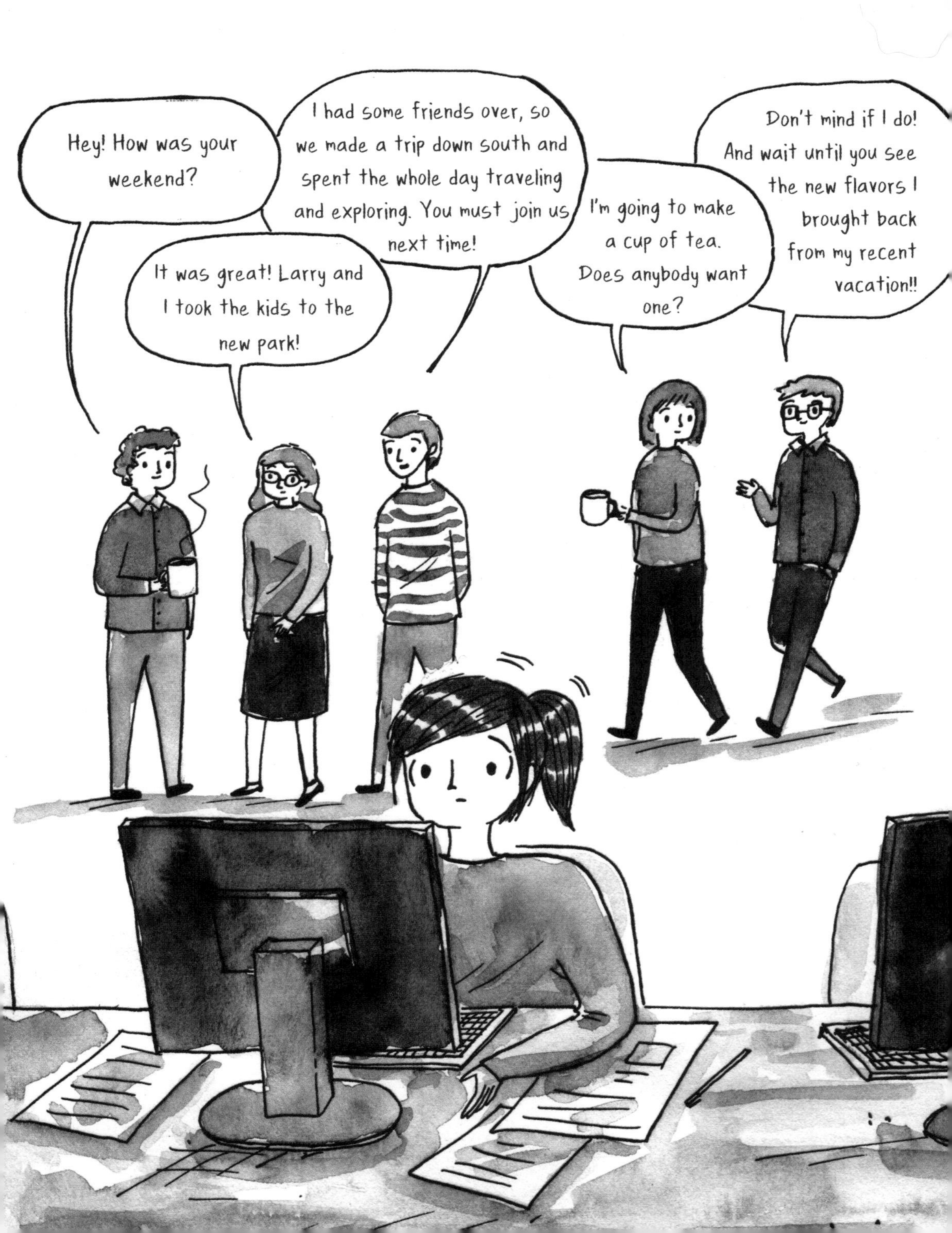
Hey! How was your weekend?
It was great! Larry and I took the kids to the new park!
I had some friends over, so we made a trip down south and spent the whole day traveling and exploring. You must join us next time!
I'm going to make a cup of tea. Does anybody want one?
Don't mind if I do! And wait until you see the new flavors I brought back from my recent vacation!!

Tea makes
everything better.

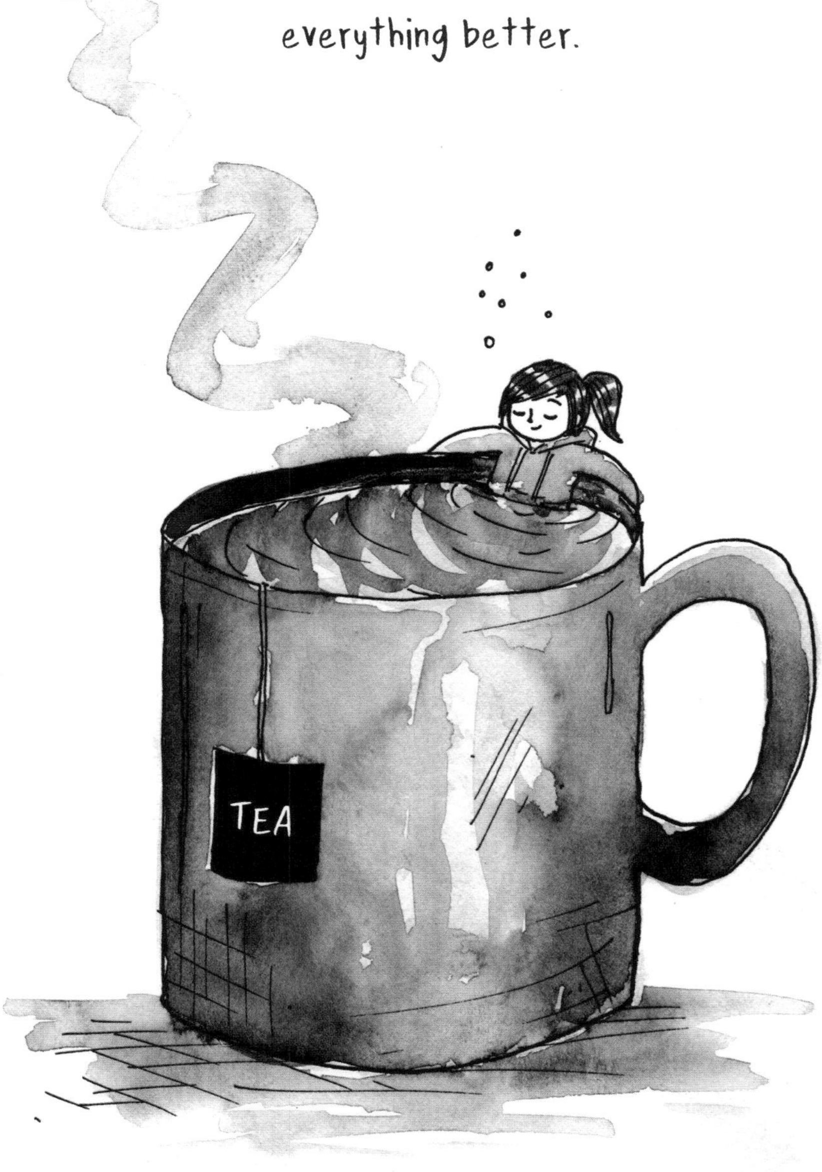
TEA

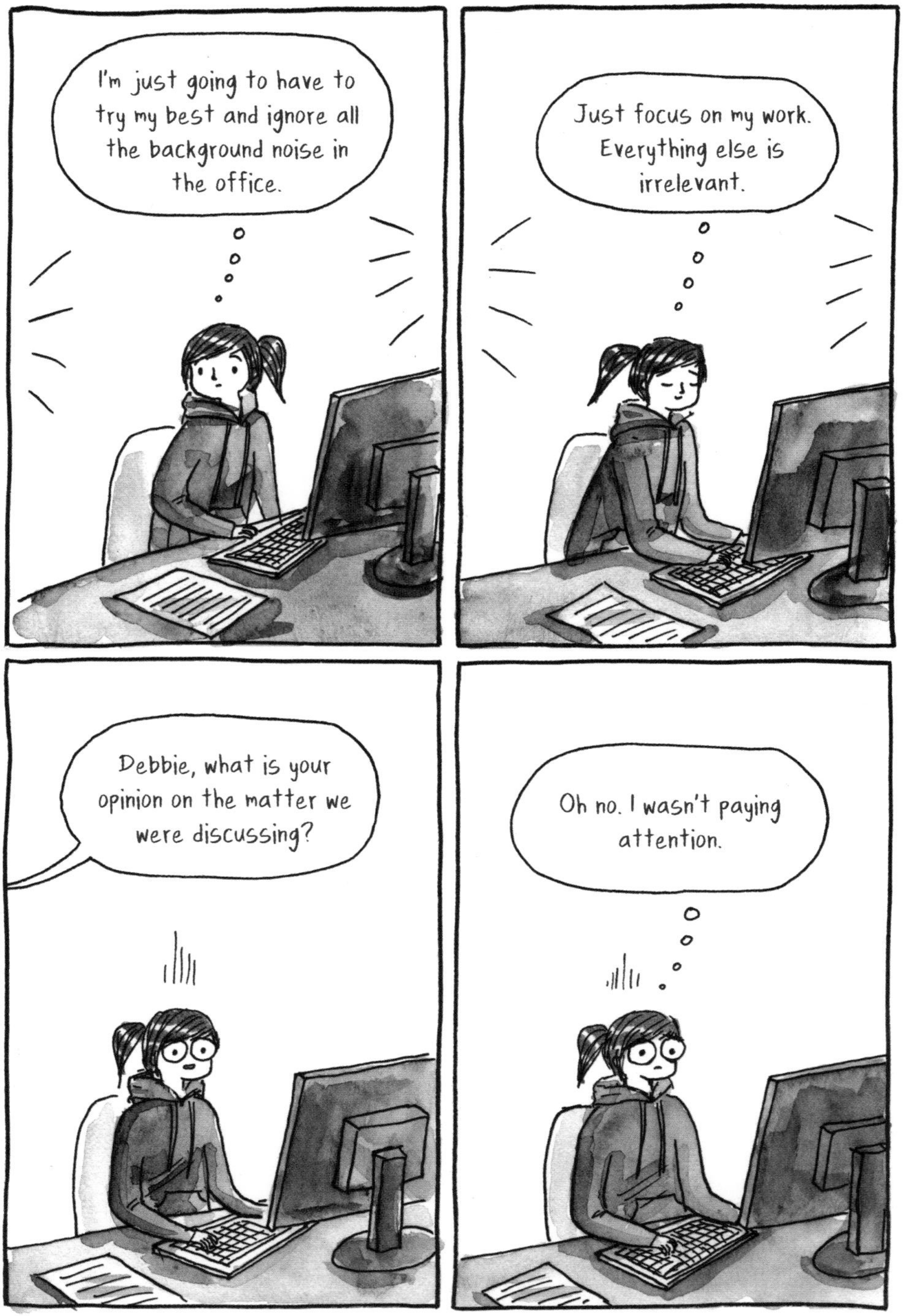
I'm just going to have to try my best and ignore all the background noise in the office.
Just focus on my work. Everything else is irrelevant.
Debbie, what is your opinion on the matter we were discussing?
Oh no. I wasn't paying attention.

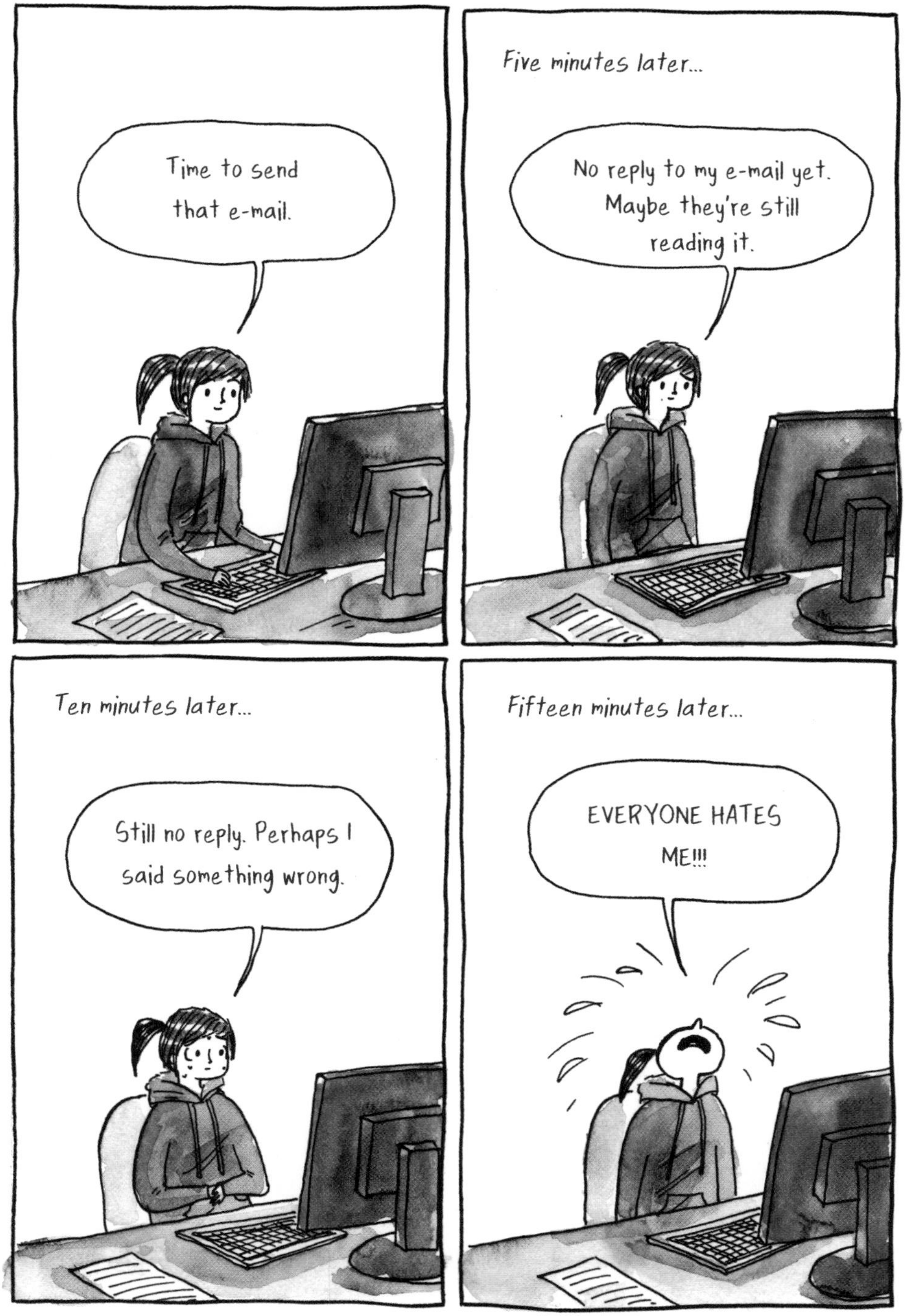
Time to send that e-mail.
Five minutes later...
No reply to my e-mail yet. Maybe they're still reading it.
Ten minutes later...
Still no reply. Perhaps I said something wrong.
Fifteen minutes later...
EVERYONE HATES ME!!!

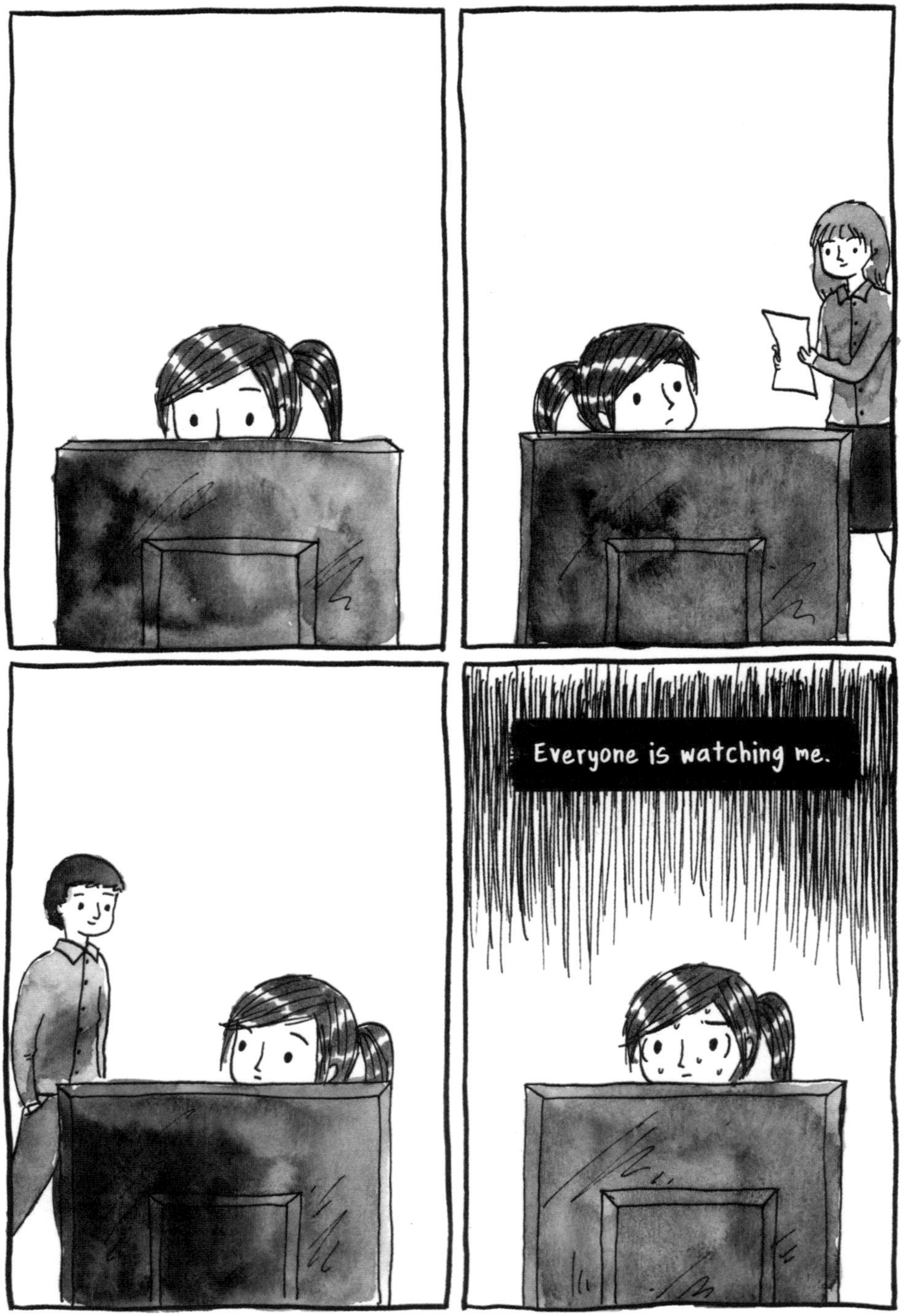
Everyone is watching me.

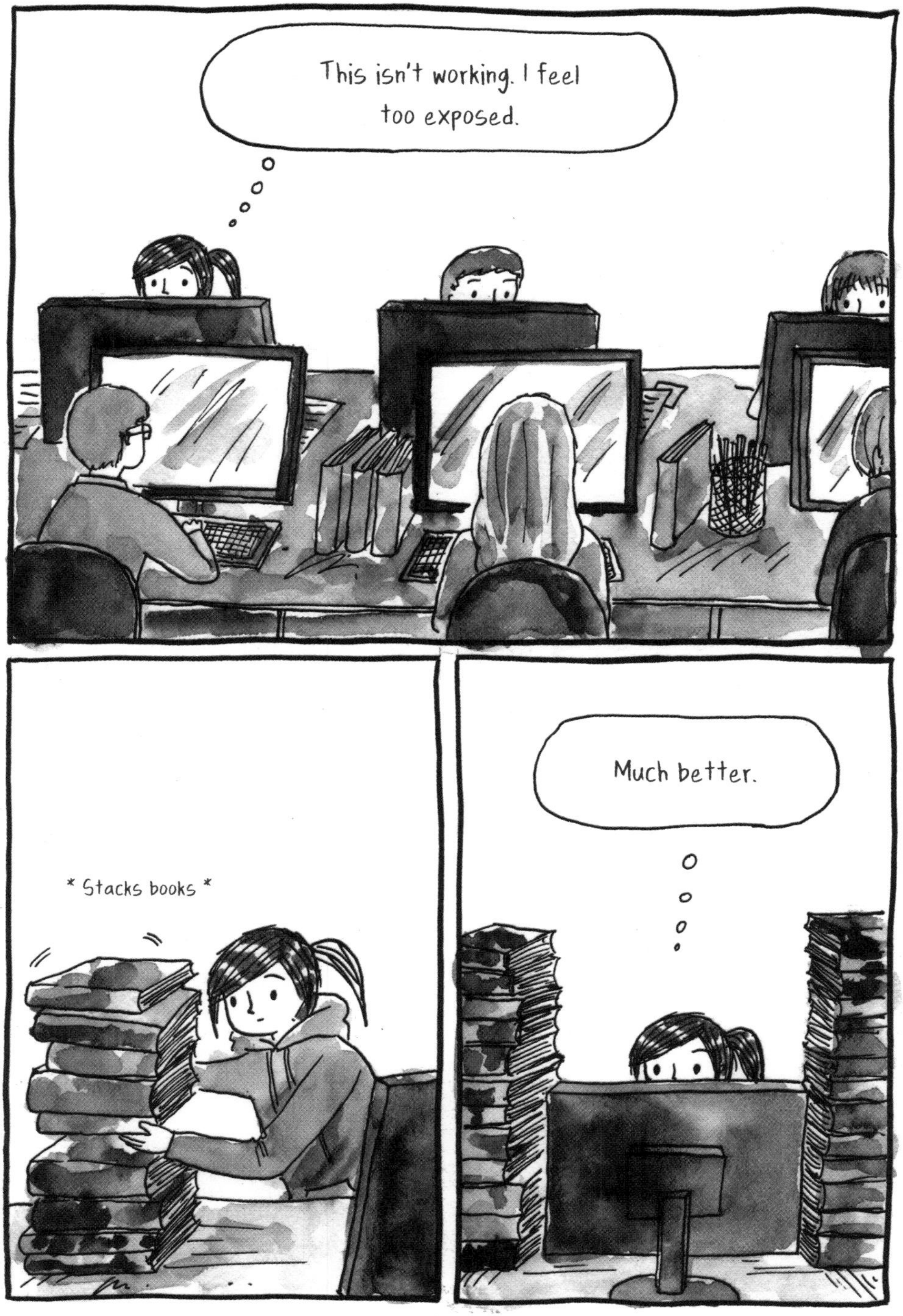
This isn't working. I feel too exposed.
* Stacks books *
Much better.

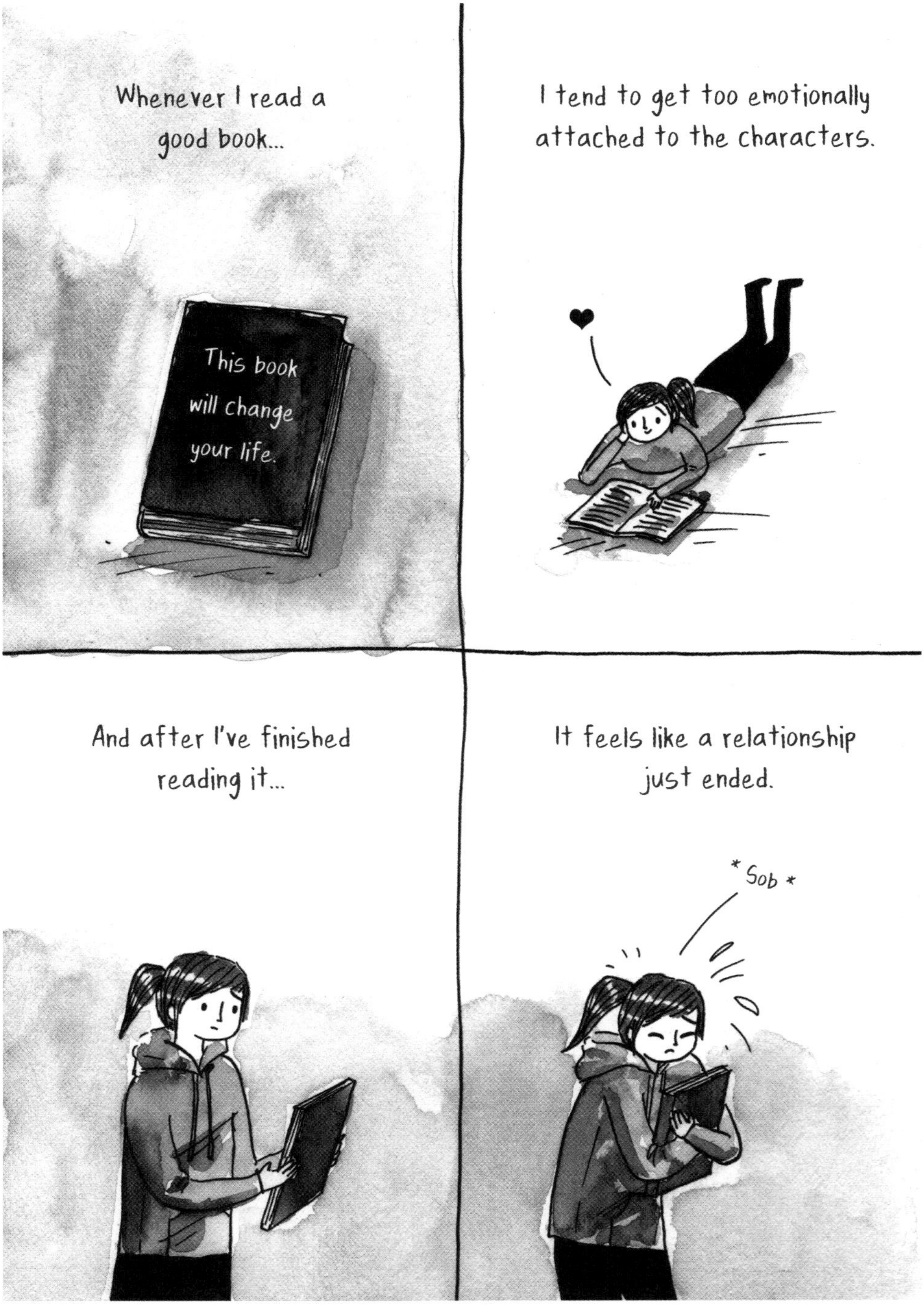
Whenever I read a good book...
This book will change your life.
I tend to get too emotionally attached to the characters.
And after I've finished reading it...
It feels like a relationship just ended.
* Sob *

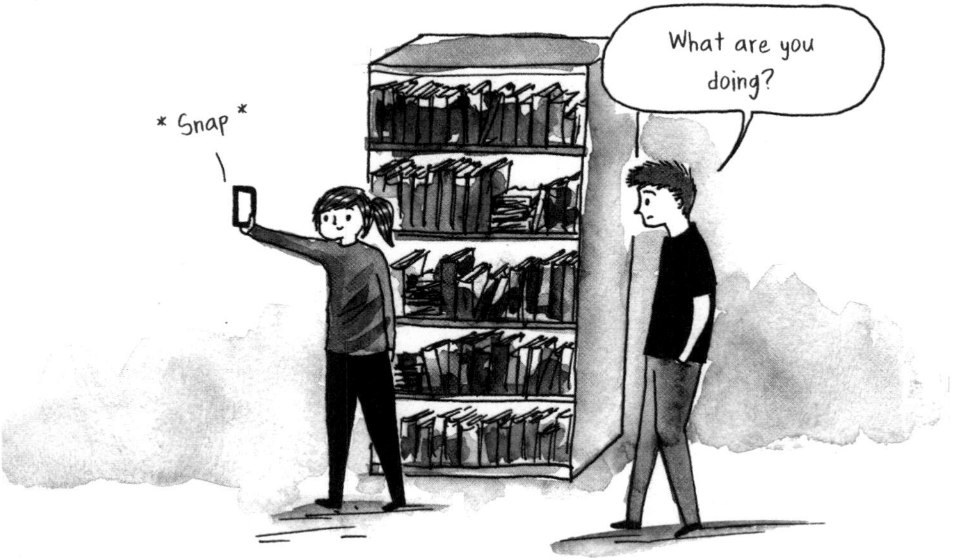
* Snap *
What are you doing?

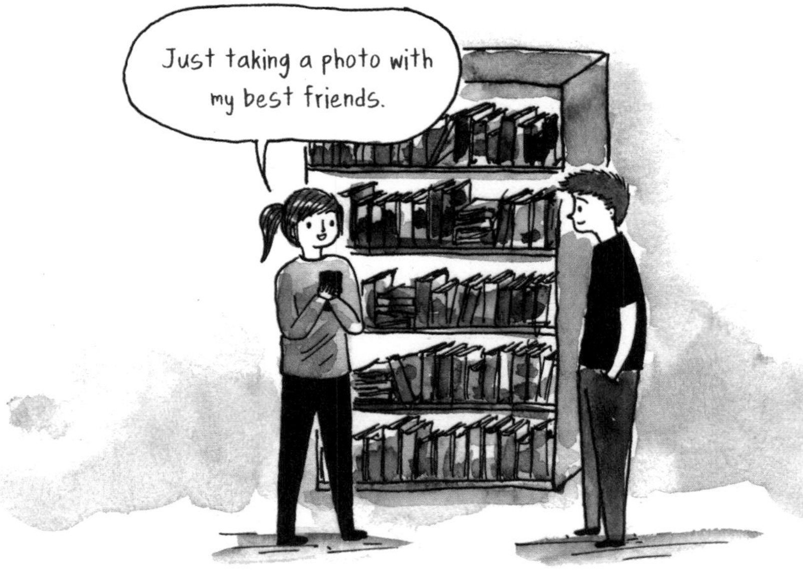
Just taking a photo with my best friends.

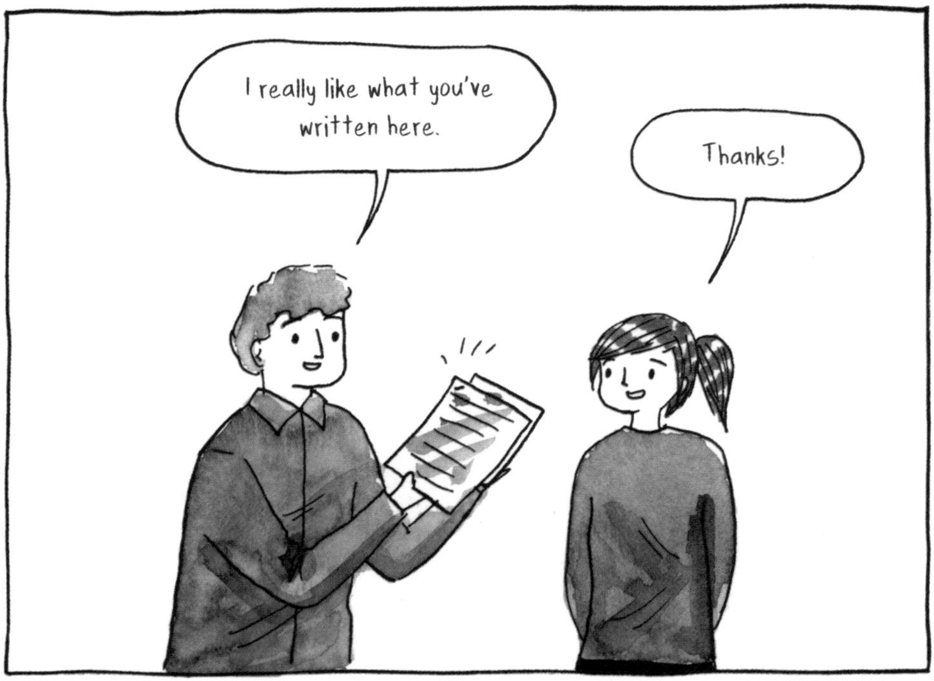
I really like what you've written here.
Thanks!

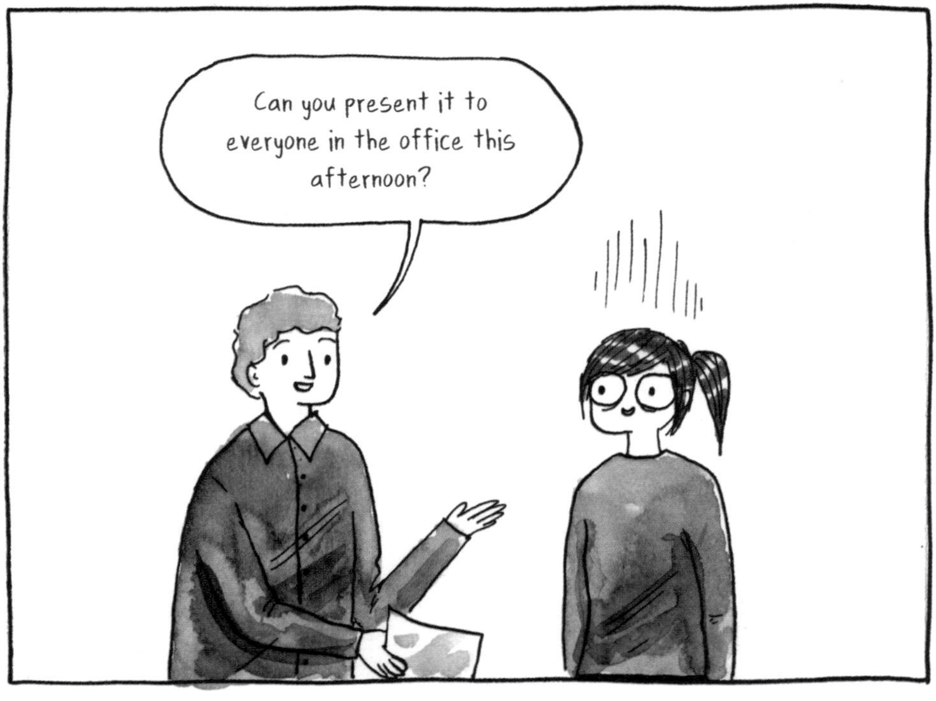
Can you present it to everyone in the office this afternoon?

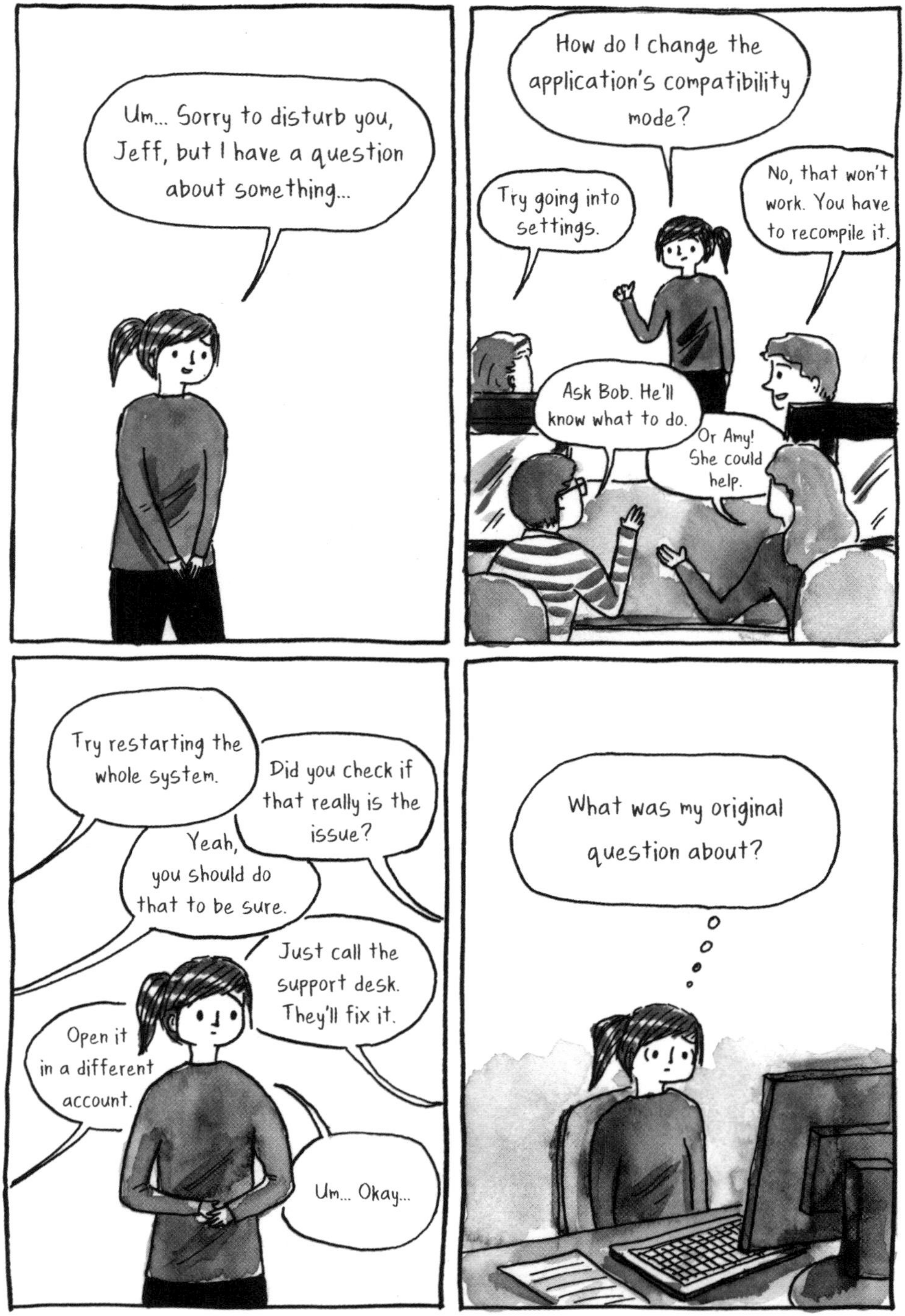
Um... Sorry to disturb you, Jeff, but I have a question about something...
How do I change the application's compatibility mode?
Try going into settings.
No, that won't work. You have to recompile it.
Ask Bob. He'll know what to do.
Or Amy! She could help.
Try restarting the whole system.
Did you check if that really is the issue?
Yeah, you should do that to be sure.
Just call the support desk. They'll fix it.
Open it in a different account.
Um... Okay...
What was my original question about?

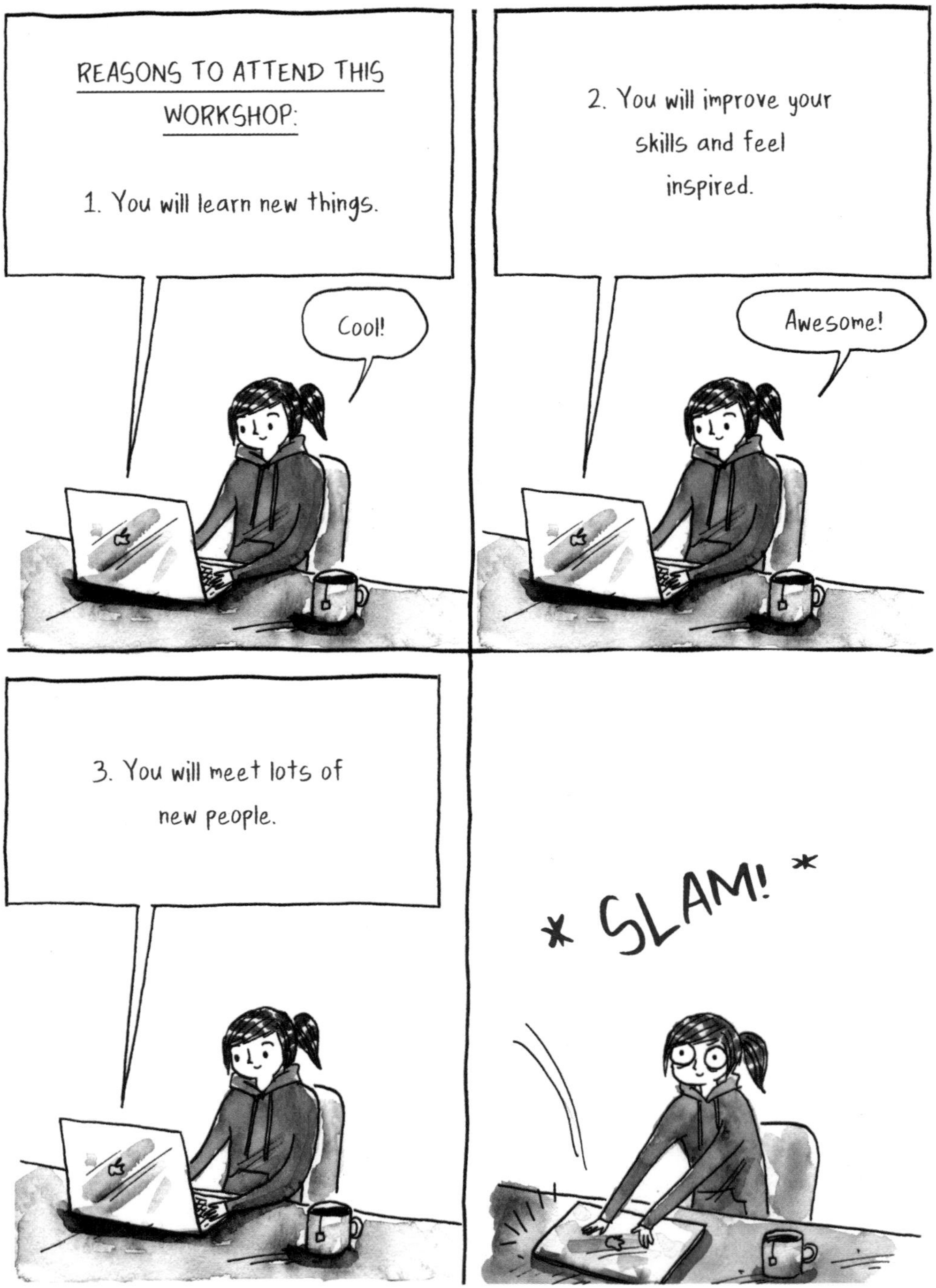
REASONS TO ATTEND THIS WORKSHOP:
1. You will learn new things.
Cool!
2. You will improve your skills and feel inspired.
Awesome!
3. You will meet lots of new people.
* SLAM! *

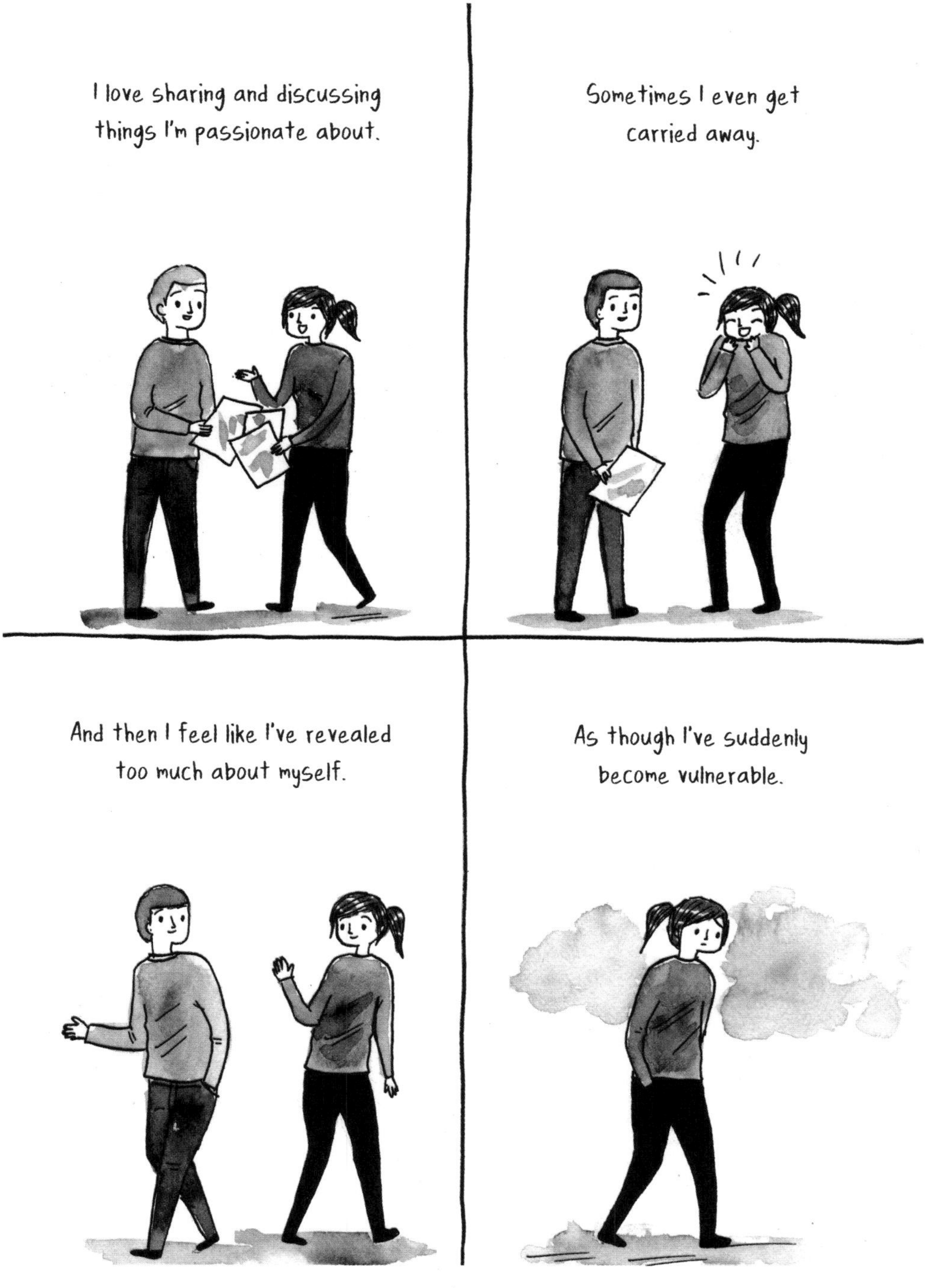
I love sharing and discussing things I'm passionate about.
Sometimes I even get carried away.
And then I feel like I've revealed too much about myself.
As though I've suddenly become vulnerable.

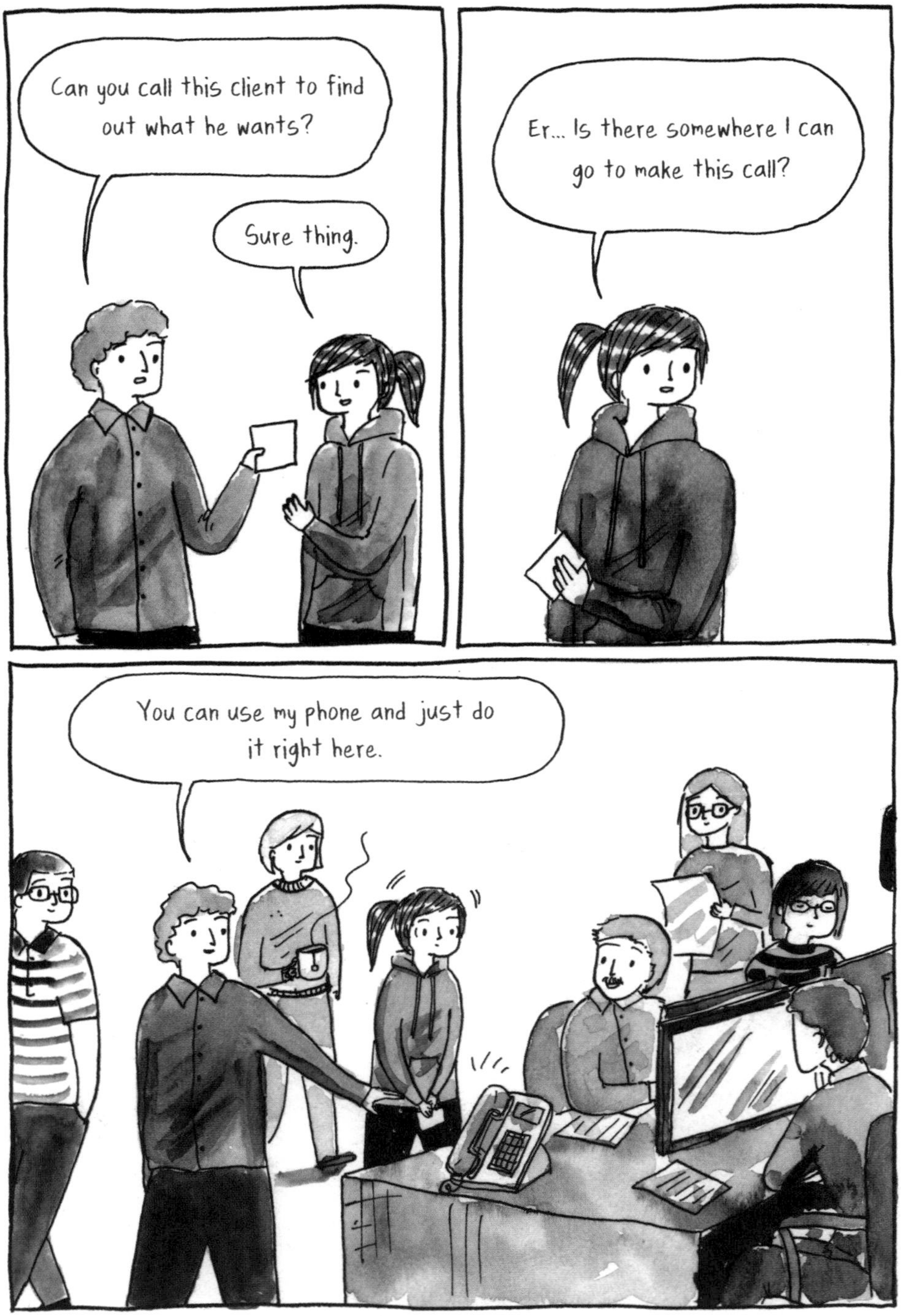
Can you call this client to find out what he wants?
Sure thing.
Er... Is there somewhere I can go to make this call?
You can use my phone and just do it right here.

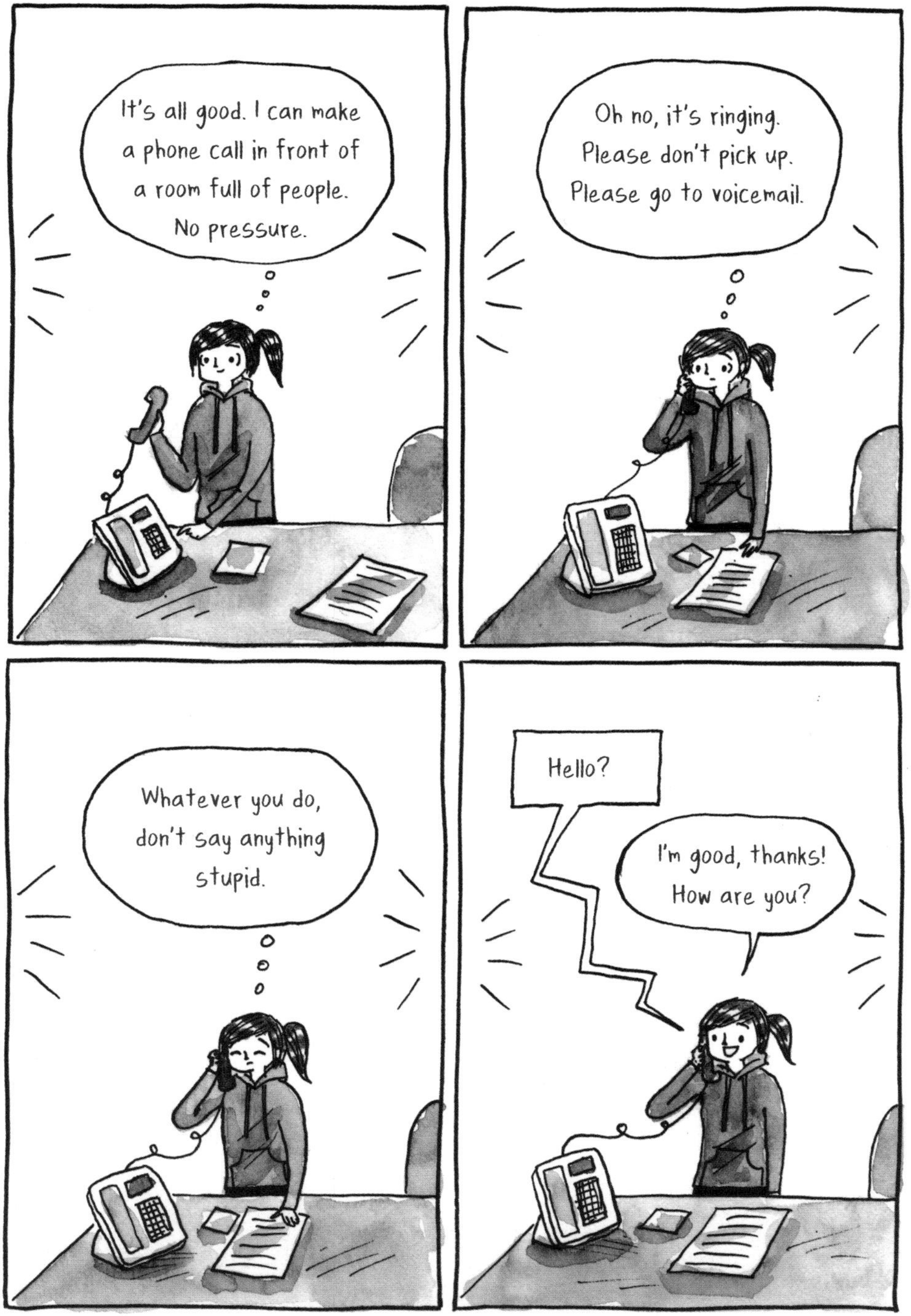
It's all good. I can make a phone call in front of a room full of people. No pressure.
Oh no, it's ringing. Please don't pick up. Please go to voicemail.
Whatever you do, don't say anything stupid.
Hello?
I'm good, thanks! How are you?

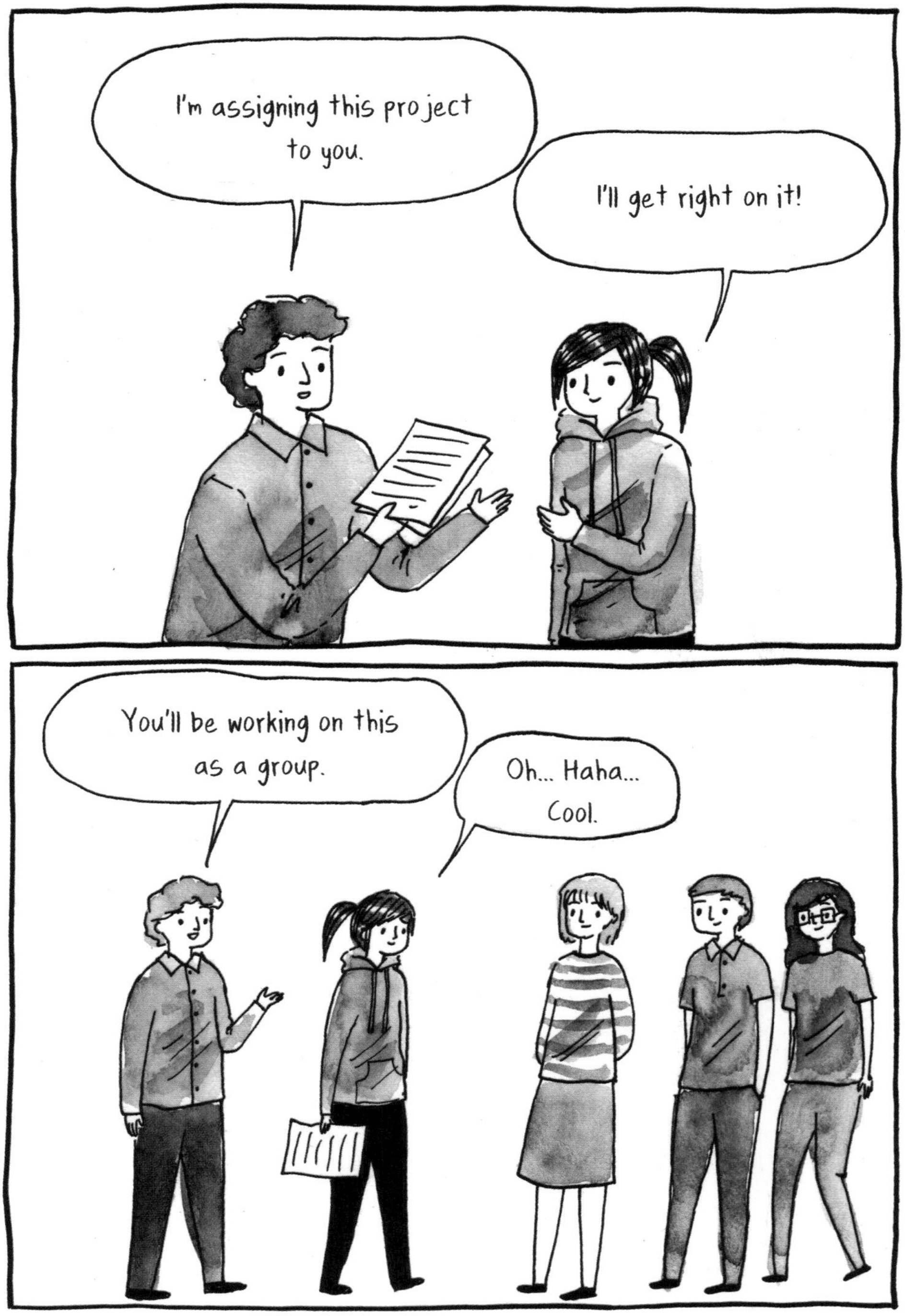
I'm assigning this project to you.
I'll get right on it!
You'll be working on this as a group.
Oh... Haha... Cool.

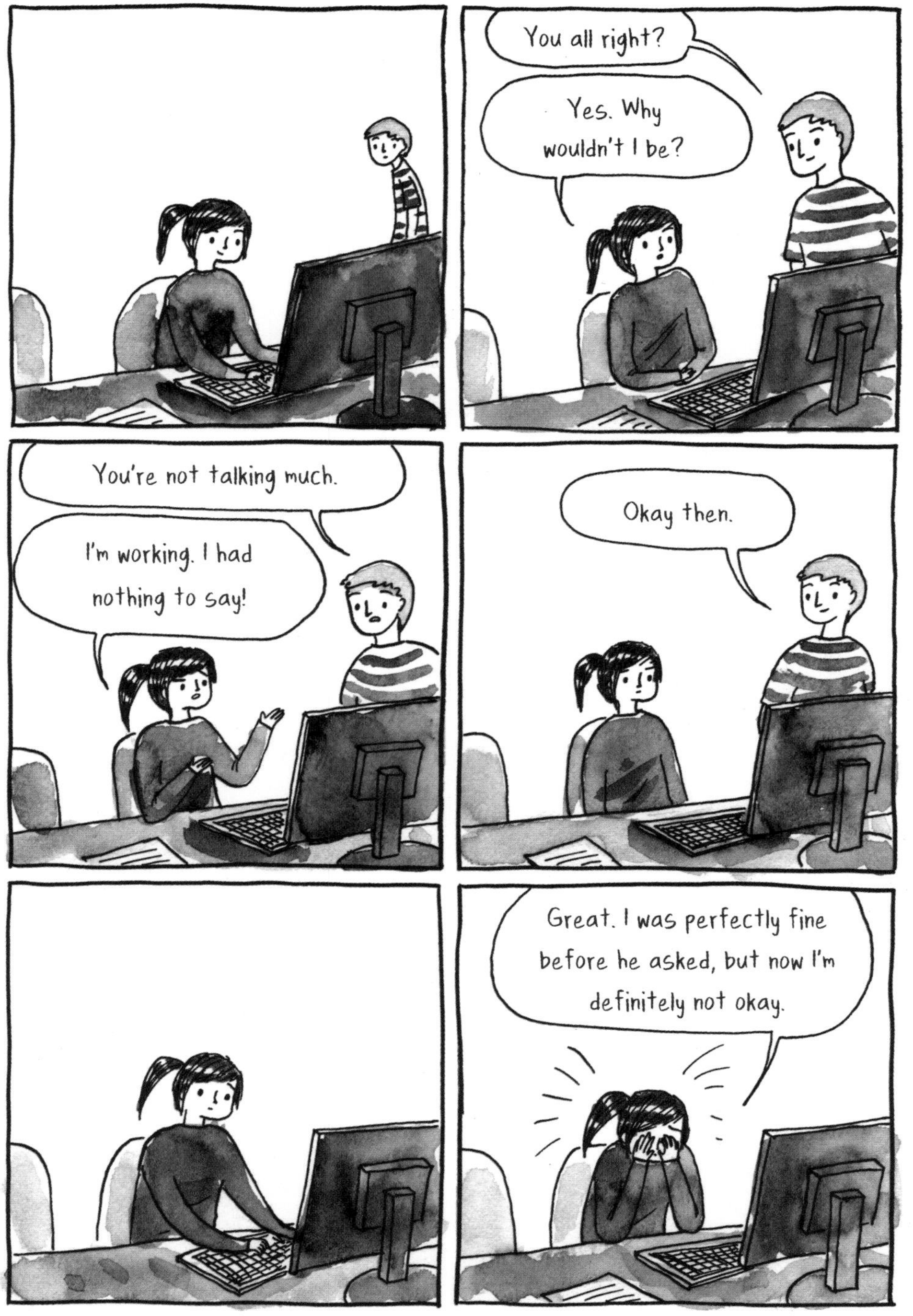
You all right?
Yes. Why wouldn't I be?
You're not talking much.
I'm working. I had nothing to say!
Okay then.
Great. I was perfectly fine before he asked, but now I'm definitely not okay.

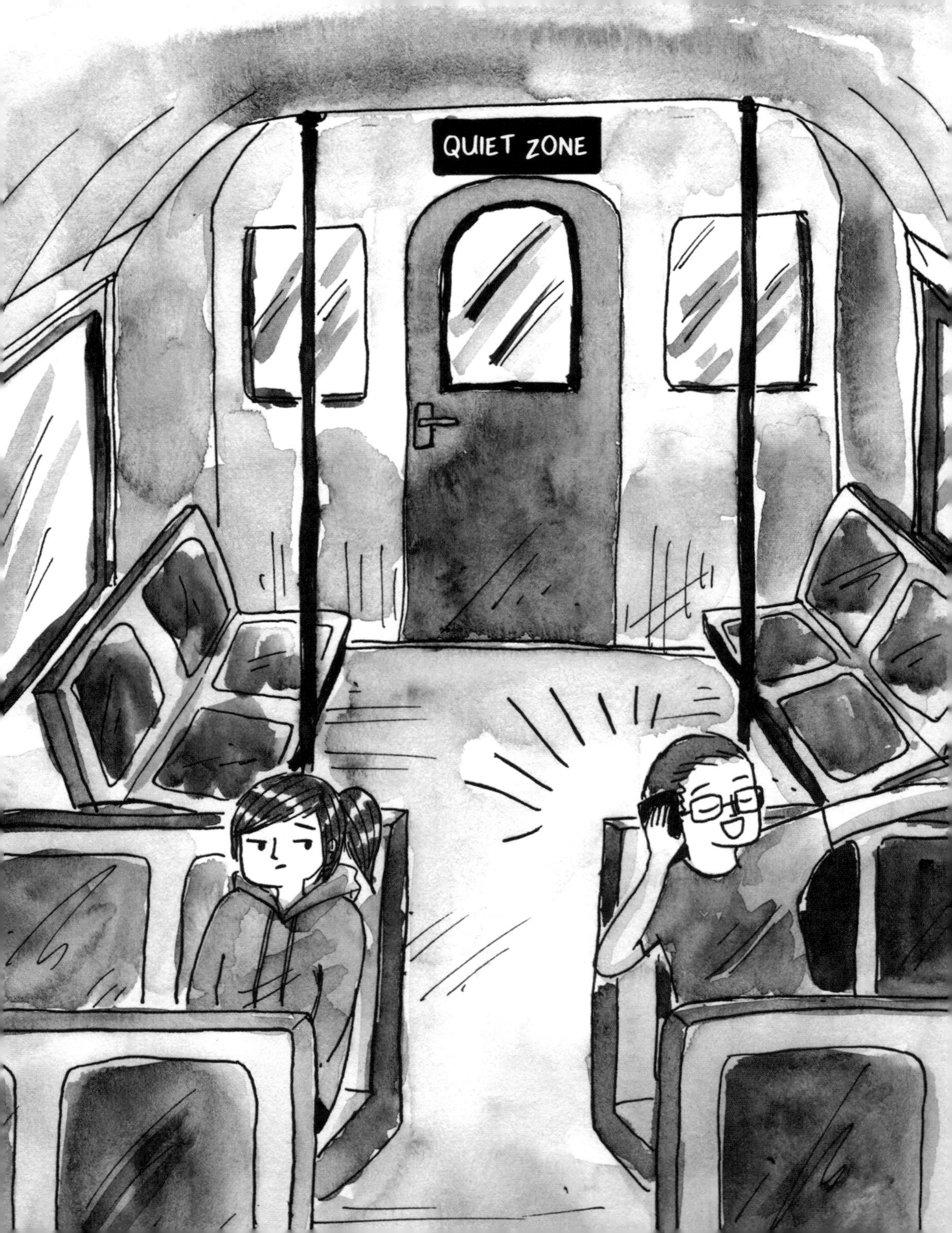
QUIET ZONE

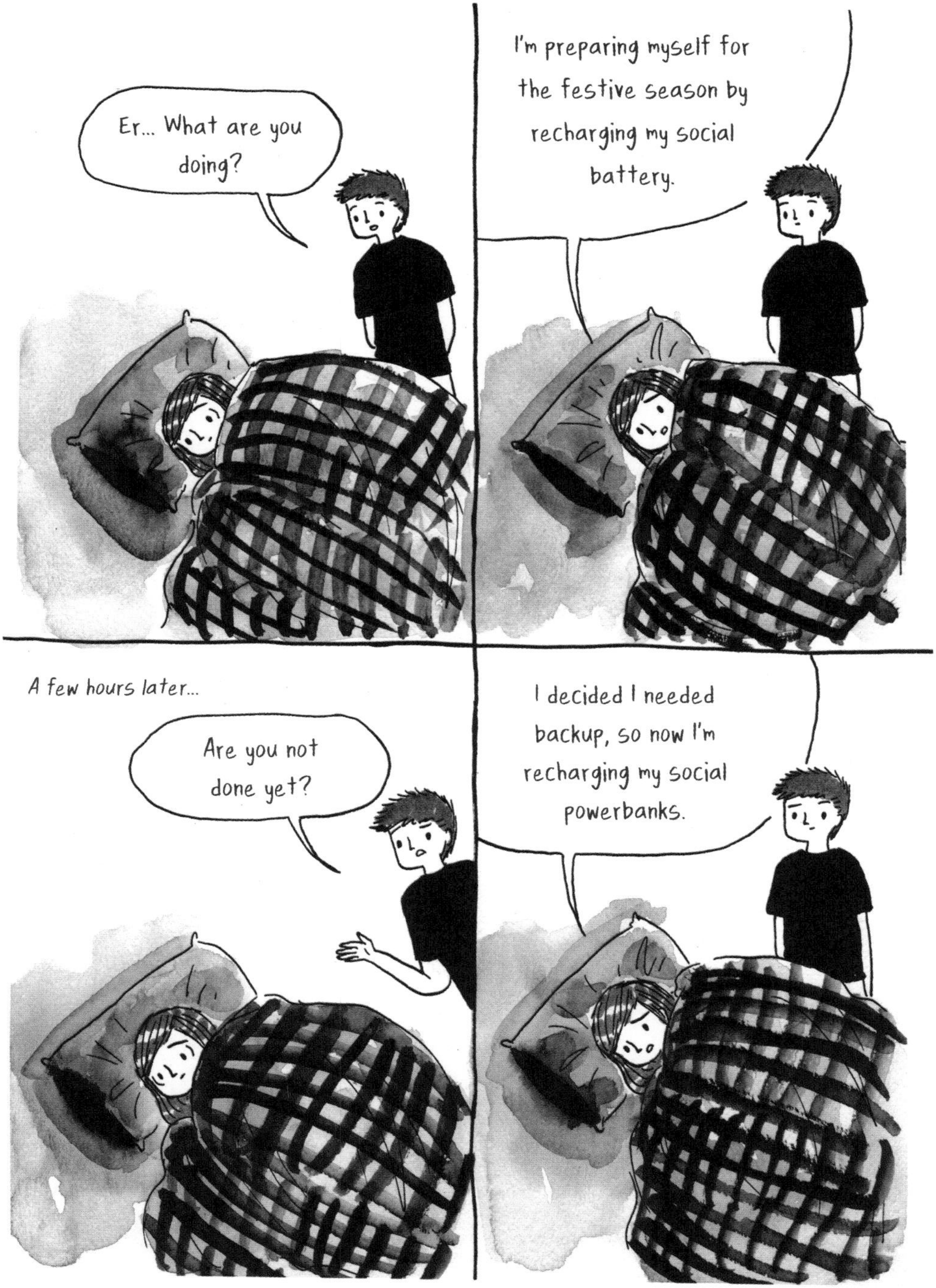
Er... What are you doing?
I'm preparing myself for the festive season by recharging my social battery.
A few hours later...
Are you not done yet?
I decided I needed backup, so now I'm recharging my social powerbanks.

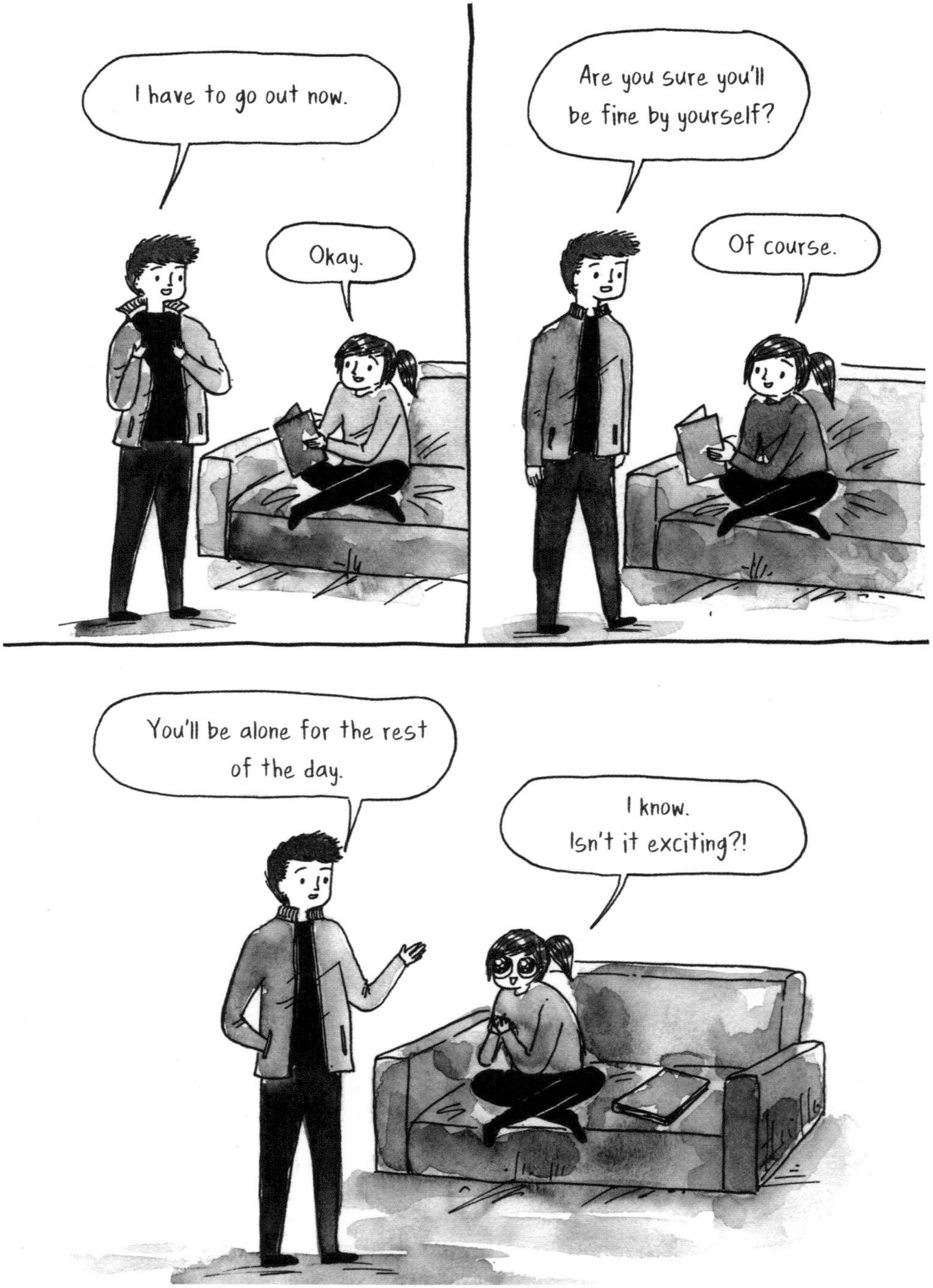
I have to go out now.
Okay.
Are you sure you'll be fine by yourself?
Of course.
You'll be alone for the rest of the day.
I know.
Isn't it exciting?!

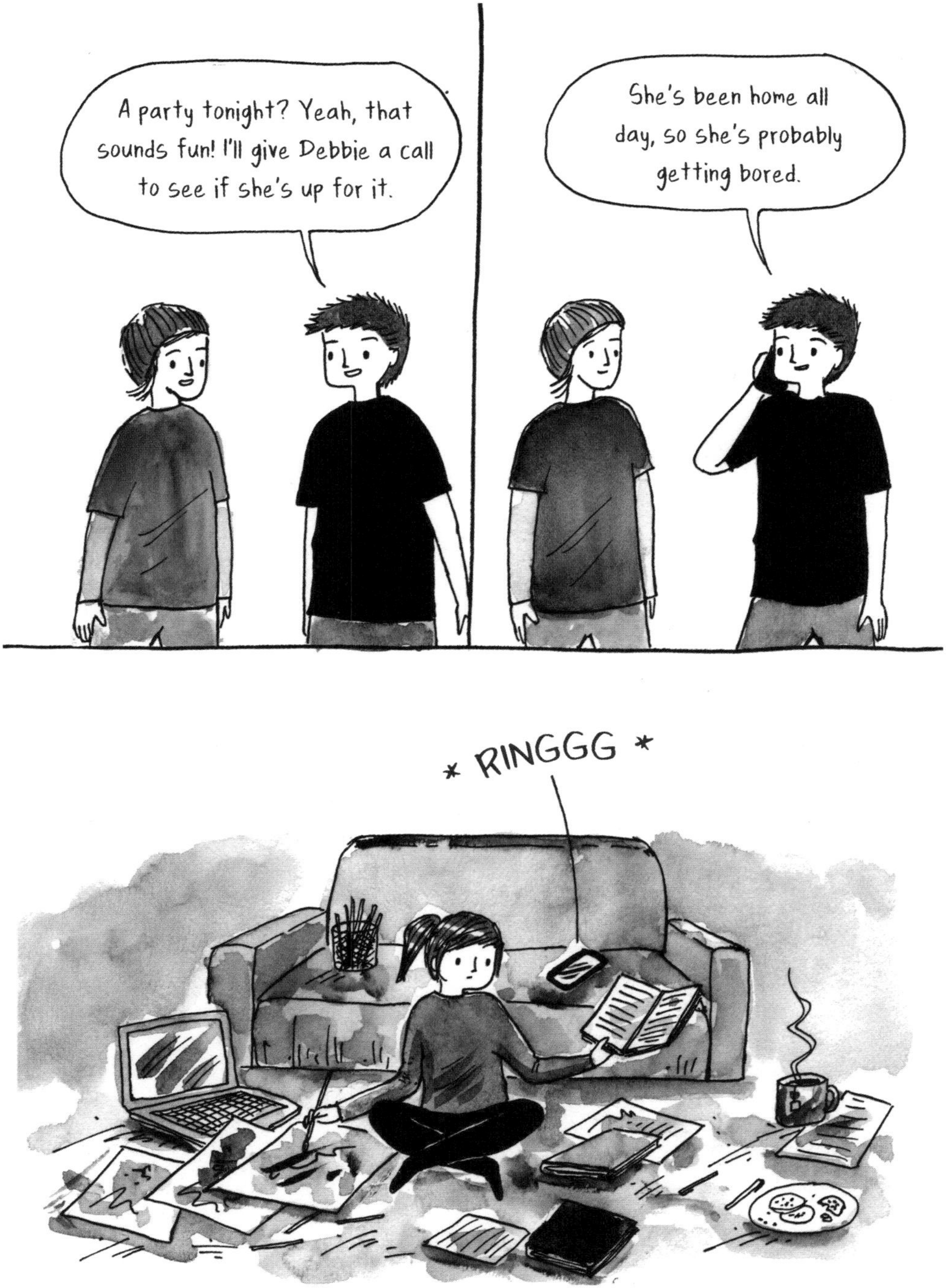
A party tonight? Yeah, that sounds fun! I'll give Debbie a call to see if she's up for it.
She's been home all day, so she's probably getting bored.
* RINGGG *

# My social battery at parties

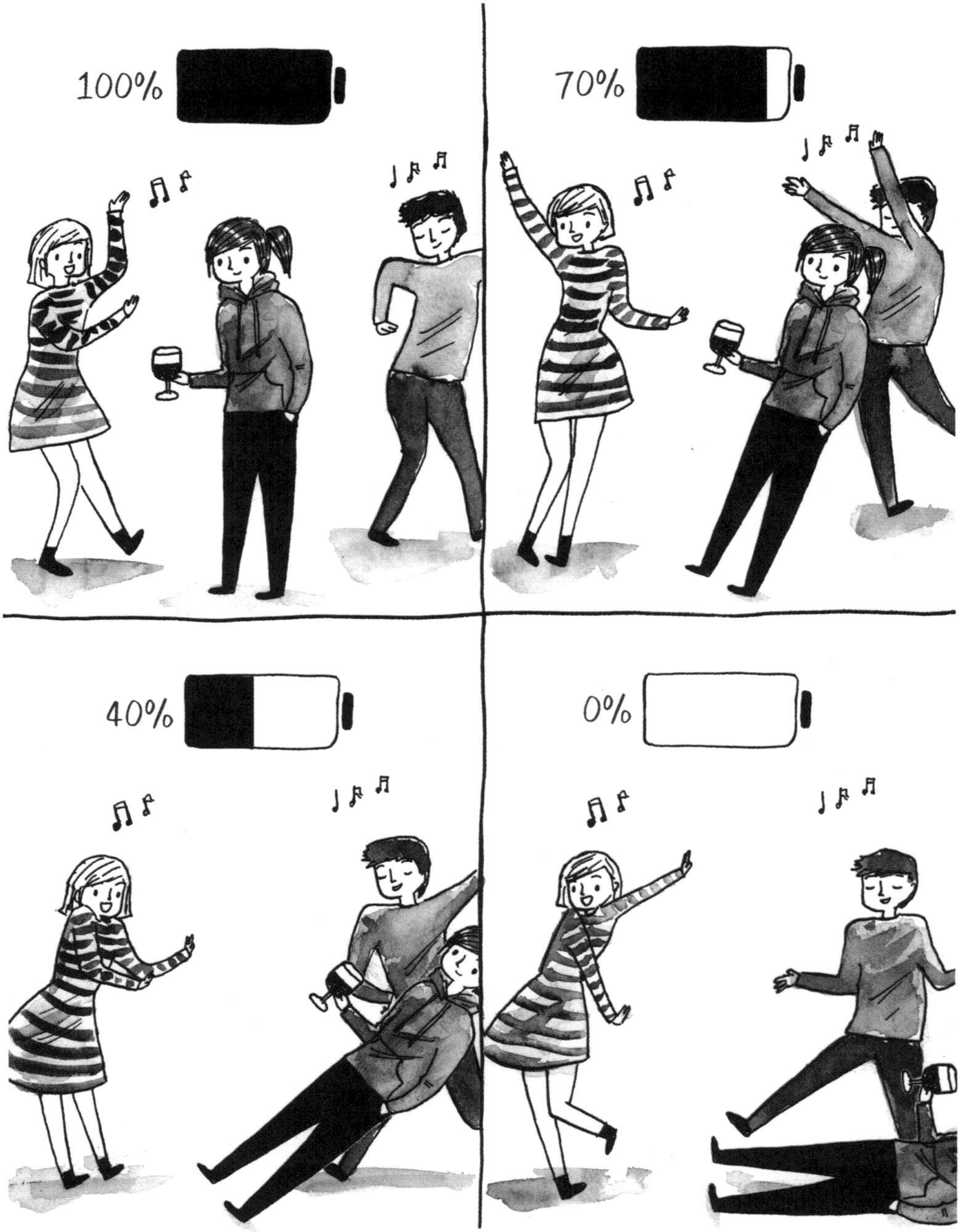
100%
70%
40%
0%

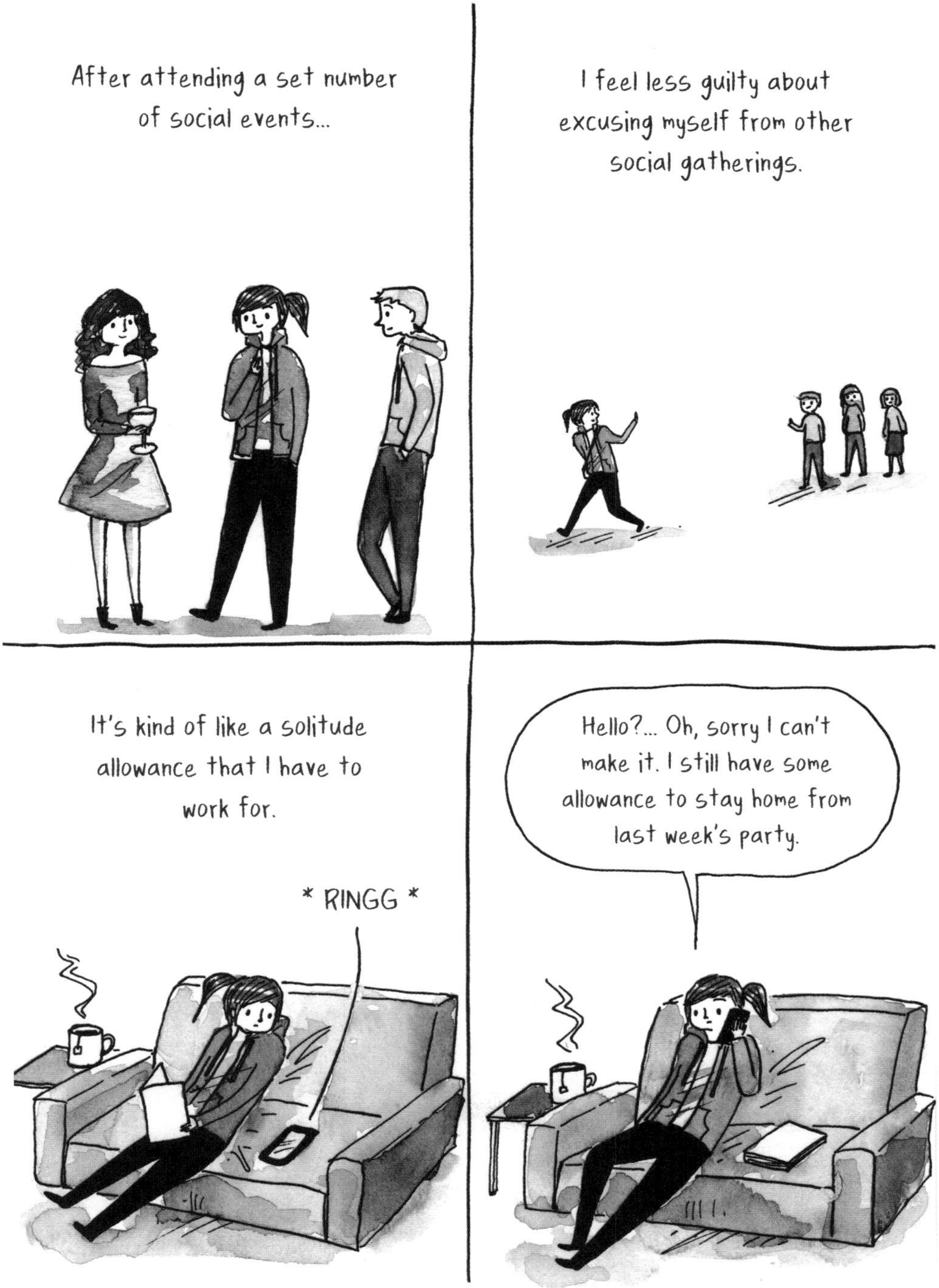
After attending a set number of social events...
I feel less guilty about excusing myself from other social gatherings.
It's kind of like a solitude allowance that I have to work for.
* RINGG *
Hello?... Oh, sorry I can't make it. I still have some allowance to stay home from last week's party.

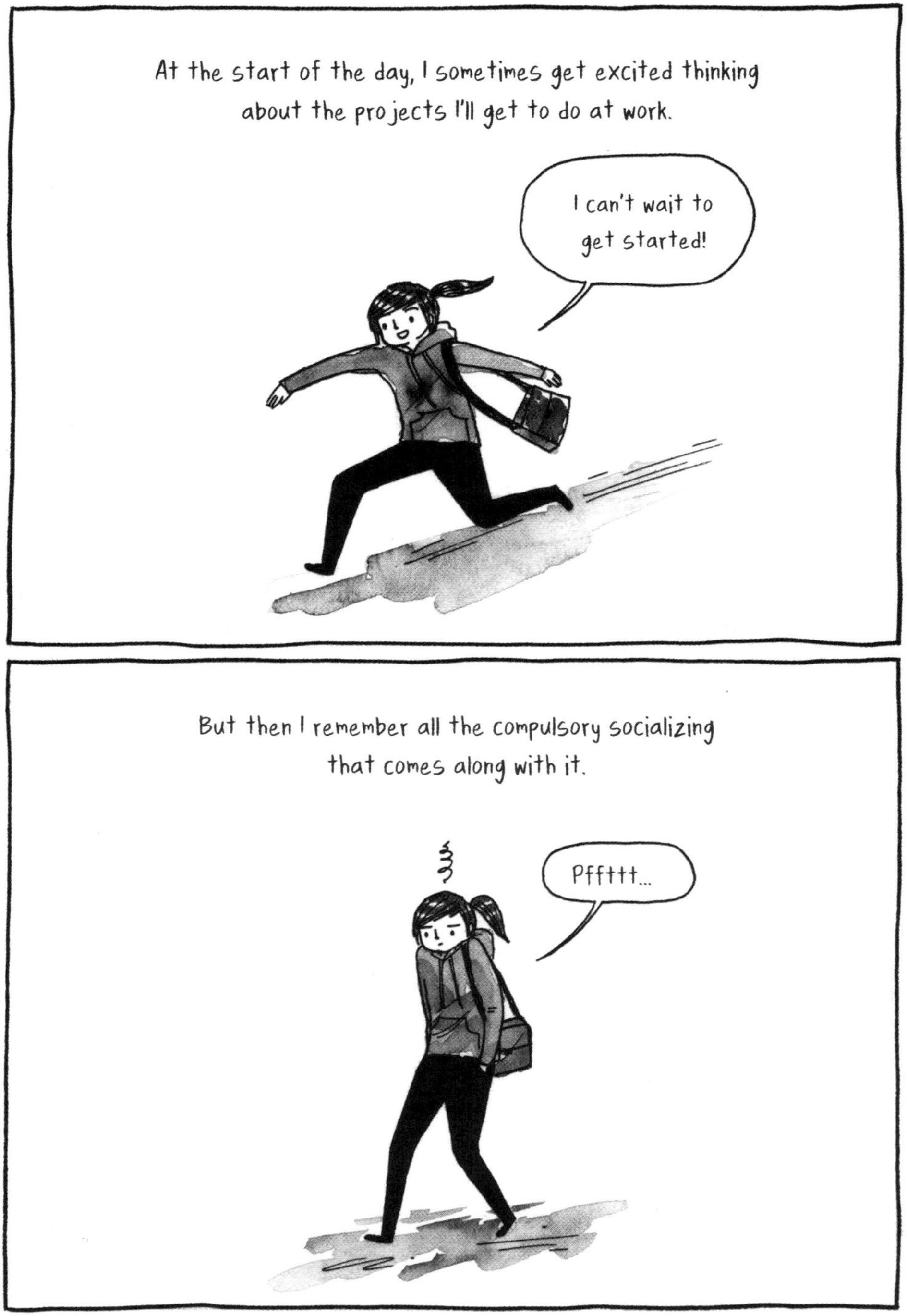
At the start of the day, I sometimes get excited thinking about the projects I'll get to do at work.
I can't wait to get started!
But then I remember all the compulsory socializing that comes along with it.
Pffttt...

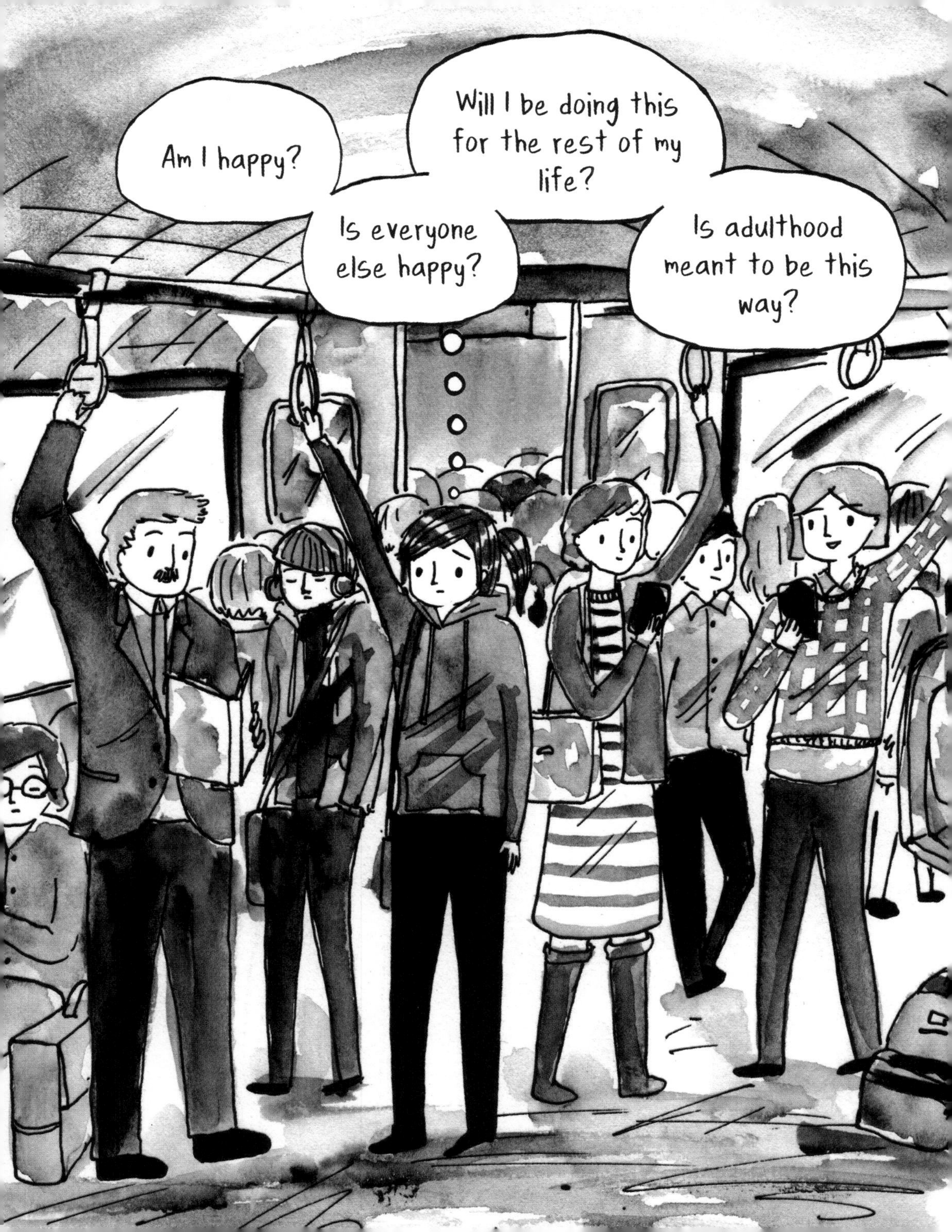
Am I happy?
Will I be doing this for the rest of my life?
Is everyone else happy?
Is adulthood meant to be this way?

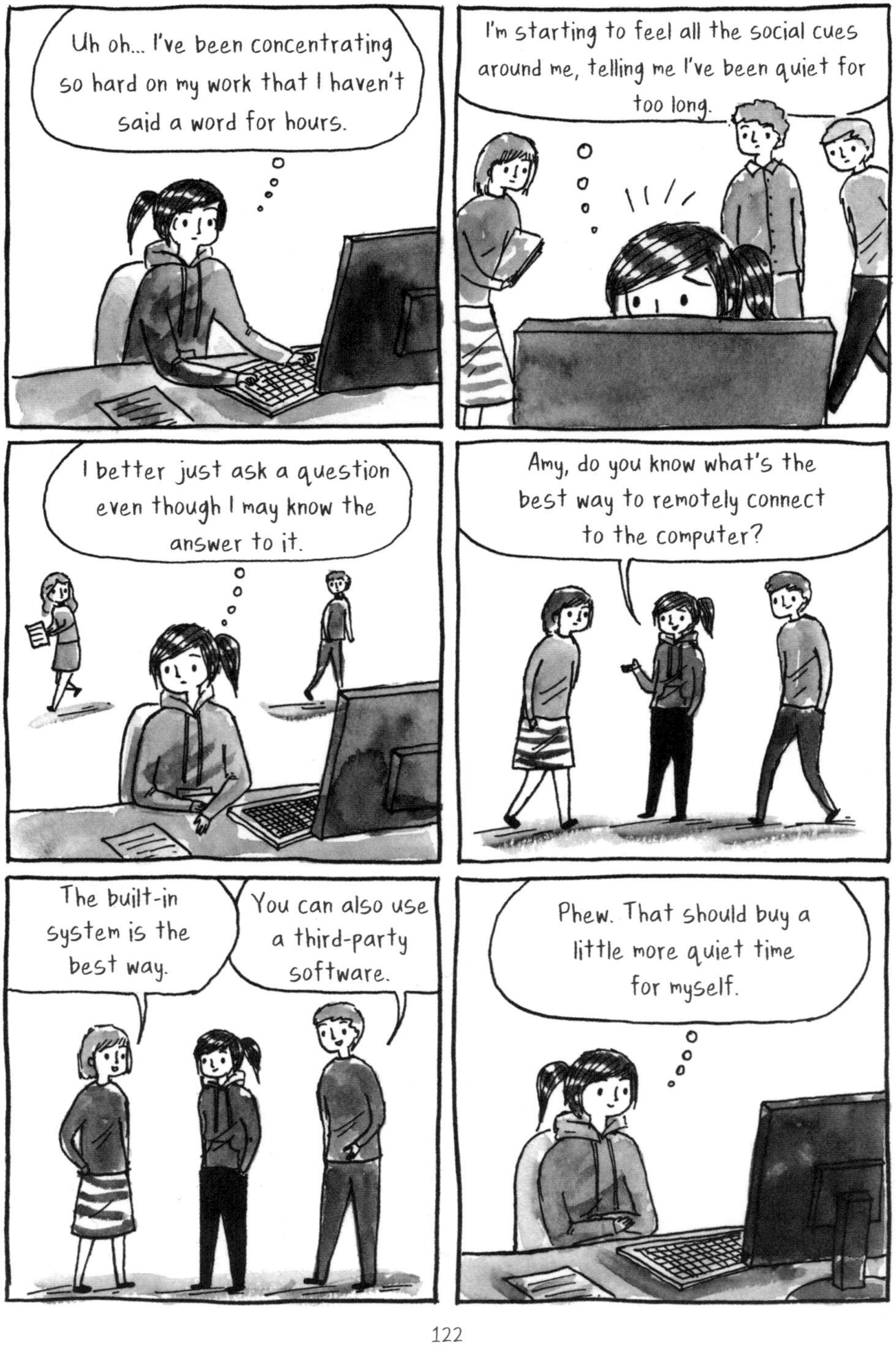
Uh oh... I've been concentrating so hard on my work that I haven't said a word for hours.
I'm starting to feel all the social cues around me, telling me I've been quiet for too long.
I better just ask a question even though I may know the answer to it.
Amy, do you know what's the best way to remotely connect to the computer?
The built-in system is the best way.
You can also use a third-party software.
Phew. That should buy a little more quiet time for myself.

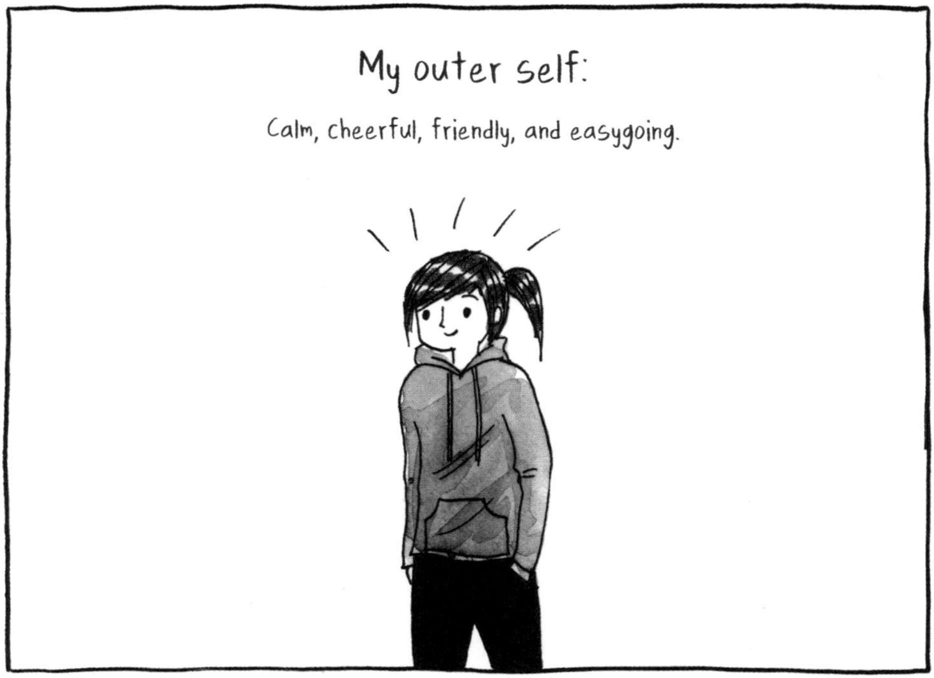
My outer self:
Calm, cheerful, friendly, and easygoing.

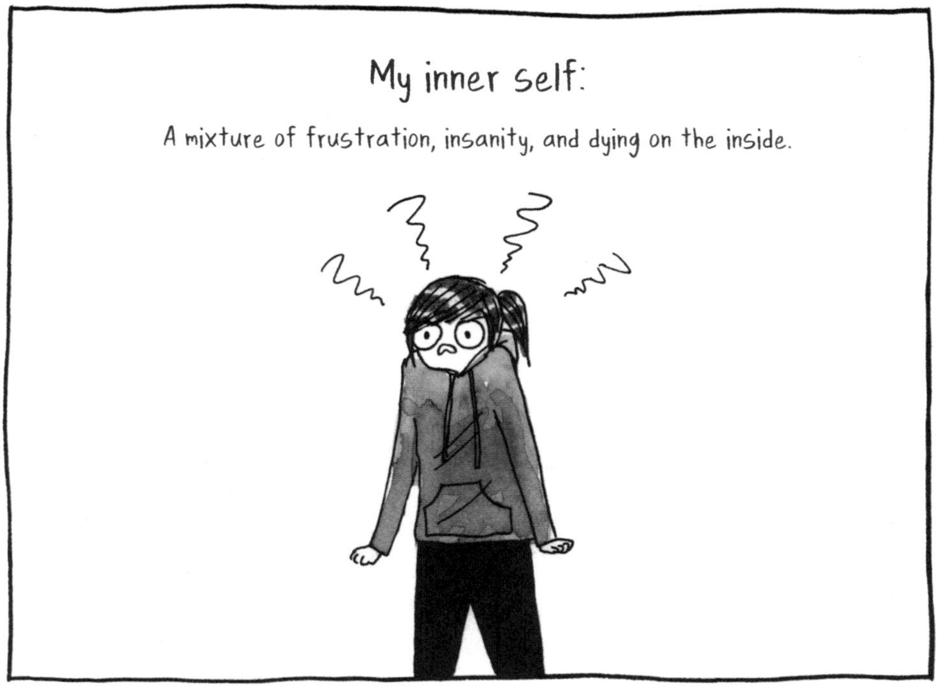
My inner self:
A mixture of frustration, insanity, and dying on the inside.

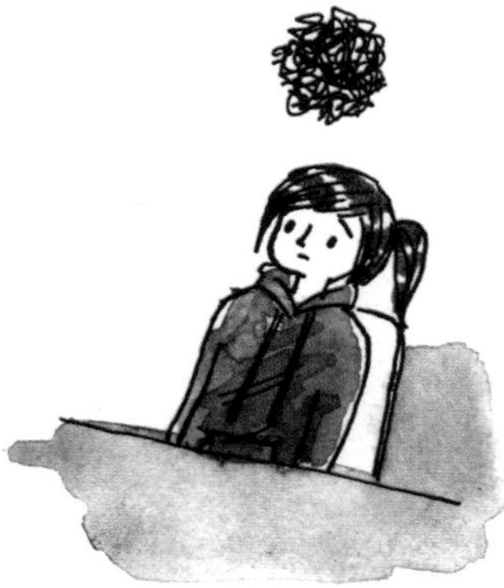

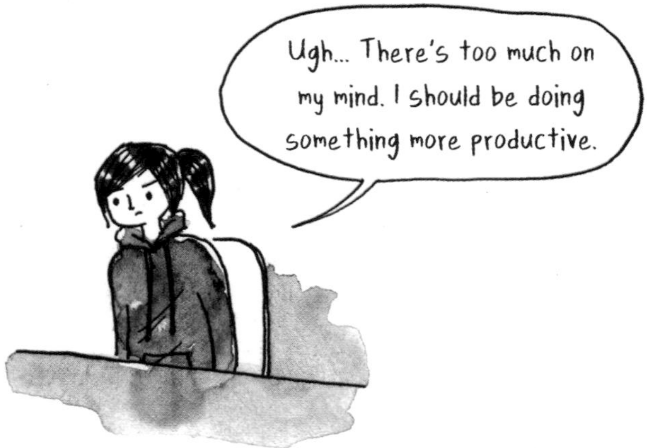

Ugh... There's too much on my mind. I should be doing something more productive.


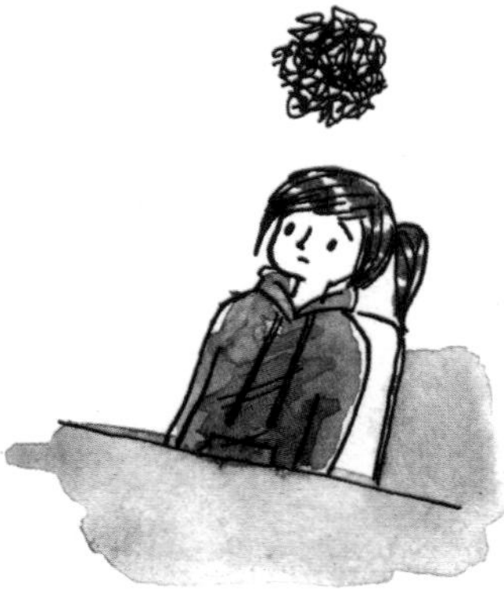

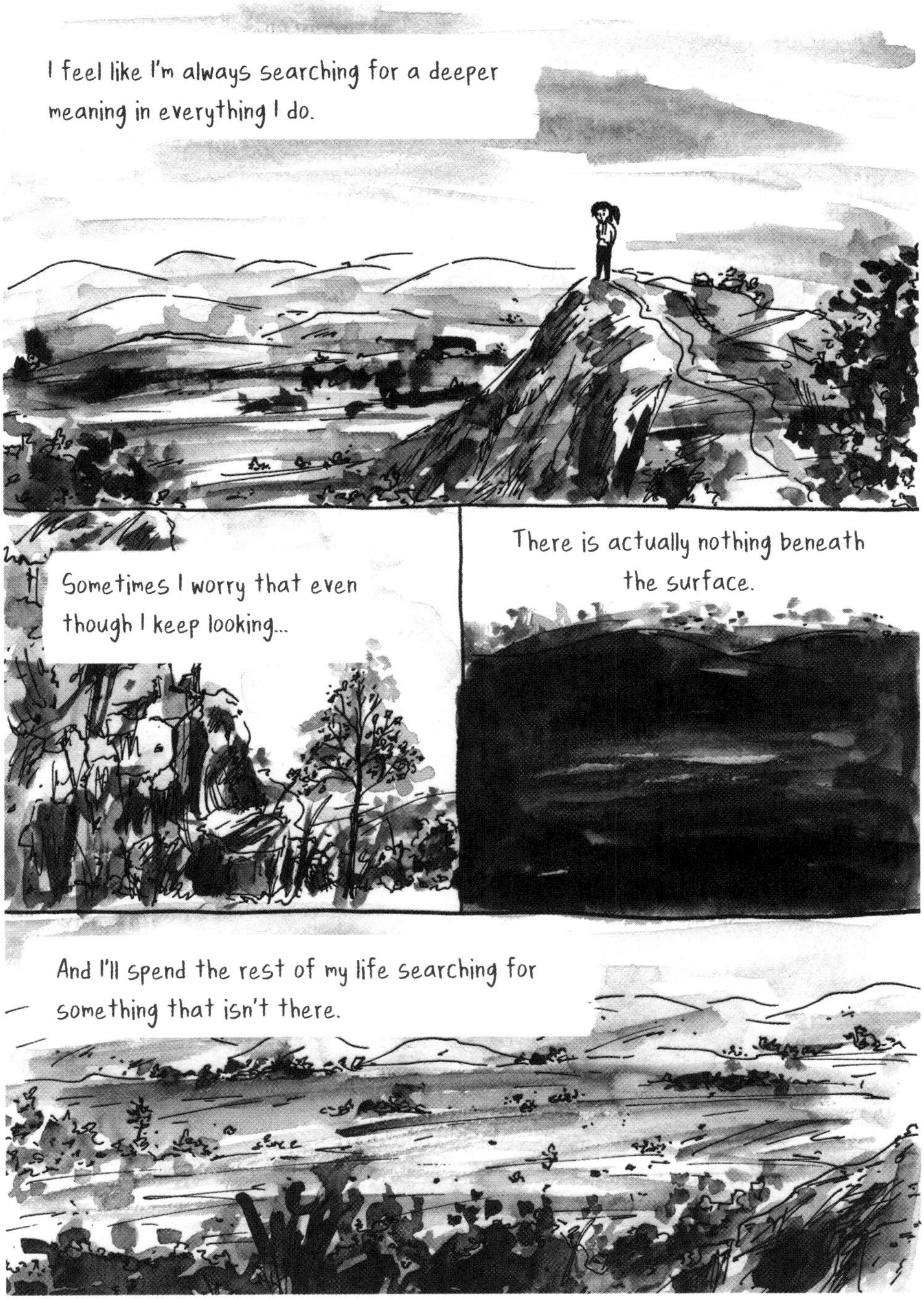
I feel like I'm always searching for a deeper meaning in everything I do.
Sometimes I worry that even though I keep looking...
There is actually nothing beneath the surface.
And I'll spend the rest of my life searching for something that isn't there.

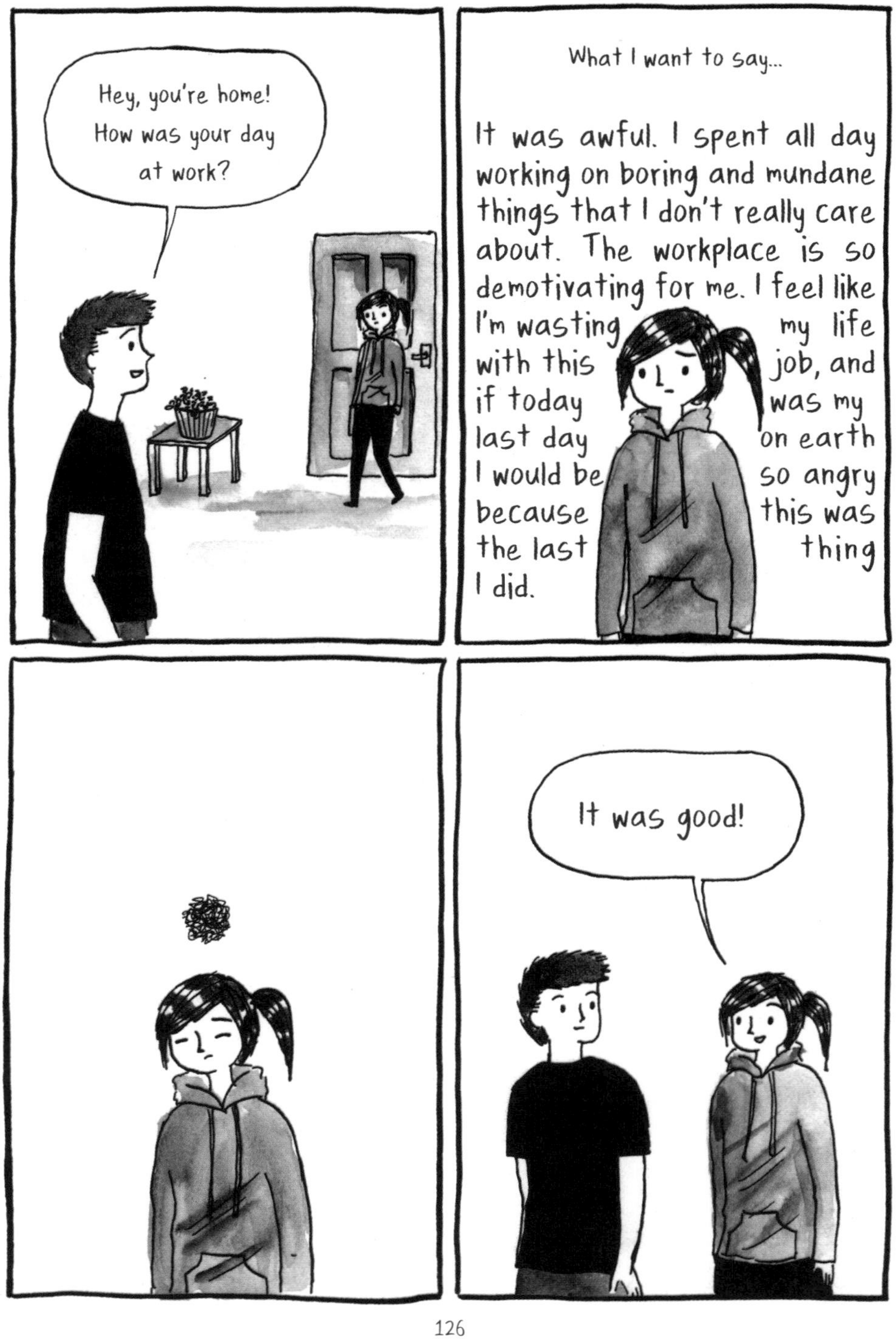
Hey, you're home! How was your day at work?
What I want to say...
It was awful. I spent all day working on boring and mundane things that I don't really care about. The workplace is so demotivating for me. I feel like I'm wasting my life with this job, and if today was my last day on earth I would be so angry because this was the last thing I did.
It was good!

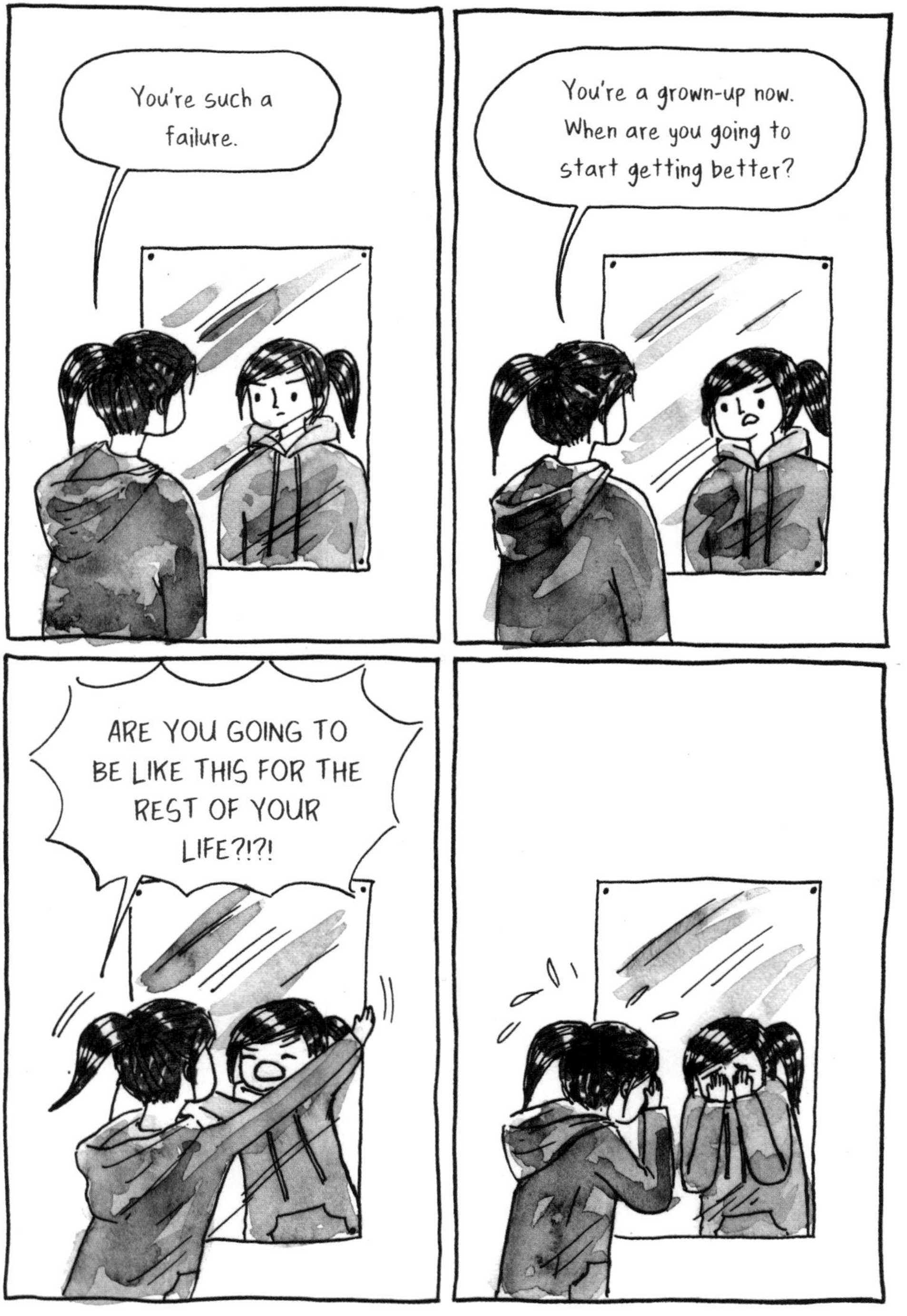
You're such a failure.
You're a grown-up now. When are you going to start getting better?
ARE YOU GOING TO BE LIKE THIS FOR THE REST OF YOUR LIFE?!?!

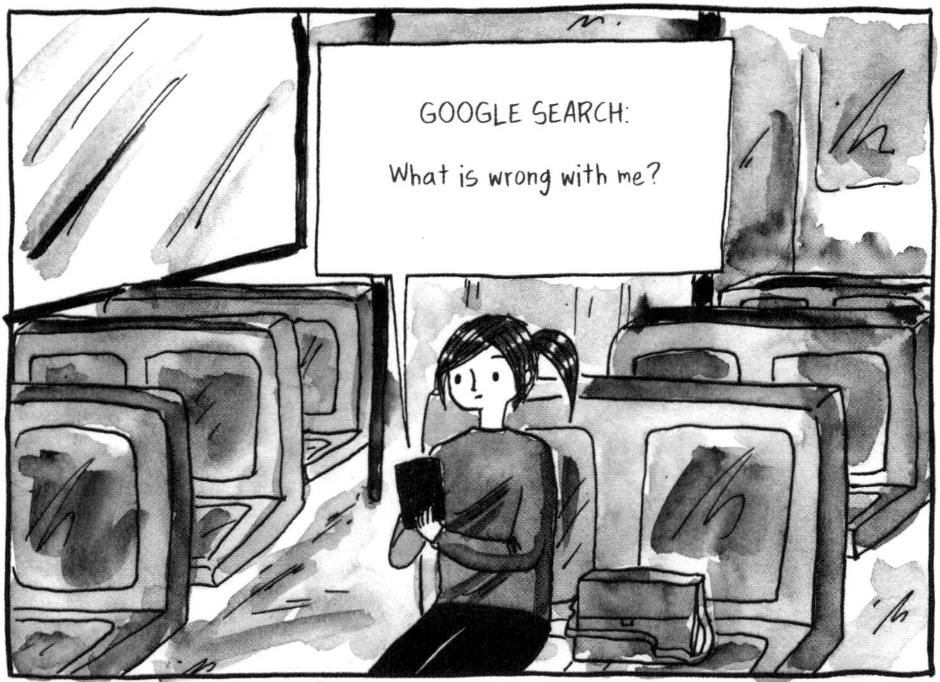
GOOGLE SEARCH:
What is wrong with me?

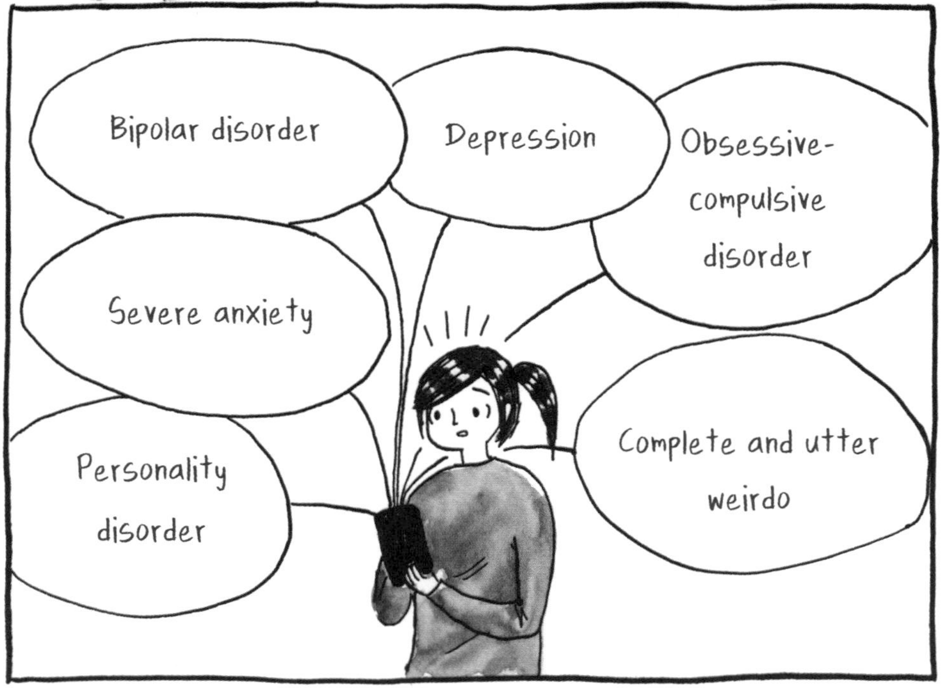
Bipolar disorder
Depression
Obsessive-compulsive disorder
Severe anxiety
Personality disorder
Complete and utter weirdo

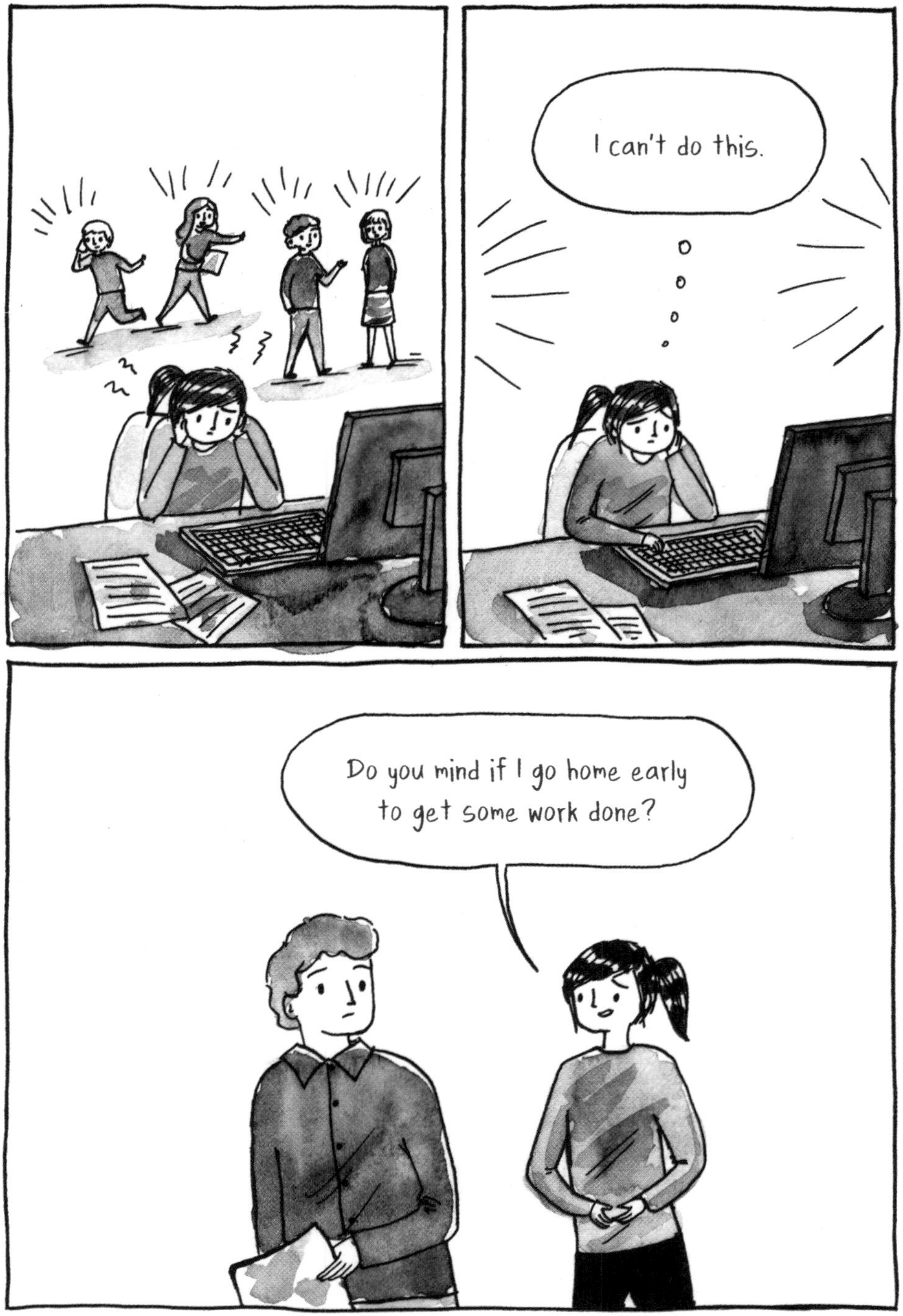
I can't do this.
Do you mind if I go home early to get some work done?

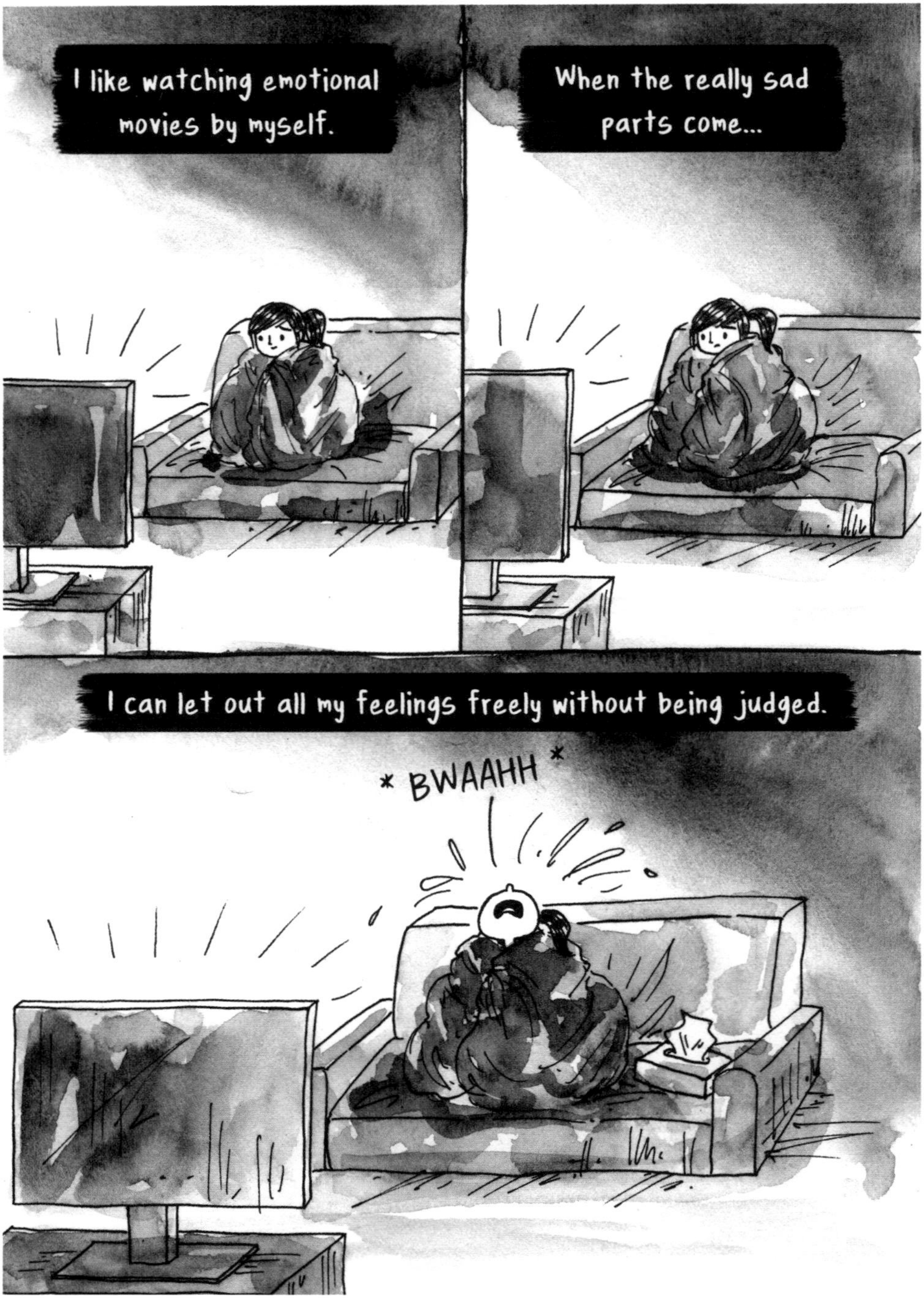
I like watching emotional movies by myself.
When the really sad parts come...
I can let out all my feelings freely without being judged.
* BWAAHH *

# Talking about my feelings

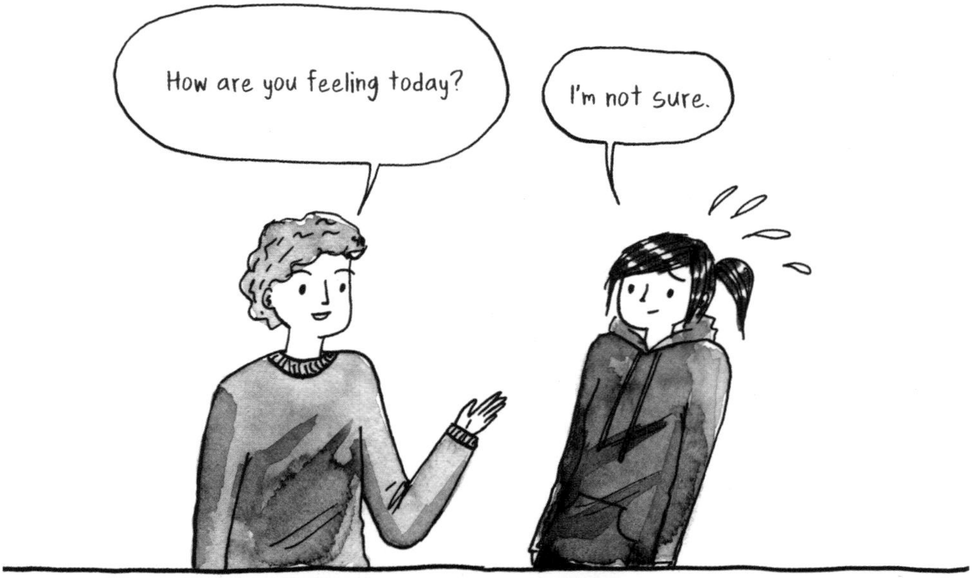
How are you feeling today?
I'm not sure.

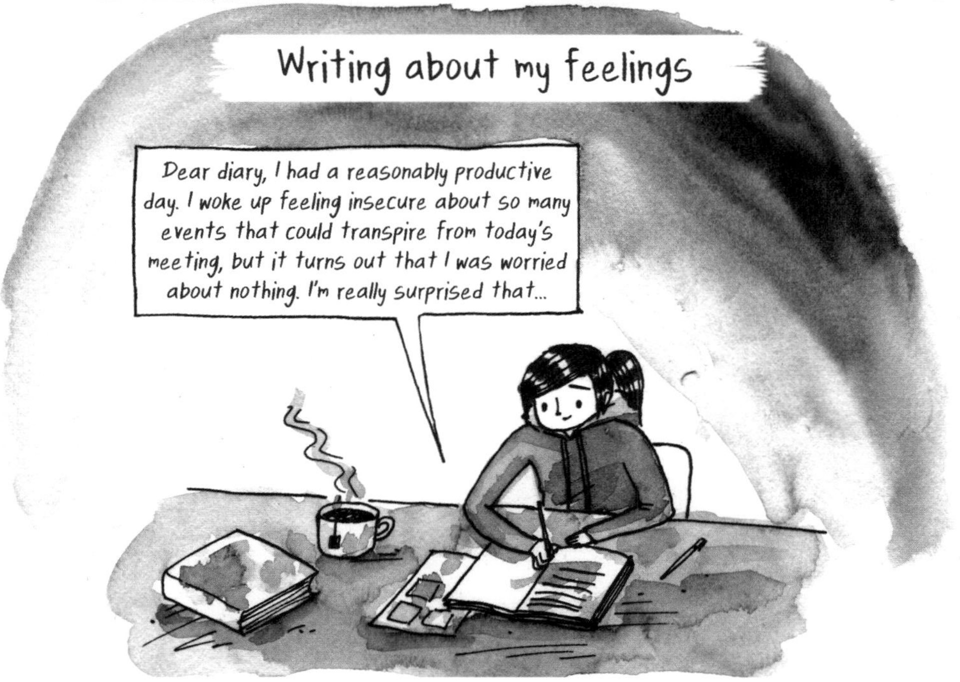
Writing about my feelings
Dear diary, I had a reasonably productive day. I woke up feeling insecure about so many events that could transpire from today's meeting, but it turns out that I was worried about nothing. I'm really surprised that...

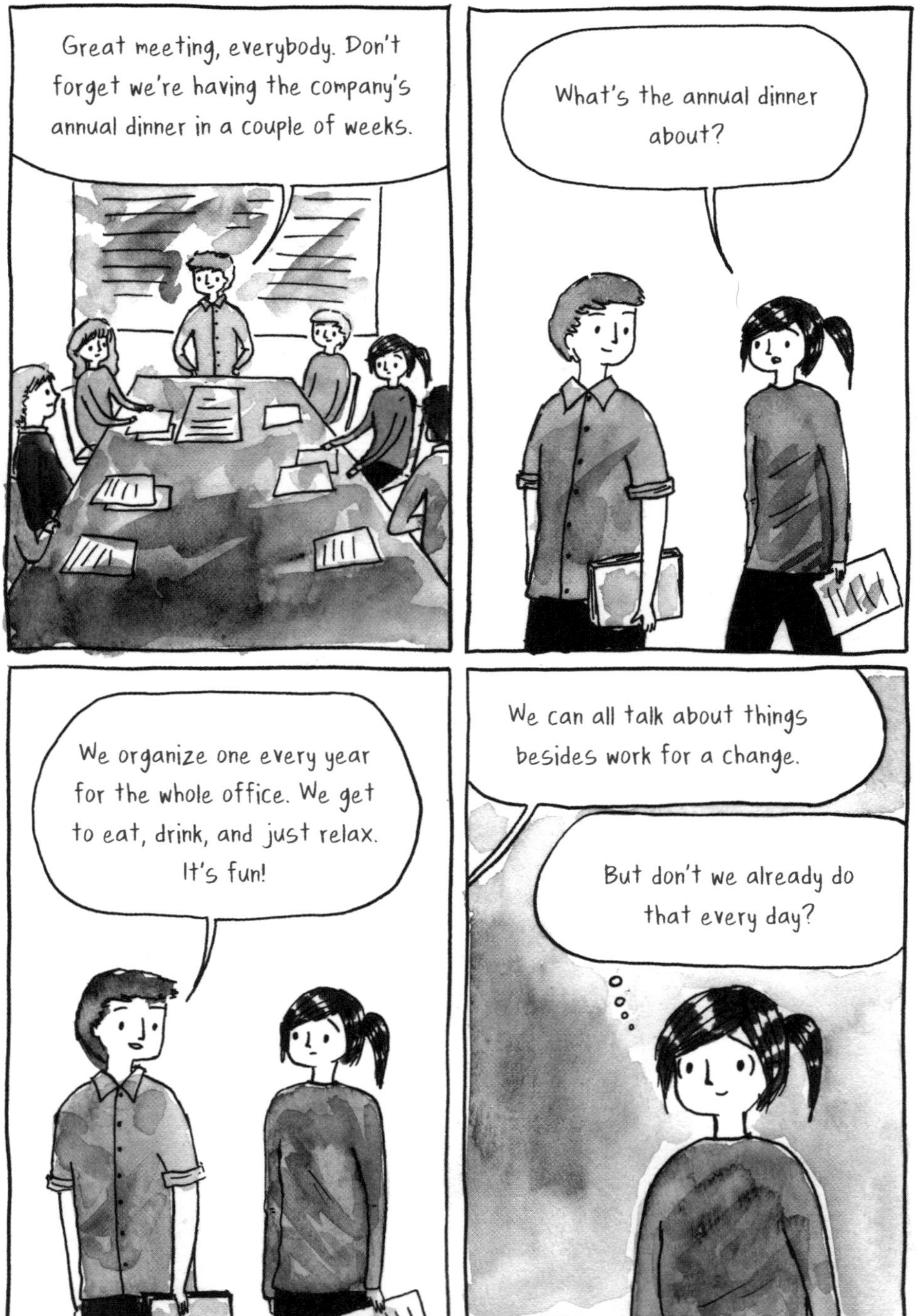

Great meeting, everybody. Don't forget we're having the company's annual dinner in a couple of weeks.
What's the annual dinner about?
We organize one every year for the whole office. We get to eat, drink, and just relax. It's fun!
We can all talk about things besides work for a change.
But don't we already do that every day?

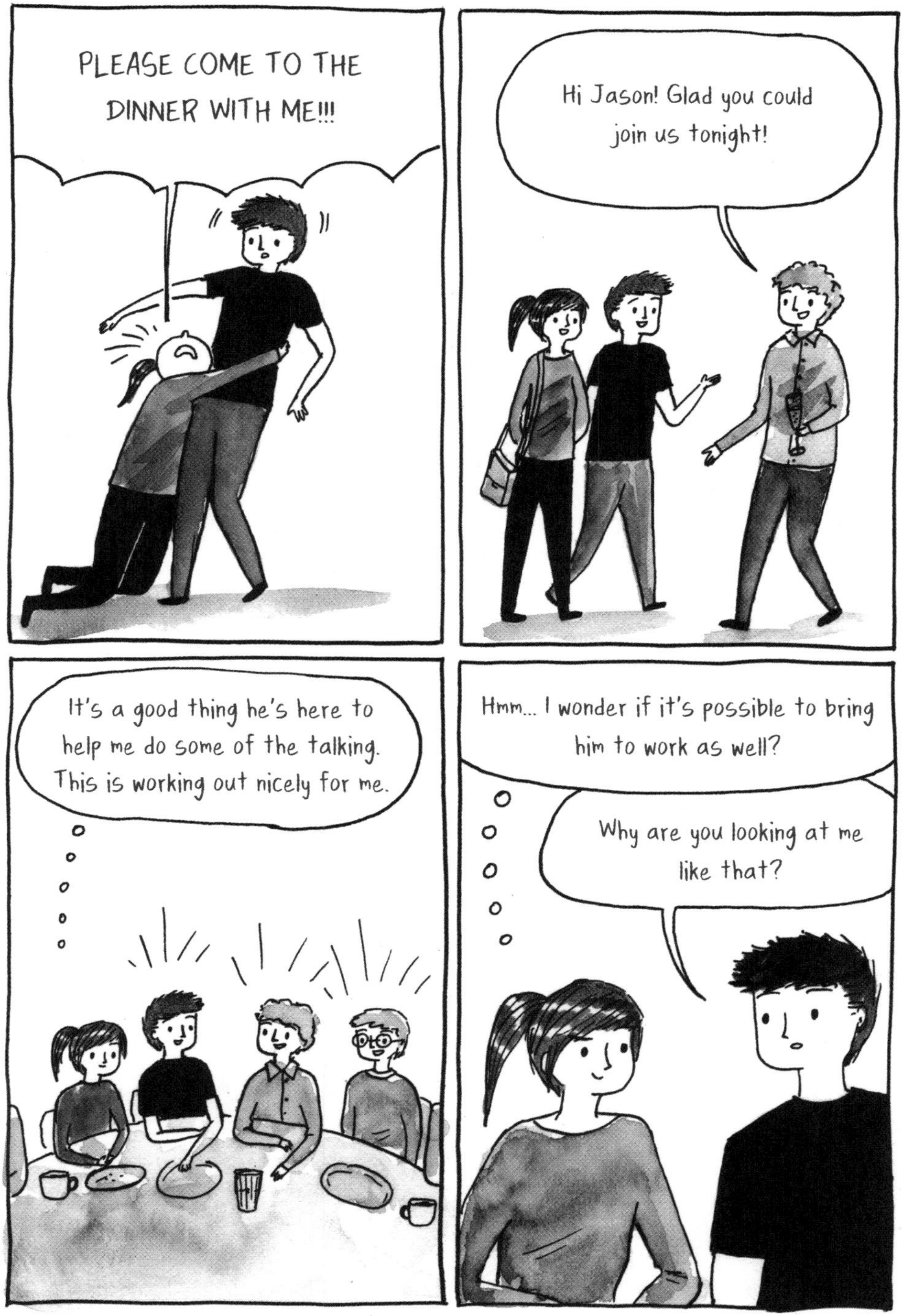
PLEASE COME TO THE DINNER WITH ME!!!
Hi Jason! Glad you could join us tonight!
It's a good thing he's here to help me do some of the talking. This is working out nicely for me.
Hmm... I wonder if it's possible to bring him to work as well?
Why are you looking at me like that?

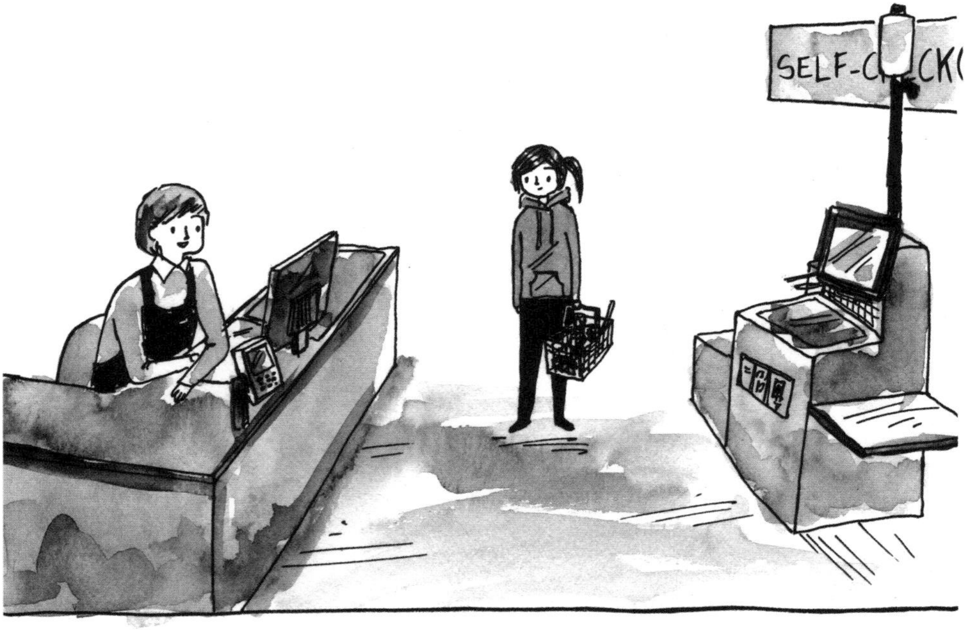

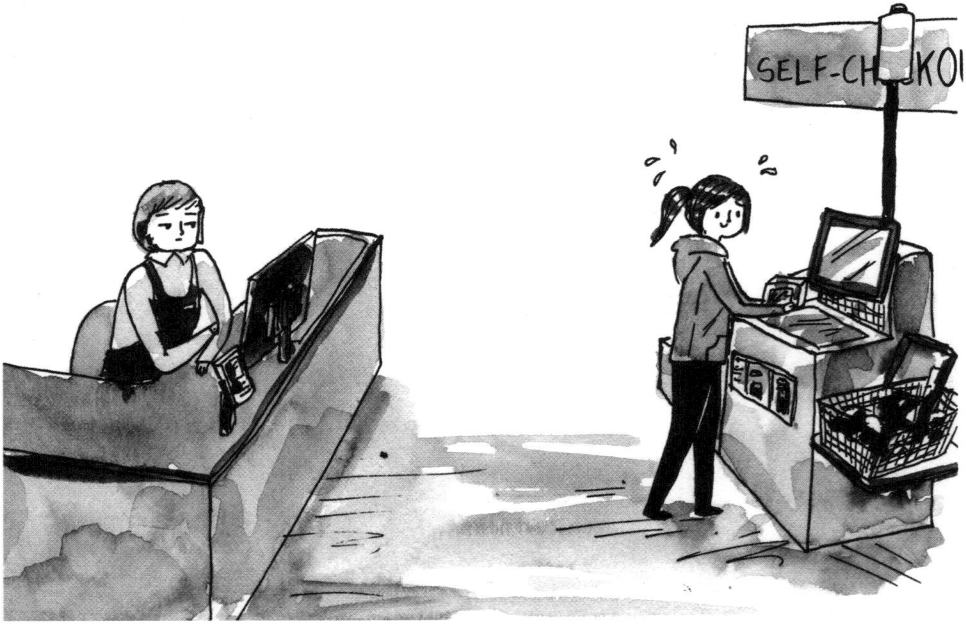

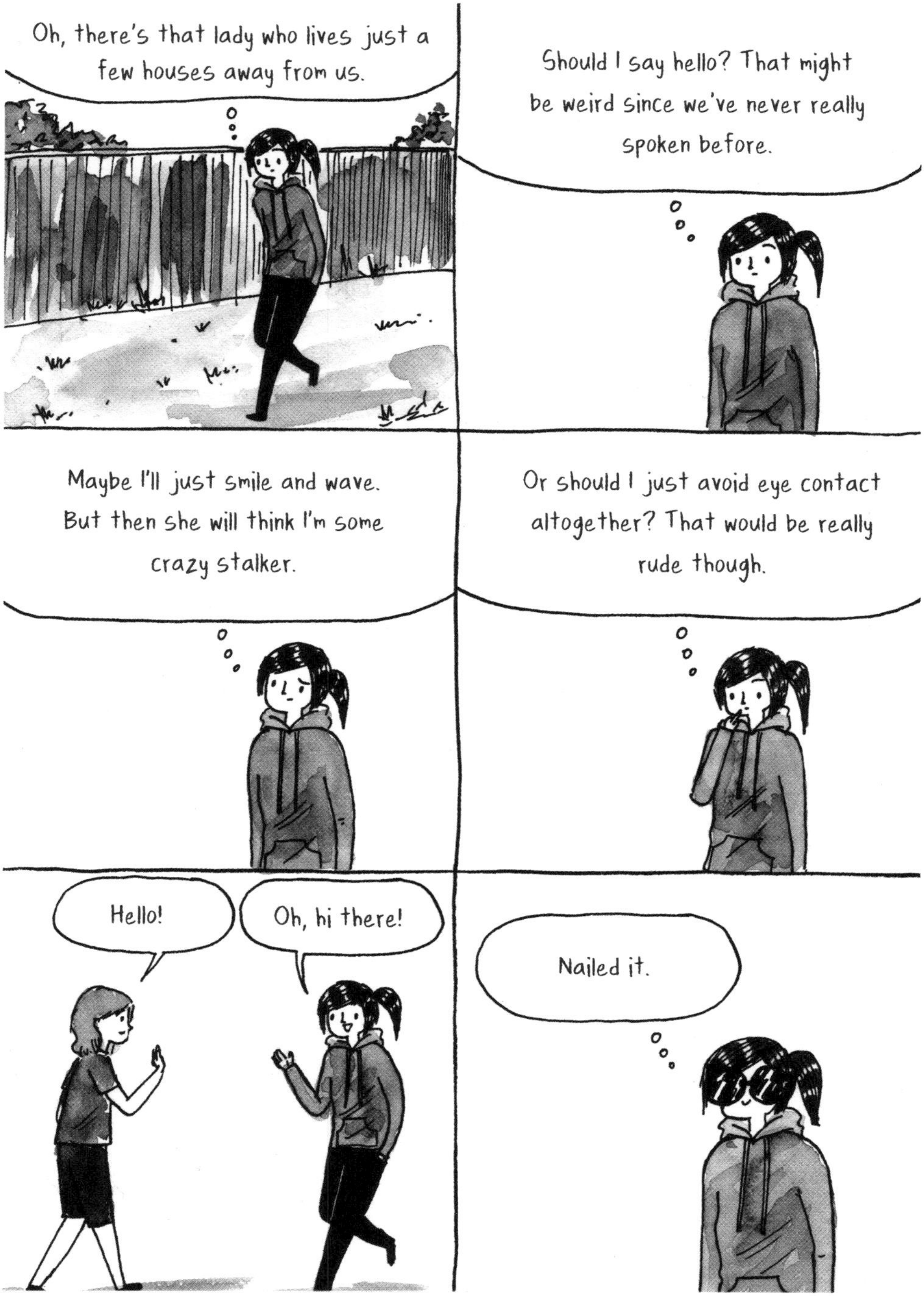
Oh, there's that lady who lives just a few houses away from us.
Should I say hello? That might be weird since we've never really spoken before.
Maybe I'll just smile and wave. But then she will think I'm some crazy stalker.
Or should I just avoid eye contact altogether? That would be really rude though.
Hello!
Oh, hi there!
Nailed it.

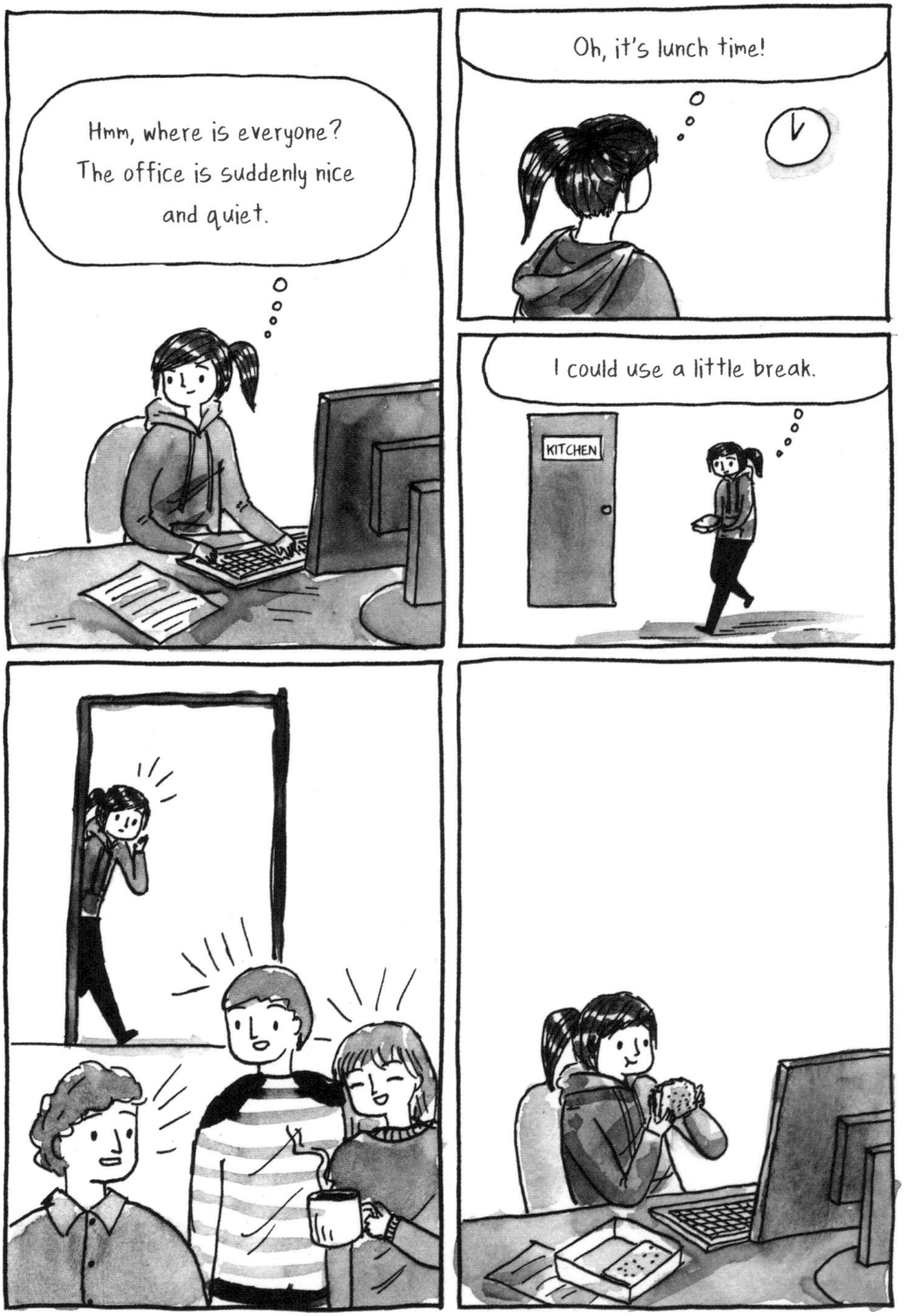
Hmm, where is everyone? The office is suddenly nice and quiet.
Oh, it's lunch time!
I could use a little break.
KITCHEN

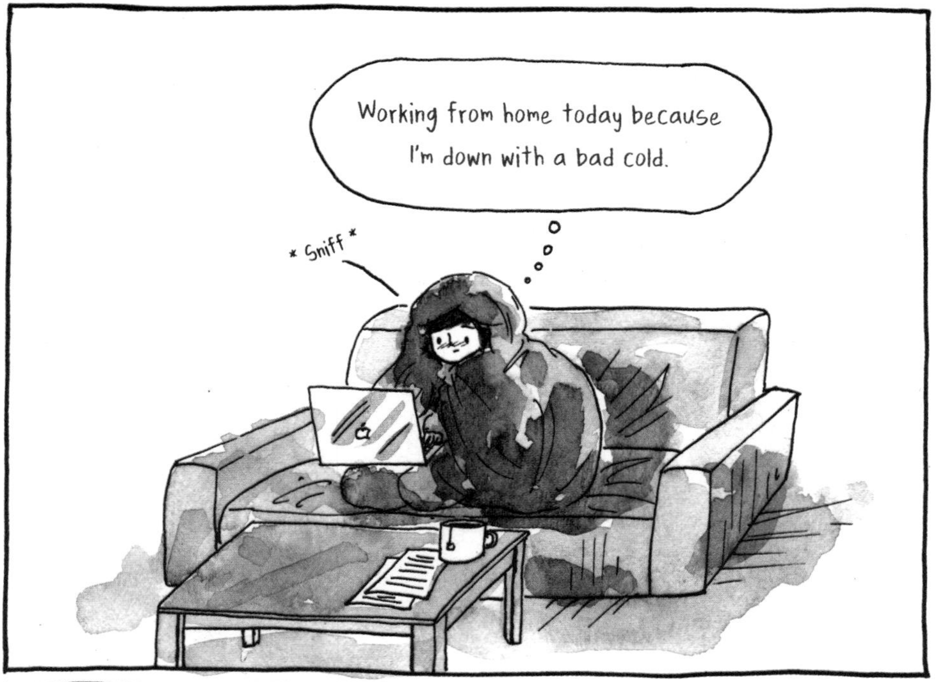
Working from home today because I'm down with a bad cold.
* Sniff *

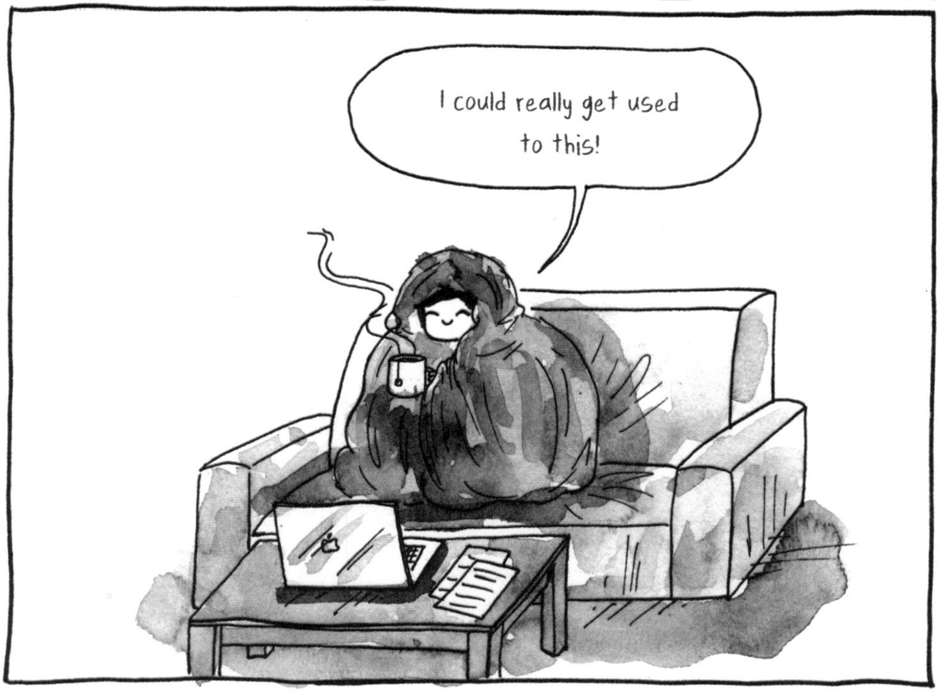
I could really get used to this!

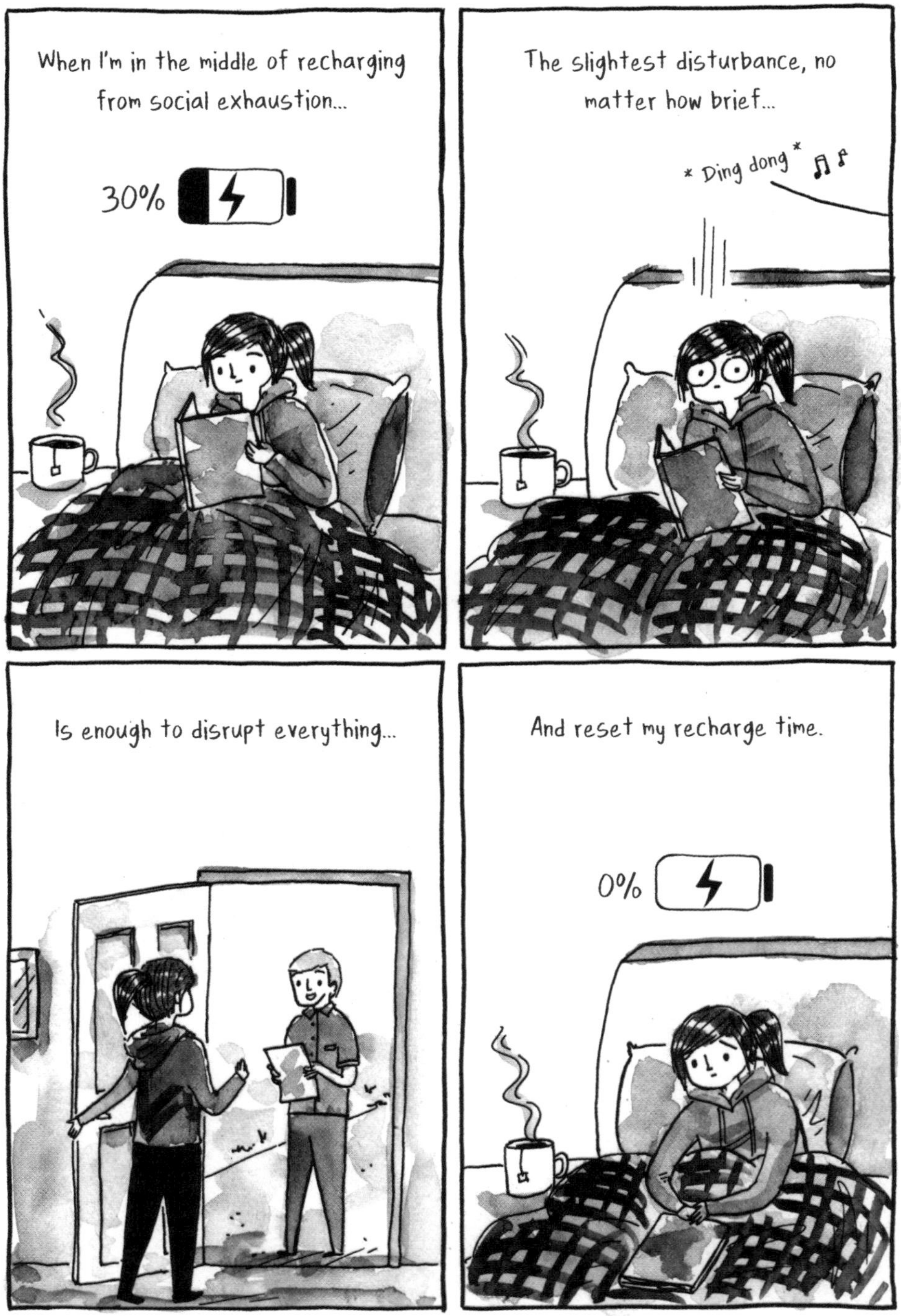
When I'm in the middle of recharging from social exhaustion...
30%
The slightest disturbance, no matter how brief...
* Ding dong *
Is enough to disrupt everything...
And reset my recharge time.
0%

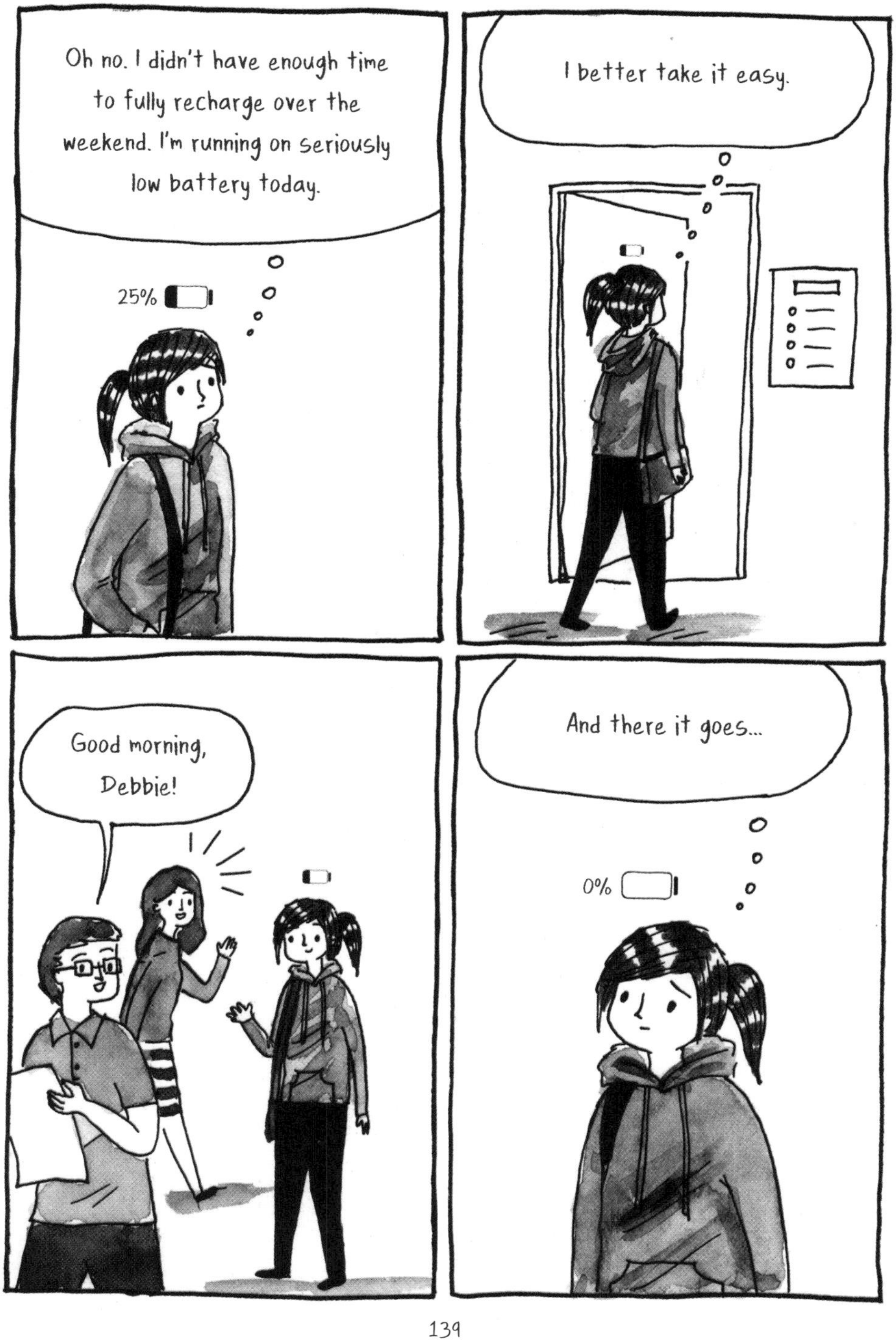
Oh no. I didn't have enough time to fully recharge over the weekend. I'm running on seriously low battery today.
25%
I better take it easy.
Good morning, Debbie!
And there it goes...
0%

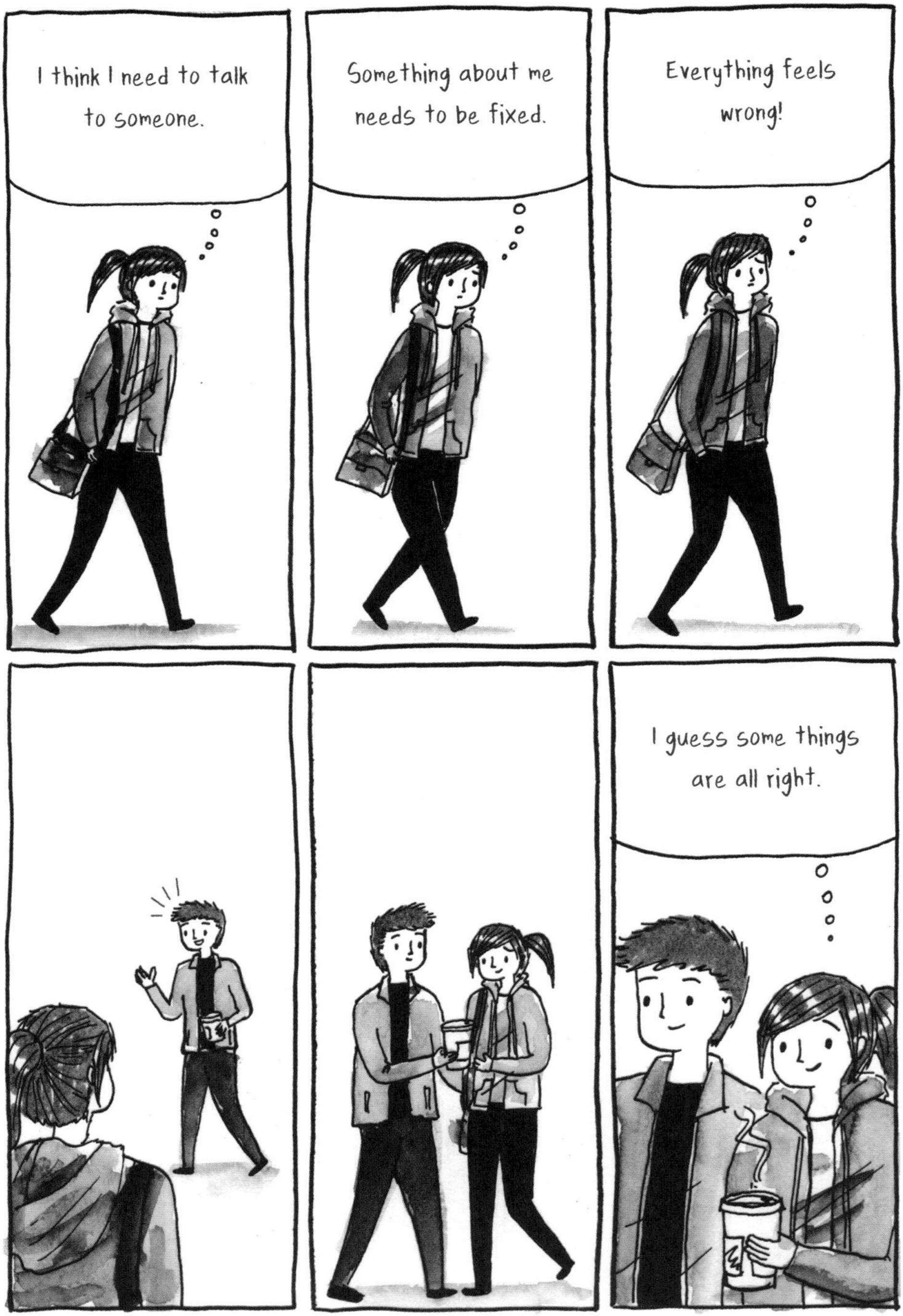
I think I need to talk to someone.
Something about me needs to be fixed.
Everything feels wrong!
I guess some things are all right.

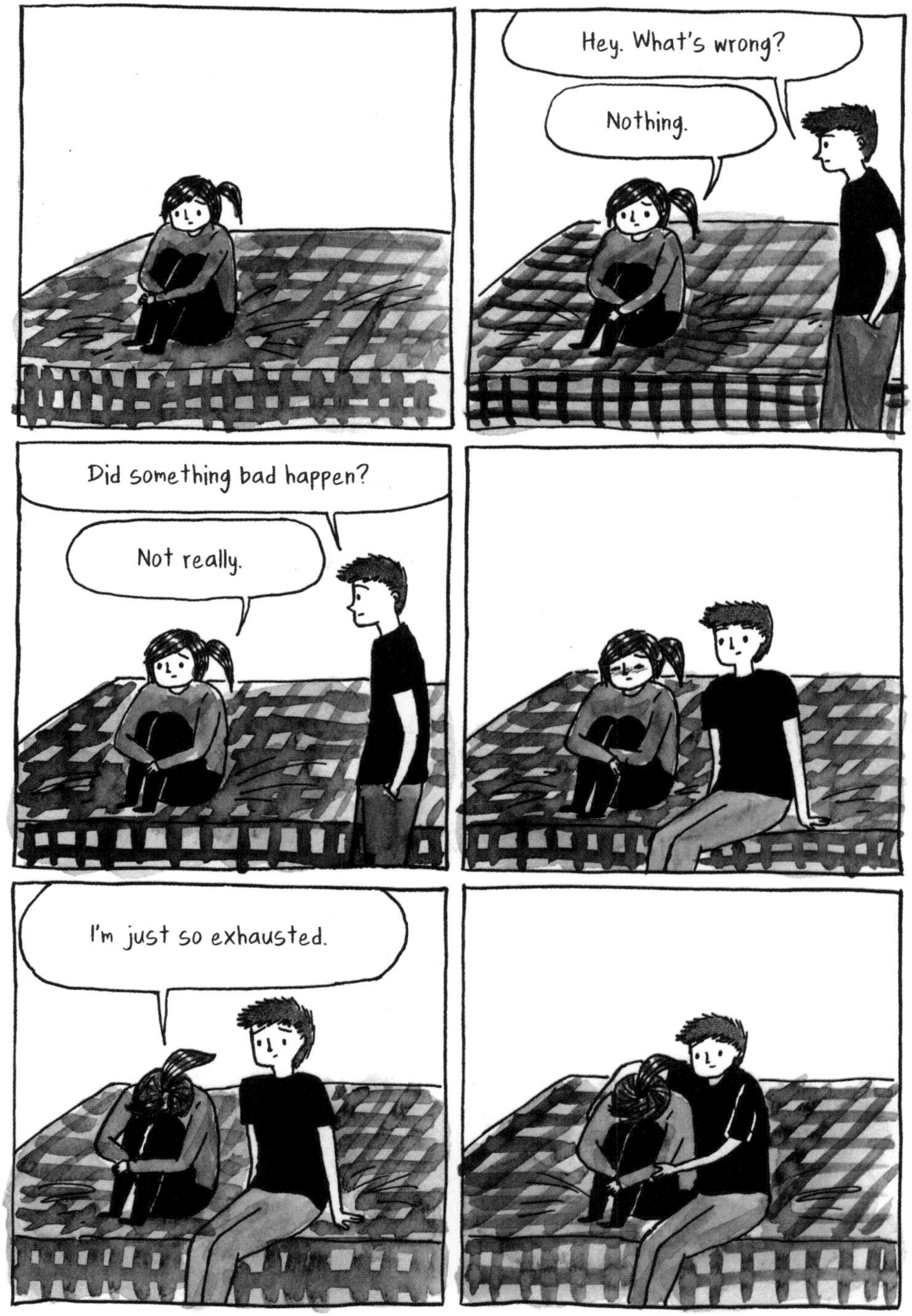
Hey. What's wrong?
Nothing.
Did something bad happen?
Not really.
I'm just so exhausted.

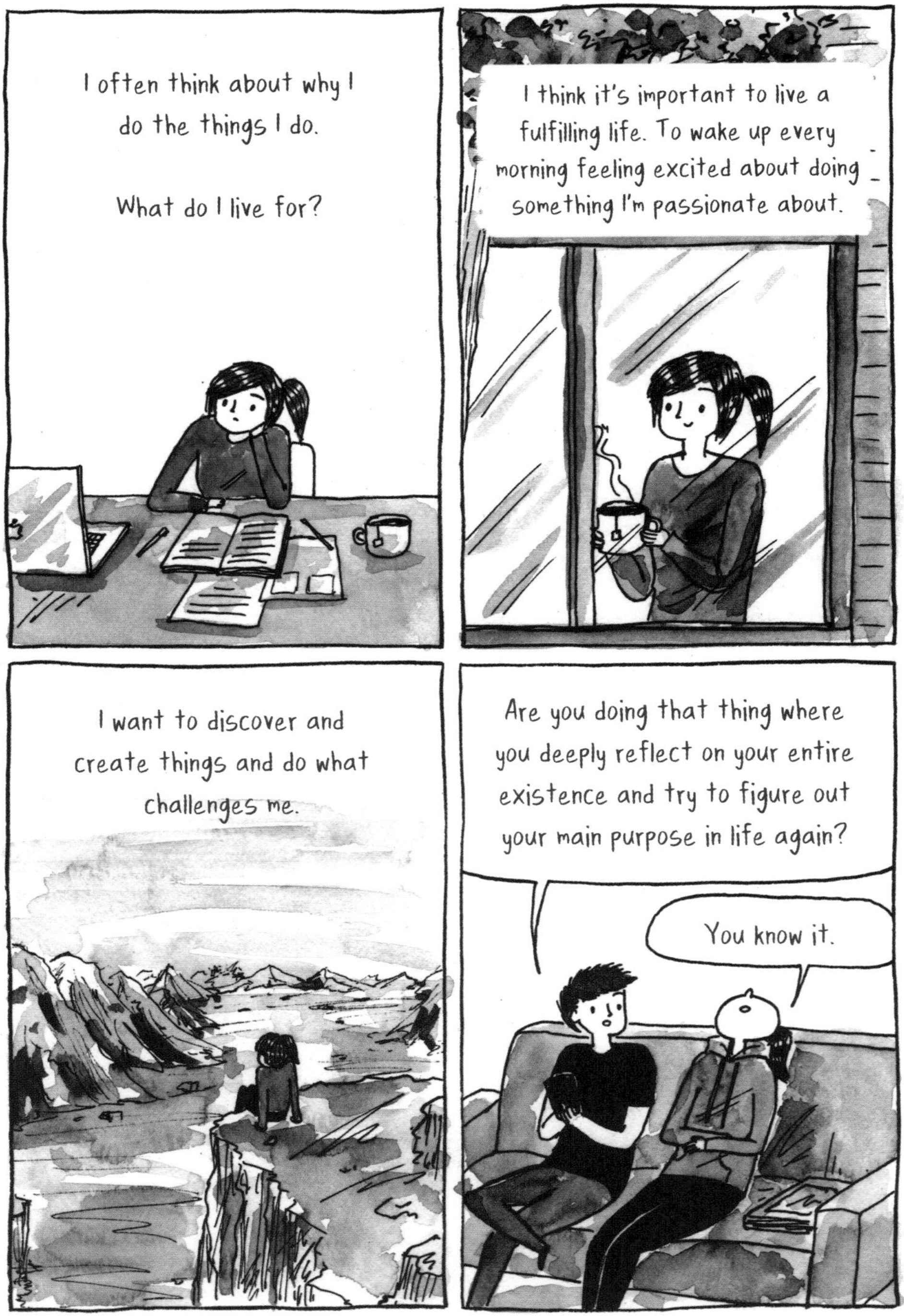
I often think about why I do the things I do.
What do I live for?
I think it's important to live a fulfilling life. To wake up every morning feeling excited about doing something I'm passionate about.
I want to discover and create things and do what challenges me.
Are you doing that thing where you deeply reflect on your entire existence and try to figure out your main purpose in life again?
You know it.

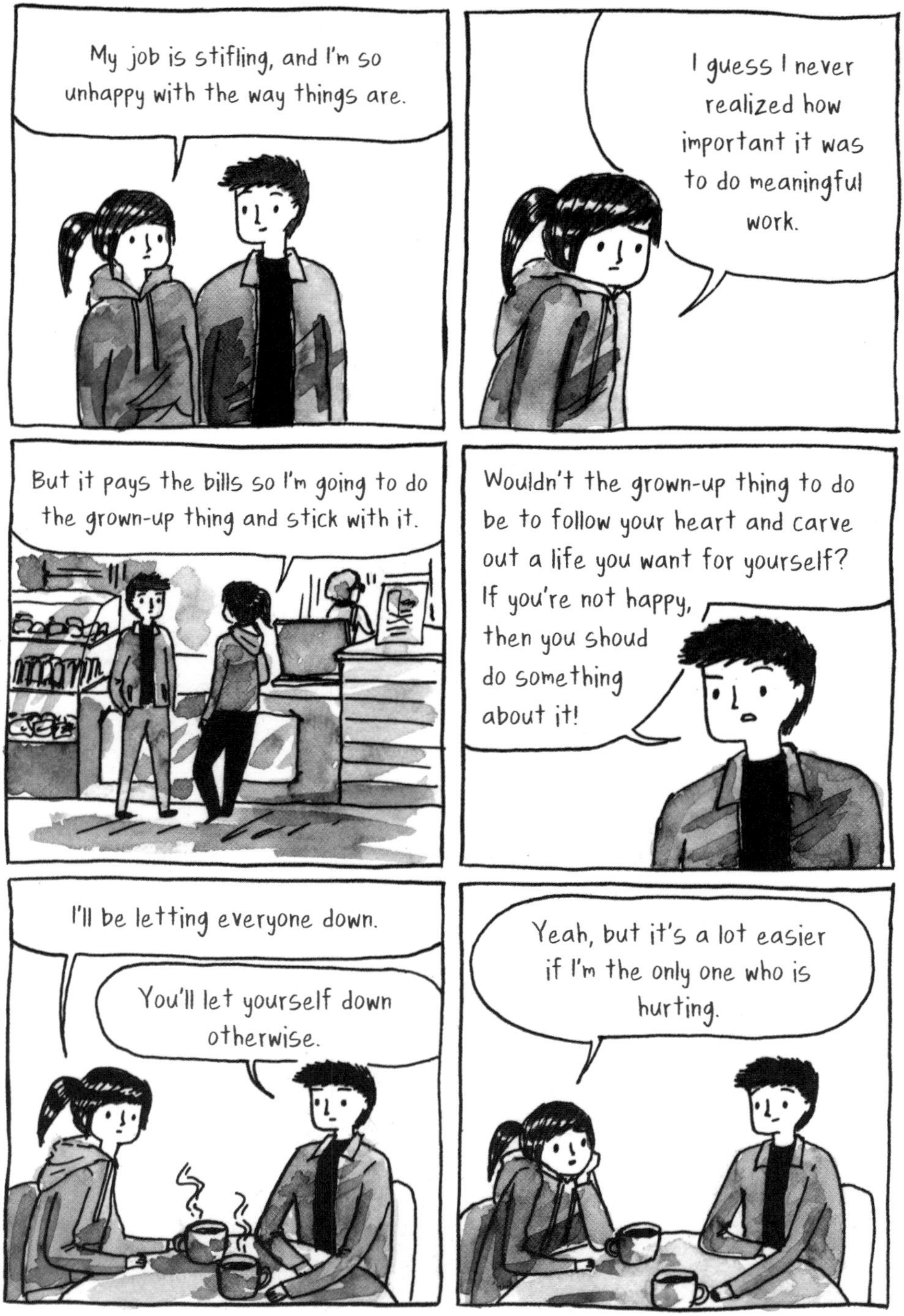
My job is stifling, and I'm so unhappy with the way things are.
I guess I never realized how important it was to do meaningful work.
But it pays the bills so I'm going to do the grown-up thing and stick with it.
Wouldn't the grown-up thing to do be to follow your heart and carve out a life you want for yourself? If you're not happy, then you shoud do something about it!
I'll be letting everyone down.
You'll let yourself down otherwise.
Yeah, but it's a lot easier if I'm the only one who is hurting.

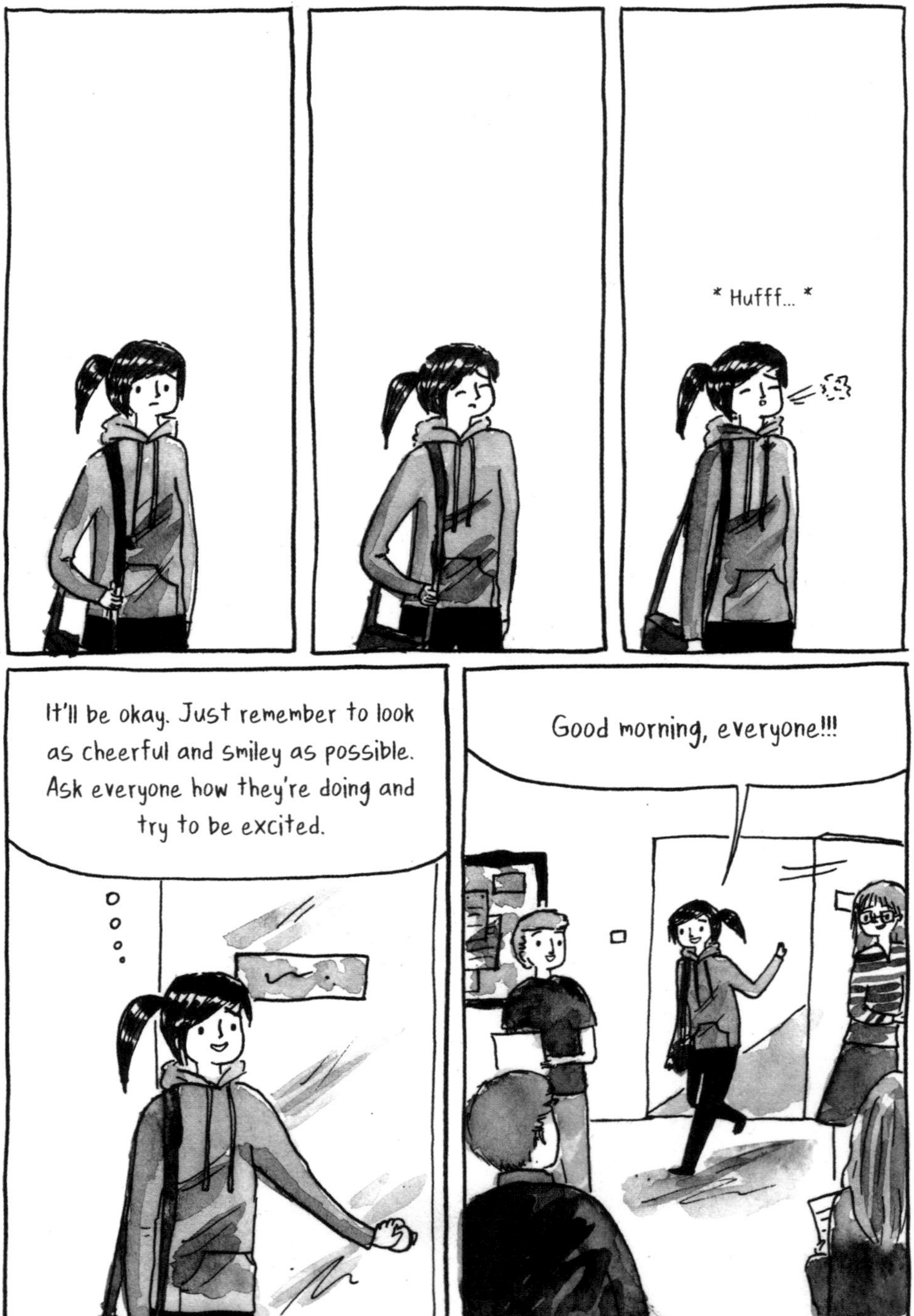
* Hufff... *
It'll be okay. Just remember to look as cheerful and smiley as possible. Ask everyone how they're doing and try to be excited.
Good morning, everyone!!!

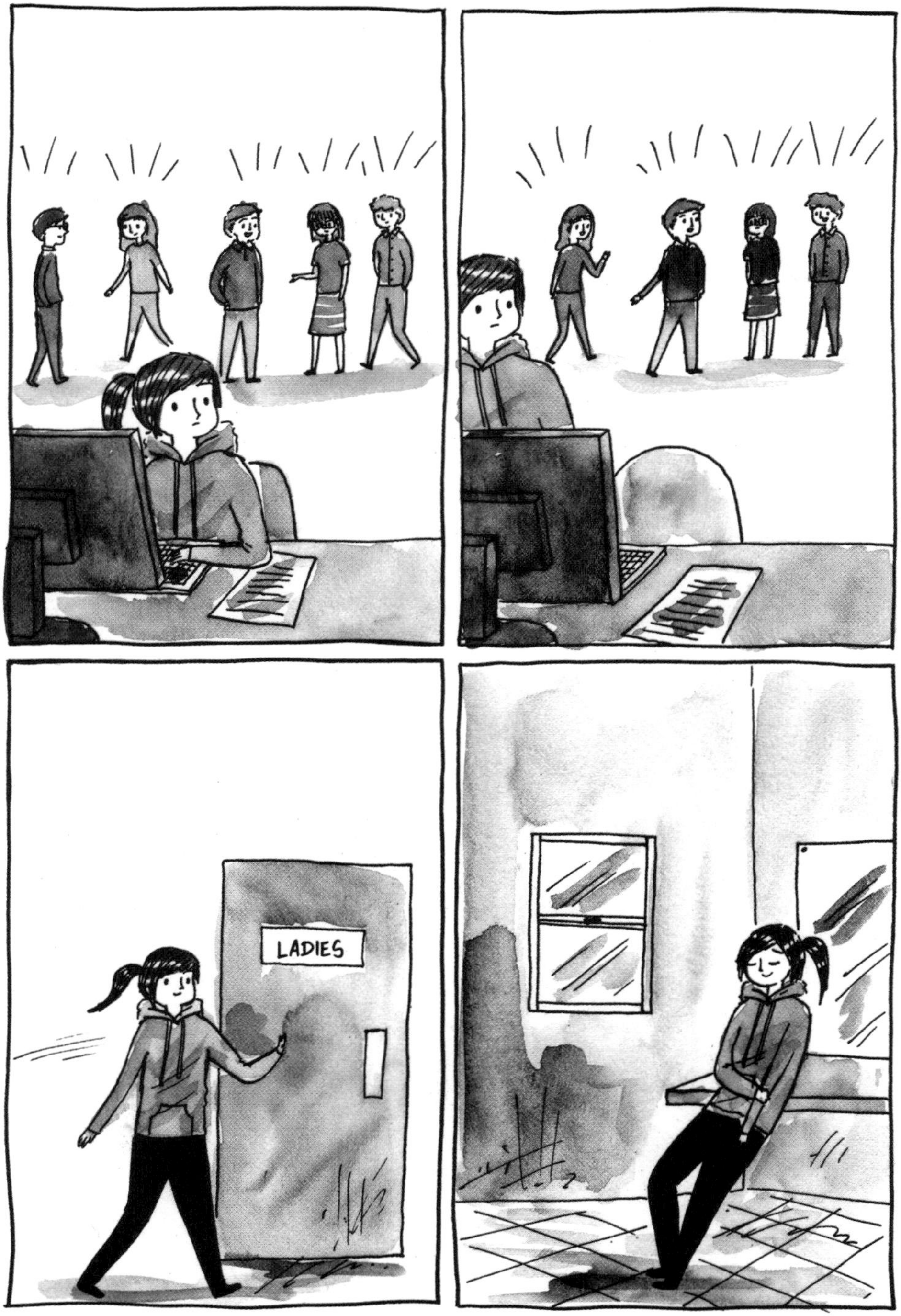
LADIES

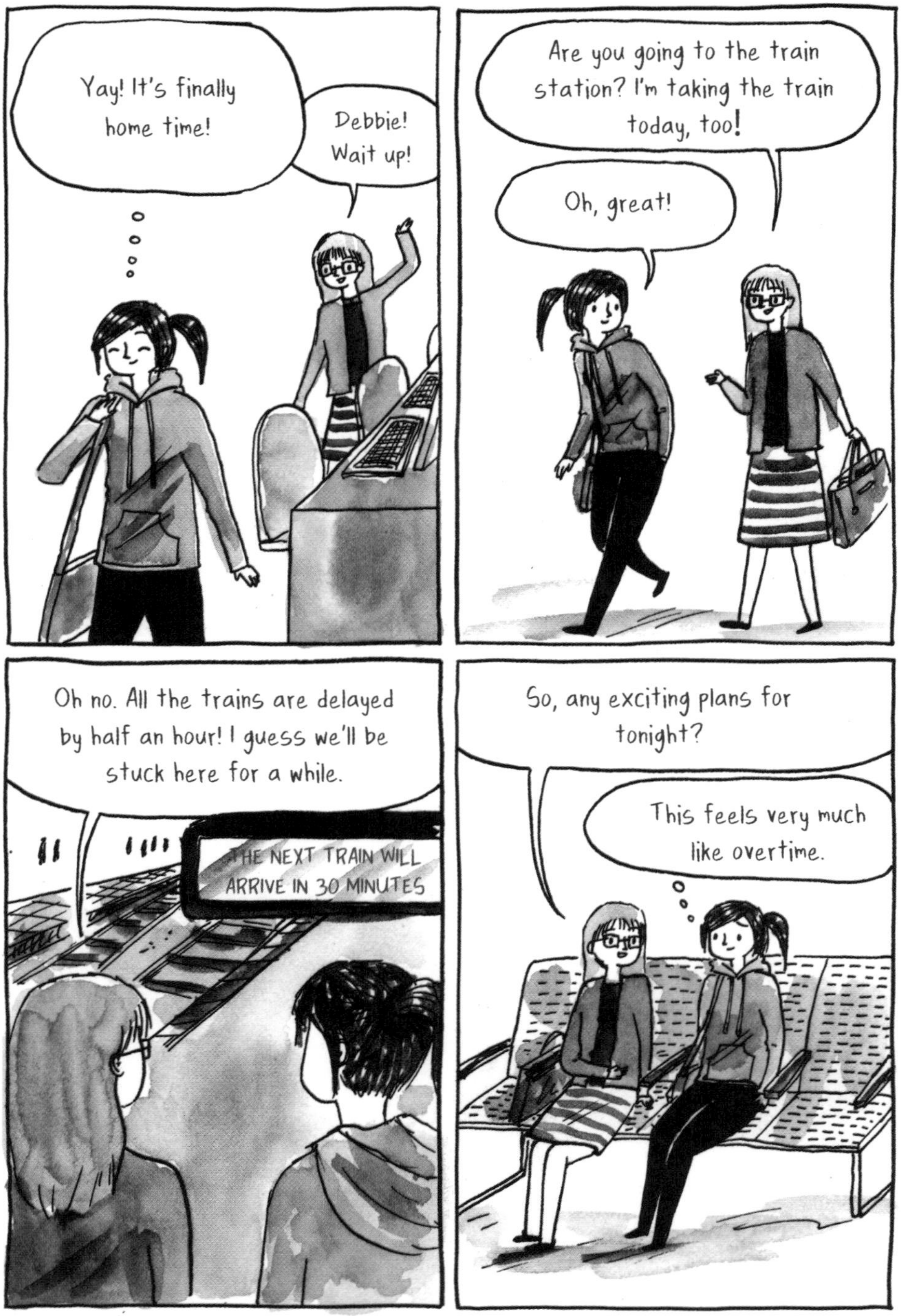
Yay! It's finally home time!
Debbie! Wait up!
Are you going to the train station? I'm taking the train today, too!
Oh, great!
Oh no. All the trains are delayed by half an hour! I guess we'll be stuck here for a while.
THE NEXT TRAIN WILL ARRIVE IN 30 MINUTES
So, any exciting plans for tonight?
This feels very much like overtime.

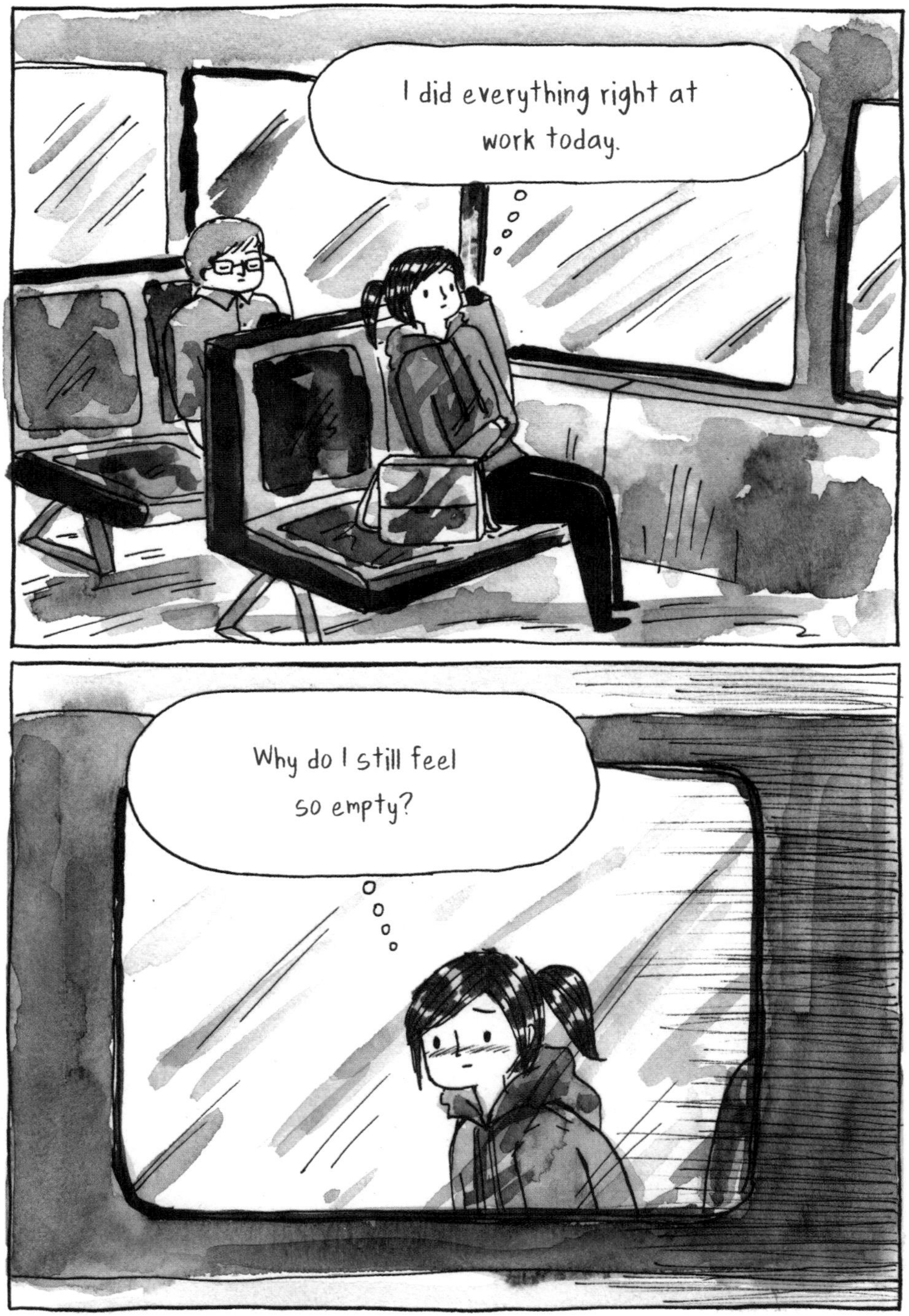
I did everything right at work today.
Why do I still feel so empty?

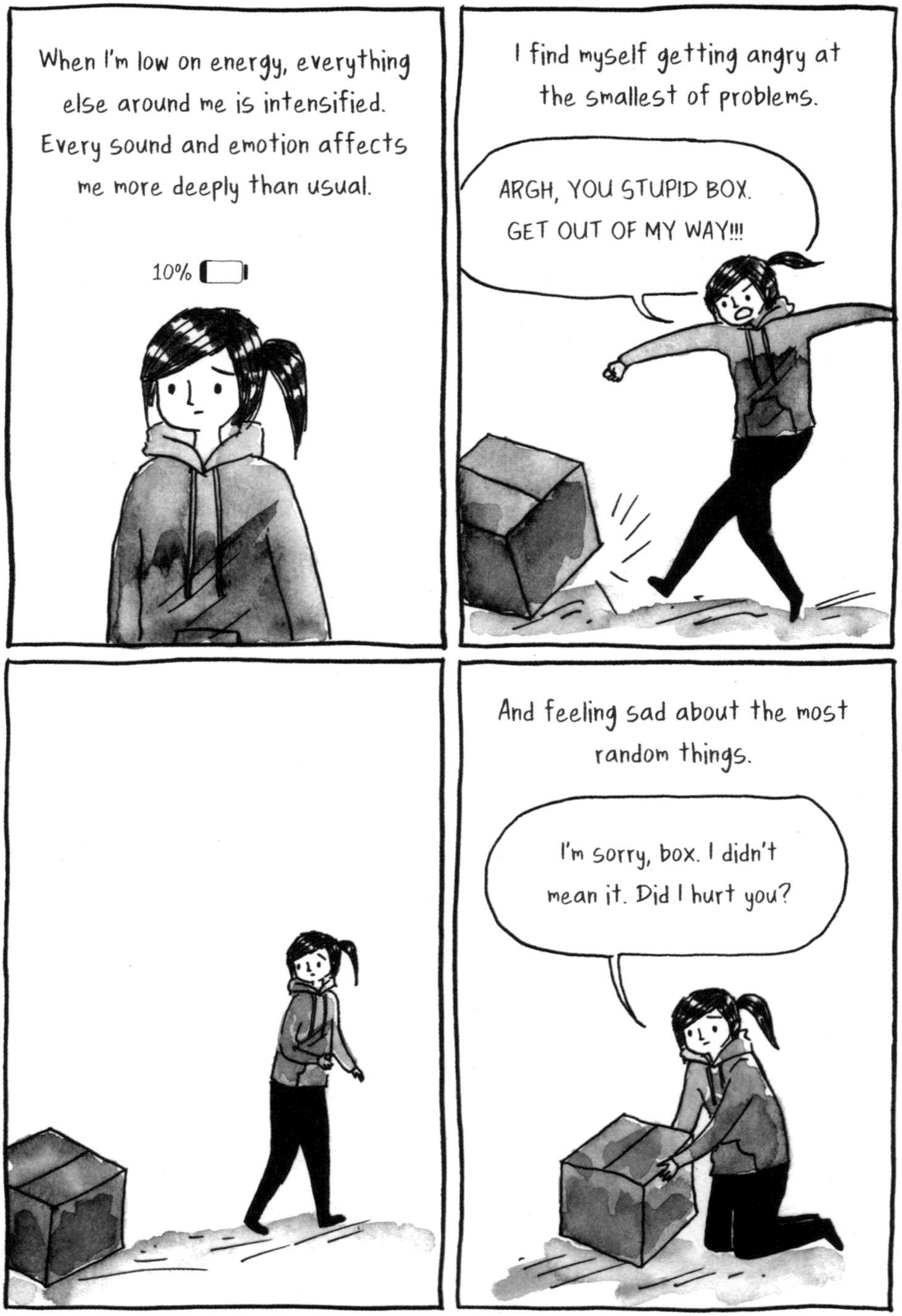
When I'm low on energy, everything else around me is intensified. Every sound and emotion affects me more deeply than usual.
10%
I find myself getting angry at the smallest of problems.
ARGH, YOU STUPID BOX. GET OUT OF MY WAY!!!
And feeling sad about the most random things.
I'm sorry, box. I didn't mean it. Did I hurt you?

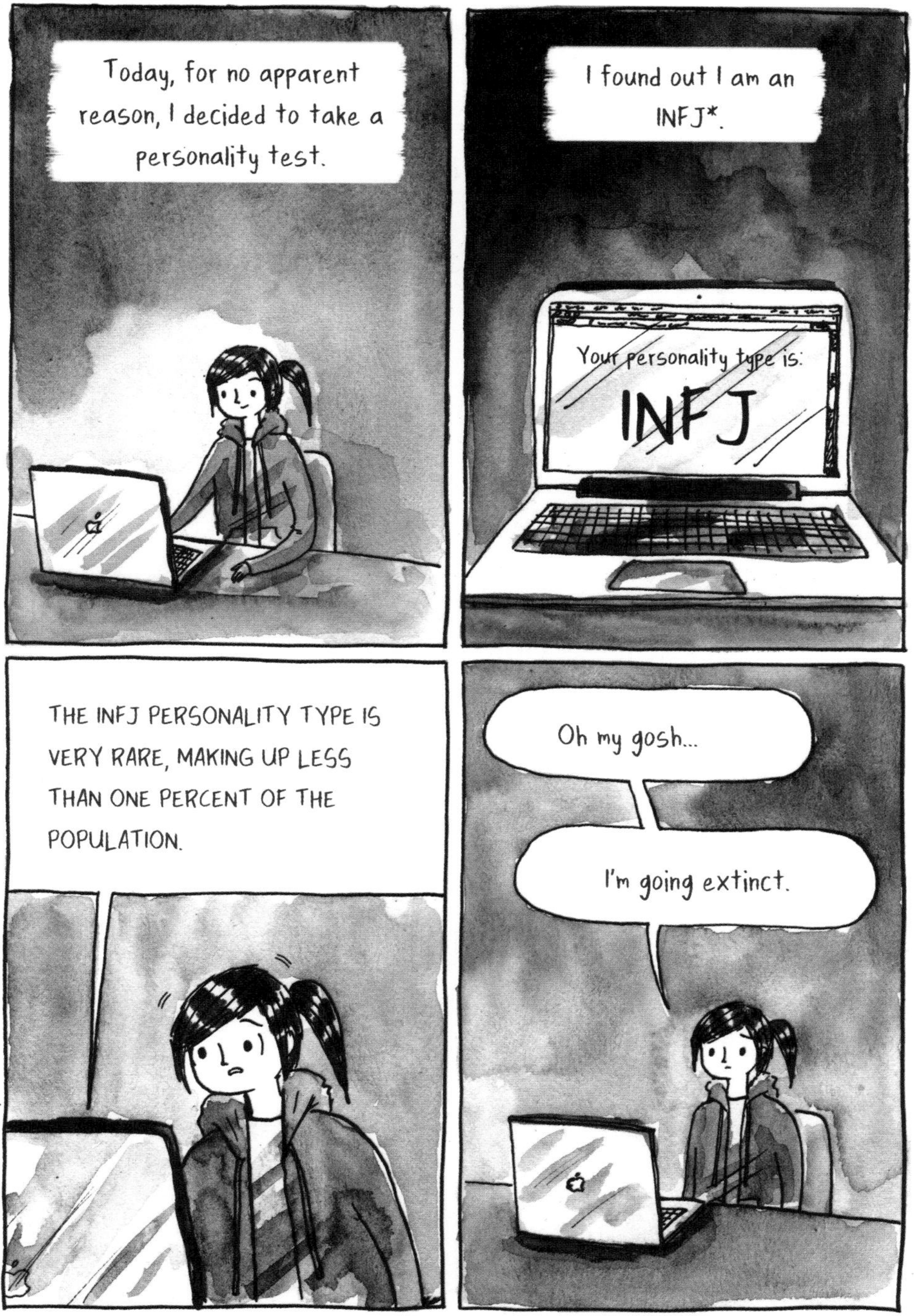
Today, for no apparent reason, I decided to take a personality test.
I found out I am an INFJ*.
Your personality type is:
INFJ
THE INFJ PERSONALITY TYPE IS VERY RARE, MAKING UP LESS THAN ONE PERCENT OF THE POPULATION.
Oh my gosh...
I'm going extinct.

*Introversion, Intuition, Feeling, and Judging. Based on the Myers-Briggs Type Indicator.

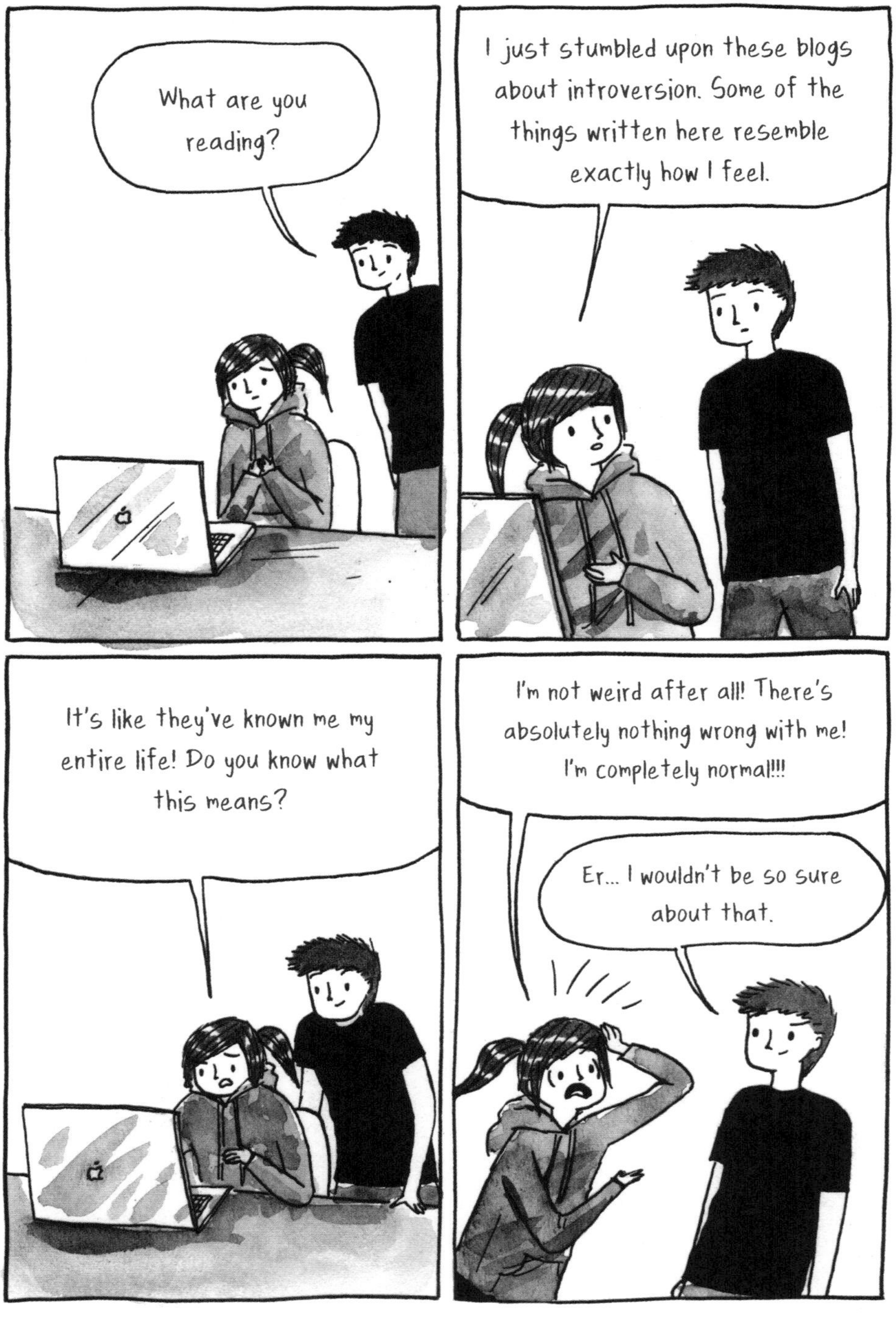
What are you reading?
I just stumbled upon these blogs about introversion. Some of the things written here resemble exactly how I feel.
It's like they've known me my entire life! Do you know what this means?
I'm not weird after all! There's absolutely nothing wrong with me! I'm completely normal!!!
Er... I wouldn't be so sure about that.

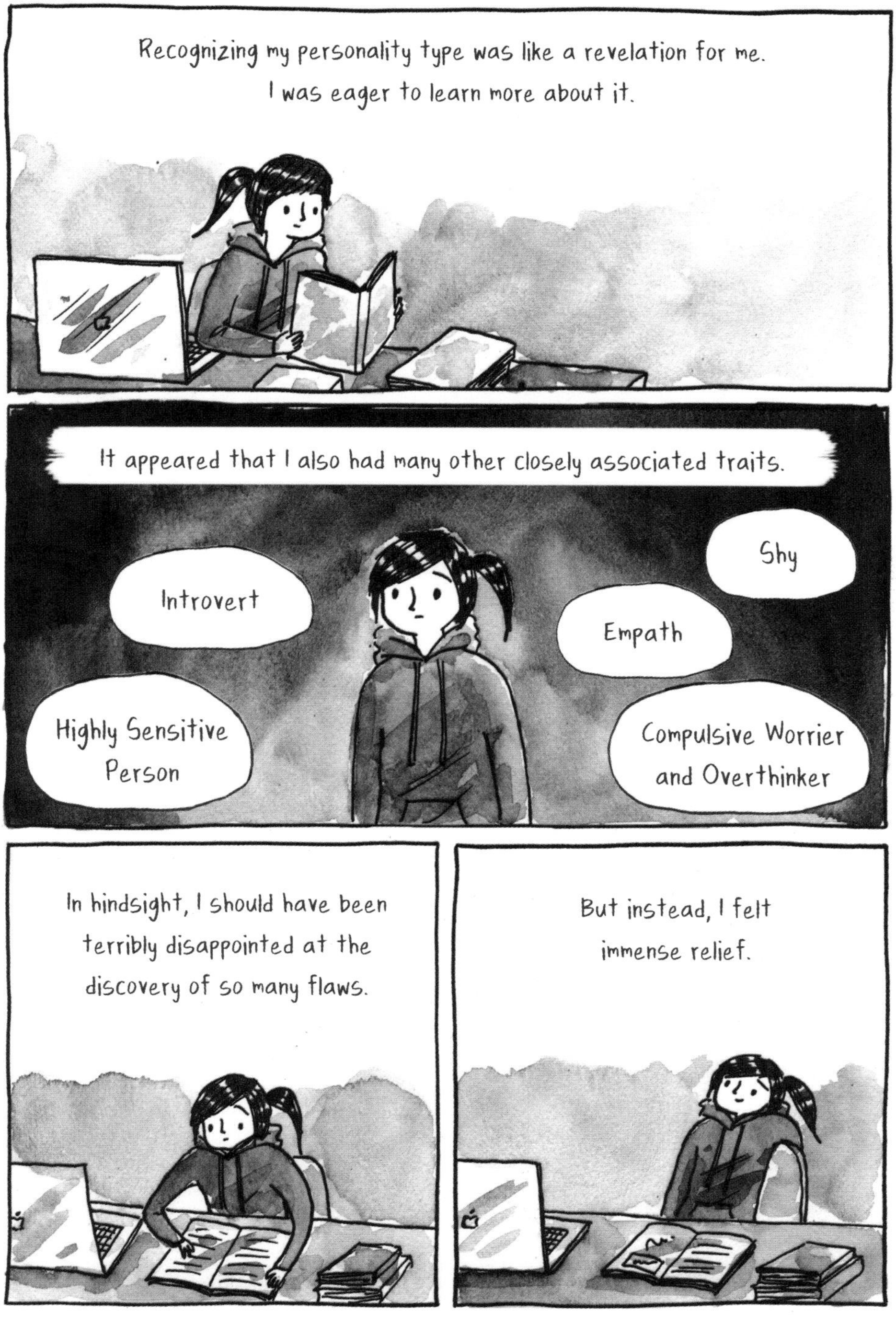
Recognizing my personality type was like a revelation for me.
I was eager to learn more about it.
It appeared that I also had many other closely associated traits.
Introvert
Shy
Empath
Highly Sensitive Person
Compulsive Worrier and Overthinker
In hindsight, I should have been terribly disappointed at the discovery of so many flaws.
But instead, I felt immense relief.

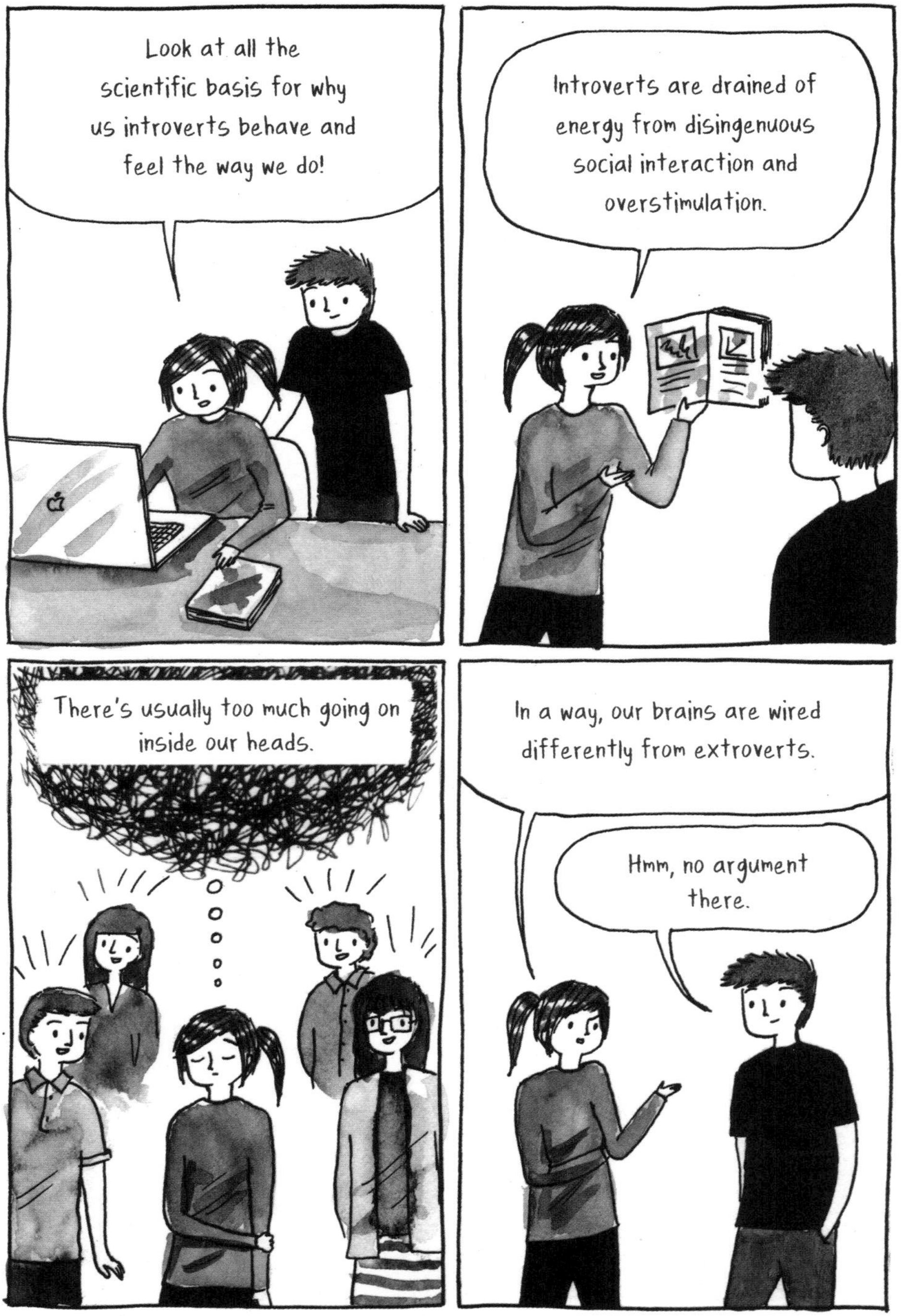
Look at all the scientific basis for why us introverts behave and feel the way we do!
Introverts are drained of energy from disingenuous social interaction and overstimulation.
There's usually too much going on inside our heads.
In a way, our brains are wired differently from extroverts.
Hmm, no argument there.

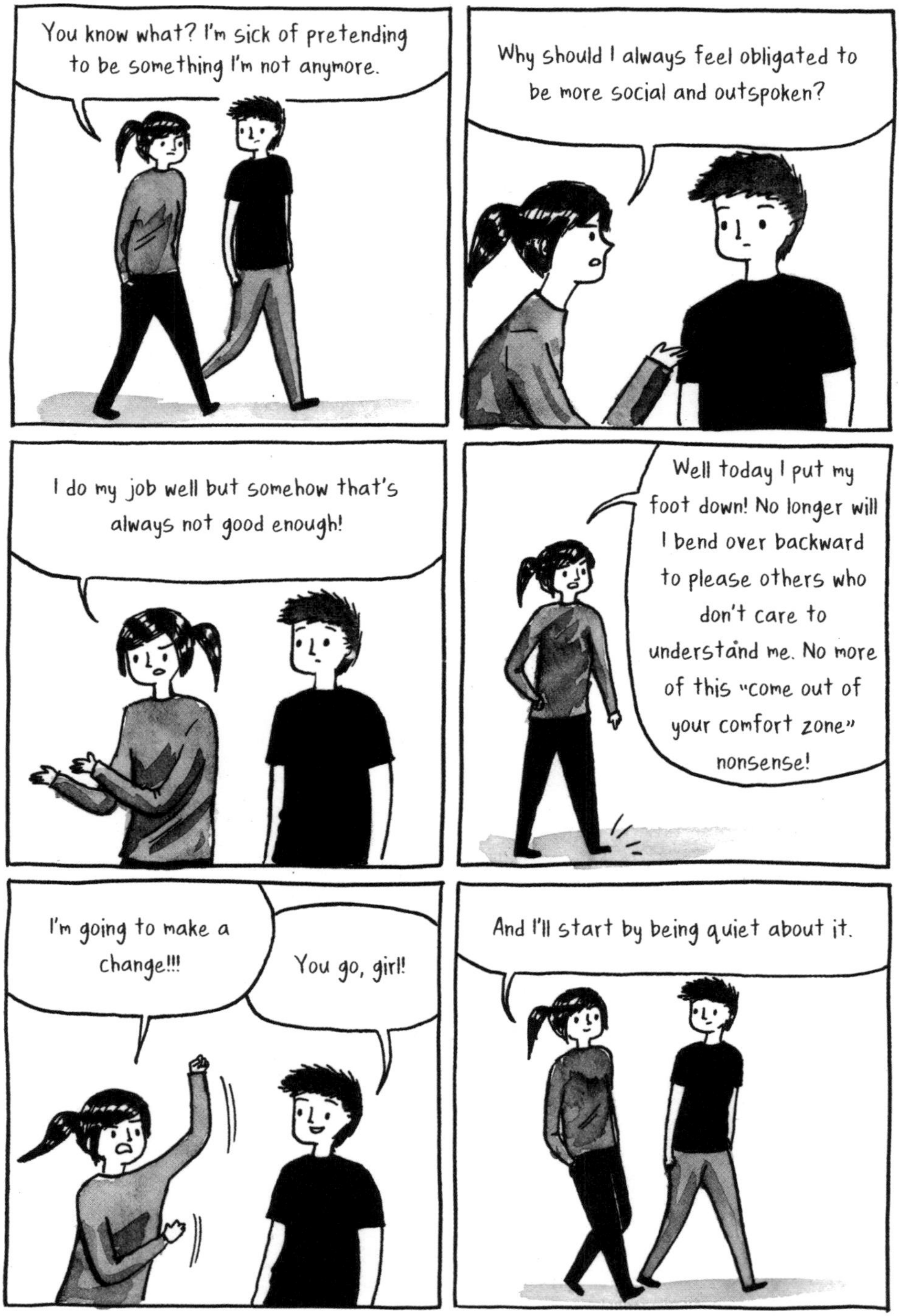
You know what? I'm sick of pretending to be something I'm not anymore.
Why should I always feel obligated to be more social and outspoken?
I do my job well but somehow that's always not good enough!
Well today I put my foot down! No longer will I bend over backward to please others who don't care to understand me. No more of this "come out of your comfort zone" nonsense!
I'm going to make a change!!!
You go, girl!
And I'll start by being quiet about it.

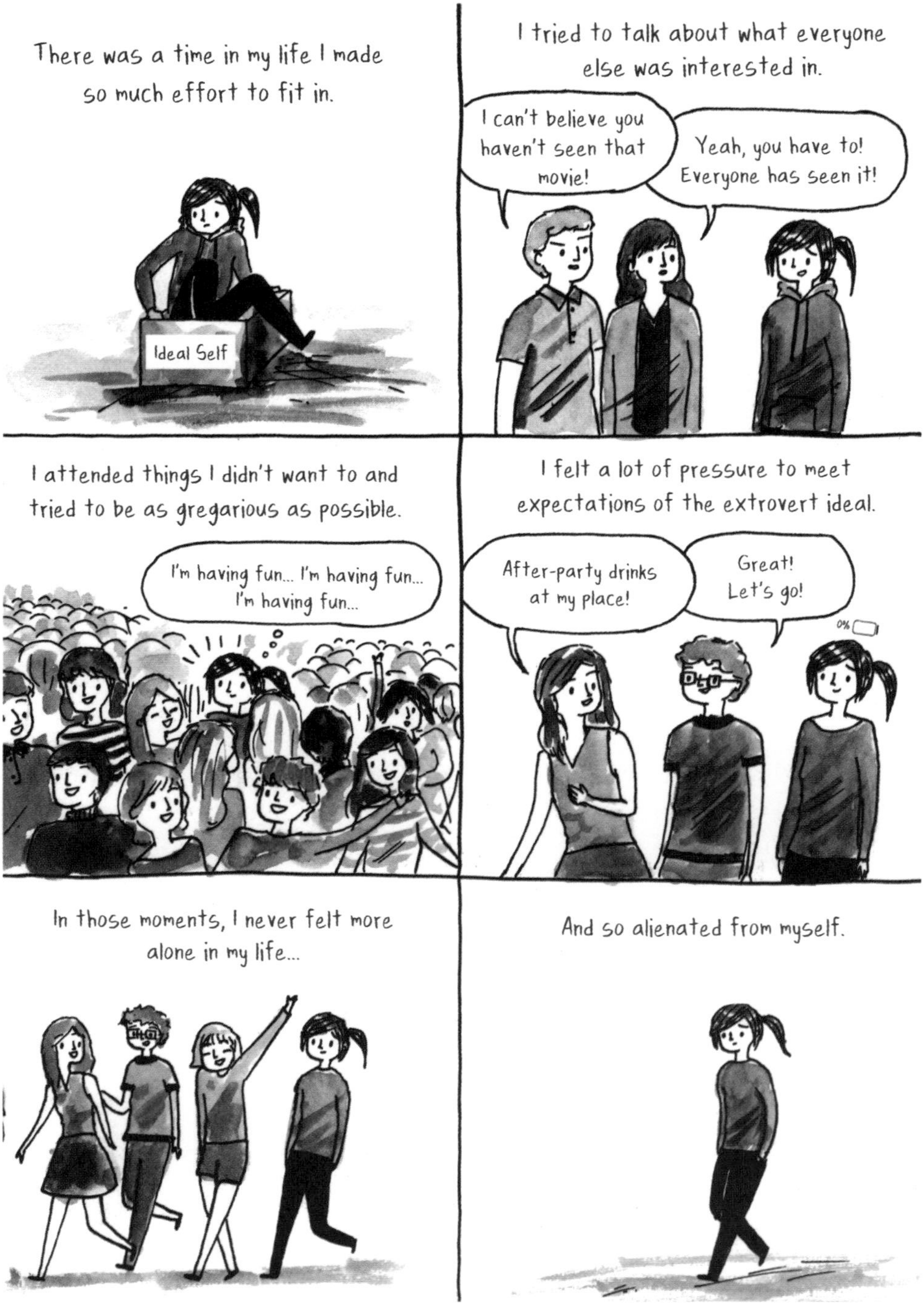
There was a time in my life I made so much effort to fit in.
Ideal Self
I tried to talk about what everyone else was interested in.
I can't believe you haven't seen that movie!
Yeah, you have to! Everyone has seen it!
I attended things I didn't want to and tried to be as gregarious as possible.
I'm having fun... I'm having fun... I'm having fun...
I felt a lot of pressure to meet expectations of the extrovert ideal.
After-party drinks at my place!
Great! Let's go!
0%
In those moments, I never felt more alone in my life...
And so alienated from myself.

I'm highly sensitive to other people's feelings and emotions.
Sometimes, I even end up absorbing them.

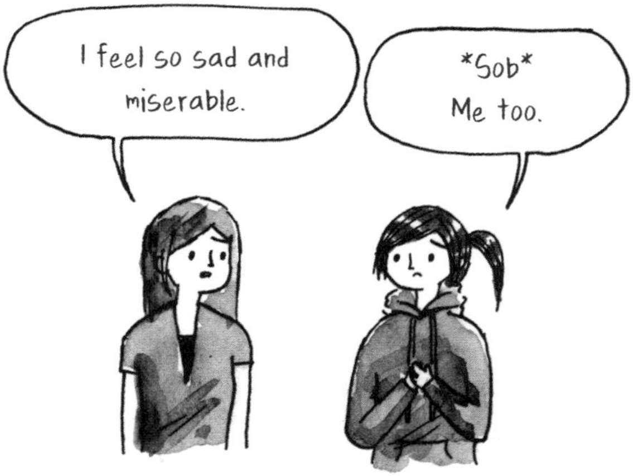
I feel so sad and miserable.
*Sob* Me too.

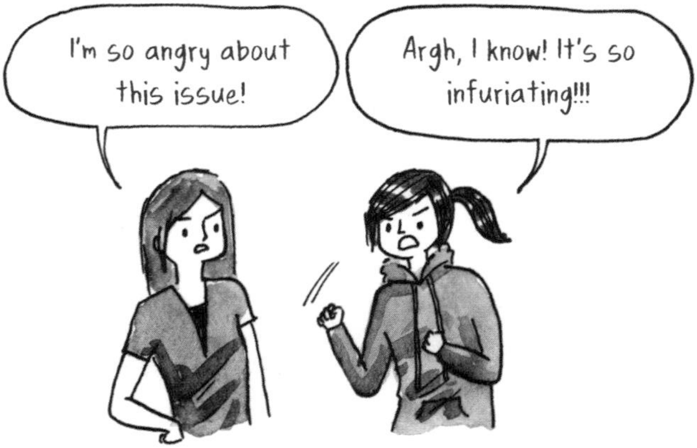
I'm so angry about this issue!
Argh, I know! It's so infuriating!!!

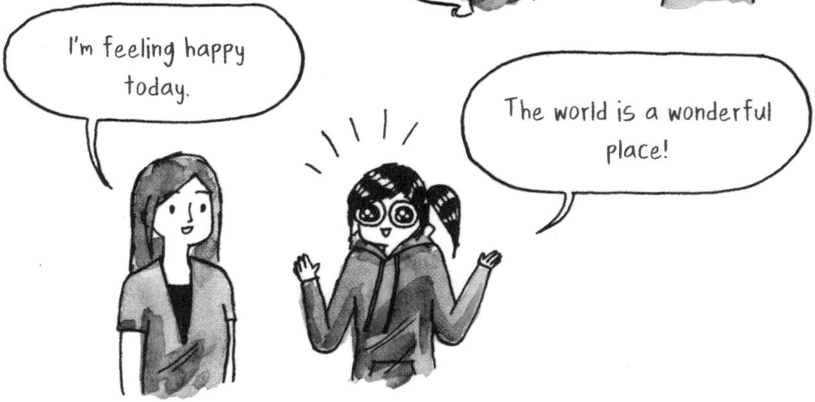
I'm feeling happy today.
The world is a wonderful place!

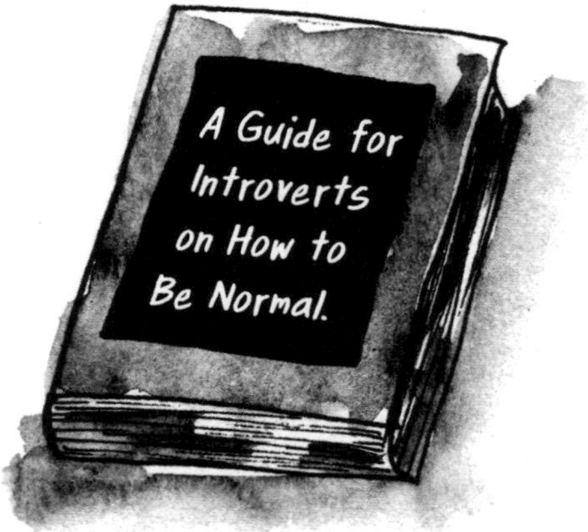
A Guide for
Introverts
on How to
Be Normal.

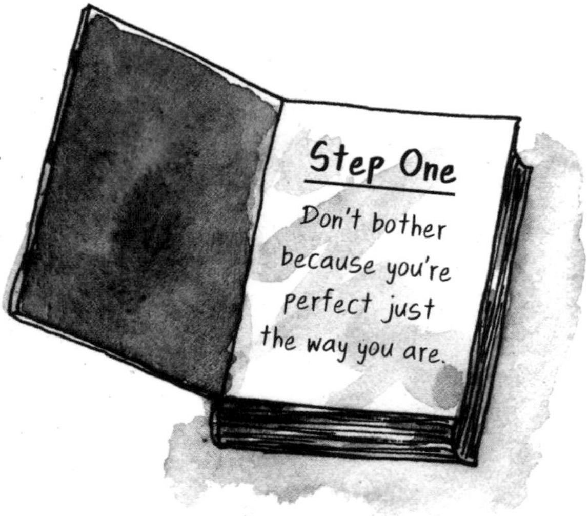
Step One
Don't bother
because you're
perfect just
the way you are.

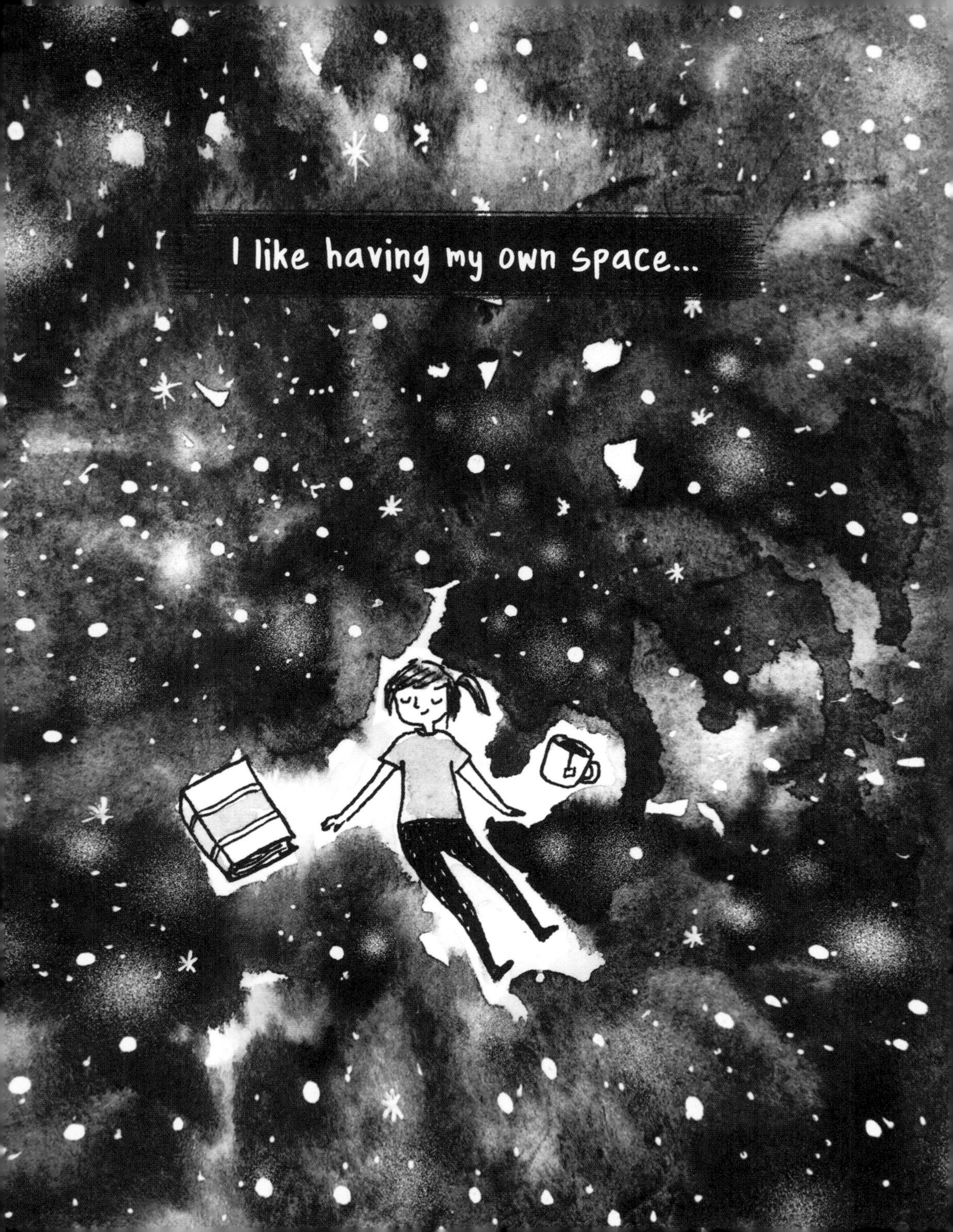
I like having my own space...

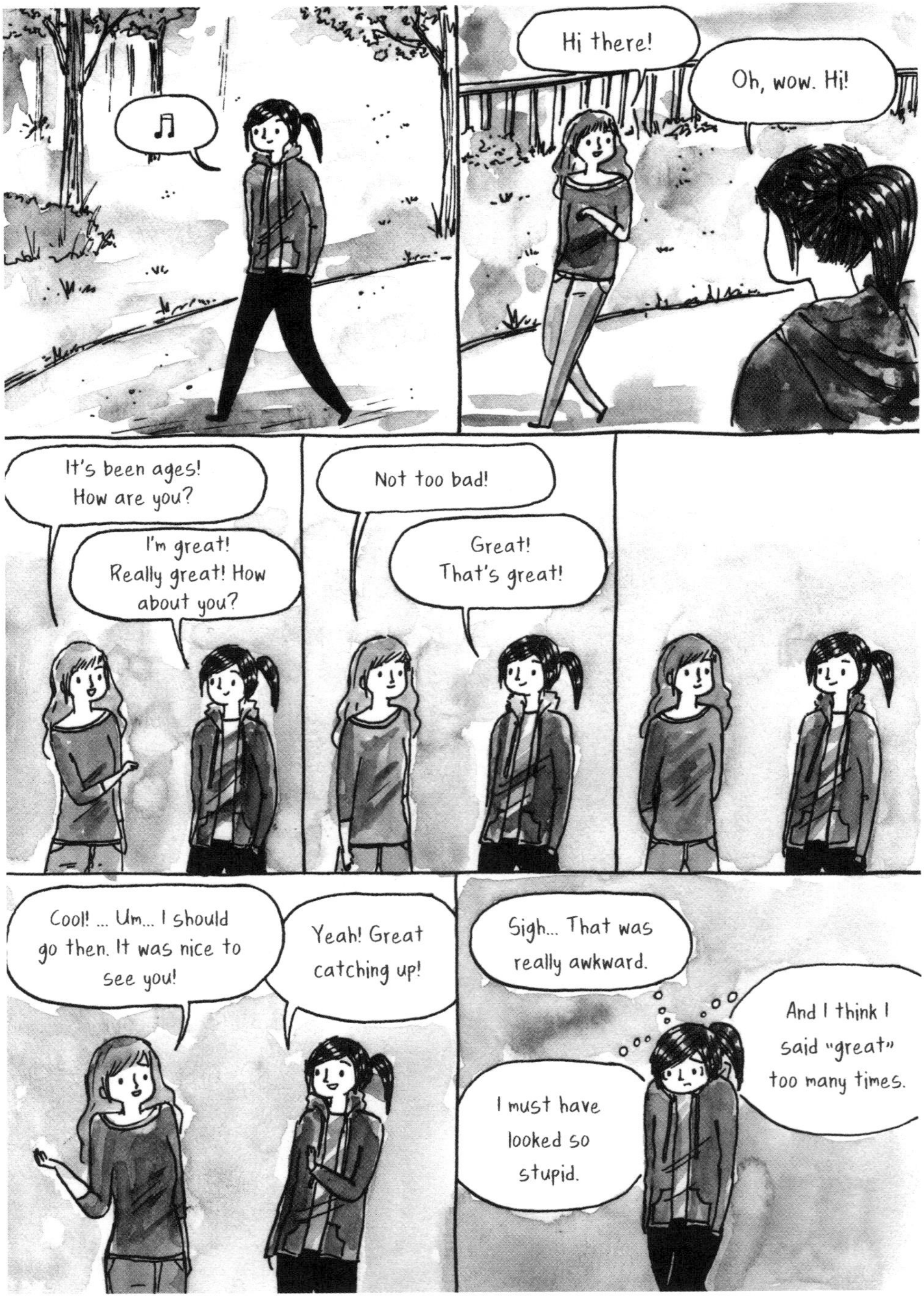
Hi there!
Oh, wow. Hi!
It's been ages! How are you?
I'm great! Really great! How about you?
Not too bad!
Great! That's great!
Cool! ... Um... I should go then. It was nice to see you!
Yeah! Great catching up!
Sigh... That was really awkward.
And I think I said "great" too many times.
I must have looked so stupid.

# An Introvert's Fashion Guide to Avoid Unexpected Social Conversations in Public

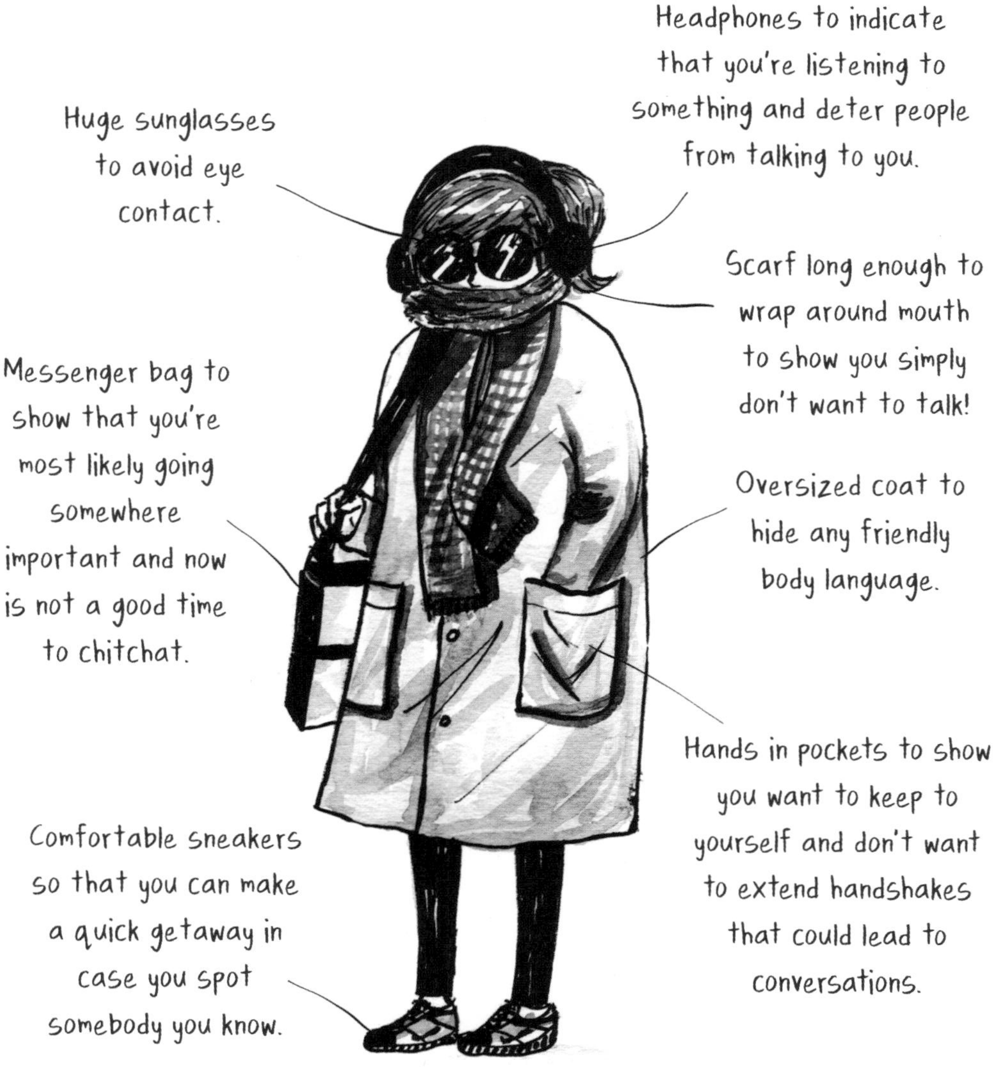
Huge sunglasses to avoid eye contact.
Headphones to indicate that you're listening to something and deter people from talking to you.
Scarf long enough to wrap around mouth to show you simply don't want to talk!
Messenger bag to show that you're most likely going somewhere important and now is not a good time to chitchat.
Oversized coat to hide any friendly body language.
Hands in pockets to show you want to keep to yourself and don't want to extend handshakes that could lead to conversations.
Comfortable sneakers so that you can make a quick getaway in case you spot somebody you know.

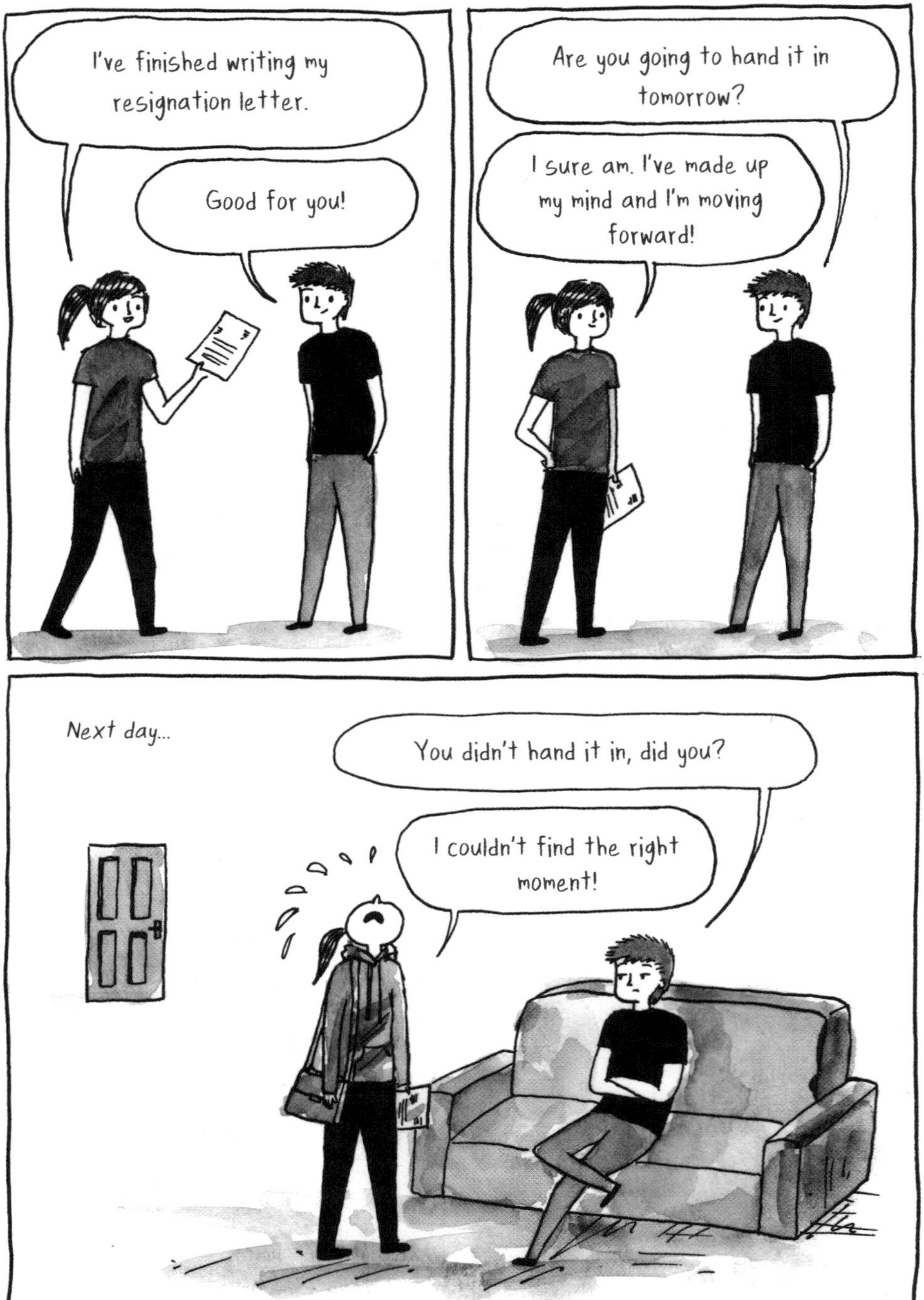
I've finished writing my resignation letter.
Good for you!
Are you going to hand it in tomorrow?
I sure am. I've made up my mind and I'm moving forward!
Next day...
You didn't hand it in, did you?
I couldn't find the right moment!

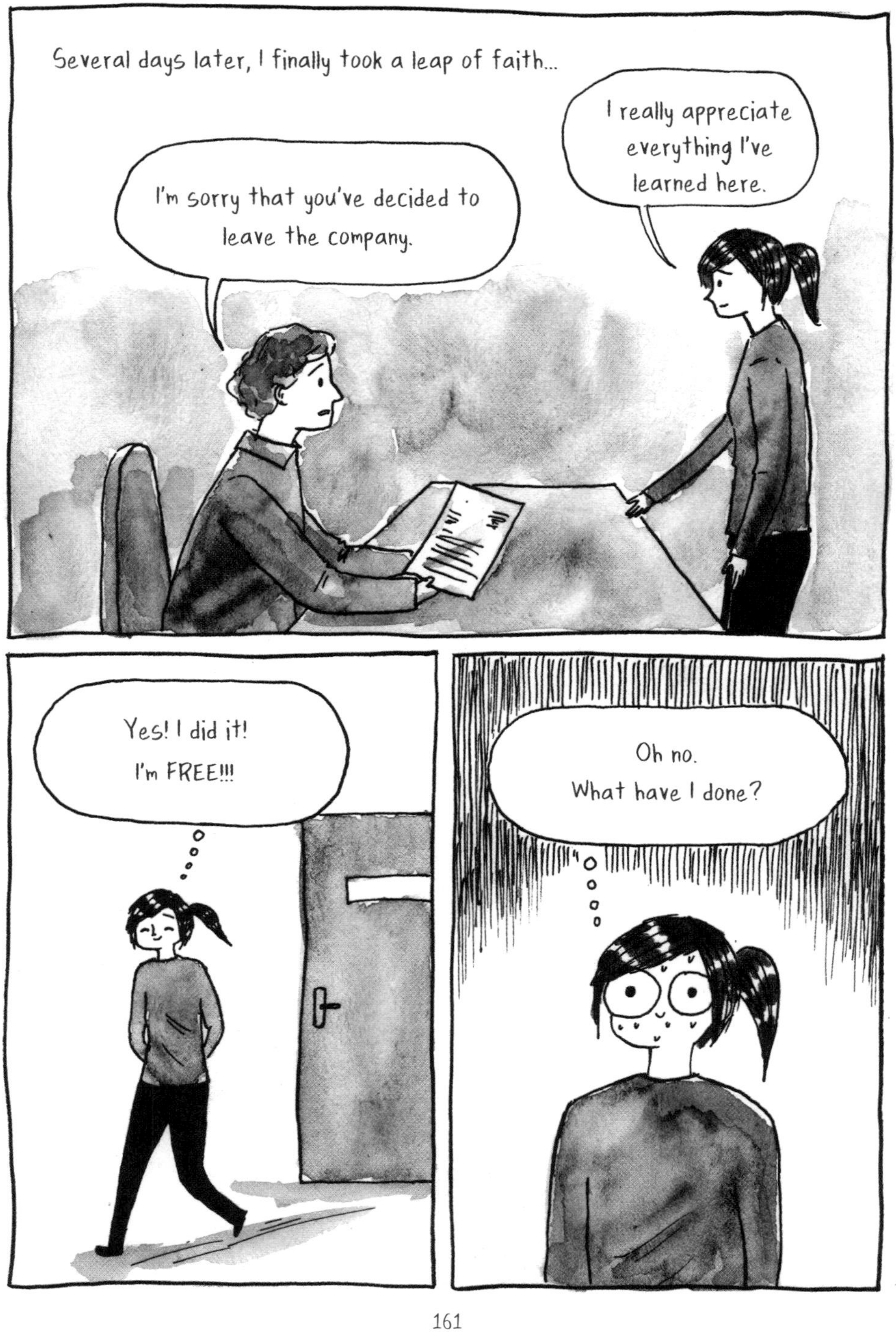
Several days later, I finally took a leap of faith...
I'm sorry that you've decided to leave the company.
I really appreciate everything I've learned here.
Yes! I did it! I'm FREE!!!
Oh no. What have I done?

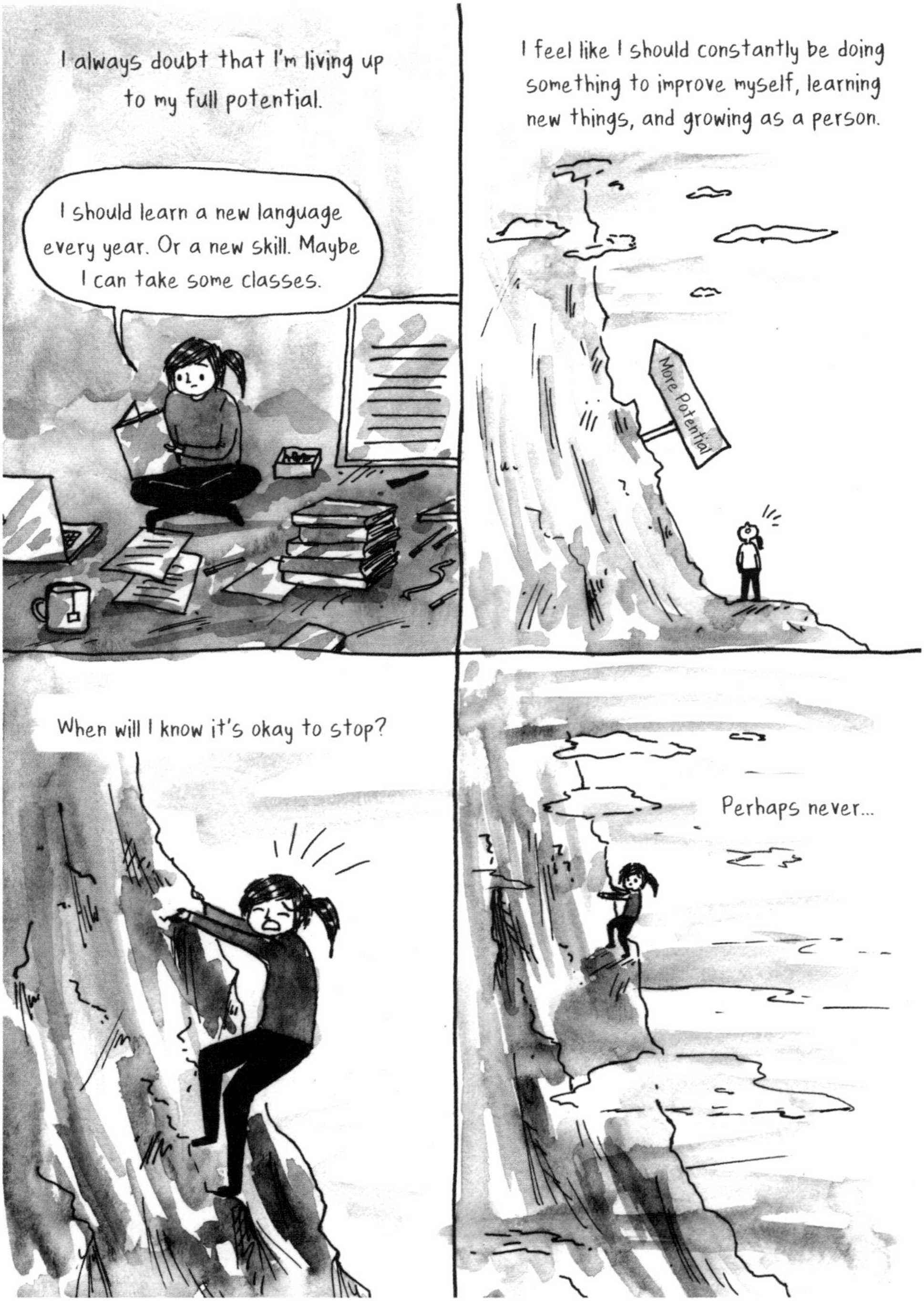
I always doubt that I'm living up to my full potential.
I should learn a new language every year. Or a new skill. Maybe I can take some classes.
I feel like I should constantly be doing something to improve myself, learning new things, and growing as a person.
More Potential
When will I know it's okay to stop?
Perhaps never...

# Solitude

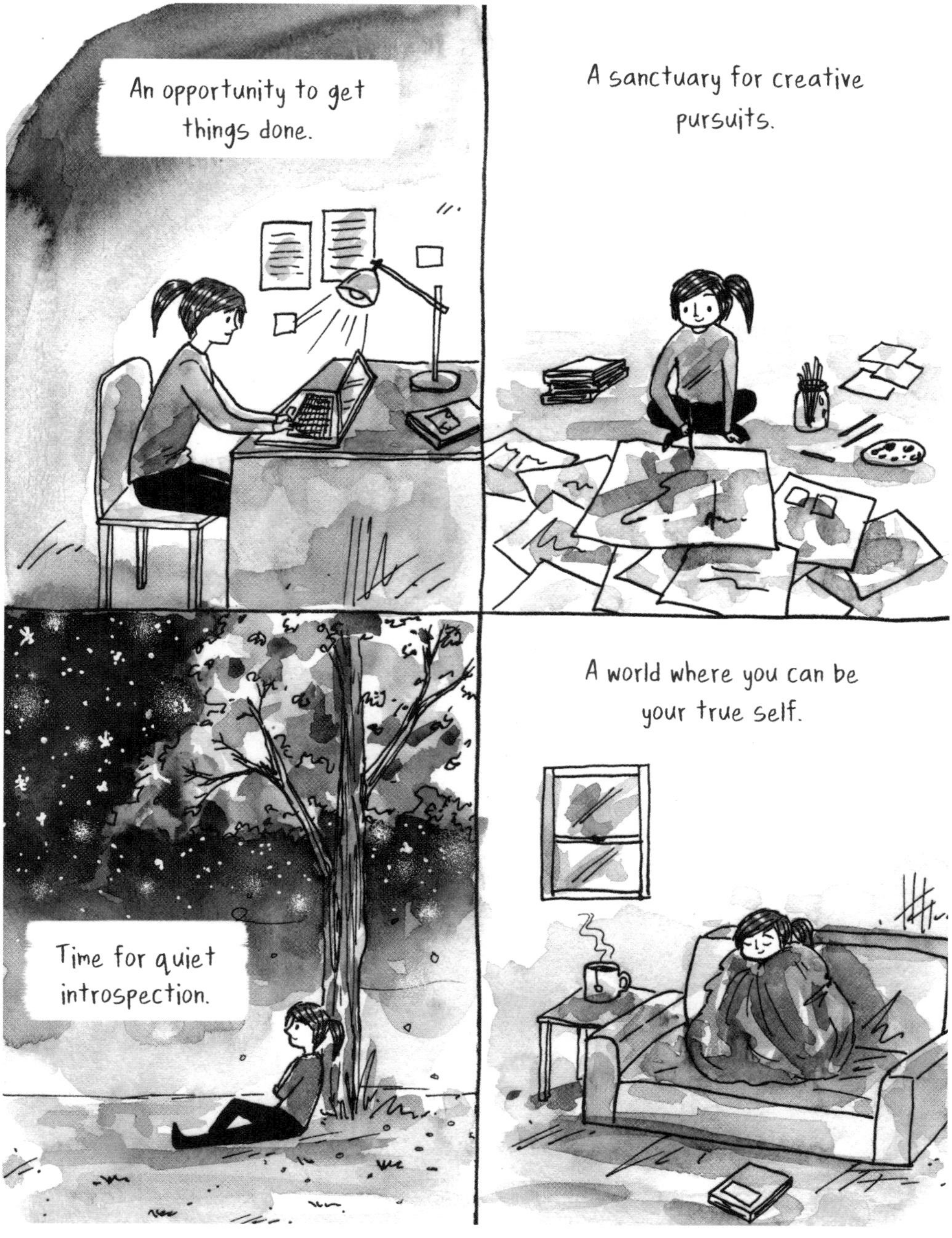
An opportunity to get things done.
A sanctuary for creative pursuits.
Time for quiet introspection.
A world where you can be your true self.

# An Introvert's Survival Kit

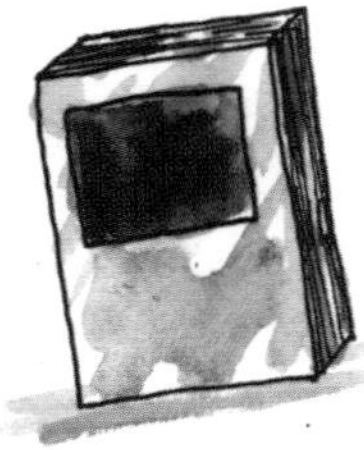

A good book

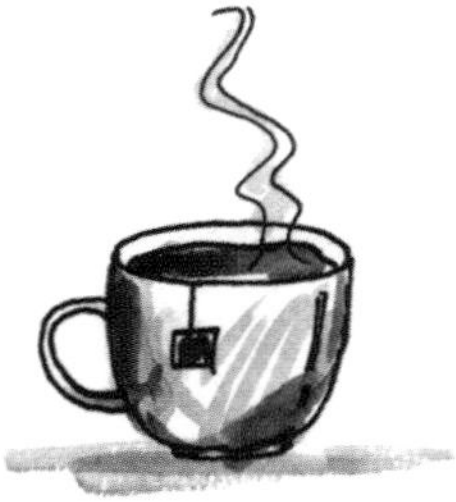

Tea

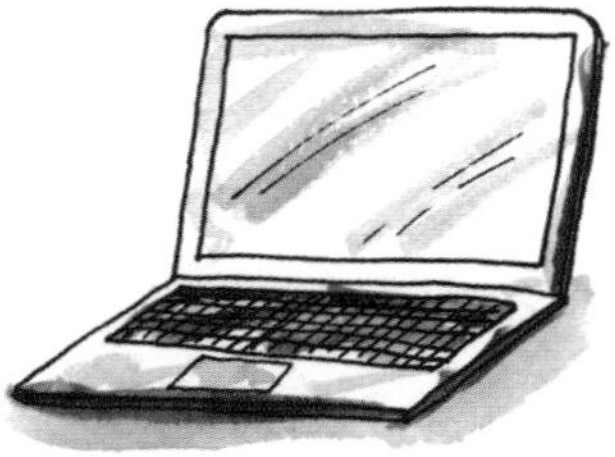

Laptop with Internet connection

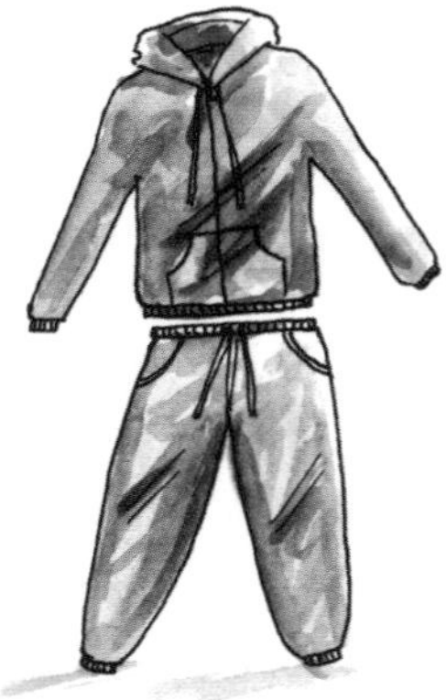

Oversized comfy clothes

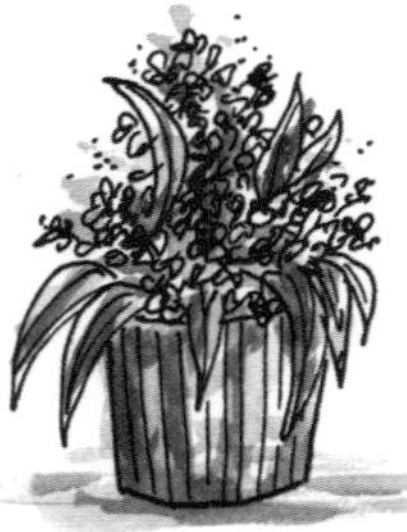

Nature

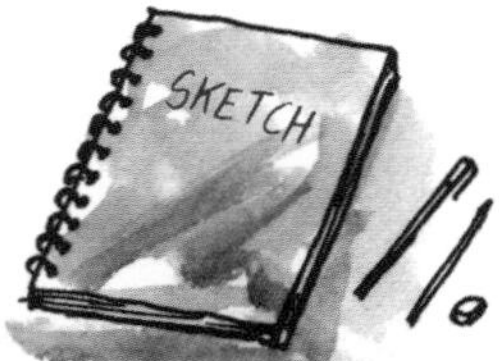
SKETCH

Writing and art supplies

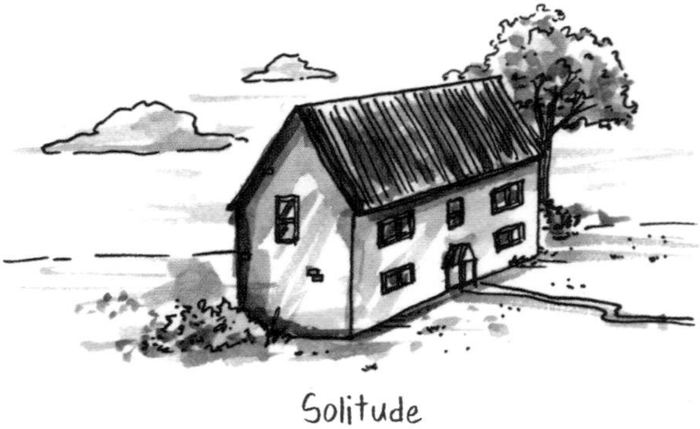

Solitude

Every time I go out, I tend to bring a book with me...

Even though I know I won't have time to read it.

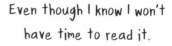

I guess it just gives me a sense of comfort...

Because it feels like I have a good friend by my side.

# Reasons I love my extrovert husband

He knows when I need to take a break.

I made you a cup of tea!

He steps in to do the socializing when I can't.

He accompanies me to new places I want to visit but would rather not go alone.

This museum is amazing!

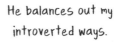

We're often together, but he understands when I need my space.

He balances out my introverted ways.

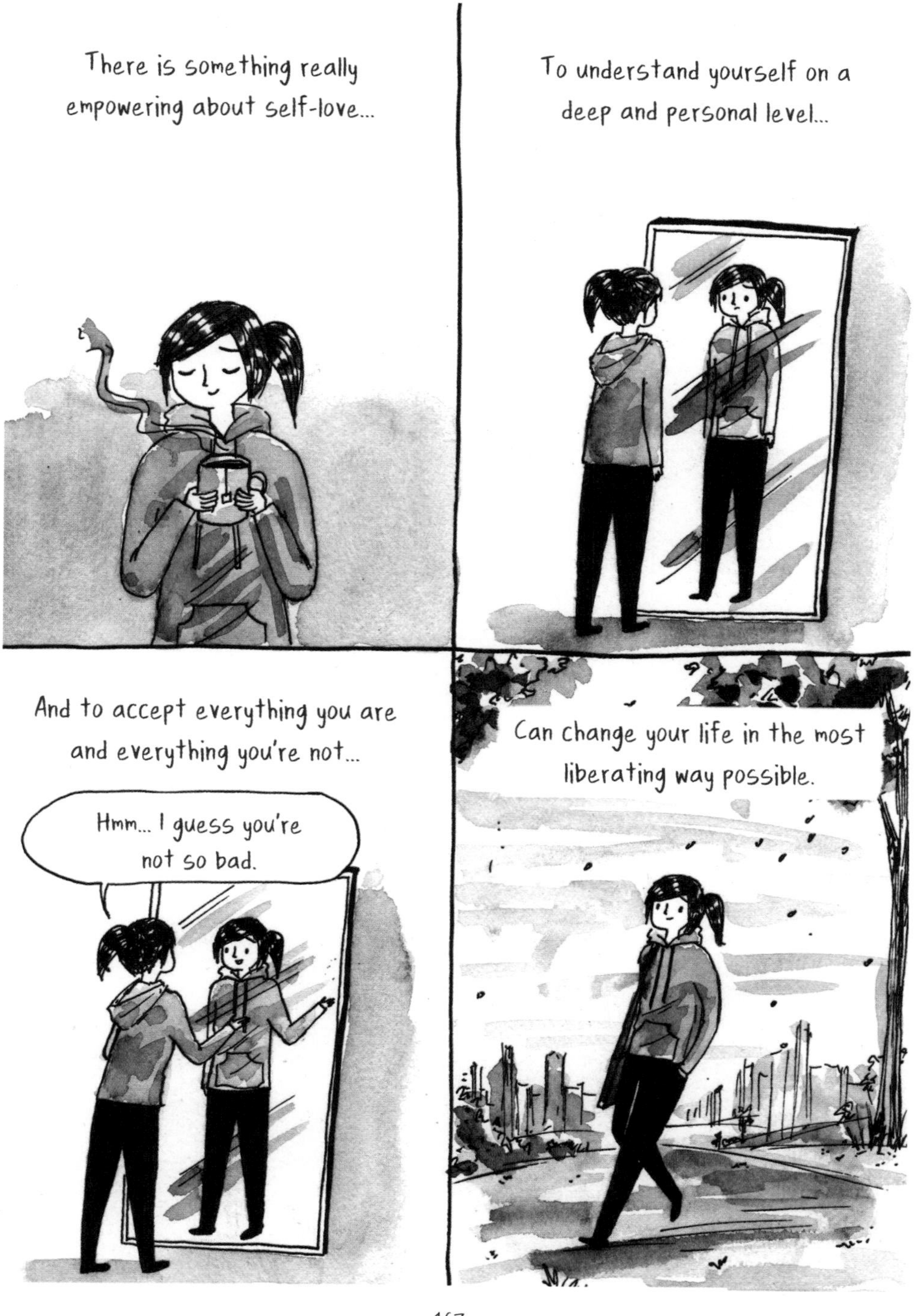
There is something really empowering about self-love...
To understand yourself on a deep and personal level...
And to accept everything you are and everything you're not...
Hmm... I guess you're not so bad.
Can change your life in the most liberating way possible.

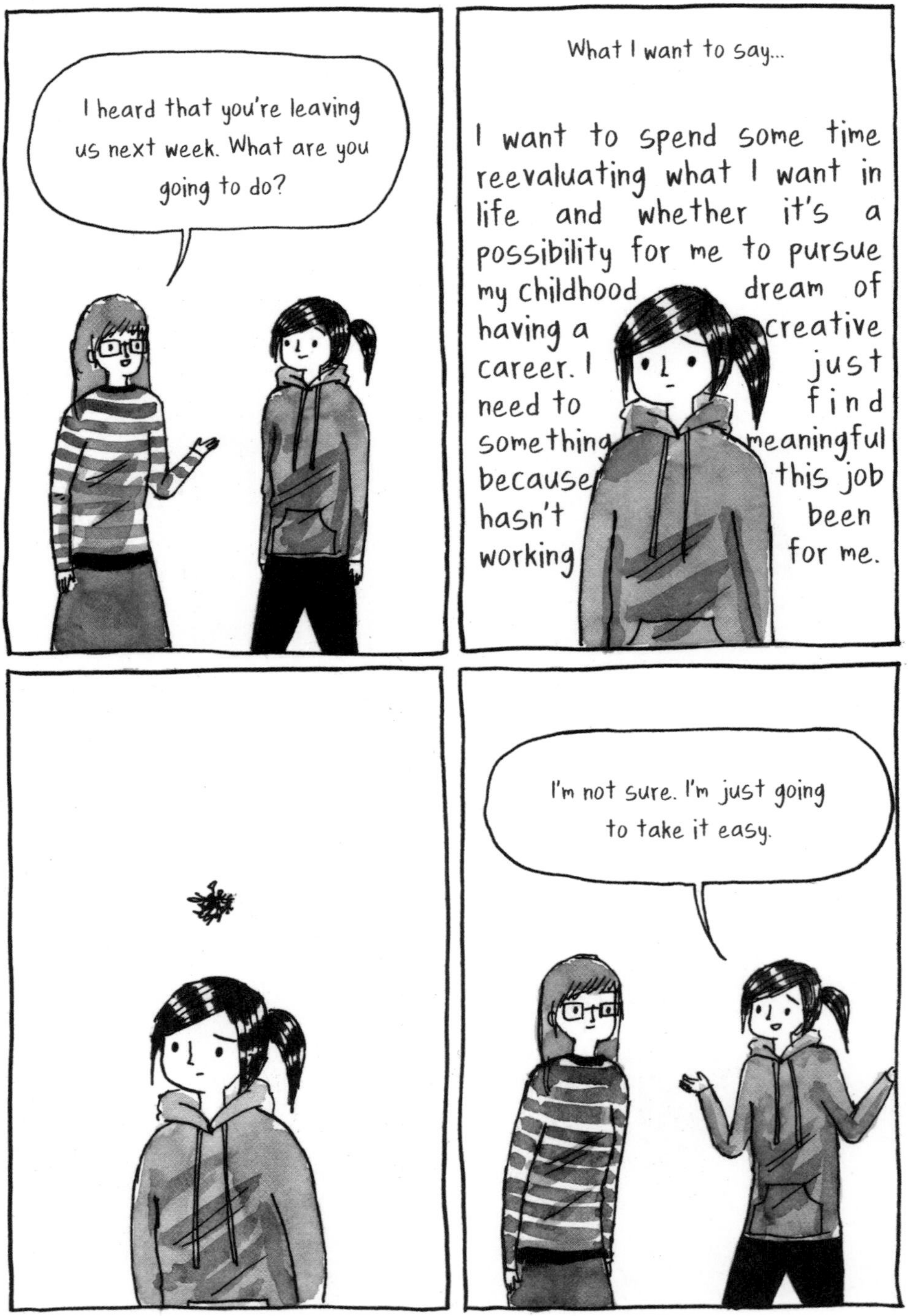
I heard that you're leaving us next week. What are you going to do?
What I want to say...
I want to spend some time reevaluating what I want in life and whether it's a possibility for me to pursue my childhood dream of having a creative career. I just need to find something meaningful because this job hasn't been working for me.
I'm not sure. I'm just going to take it easy.

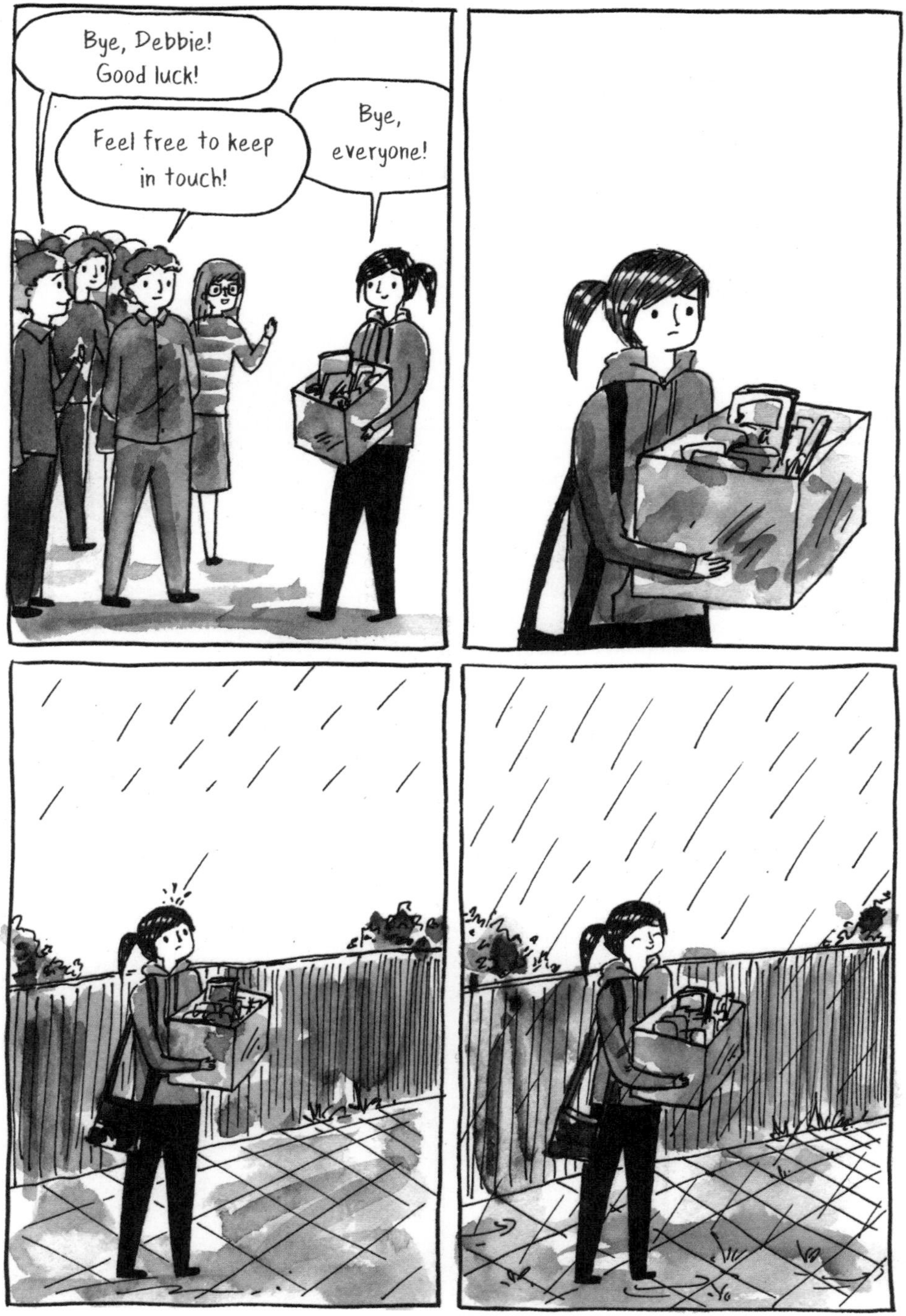
Bye, Debbie! Good luck!
Feel free to keep in touch!
Bye, everyone!

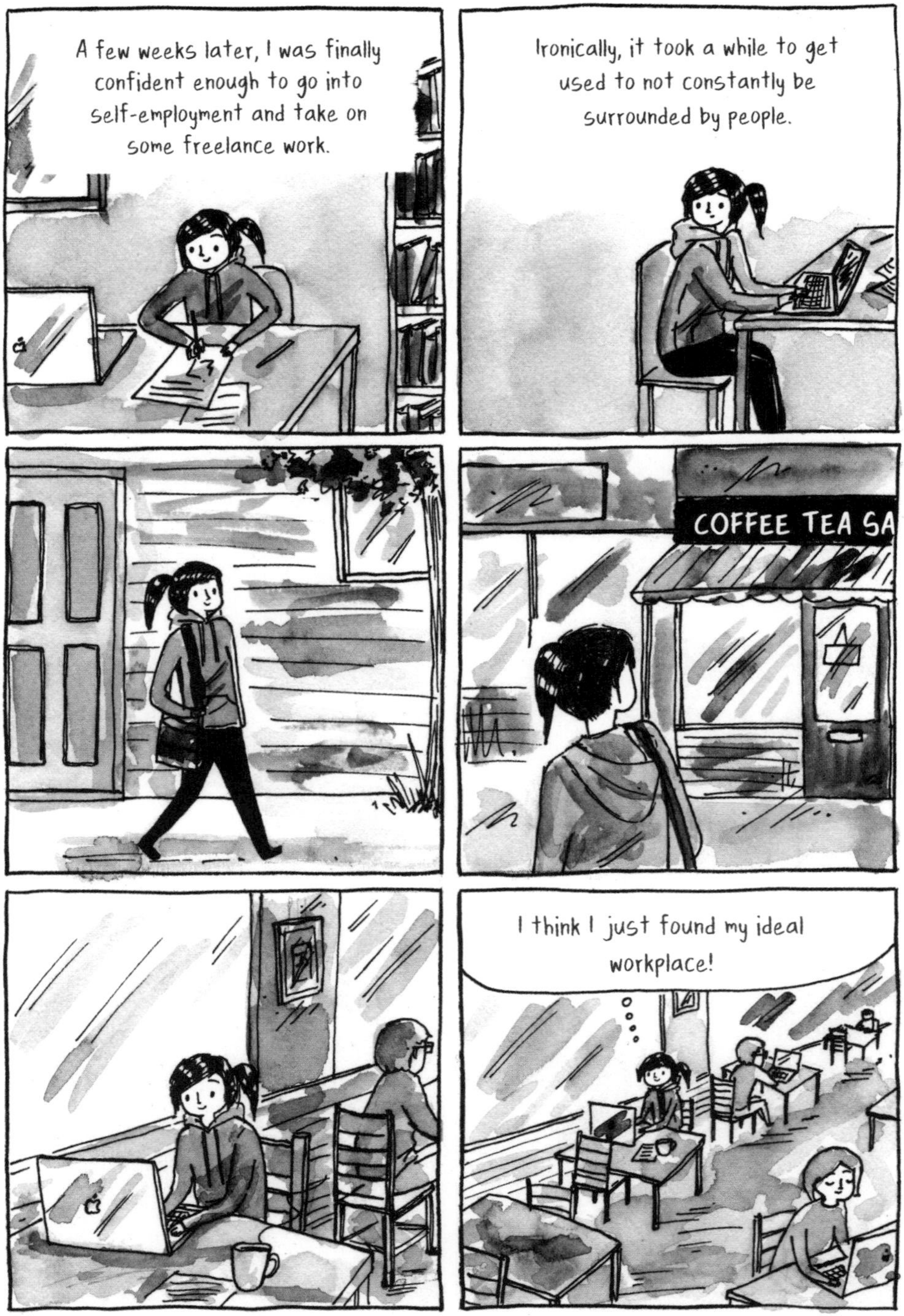
A few weeks later, I was finally confident enough to go into self-employment and take on some freelance work.
Ironically, it took a while to get used to not constantly be surrounded by people.
COFFEE TEA SA
I think I just found my ideal workplace!

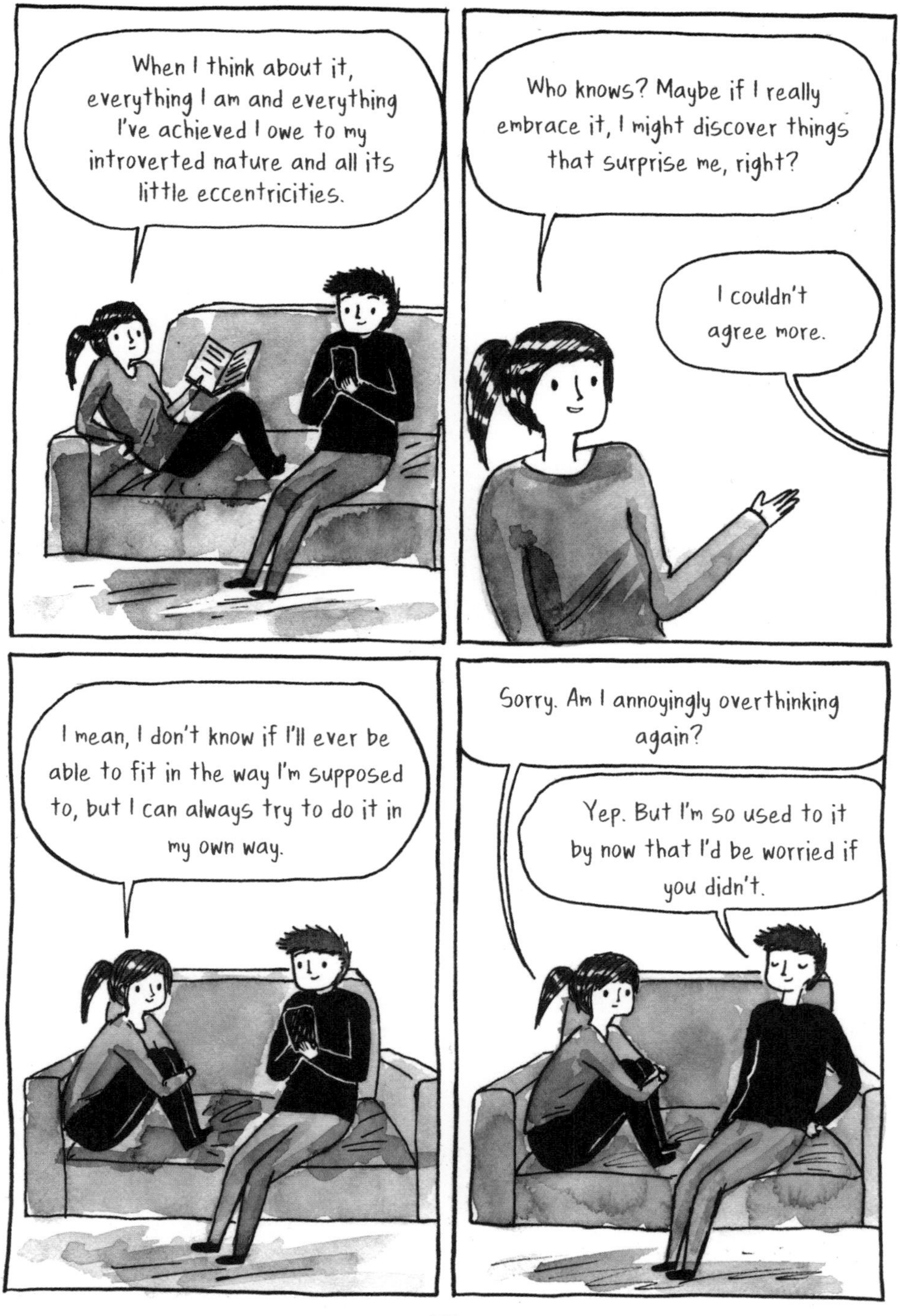
When I think about it, everything I am and everything I've achieved I owe to my introverted nature and all its little eccentricities.
Who knows? Maybe if I really embrace it, I might discover things that surprise me, right?
I couldn't agree more.
I mean, I don't know if I'll ever be able to fit in the way I'm supposed to, but I can always try to do it in my own way.
Sorry. Am I annoyingly overthinking again?
Yep. But I'm so used to it by now that I'd be worried if you didn't.

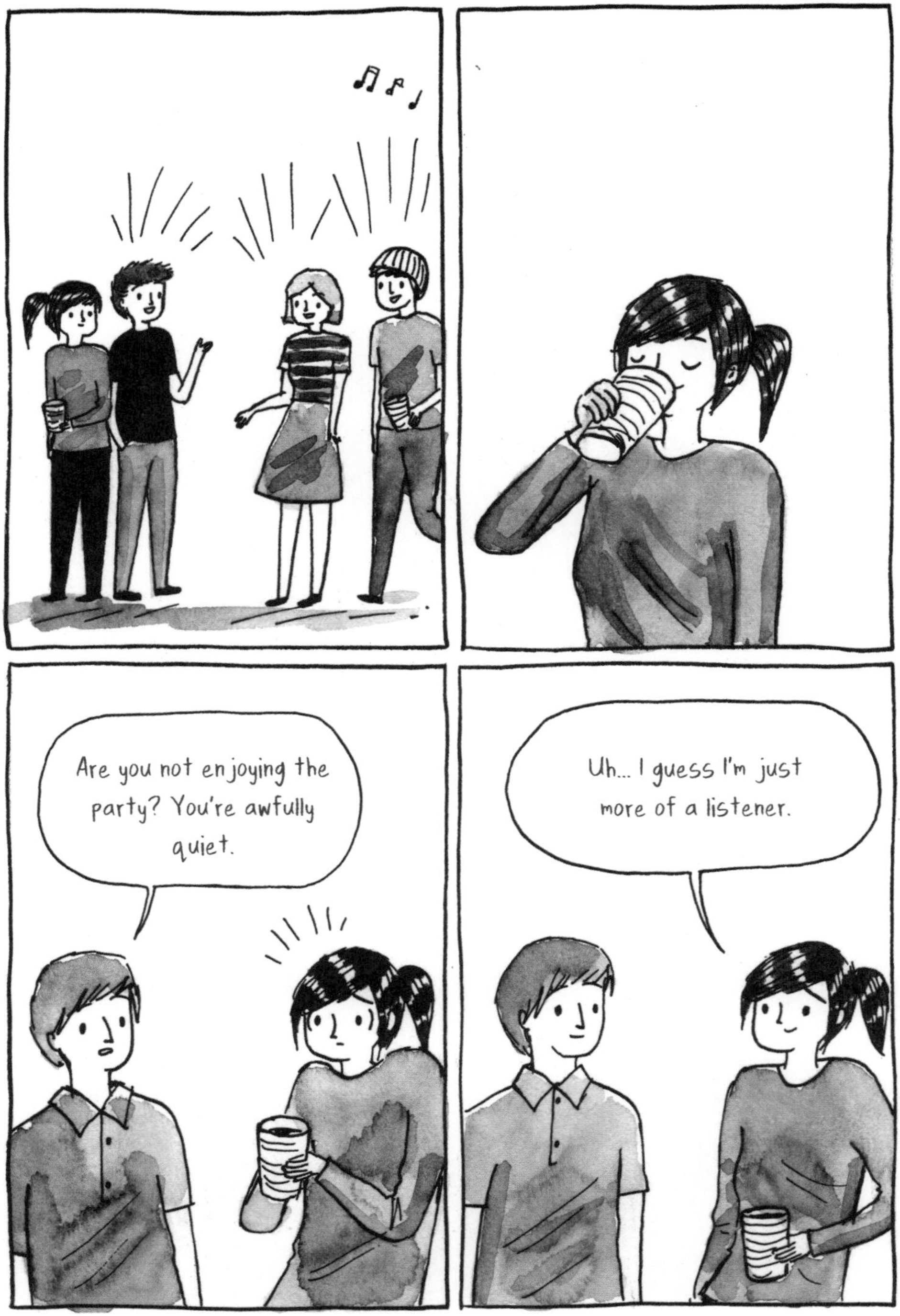
Are you not enjoying the party? You're awfully quiet.
Uh... I guess I'm just more of a listener.

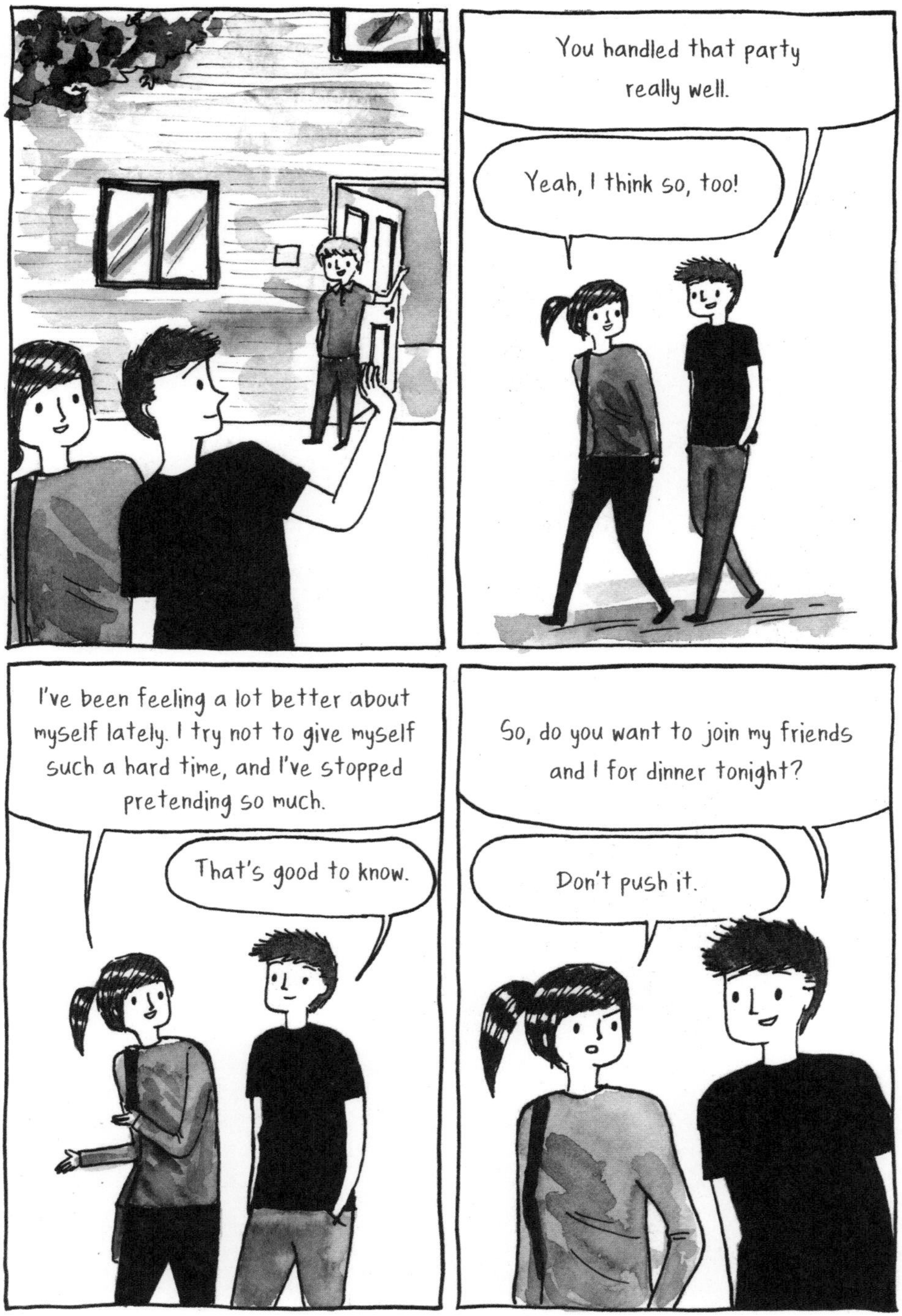
You handled that party really well.
Yeah, I think so, too!
I've been feeling a lot better about myself lately. I try not to give myself such a hard time, and I've stopped pretending so much.
That's good to know.
So, do you want to join my friends and I for dinner tonight?
Don't push it.

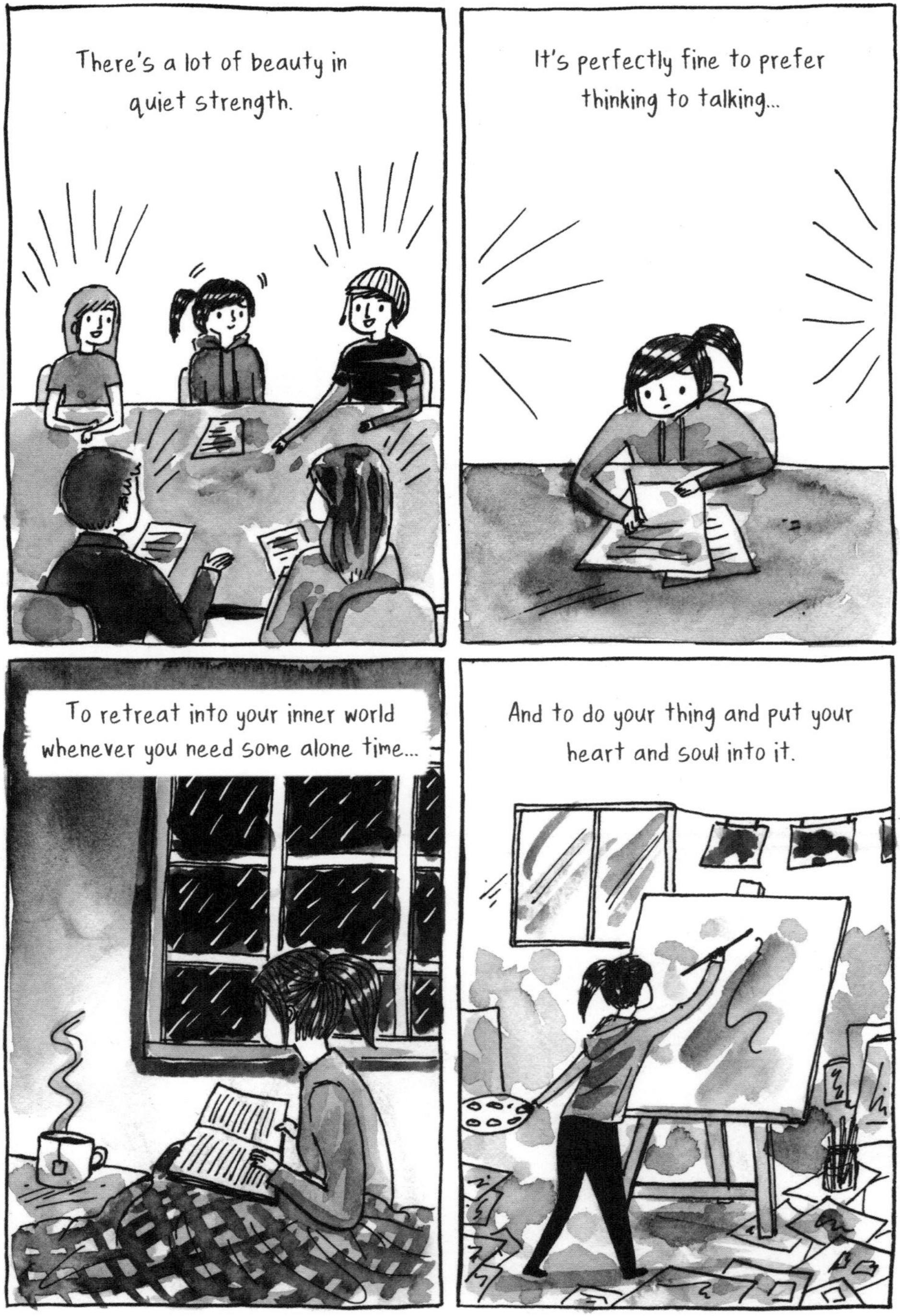
There's a lot of beauty in quiet strength.
It's perfectly fine to prefer thinking to talking...
To retreat into your inner world whenever you need some alone time...
And to do your thing and put your heart and soul into it.

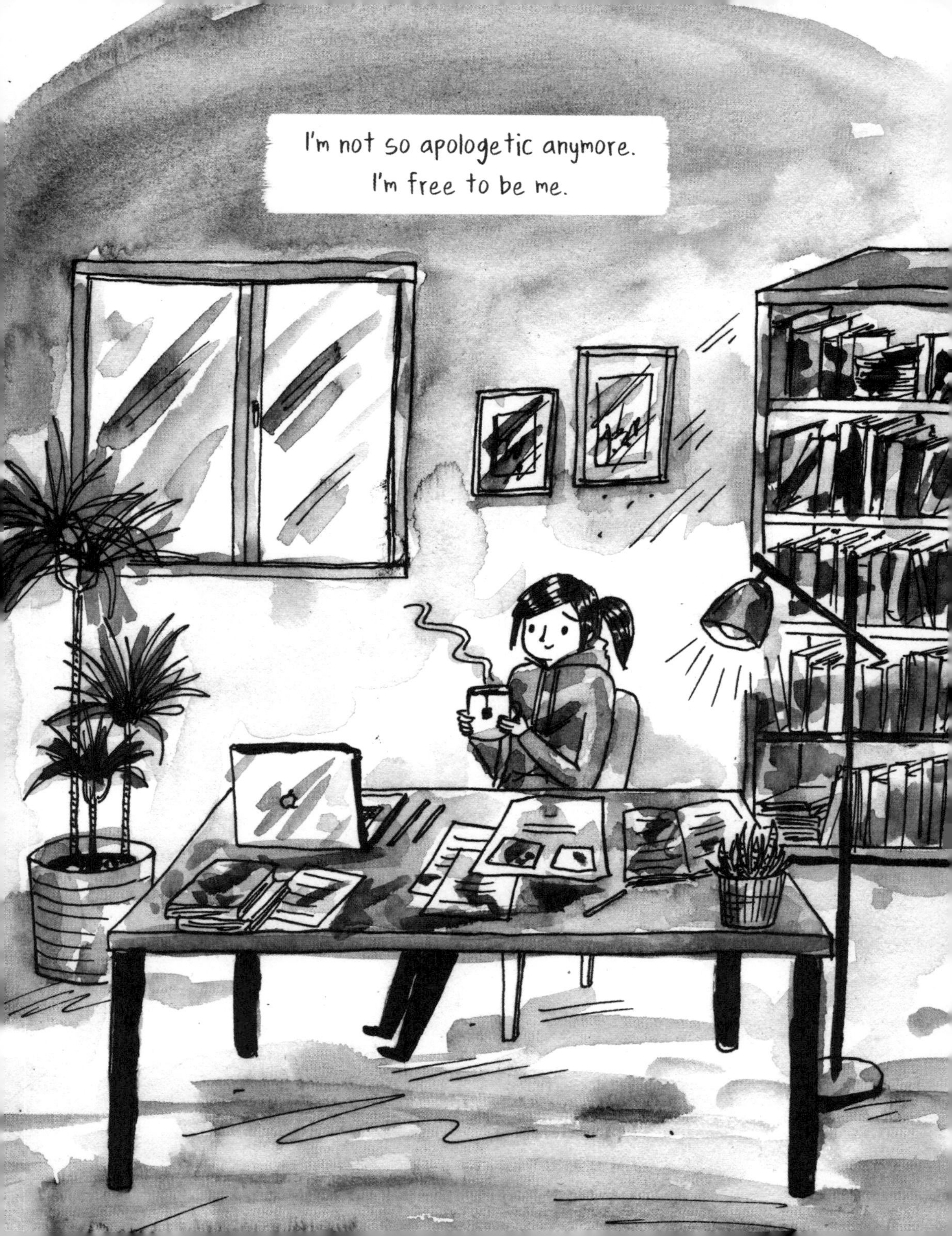
I'm not so apologetic anymore.
I'm free to be me.

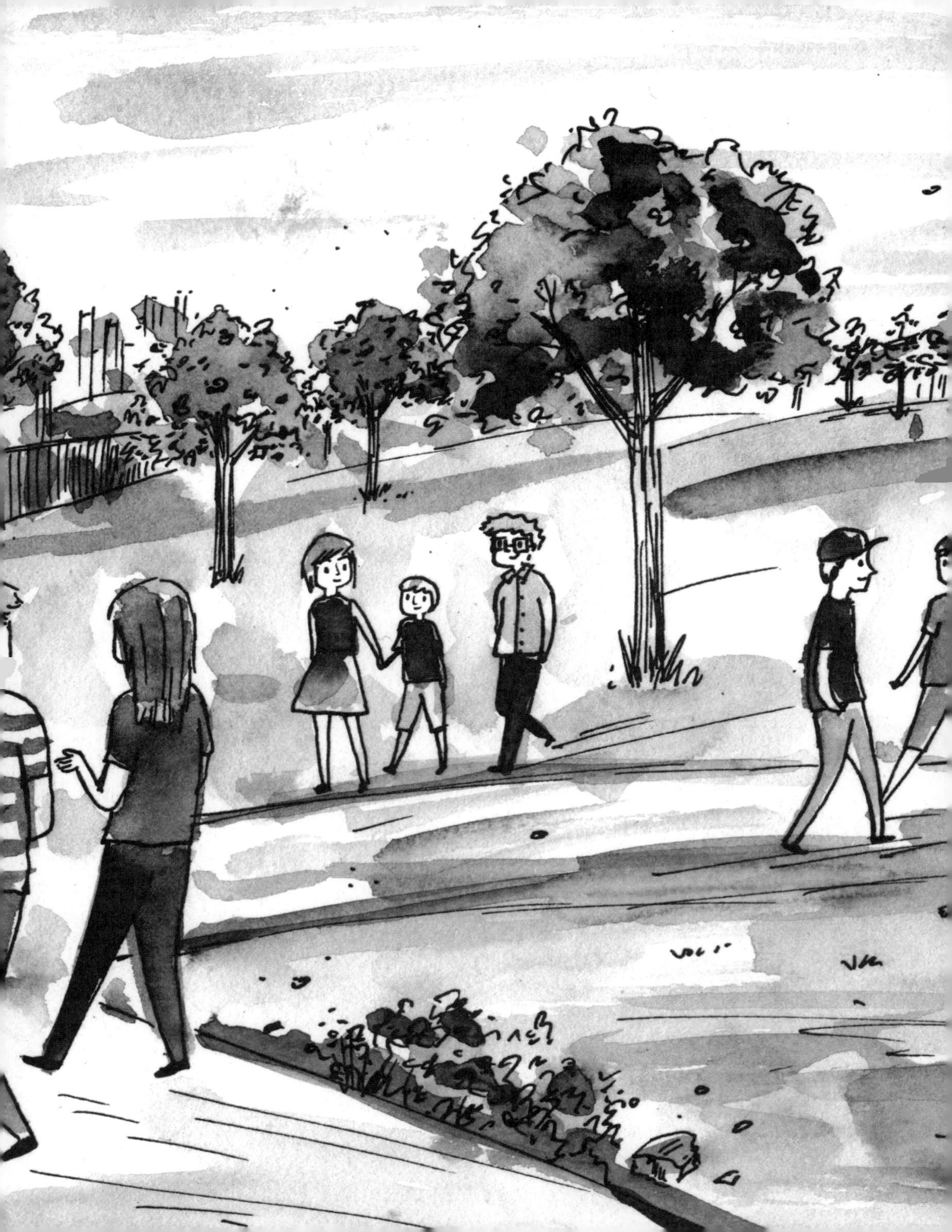

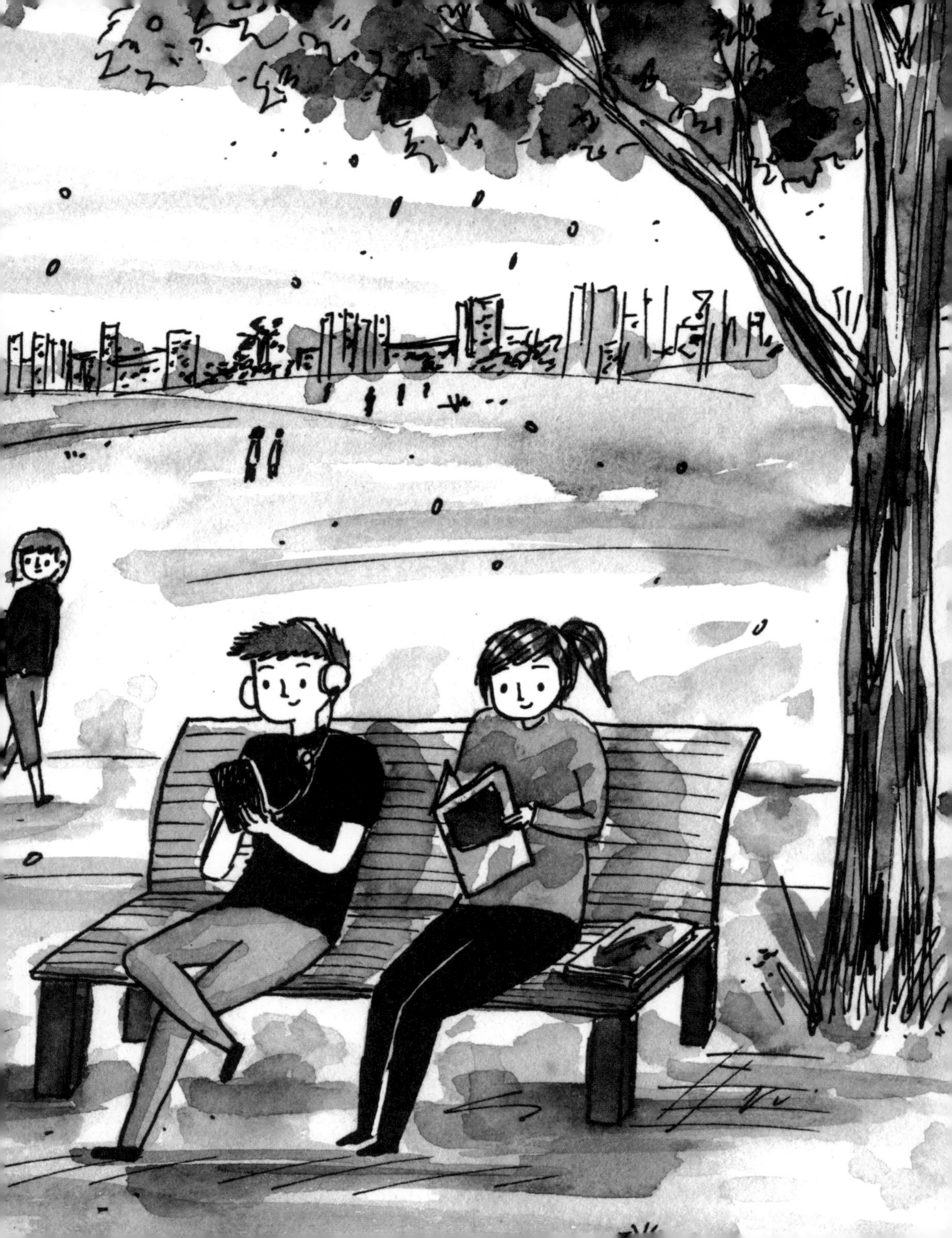

# Acknowledgments

I would like to thank everyone at Andrews McMeel, especially my editor, Patty Rice, for helping me bring this book to life. A huge thank you to my brilliant agent, Laurie Abkemeier, for all her support and guidance.

I am incredibly grateful to everyone who has been following my work online over the years, for all the amazing messages and the encouragement to keep going.

Thank you to my dad for being my number one fan since the day I started drawing, for inspiring me and for being my hero. To my mom, for always being there for me no matter what. Thank you to my sister, who listens to all my worries, and my brother who read all the comics I drew when we were kids.

Lastly, I want to thank my husband, Jason, for being so patient and supportive of everything I do, and for letting me turn him into a cartoon every day.

## About the Author

Debbie Tung is a cartoonist and illustrator from Birmingham, England. Her comics are based on simple (and sometimes awkward) everyday life moments and her love for books and tea. She lives with her husband and works from home in her quiet little studio.

Andrews McMeel Publishing
a division of Andrews McMeel Universal
1130 Walnut Street, Kansas City, Missouri 64106

www.andrewsmcmeel.com

18 19 20 21 22 SDB 10 9 8 7 6 5 4 3

ISBN: 978-1-4494-8606-8

Library of Congress Control Number: 2017932227

Editor: Patty Rice
Designer/Art Director: Diane Marsh
Production Editor: Erika Kuster
Production Manager: Tamara Haus

ATTENTION: SCHOOLS AND BUSINESSES
Andrews McMeel books are available at quantity discounts with
bulk purchase for educational, business, or sales promotional
use. For information, please e-mail the Andrews McMeel Publishing
Special Sales Department: specialsales@amuniversal.com.